OXFORD
UNIVERSITY PRESS

fourth edition

English File

Elementary
Teacher's Guide

WITH TEACHER'S RESOURCE CENTRE

Christina Latham-Koenig
Clive Oxenden
Jerry Lambert

Paul Seligson
with Anna Lowy
Krysia Mabbott

OXFORD
UNIVERSITY PRESS

Great Clarendon Street, Oxford, OX2 6DP, United Kingdom

Oxford University Press is a department of the University of Oxford.
It furthers the University's objective of excellence in research, scholarship,
and education by publishing worldwide. Oxford is a registered trade
mark of Oxford University Press in the UK and in certain other countries

© Oxford University Press 2019

The moral rights of the author have been asserted

First published in 2019

2024
10 9

ISBN: 978 0 19 403282 7   Teacher's Guide

Printed in China

This book is printed on paper from certified and well-managed sources

ACKNOWLEDGEMENTS

Back cover photograph: Oxford University Press building/David Fisher

*The authors would like to thank all the teachers and students round the world whose
feedback has helped us to shape* English File.

The authors would also like to thank: all those at Oxford University Press (both
in Oxford and around the world) and the design team who have contributed
their skills and ideas to producing this course.

*Finally very special thanks from Clive to Maria Angeles, Lucia, and Eric, and from
Christina to Cristina, for all their support and encouragement. Christina would also like
to thank her children Joaquin, Marco, and Krysia for their constant inspiration.*

The publisher would like to thank the following for permission to reproduce photographs:
Age Fotostock p.191 (reading/Alan Marsh); Alamy pp.169 (colleagues/
NICOLAS HERRBACH Stock Photo), 169 (students/Lev Dolgachov Stock Photo),
171 (newspaper/Nikreates), 171 (chairs/Maksym Bondarchuk Stock Photo),
171 (umbrella/Image Source Stock Photo), 171 (wallet/L A Heusinkveld
Stock Photo), 185 (concert/Anthony Brown Stock Photo), 185 (BBC Proms/
Milton Cogheil Stock Photo), 186 (Mother Teresa/Tim Graham Stock Photo),
191 (shopping/Blend Images Stock Photo), 191 (colleagues/Image Source
Plus Stock Photo), 191 (sale/Westend61 GmbH Stock Photo), 195 (city/
eye35 Stock Photo), 200 (architect/Cultura Creative (RF) Stock Photo),
217 (scissors), 217 (laptop/Ellen Isaacs Stock Photo), 217 (pens/Zoonar GmbH
Stock Photo), 217 (headphones/Zoonar GmbH Stock Photo), 217 (photos/
Mauricio Jordan Stock Photo), 217 (parasol/Anatoly Vartanov Stock Photo),
217 (glasses/Sirpa/Stockimo Stock Photo), 217 (credit card/Artur Marciniec
Stock Photo), 217 (keys/Tronin Vladimir Stock Photo), 231 (snowman/D.
Hurst Stock Photo), 231 (birthday/Rawpixel Ltd Stock Photo), 231 (cafe/
MBI Stock Photo), 231 (bicycle/Tony Tallec Stock Photo), 237 (star homes/
Andreas von Einsiedel Stock Photo), 238 (star homes/Andreas von Einsiedel
Stock Photo), 258 (geishas/Jon Arnold Images Ltd Stock Photo), 258 (dancers/
Nate Clicks Stock Photo), 260 (ticket), 262 (guitar/Hero Images Inc. Stock
Photo), 263 (nurse), 263 (policewoman/Janine Wiedel), 263 (journalist),
263 (musician), 267 (sprint/Yon Marsh Stock Photo), 267 (painting/
Blend Images Stock Photo), 273 (yoghurt/Shotshop GmbH Stock Photo),
273 (kiwi/Maya Kovacheva Stock Photo); Corbis UK Ltd. pp.263 (dentist/
Benelux), 263 (waiter), 263 (lawyer/Ocean), 263 (builder), 263 (engineer);
Getty Images pp.186 (Picasso/ullstein bild), 217 (watch), 217 (lamp/Digital
Vision/Creative Crop), 222 (Cristiano Ronaldo), 222 (Tom Hiddleston/
WireImage), 234 (Anthony Hopkins/Moviepix), 234 (Elizabeth Arden/Hulton
Archive), 235 (Anthony Hopkins/Moviepix), 235 (Elizabeth Arden/Hulton
Archive), 237 (dream flats/Arcaid Images), 238 (dream flats/Arcaid Images),
258 (China/Gallo Images), 258 (mosque/E+/Leonardo Patrizi), 258 (sombrero/
Image Source), 262 (reading/Digital Vision/Dougal Waters), 263 (architect/
Photolibrary/Tetra Images), 263 (soldier), 263 (hairdresser/Frank Gaglione/
Stockbyte), 263 (doctor/Thomas Tolstrup), 263 (actor), 263 (pilot); Guinness
GB p.258 (Guinness); iStockphoto pp.171 (keys), 171 (pizza), 171 (tissue box),
171 (sandwiches), 184 (cleaning), 195 (desert), 217 (coins), 217 (magazines),
217 (wallet), 258 (Eiffel Tower), 258 (tango), 258 (Poland), 258 (Ethiopia),
258 (cathedral), 258 (Prague), 262 (listening), 267 (flowers), 273 (cheese cake),
273 (lettuce/E+/Creativeye99), 273 (mushrooms), 273 (vegetables); Oxford
University Press pp.171 (lamp/exopixel/Shutterstock), 171 (headphones/Mark
Mason), 171 (pencils/Yganko/Shutterstock), 249 (), 188 (fireworks), 258 (paella/
Christina Latham-Koenig), 260 (coin/MM Studios), 260 (key/MM Studios),
260 (diary/Shutterstock), 260 (laptop/Shutterstock), 260 (watch/MM Studios),
260 (magazine/MM Studios), 260 (ID card/MM Studios), 260 (sunglasses/MM
Studios), 260 (scissors/MM Studios), 260 (file/MM Studios), 260 (purse/MM
Studios), 260 (wallet/MM Studios), 260 (umbrella/MM Studios), 273 (apple/
Alex Staroseltsev/Shutterstock), 273 (bread/Robert Milek/Shutterstock),
273 (carrots/Ivonne Wierink/Shutterstock), 273 (egg/rangizzz/Shutterstock),
273 (fish/Ivaschenko Roman/Shutterstock), 273 (grapes/Evgeny Karandaev/
Shutterstock), 273 (burger/rvlsoft/Shutterstock), 273 (ice cream), 273 (juice/
Ljupco Smokovski/Shutterstock), 273 (nuts/Maks Narodenko/Shutterstock),
273 (onions/mylisa/Shutterstock), 273 (peas/Egor Rodynchenko/Shutterstock),
273 (rice/oriori/Shutterstock), 273 (tomato/Rob Stark/Shutterstock),
273 (watermelon/Alex Staroseltsev/Shutterstock), 273 (sandwich/
ampFotoStudio/Shutterstock); PPR/Lindt & Spruengli AG p.258 (chocolate);
Press Association Images pp.222 (Samuel L Jackson/Doug Peters), 222 (Jennifer
Lawrence/ABACA USA), 222 (Hugh Jackman/EMPICS Entertainment),
222 (Rihanna/Doug Peters), 222 (Brad Pitt/AFF), 222 (Adele/ABACA), 222 (Taylor
Swift/AFF), 222 (Benedict Cumberbatch/AFF), 222 (Charlize Theron/AFF); Rex
Features – Shutterstock p.222 (Scarlett Johansson/Theo Kingma); Shutterstock
pp.171 (mobile phone/Nick Merkulov), 173 (etorres), 175 (ESLINE), 184 (eating/
Monkey Business Images), 195 (train station/cowardlion), 200 (pasta/Mint and
Lemon), 217 (charger/Pongsathon Ladasuwankul), 258 (Mercedes/Bhakpong),
258 (boomerangs/Stepan Bormotov), 263 (receptionist), 263 (cleaner),
263 (vet), 274 (skeleton); Superstock Ltd. p.186 (Barack Obama); Zooid Pictures
p.217 (license).

Illustrations by: Adrian Barclay Illustration pp.179, 181, 187, 198, 201, 272;
Bess Harding pp.177, 181, 198, 201, 223, 232, 248, 264; Atsushi Hara pp.224;
Hannah Davies pp.246; Bill Brown pp.168, 172, 174, 193, 197, 233, 239, 240;
Jerome Mireault pp.189; Kath Walker pp.228, 244, 266; Mark Duffin p.190;
Oxford University Press pp.265; Paul Boston pp.259; Roger Penwill pp.170,
179, 180, 196, 199, 223, 241, 268; Sophie Joyce pp.177, 192, 223.

Grammar photocopiable activities written by: Amanda Begg

Contents

Syllabus checklist

		GRAMMAR	VOCABULARY	PRONUNCIATION
1				
6	**A** Welcome to the class	verb *be* ⊞, subject pronouns: *I, you*, etc.	days of the week, numbers 0–20	vowel sounds, word stress
8	**B** One world	verb *be* ⊟ and ?	countries, numbers 21–100	/ə/, consonant sounds /tʃ/, /ʃ/, /dʒ/, word stress
10	**C** What's your email?	possessive adjectives: *my, your*, etc.	classroom language	/əʊ/, /uː/, /ɑː/, the alphabet, sentence stress
12	**Practical English** Episode 1	checking in **V** in a hotel		
2				
14	**A** Are you tidy or untidy?	singular and plural nouns	things, *in, on, under*	final *-s* and *-es*
16	**B** Made in America	adjectives	colours, adjectives, modifiers: *very / really, quite*	long and short vowel sounds
18	**C** Slow down!	imperatives, *let's*	feelings	linking
20	**Revise and Check 1&2**			
3				
22	**A** Britain: the good and the bad	present simple ⊞ and ⊟	verb phrases: *cook dinner*, etc.	third person *-s*
24	**B** 9 to 5	present simple ?	jobs	/ɜː/ and /ə/
26	**C** Love me, love my dog	word order in questions	question words	sentence stress
28	**Practical English** Episode 2	buying a coffee **V** telling the time		
4				
30	**A** Family photos	possessive *'s*, *Whose…?*	family	/ʌ/, the letter *o*
32	**B** From morning to night	prepositions of time (*at, in, on*) and place (*at, in, to*)	daily routine	linking
34	**C** Blue Zones	position of adverbs, expressions of frequency	months, adverbs and expressions of frequency	the letter *h*
36	**Revise and Check 3&4**			
5				
38	**A** Vote for me!	*can / can't*	verb phrases: *buy a newspaper*, etc.	sentence stress
40	**B** A quiet life?	present continuous: *be* + verb + *-ing*	noise: verbs and verb phrases	/ŋ/
42	**C** A city for all seasons	present simple or present continuous?	the weather and seasons	places in London
44	**Practical English** Episode 3	buying clothes **V** clothes		
6				
46	**A** A North African story	object pronouns: *me, you, him*, etc.	words in a story	/aɪ/, /ɪ/, and /iː/
48	**B** The third Friday in June	*like* + (verb + *-ing*)	the date, ordinal numbers	/ð/ and /θ/, saying the date
50	**C** Making music	revision: *be* or *do*?	music	/j/, giving opinions
52	**Revise and Check 5&6**			

SPEAKING	LISTENING	READING
saying hello, saying goodbye	recognizing names recognizing places and numbers	
Where are you from? Where is it from? Where are they from?	*Where are you from? Where is it from? Where are they from?*, numbers	
giving personal information	classroom language; understanding personal information	classroom language

SPEAKING	LISTENING	READING
saying where things are	listening for detail	
describing things; the same or different?		identifying paragraph headings
What's the matter?	inferring mood, understanding specific advice	

SPEAKING	LISTENING	READING
things I like and don't like about my country		identifying attitude
guess the job	understanding specific information	
getting to know somebody	identifying who's who	

SPEAKING	LISTENING	READING
talking about family	identifying the main / supporting information	
a typical weekend	inferring feelings	understanding specific information
retelling the main information in a short text	listening for detail	inferring information

SPEAKING	LISTENING	READING
talking about abilities	focusing on practical information	
spot the difference	identifying a situation from context	
the weather and seasons; what to do in London	the weather and seasons	finding specific information

SPEAKING	LISTENING	READING
reading habits, retelling a story	checking predictions	understanding a traditional story
favourite times	understanding dates	understanding feelings and opinions
music questionnaire; giving opinions	understanding specific information	

Course overview

Introduction

Our aim with *English File fourth edition* has been to make every lesson better and to make the package more student- and teacher-friendly. As well as the main A, B, C Student's Book lessons, there is a range of material that you can use according to your students' needs, and the time and resources you have available. Don't forget:

- videos that can be used in class in every File: Practical English, Video Listening, and Can you understand these people?
- Quick Tests and File tests for every File, as well as Progress Tests, an End-of-course Test, and an Entry Test, which you can use at the beginning of the course
- photocopiable Grammar and Communicative activities for every A, B, C lesson, and a Vocabulary activity for every Vocabulary Bank

Online Practice and the **Workbook** provide review, support, and practice for students outside the class.

The **Teacher's Guide** suggests different ways of exploiting the Student's Book depending on the level of your class. We very much hope you enjoy using *English File fourth edition*.

What do Elementary students need?

We believe that in 9 out of 10 cases when a student signs up for English classes, their goal is to speak. Speaking a foreign language is very hard, so students need a great deal of motivation to encourage them to speak in English.

Grammar, Vocabulary, and Pronunciation

If we want students to speak English with confidence, we need to give them the tools they need – Grammar, Vocabulary, and Pronunciation (G, V, P). We believe that 'G + V + P = confident speaking', and in *English File Elementary* all three elements are given equal importance. Each lesson has clear G, V, P aims to keep lessons focused and give students concrete learning objectives and a sense of progress.

Grammar

- Clear and memorable presentations of new structures
- Regular and varied practice in useful and natural contexts
- Student-friendly reference material

We have tried to provide contexts for new language that will engage students, using real-life stories and situations, humour, and suspense. The **Grammar Banks** give students a single, easy-to-access grammar reference section, with example sentences with audio, clear rules, and common errors. There are at least two practice exercises for each grammar point. Students can look again at the grammar presented in the lesson on **Online Practice**. The **Workbook** provides a variety of practice exercises and the opportunity for students to use the new grammar to express their own ideas.

Vocabulary

- A focus on high-frequency words and phrases
- Opportunities to personalize new vocabulary
- Accessible reference material

Every lesson focuses on high frequency vocabulary and common lexical areas, but keeps the load realistic. All new vocabulary is given with the phonemic script alongside, to help students with the pronunciation of new words.

Many lessons are linked to the **Vocabulary Banks** which help present and practise the vocabulary in class, give an audio model of each word, and provide a clear reference so students can revise and test themselves in their own time. Students can review the meaning and the pronunciation of new vocabulary on **Online Practice**, and find further practice in the **Workbook**.

Pronunciation

- A solid foundation in the sounds of English.
- Targeted pronunciation development.
- Awareness of rules and patterns.

Elementary learners are often frustrated by English pronunciation, particularly the sound–spelling relationships, silent letters, and weak forms. There is a pronunciation focus in every lesson, which integrates clear pronunciation into grammar and vocabulary practice. There is an emphasis on the sounds most useful for communication, on word stress, and on sentence rhythm. **Online Practice** contains the Sound Bank videos which show students the mouth positions to make English vowels and consonants. They can also review the pronunciation from the lesson at their own speed. There is more practice of pronunciation in the **Workbook**, with audio, which can be found on **Online Practice**.

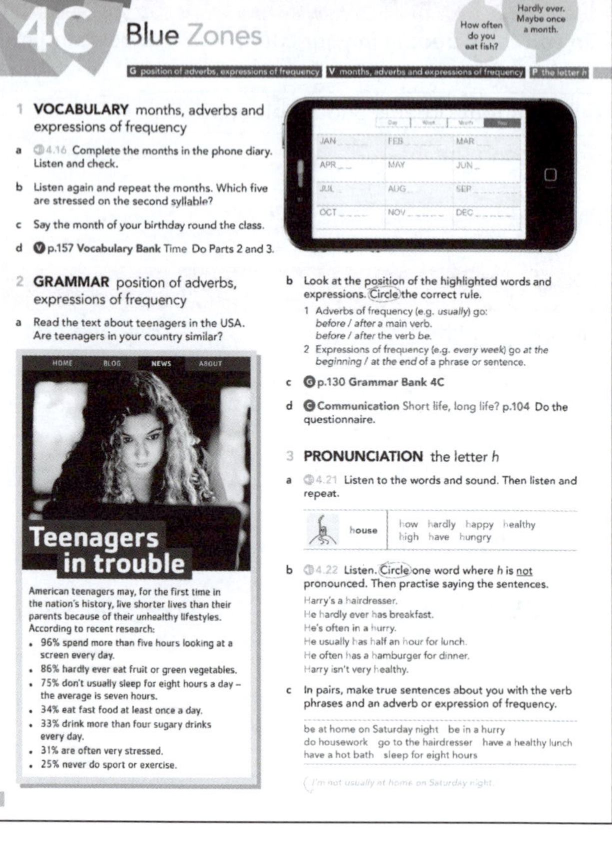

Speaking

- Topics that will inspire students' interest
- Achievable, motivating tasks
- Regular opportunities to use new language

English File motivates students to speak by providing varied and achievable tasks, and the language (G + V + P) that they need in order to communicate with confidence. In addition to the Speaking stage, students are encouraged to speak all through each lesson, responding to texts and listenings, and practising grammar and vocabulary orally. Every two Files, students can use **Online Practice** to record themselves doing a short task.

Listening

- A reason to listen
- Confidence-building tasks
- Help with connected speech

The listenings in *English File* are based on a variety of entertaining and realistic situations. The tasks focus on helping students to get the gist on the first listen and then being able to understand more the second time. On **Online Practice**, for each File students can find further listening practice related to the topic. They can also access the listening activities from every lesson, to practise in their own time, and to read the script to check anything that they have found difficult.

Reading

- Engaging topics and stimulating texts.
- Manageable tasks that help students to read.

Many students need to read in English for their work or studies, and reading is also important in helping to build vocabulary and to consolidate grammar. The key to encouraging students to read is to give them motivating but accessible material and tasks they can do. In *English File Elementary* reading texts have been adapted from a variety of real sources (the British press, magazines, news websites) and have been chosen for their intrinsic interest and ability to generate discussion.

Writing

- Clear models
- The 'nuts and bolts' of writing on a word and sentence level

The growth of the internet and email means that people worldwide are writing in English more than ever before both for business and personal communication. *English File Elementary* provides guided writing tasks covering a range of writing types from a formal email to a social media post. Students can use **Online Practice** to develop their writing skills further. The Discussion board also provides opportunities for informal written interaction.

Practical English

- Understanding high-frequency phrases
- Knowing what to say in typical situations

The Practical English lessons give students practice in key language for situations such as checking into a hotel or ordering a meal in a restaurant. To make these everyday situations come alive, there is a storyline involving two main characters, Jenny (from New York) and Rob (from London). There is a clear distinction between what students will hear and need to understand and what they need to say. The lessons also highlight other key 'Social English' phrases. On **Online Practice**, students can use the interactive video to record themselves and hear their own voice in the complete conversation. They can also listen and record the Social English phrases. The **Workbook** provides practice of all the language from the Practical English lessons.

Revision

- Regular review
- Motivating reference and practice material
- A sense of progress

Students will usually only assimilate and remember new language if they have the chance to see it and use it several times. Grammar, Vocabulary, and Pronunciation are recycled throughout the course. After every two Files there is a two-page Revise & Check section. The left-hand page revises the grammar, vocabulary, and pronunciation of each File. The right-hand page provides a series of skills-based challenges, including street interviews, and helps students to measure their progress in terms of competence. These pages are designed to be used flexibly according to the needs of your students. On **Online Practice**, for each File, there are three **Check your progress** activities. The first is a multiple choice activity for students to test themselves on the Grammar and Vocabulary from the File. The second is a dictation related to the topic and the language of the File for students to practise the new language in context. Finally, there is a **Challenge** activity, which involves a mini-research project based on a topic from the File. Every two Files, the **Workbook** contains a *Can you remember...?* page, which provides a cumulative review of language students have covered in the **Student's Book**.

Course overview

For students

Student's Book

The Student's Book has 12 Files. Each File is organized like this:

A, B, and C lessons

Each File contains three two-page lessons which present and practise **Grammar**, **Vocabulary**, and **Pronunciation** with a balance of reading and listening activities, and lots of opportunities for speaking. Every two Files (starting from File 2), the C lesson ends with a **Video Listening** section. All lessons have clear references to the **Grammar Bank**, **Vocabulary Bank**, and where relevant, to the **Sound Bank** at the back of the book.

Practical English

Every two Files (starting from File 1), there is a two-page lesson with integral video which teaches functional 'survival English' (for example language for checking into a hotel or ordering a meal) and also 'Social English' (useful phrases like *Nice to meet you, Let's go.*). The video is in the form of a drama, featuring the two main characters, Rob and Jenny. The lessons have a storyline which runs through the level.

Revise & Check

Every two Files (starting from File 2) there is a two-page section revising the **Grammar**, **Vocabulary**, and **Pronunciation** of each File and providing **Reading**, **Listening**, and **Speaking**. The *'Can you…?'* section challenges students with engaging reading texts and street interview videos, which give students exposure to real-life English.

The back of the Student's Book

The lessons contain references to these sections: Communication, Writing, Listening, Grammar Bank, Vocabulary Bank, and Sound Bank.

The Student's Book is also available as an eBook.

Online Practice

For students to practise and develop their language and skills or catch up on a class they have missed.

- **Look again:** students can review the language from every lesson.
- **Practice:** students can develop their skills with extra Reading, Writing, Listening, and Speaking practice.
- **Check your progress:** students can test themselves on the main language from the lesson and get instant feedback, and try an extra challenge.
- **Interactive video** to practise the language from the Practical English lessons.
- **Sound Bank videos** to learn and practise pronunciation of English sounds.
- **Resources:** All Student's Book audio, video, scripts, wordlists, dyslexia-friendly texts, and CEFR Language Portfolio.

Workbook

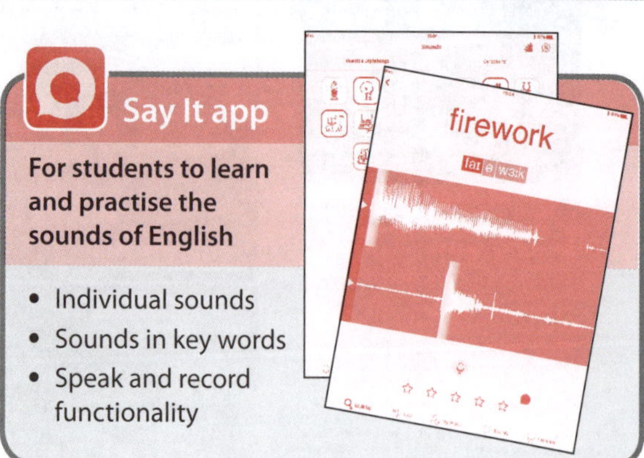

For language practice after class.

- All the Grammar, Vocabulary, and Practical English
- Pronunciation exercises with audio. The audio can be accessed on **Online Practice**
  - *Can you remember…?* exercises for students to check their progress
- Available with or without key

"

For teachers

Teacher's Guide

Step-by-step procedural notes for all
the lessons including:

- an optional 'books-closed' lead-in
  for every lesson.
- **Extra challenge** suggestions
  for ways of exploiting the
  Student's Book material in a more
  challenging way if you have a
  stronger class.
- **Extra support** suggestions for
  ways of adapting activities or exercises to make them
  work with weaker students.
- **Extra ideas** for optional activities.

All lesson plans include answer keys and audio scripts.
Over 90 pages of photocopiable activities.

Grammar

see pp. 165–203

- An activity for every Grammar Bank, which can be used in
  class or for self-study extra practice

Communicative

see pp.204–252

- Extra speaking practice for every A, B, C lesson

Vocabulary

see pp.253–275

- An activity for every Vocabulary Bank, which can be used
  in class or for self-study extra practice

There is more information on page 164 of this Teacher's
Guide about the photocopiable worksheets and tips on how
best to use them.

Teacher's Resource Centre

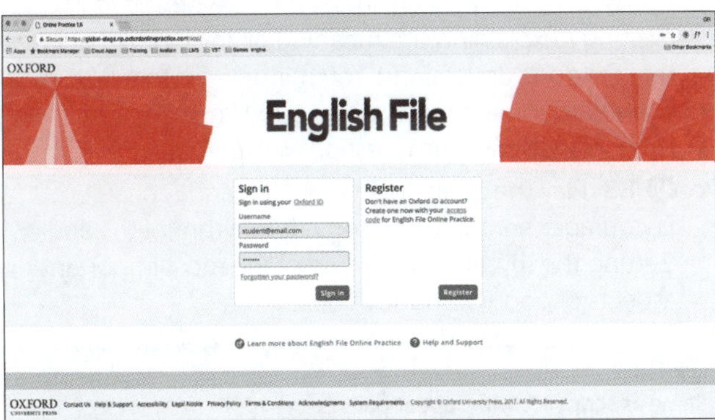

- All the Student's Book audio/video files and scripts
- Detailed lesson plans from the Teacher's Guide
- Answer keys
- All the photocopiable activities from the Teacher's Guide,
  including customisable versions
- All the Workbook audio files and scripts
- Tests and assessment material, including: an Entry Test;
  Progress Tests; an End-of-course Test; a Quick Test for every
  File; and complete test for every File. There are A and B
  versions of all the main tests and audio files for all the
  Listening tests
- CEFR documents

Classroom Presentation Tool

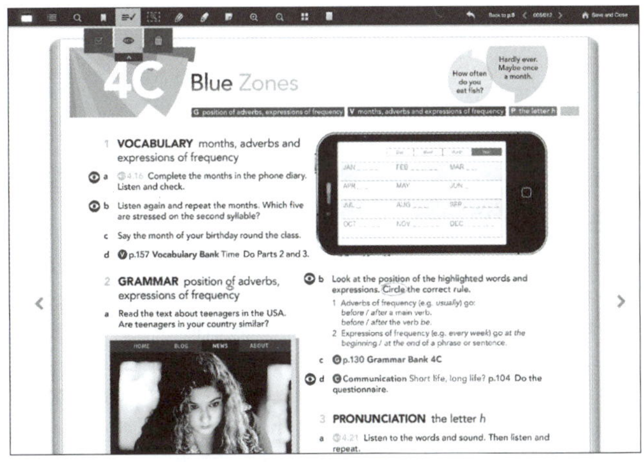

- The complete Student's Book
- Photocopiable activities from the Teacher's Guide
- All class audio and video, with interactive scripts
- Answer keys for exercises in the Student's Book and
  photocopiable activities
- Dyslexia-friendly texts

Class audio

All the listening materials for the Student's Book can be
found on the **Teacher's Resource Centre**, **Classroom
Presentation Tool**, **Online Practice**, **Student's eBook**, and
the **Class Audio CDs**.

Video

Video listening

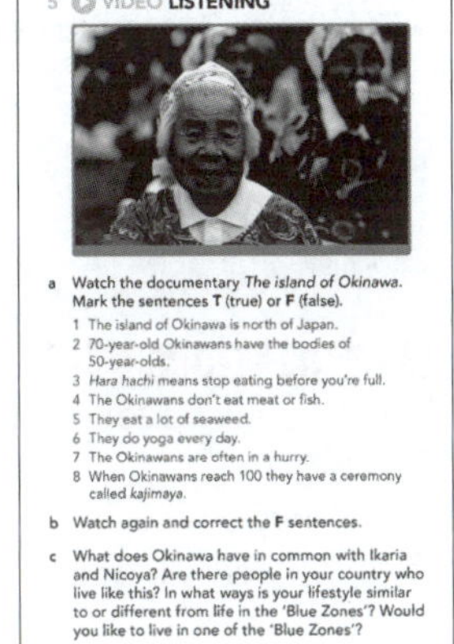

- Short documentary, drama, or
  animation for students at the
  end of even-numbered
  C lessons (2C, 4C, 6C, etc.)

Practical English

- A unique series of videos that
  goes with the Practical English
  lessons in the Student's Book

Revise & Check video

- Street interviews filmed in
  London, New York, and Oxford
  to accompany the
  Revise & Check section

All the video materials for the Student's Book can be
found on the **Teacher's Resource Centre**, **Classroom
Presentation Tool**, **Online Practice**, **Student's eBook**,
and the **Class DVD**.

1A Welcome to the class

G verb *be* [+], subject pronouns: *I*, *you*, etc.
V days of the week, numbers 0–20
P vowel sounds (/ɪ/, /iː/, /æ/, /e/, /eɪ/, /aɪ/), word stress

Lesson plan

The context of this first lesson is a young man who meets a woman at a salsa class. He then introduces her to his friend, who clearly likes her and joins the class. The lesson starts with five conversations where Sts practise basic greetings, asking names, etc. They then focus on the grammar of the verb *be* in positive sentences and on subject pronouns. In Pronunciation, Sts are introduced to word stress and the *English File* system of teaching the sounds of English. Here they begin by focusing on six vowel sounds. There is a vocabulary focus on the days of the week and numbers 0–20, and the lesson finishes with a listening and speaking activity, which pulls together the various strands of the lesson.

There is an Entry Test on the *Teacher's Resource Centre* which you can give Sts before starting the course.

More materials

For teachers

Photocopiables
Grammar verb *be* [+], subject pronouns *p.168*
Vocabulary Days of the week / Numbers 0–20 *p.257* (instructions *p.253*)
Communicative You say, you answer *p.214* (instructions *p.204*)

Teacher's Resource Centre
Entry test

For students
Workbook 1A
Online Practice 1A

OPTIONAL LEAD-IN (BOOKS CLOSED)
Pre-teach conversation 2 in **b** by introducing yourself. Say *Hi / Hello, I'm* (…), and ask three or four Sts *What's your name?* When they answer, pretend sometimes not to have heard them properly, and say *Sorry?* and put your hand to your ear.

1 LISTENING & SPEAKING recognizing names

a 1.2 Books open. Focus on the people in the photo story. Then tell Sts to listen to the conversations and label the four people in pictures 1–4.

Play the audio once or twice if necessary.

Check answers.

EXTRA SUPPORT Read through the script and decide if you need to pre-teach any new lexis before Sts listen.

A Carla **B** Matt **C** Sally **D** Ben

1.2
C = Carla, M = Matt, S = Sally, B = Ben

1
C Hello, everybody. Welcome to the class. I'm Carla. I'm your teacher.
2
M Hi, I'm Matt. What's your name?
S Sally.
M Sorry?
S Sally!
3
M What's your phone number?
S It's 07894 132 456.
4
B Hi, Matt.
M Hello. This is Sally. She's in my salsa class.
B Nice to meet you. My name's Ben.
S Nice to meet you, too.
M Bye, Sally.
S Goodbye, Matt. Bye, Ben.
5
B Hi, Sally.
S Ben! Are you in the salsa class, too?
B Yes, I am. How are you?
S I'm very well, thank you. And you?
B Fine, thanks. … Great! You're my partner!
S Yes! See you later, Matt.

b Play the audio again for Sts to listen and complete the gaps. Point out that the first one (*name*) has been done for them. Play it again if necessary.

Check answers and write the words on the board.

2 Sorry **3** number **4** Hi **5** meet **6** you **7** thank **8** Fine

EXTRA SUPPORT Write the seven missing words in jumbled order on the board.

Finally, go through each line of the conversations eliciting / explaining the meaning of any words / phrases that Sts don't understand. You might want to tell Sts that nowadays some people say *I'm good* (instead of *I'm fine. / Fine.*) in answer to the question *How are you?*.

c 1.3 Play the audio for Sts to listen and repeat. Encourage them to try to copy the rhythm of the audio. Getting the rhythm right is one of the most important aspects of good pronunciation.

1.3
Same as script 1.2 with repeat pauses

EXTRA IDEA Put Sts in groups of three, and tell them to take roles (Sally, Matt, and Ben). Tell them to focus on the pictures and explain that they are going to act out the conversations. If there's time, get Sts to swap roles.

d Focus on the exercise. Explain that *Hello* and *Hi* mean the same, but *Hi* is more informal.

Get Sts, in pairs, to complete the gaps with words from the list.

Check answers and highlight that the words / phrases on the right are more informal than those on the left.

My name's... = **I'm**   Very well = **Fine**   Thank you = **Thanks**
Goodbye = **Bye**

 Write the phrases in the left-hand column
on the board first.

e Focus on the example sentences in the speech bubbles.

 Explain that in English some words are
said more strongly than others, e.g. in *Nice to meet you, Nice*
and *meet* are pronounced more strongly than *to* and *you*.
Model and drill the phrase, and encourage Sts to try to copy
the rhythm.

Tell Sts to imagine that they're at a party where they don't
know anyone. Get them to stand up.

Now tell Sts to introduce themselves to at least five other
Sts. Encourage them to shake hands, or use a locally
appropriate gesture, say *Nice to meet you,* and say *Sorry?* if
they don't hear the other student's name.

2 GRAMMAR   verb *be* ⊞, subject pronouns

a Focus on the instructions and on the first sentence, *I am
Carla.* Then read the second sentence, *I'm Carla,* and
explain that *I'm* is the contraction of the two words *I* and
am. Tell Sts that when people speak, they normally use
contractions.

Give Sts a minute to complete the other four gaps and
check answers.

2 I**'m** Matt.   **3** My name**'s** Ben.   **4** You**'re** my partner.
5 She**'s** in my salsa class.

b Tell Sts to go to **Grammar Bank 1A** on *p.124*. Explain that
all the grammar rules and exercises are in this section of
the book.

Grammar notes

Highlight that fluent speakers of English often use
contractions in conversation, especially when the subject
is a pronoun.

Highlight also that in English there is only one form of
you, which is used for singular and plural, and for formal or
informal situations. In your Sts' language(s), there may be
different pronouns for second person singular and plural,
and also formal and informal forms.

 If you have a monolingual class, don't be
afraid of using your Sts' L1 to talk about the grammar rules.
At this level, it is unrealistic to expect Sts to fully understand
grammar rules in English.

1.4 Focus on the example sentences and play the
audio for Sts to listen and repeat. Focus particularly on the
pronunciation of the contractions, especially *You're* /jʊə/,
We're /wɪə/, and *They're* /ðeə/. Then go through the rules
with the class.

Now focus on the exercises for **1A** on *p.125*. Sts do the
exercises individually or in pairs.

Check answers, getting Sts to read the full sentences.

a
1 are   **2** is   **3** are   **4** is   **5** am   **6** is   **7** are   **8** is   **9** is
10 am

b
1 It's…   **2** They're…   **3** I'm…   **4** You're…
c
1 He's…   **2** We're…   **3** She's…   **4** It's…   **5** They're…

Tell Sts to go back to the main lesson **1A**.

 If you think Sts need more practice, you
may want to give them the **Grammar** photocopiable
activity at this point.

c ◆ **1.5** Play the audio and get Sts to listen and repeat the
pronouns and contractions.

1.5
1 I, I'm
2 you, you're
3 he, he's
4 she, she's
5 it, it's
6 we, we're
7 they, they're

 Write the words on the board so that Sts
know what they are saying.

d ◆ **1.6** Focus on the example and tell Sts they're going
to hear a full form of the verb and that they must say the
contracted form.

Play the audio, pausing after each phrase, and elicit a
response from the whole class.

1.6
1 I am (*pause*) I'm
2 you are (*pause*) you're
3 he is (*pause*) he's
4 she is (*pause*) she's
5 it is (*pause*) it's
6 we are (*pause*) we're
7 they are (*pause*) they're

Now repeat the activity with individual Sts.

e Point to a male student whose name you remember and
say *He's (Antonio).* Then point to a female student and elicit
She's (María).

Put Sts in pairs and ask them to continue naming other
Sts, using *He's / She's.*

f Focus on the example sentences in the speech bubbles.
Tell Sts to stand up and speak to the other Sts.

3 PRONUNCIATION   vowel sounds, word stress

Pronunciation notes

It is important to point out to Sts that with vowels (*a, e, i,
o, u*), there is no one-to-one relation between a letter and
a sound, e.g. the letter *e* can be pronounced in more than
one way, e.g. *he, very,* and *they*. However, reassure your
Sts that there are common combinations of letters which
are usually pronounced the same way and these will be
pointed out to them as the course progresses.

a ◆ **1.7** Focus on the **Vowel sounds** box and go through
it with the class. Tell Sts that English has 20 vowel sounds,
and that the *English File* pronunciation system has an
example word to help them remember each sound.
Learning the sounds will help them to pronounce words
more clearly and confidently.

Focus on the six sound pictures (*fish*, *tree*, etc.). Explain that the phonetic symbol in the picture represents the sound. The phonetic alphabet is used worldwide to show how words are pronounced. Learning to recognize these symbols will help Sts to check the pronunciation of a word in a dictionary.

Tell Sts that the two dots in the symbol /iː/ mean that it's a long sound.

Now tell Sts that diphthongs, e.g. /eɪ/ and /aɪ/, are two sounds together (/e/ and /ɪ/, /æ/ and /ɪ/).

Now focus on the example words in the column under each sound picture, e.g. *it*, *this*, *in*. Explain that the pink letters are the same sound as the picture word they're under. Demonstrate for Sts, e.g. say *fish*, *it*, *this*, *in*; *tree*, *he*, *we*, *meet*, etc.

Play the audio for Sts just to listen.

◖ 1.7
See words and sounds in Student's Book on *p.7*

Now play the audio again for Sts to listen and repeat. Get Sts to repeat the first picture word (*fish*), then the sound (/ɪ/), and then the group of three words (*it*, *this*, *in*). However, you may wish to get Sts to repeat after each individual word rather than the group of three.

EXTRA SUPPORT If these sounds are difficult for your Sts, it will help to show them the mouth position. You could model this yourself or use the Sound Bank videos on the *Teacher's Resource Centre*.

b ◖ **1.8** Tell Sts they're going to hear ten words and that they must write them in their notebooks.

Play the audio, pausing after each word to give Sts time to write.

Check answers by getting Sts to write the words on the board.

◖ 1.8
Hi   Bye   meet   they   he   thanks   we   very   this   name

---

c ◖ **1.9** Focus on the **Word stress** box and go through it with the class. Elicit / Explain the meaning of *syllable* (= units into which a word is divided).

Now focus on the words. These are words that many Sts will probably already know, and some are 'international', e.g. *hotel*, *internet*. Write AIRPORT on the board. Elicit / Teach that it has two syllables. Then explain that all words of two or more syllables have one which is stressed (pronounced more strongly than the other(s)). Then say *airport* both ways (*airport* and *airport*) and ask Sts which way they think is correct (*airport*). Underline AIR on the board, and tell Sts to underline the stressed syllable when they learn new words, especially if it isn't where they would expect it.

! Warn Sts that even if the same or a similar word exists in their language, the stress may be on a different syllable.

Play the audio once the whole way through for Sts just to listen.

◖ 1.9
<u>air</u>port   com<u>pu</u>ter   <u>e</u>mail   ho<u>tel</u>   <u>in</u>ternet   mu<u>se</u>um   <u>pas</u>ta   <u>piz</u>za
<u>sal</u>ad   <u>sand</u>wich   uni<u>ver</u>sity   <u>web</u>site

---

Now play it again, pausing after each word for Sts to underline the stressed syllable.

Check answers.

See underlining in script 1.9

EXTRA IDEA If Sts have got dictionaries with them, for example on their phones, get them to look up a word, e.g. *airport*, and show them that stress is marked in dictionaries with an apostrophe before the stressed syllable, e.g. /ˈeəpɔːt/. If not, copy a dictionary entry onto the board, or use an online dictionary entry if you have an interactive board.

d Get Sts to copy the chart and write the words from **c** under the correct heading. Point out that the first one (*airport*) has been done for them.

Get Sts to compare with a partner, and then check answers.

food	technology	places
pasta	computer	*airport*
pizza	email	hotel
salad	internet	museum
sandwich	website	university

e Write the three categories on the board. Then give Sts, in pairs, one minute to try to add more English words to each column.

Write their answers on the board. Underline the stressed syllable, and model and drill the correct pronunciation.

4 VOCABULARY days of the week, numbers 0–20

a ◖ **1.10** Focus on the picture and elicit that the two people are Ben and Sally.

Play the audio for Sts to complete the gaps.

Check answers.

◖ 1.10
Ben See you on Saturday. Bye.
Sally Bye, Ben.

---

b Tell Sts to go to **Vocabulary Bank** Days and numbers on *p.148* and get them to do **Parts 1** and **2**. Explain that these pages (**Vocabulary Banks**) are their vocabulary section where they will first do the exercises, and will then have the pages for reference to help them learn and remember the words.

Focus on **1 Days of the week** and get Sts to do **a** individually or in pairs.

◖ **1.11** Now do **b**. Play the audio for Sts to listen and check.

Check answers.

◖ 1.11
Days and numbers, 1 Days of the week
Monday Tuesday Wednesday Thursday Friday Saturday Sunday

Now either use the audio to drill the pronunciation of the days, or model and drill them yourself. Ask Sts where the stress is (always on the first syllable). Give further practice of any words your Sts find difficult to pronounce. Sts may have problems with *Tuesday* /ˈtjuːzdeɪ/, *Wednesday* /ˈwenzdeɪ/, and *Thursday* /ˈθɜːzdeɪ/. You could write these on the board and cross out the silent *d* in *Wednesday*, and highlight the vowel sounds in *Tuesday* and *Thursday*.

◗ **1.12** Now focus on the instructions for **c**, and play the audio for Sts just to listen.

◗ **1.12**
See phrases in Student's Book on *p.148*

Highlight the stressed syllables (week<u>end</u>, <u>week</u>day, <u>to</u>day, etc.). Elicit / Explain the meaning of any words Sts don't know.

Now either use the audio to drill the pronunciation of the phrases, or model and drill them yourself. Give further practice of any words your Sts find difficult to pronounce.

Then focus on **Activation**. Get Sts to cover the days of the week with a piece of paper and say them in order. Now ask them *What day is it today? And tomorrow?*

Finally, go through the **Capital letters** box with the class.

Now focus on **2 Numbers 0–20** and get Sts to do **a** individually or in pairs

> **Vocabulary notes**
> Highlight the spelling changes between *three* and *thirteen*, and *five* and *fifteen*. You could also point out to Sts that numbers in English have only one form and never change.

◗ **1.13** Now do **b**. Play the audio for Sts to listen and check.

Check answers.

> **5** five **7** seven **11** eleven **12** twelve **15** fifteen
> **18** eighteen **20** twenty

◗ **1.13**
2 Numbers 1-20
zero, one, two, three, four, five, six, seven, eight, nine, ten, eleven, twelve, thirteen, fourteen, fifteen, sixteen, seventeen, eighteen, nineteen, twenty

---

Now either use the audio to drill the pronunciation of the numbers, or model and drill them yourself. Explain / Elicit that numbers 13–19 are stressed on the second syllable. Give further practice of any numbers your Sts find difficult to pronounce.

❗ When we count in a list, *1, 2, 3, 4*, etc., we usually stress numbers 13–19 on the first syllable. However, at all other times, when we say them in isolation, e.g. *Room 13*, they are stressed on the second syllable. We recommend that you teach this pronunciation, as it is important for Sts to later distinguish between, e.g. 13 (thir<u>teen</u>) and 30 (<u>thir</u>ty).

 Most Sts will probably know how to count to ten, but may be less confident with 11–20. Get the class to try to count from 0 to 20. You start with the number 0 and get a student to say the next number. Try to elicit all numbers from 0 to 20. Then do the same counting backwards, starting from 20.

Now focus on **Activation**. Get Sts to cover the words with a piece of paper, leaving the numbers visible.

Finally, go through the **Phone numbers** box with the class. Highlight that *0* is usually pronounced /əʊ/ in telephone numbers, although *zero* can also be used.

Tell Sts to go back to the main lesson **1A**.

 If you think Sts need more practice, you may want to give them the **Vocabulary** photocopiable activity at this point.

c ◗ **1.14** Focus on the example and tell Sts they will hear two words (days of the week or numbers), and they have to say the next word in the sequence.

Play the audio, pausing after the two words, and elicit a response from the whole class.

◗ **1.14**
Monday, Tuesday, *(pause)* Wednesday
eighteen, nineteen, *(pause)* twenty
Tuesday, Wednesday, *(pause)* Thursday
eight, nine, *(pause)* ten
thirteen, fourteen, *(pause)* fifteen
Friday, Saturday, *(pause)* Sunday
Sunday, Monday, *(pause)* Tuesday
ten, eleven, *(pause)* twelve
sixteen, seventeen, *(pause)* eighteen

Now repeat the activity, eliciting responses from individual Sts.

d Model and drill the question. Get Sts to ask three Sts sitting near them. They should write down the phone numbers so that they can check them.

❗ Tell Sts they can invent their phone numbers if they prefer.

Get feedback from the class.

5 LISTENING & SPEAKING recognizing places and numbers

a ◗ **1.15** Focus on the six places (*airport, sandwich bar*, etc.) and make sure Sts understand them. Tell Sts they're going to listen to six short conversations. The first time they listen they should just try to understand where the conversation is taking place and write a number 2–6 in the boxes. Point out that the first one has been done for them.

❗ Make sure Sts write 2–6 in the boxes before the words *airport, sandwich bar*, etc., and <u>not</u> in the spaces, e.g. after *Gate number*.

Play the audio once for Sts to identify the place. Play again if necessary, and then check answers.

 Read through the script and decide if you need to pre-teach any new lexis before Sts listen.

> **2** language school **3** airport **4** taxi **5** hotel **6** museum

(script in Student's Book on *p.118*)

1 A A cheese and tomato sandwich, please.
   B That's five pounds twenty.
2 A So, Anna, your classes are on Tuesday and Thursday mornings.
   B *Que*? Sorry?
3 The British Airways flight to Rome is now boarding at Gate number nine.
4 A Where to, madam?
   B Manchester Road, please. Number sixteen.
5 A Here's your key, sir. Room twelve.
   B Thank you.
6 A Here we are.
   B Oh no. It's closed.
   A Look, it says 'Closed on Monday'!

b Focus on the words on the right in **a**. Elicit / Explain the meaning of *Gate*, etc. Now tell Sts to listen again, but this time to focus on the numbers and days they hear in each conversation.

Play the audio once or twice as necessary, pausing between each conversation to give Sts time to write the numbers or days in the gaps.

Get Sts to compare with a partner, and then check answers by playing the audio a final time and eliciting the numbers and days for each one.

1	sandwich bar	**5** pounds **20**
2	language school	Classes on **Tuesday** and **Thursday** mornings
3	airport	Gate number **9**
4	taxi	**16** Manchester Road
5	hotel	Room **12**
6	museum	Closed on **Mondays**

EXTRA SUPPORT If there's time, you could get Sts to listen again with the script on *p.118*, so they can see exactly what they understood / didn't understand. Translate / Explain any new words or phrases.

c ⓘ **1.16** Focus on the examples and tell Sts they're going to hear a sentence and they must respond to it.

Play the audio, pausing after each sentence to elicit a response from the whole class.

ⓘ **1.16**
1 Hello. Nice to meet you. (*pause*)
2 What day is it today? (*pause*)
3 Hi. What's your name? (*pause*)
4 What's your phone number? (*pause*)
5 Bye. See you on Monday. (*pause*)
6 Have a nice weekend. (*pause*)
7 Hi. This is Anna. (*pause*)
8 Hello. How are you? (*pause*)

Now repeat the activity, eliciting responses from individual Sts.

1B One world

G verb *be* ⊟ and ⁇
V countries, numbers 21–100
P /ə/, consonant sounds /ʧ/, /ʃ/, /ʤ/, word stress

Lesson plan

The context of this lesson is the Olympics, a time when people from many nationalities gather together in one place. Sts complete their study of the verb *be* and learn how to say where they and other people are from. They start the lesson by learning vocabulary for countries and nationalities, and this language is then practised in a world quiz. Next, Pronunciation covers the schwa /ə/, a sound which occurs in many English words, and three consonant sounds, which are difficult for many nationalities. The Grammar section, *be* in negative sentences and questions, is then presented through three interviews between a journalist and sports fans from different countries. Sts then practise asking where people are from. There is then a second Vocabulary section where Sts learn numbers 21–100, and a Pronunciation and Listening section which focuses on word stress in numbers, and practises numbers through listening and playing *Bingo*.

More materials
For teachers
Photocopiables
Grammar verb *be* ⊟ and ⁇ *p.169*
Vocabulary The world *p.258* (instructions *p.253*)
Communicative Nationalities bingo *p.215* (instructions *p.204*)
For students
Workbook 1B
Online Practice 1B

OPTIONAL LEAD-IN (BOOKS CLOSED)

Write the word CONTINENT on the board and elicit / teach its meaning. Ask Sts how many continents there are (*six*) and if they can name them (from largest to smallest: *Asia, Africa, North America, South America, Europe, Australia*). Answers to this question might differ as some people say there are five continents (counting North and South America as one); some also include *Antarctica*.

1 VOCABULARY countries

a ◉ **1.17** Books open. Focus on the four countries and make sure Sts know what they are.

Now tell Sts that they are going to hear music from these countries and they must write a number 1–4 in the boxes. Play the audio once for Sts to listen and complete the task. Check answers.

1 Scotland **2** Brazil **3** Mexico **4** Russia

◉ **1.17**
1 *Scottish music*
2 *Brazilian music*
3 *Mexican music*
4 *Russian music*

b Tell Sts to go to **Vocabulary Bank Countries** on *p.149*.

Focus on **1 Continents** and get Sts to do **a** individually or in pairs.

◉ **1.18** Now do **b**. Play the audio for Sts to listen and check.

Check answers.

◉ **1.18**
Countries, 1 Continents
4 Africa (*pause*) African
5 Asia (*pause*) Asian
6 Australia (*pause*) Australian
3 Europe (*pause*) European
1 North America (*pause*) North American
2 South America (*pause*) South American

Now either use the audio to drill the pronunciation of the words, or model and drill them yourself. Give further practice of any words your Sts find difficult to pronounce.

Focus on the instructions for **c**. Get Sts to cover the words with a piece of paper, leaving the map visible. Sts look at the map and try to remember both the continents and adjectives.

Finally, focus on the compass points, and model and drill the pronunciation: *north* /nɔːθ/, *east* /iːst/, *south* /saʊθ/, *west* /west/.

Focus on **2 Countries and nationalities** and get Sts to do **a** individually or in pairs.

Vocabulary notes
The nationality word is normally the same as the word for the language of the country, e.g. in *Italy* the language is *Italian*, in *Hungary* the language is *Hungarian*. However, some countries are different, for example in *Brazil* the language is *Portuguese*, and in some countries like *Switzerland* there are several official languages (*German, French, Italian*, and *Romansch*).

◉ **1.19** Play the audio for Sts to listen and check. Check answers.

🔊 **1.19**
2 Countries and nationalities
3 England (*pause*) English
6 Ireland (*pause*) Irish
2 Poland (*pause*) Polish
5 Scotland (*pause*) Scottish
1 Spain (*pause*) Spanish
4 Turkey (*pause*) Turkish
9 Germany (*pause*) German
7 Mexico (*pause*) Mexican
8 the United States (*pause*) American
14 Argentina (*pause*) Argentinian
10 Brazil (*pause*) Brazilian
12 Egypt (*pause*) Egyptian
11 Hungary (*pause*) Hungarian
13 Italy (*pause*) Italian
15 Russia (*pause*) Russian
17 China (*pause*) Chinese
16 Japan (*pause*) Japanese
20 the Czech Republic (*pause*) Czech
18 France (*pause*) French
19 Switzerland (*pause*) Swiss

Now either use the audio to drill the pronunciation of the words, or model and drill them yourself. Give further practice of any words your Sts find difficult to pronounce.

If your Sts' country is not in the list, teach it with the nationality adjective, and elicit which group the adjective belongs to.

Focus on the **Capital letters** and **The United Kingdom** box and go through it with the class.

Now focus on the instructions for **b**. Get Sts to cover each group of words with a piece of paper, leaving the flags visible. Sts look at the flags and try to remember both the countries and nationalities.

Finally, focus on **Activation** and the example. Put Sts in pairs and get them to tell their partner in which continent the six countries are, or, still in pairs, **A** could say a country, e.g. *Italy*, and **B** says where the country is, e.g. *Italy is in Europe*.

Tell Sts to go back to the main lesson **1B**.

 If you think Sts need more practice, you may want to give them the **Vocabulary** photocopiable activity at this point.

c Tell Sts they are going to do a quiz in small groups. Before they start, draw their attention to the example speech bubbles. Focus on the expressions *I think…* and *I'm not sure*. Teach / Elicit their meaning and drill the pronunciation.

Put Sts in small groups of three or four and set them a time limit to do questions 1–4 in *The World Quiz*. Tell them that the answers to questions 2, 3, and 4 are the 20 countries in the **Vocabulary Bank**, and let them refer to it.

Check answers and find out which group got the most correct answers.

1
a Europe **b** Asia **c** Africa **d** Australia **e** North America
f South America
2
a Argentina **b** England **c** Turkey **d** Scotland **e** the USA
f Italy
3
a Germany **b** Spain **c** Ireland **d** Poland **e** Switzerland
f Hungary
4
a Chinese **b** French **c** Czech **d** Russian **e** Brazilian
f Mexican **g** Egyptian **h** Japanese

2 PRONUNCIATION /ə/, /tʃ/, /ʃ/, /dʒ/

Pronunciation notes

The /ə/ sound occurs before or after stressed syllables and is the most common vowel sound in English. Final unstressed *-er* is always pronounced /ə/.

/tʃ/ the letters *ch* and *tch* are usually pronounced /tʃ/, e.g. *children*, *watch*.

/ʃ/ the letters *sh* are always pronounced /ʃ/, e.g. *she, shop*. The letters *s* and double *ss* are very rarely pronounced /ʃ/, e.g. only in *sure, sugar, Russian, passion*, and a few other words.

/dʒ/ *j* is always pronounced /dʒ/, e.g. *Japanese*. *g* is usually pronounced /dʒ/ before *e* or *i* (e.g. *German, giraffe*), but is pronounced /g/ before all other consonants, e.g. *gate, goodbye*, and sometimes before *e* and *i*, e.g. *get, give*, etc.

a 🔊 **1.20** Focus on **The /ə/ sound** box and go through it with the class. Model and drill the sound. Before you play the audio, you may want to point out that some words, e.g. *computer*, can have more than one /ə/ sound in them (it has two). Also show Sts that the stressed syllable has been underlined in the example words.

Play the audio for Sts just to listen to the sound and the four example words in the list.

🔊 **1.20**
See words in Student's Book on *p.8*

Now play the audio again for Sts to listen and repeat.

b 🔊 **1.21** Focus on the **Consonant sounds** box and go through it with the class.

Now focus on the three sound pictures (*chess, shower, jazz*). Remind Sts that the phonetic symbol in the picture represents the sound.

Play the audio once for Sts just to listen.

🔊 **1.21**
See sentences in Student's Book on *p.8*

Now play the audio again, pausing after each sound and sentence for Sts to repeat. Play again if necessary.

Put Sts in pairs to practise saying the sentences.

 If these sounds are difficult for your Sts, it will help to show them the mouth position. You could model this yourself or use the Sound Bank videos on the *Teacher's Resource Centre*.

c 🔊 **1.22** Here Sts recycle some of the country and nationality words that they learned in the **Vocabulary Bank**.

Tell Sts they will hear the name of a country and they must say the nationality. Focus on the example.

Play the audio, pausing after each country, and elicit the nationality from the class.

🔊 **1.22**
1 Scotland (*pause*) Scottish
2 Turkey (*pause*) Turkish
3 China (*pause*) Chinese
4 Germany (*pause*) German
5 Hungary (*pause*) Hungarian
6 Brazil (*pause*) Brazilian
7 France (*pause*) French
8 Poland (*pause*) Polish
9 Argentina (*pause*) Argentinian
10 Japan (*pause*) Japanese

Now repeat the activity, eliciting responses from individual Sts. Give further practice of any words your Sts find difficult to pronounce.

3 GRAMMAR verb *be* ☐ and ☐

a 🔊 **1.23** Focus on the instructions, and on the photos and conversations.

Play the audio, pausing after each interview for Sts to write the country or nationality.

Check answers.

1 Spain, Spanish **2** Australia **3** German, Switzerland

🔊 **1.23**
(script in Student's Book on *p.118*)
1 A Hi. Where are you from?
   B We're from Oviedo, in Spain.
   A OK. Good luck to the Spanish team!
   B Thank you!
2 A Hello. I'm Mike from UK News. Where are you from?
   B I'm from Australia.
   A Are you from Sydney?
   B No, I'm not. I'm from Cairns.
   A Where's Cairns? Is it near Sydney?
   B No, it isn't. It's in the north. Am I on TV?
   A Yes, you are.
   B Wow!
3 A Hi. Are you German?
   B No, we aren't. We're from Switzerland.
   A Oh, sorry!

b Give Sts two minutes to read the interviews again and complete the chart. Point out the example (*you aren't*).

Get Sts to compare with a partner, and then check answers by copying the chart onto the board and getting Sts to tell you how to complete it.

⊞	*I'm*	*you're*	*it's*
⊟	**I'm not**	*you aren't*	**it isn't**
☐	**Am I**	**Are you**	**Is it**

Finally, go through the interviews, eliciting / explaining the meaning of any words or phrases that Sts don't understand. You might want to point out to Sts the different use of *sorry* in the last interview. In **1A** Sts saw *Sorry* being used to ask someone to repeat something. Here the interviewer uses it to apologize – to show he feels bad about getting the nationality wrong.

c Tell Sts to go to **Grammar Bank 1B** on *p.124*.

🔊 **1.24** Focus on the example sentences and play the audio for Sts to listen and repeat. Then go through the rules with the class.

Now focus on the exercises for **1B** on *p.125*. Sts do the exercises individually or in pairs.

Check answers, getting Sts to read the full sentences.

a **1** I'm not British.
   2 They aren't Brazilian.
   3 It isn't in South America.
   4 You aren't French.

b **1** Am I in room 10? Yes, you are.
   2 Is it Spanish? No, it isn't.
   3 Are they students? No, they aren't.
   4 Is he from the USA? Yes, he is.
   5 Are you Mike Bell? No, I'm not.

c **1** 's **2** Are **3** 'm **4** 'm **5** Are **6** 'm **7** Is **8** isn't **9** 's **10** Are **11** 'm

Tell Sts to go back to the main lesson **1B**.

EXTRA SUPPORT If you think Sts need more practice, you may want to give them the **Grammar** photocopiable activity at this point.

d 🔊 **1.25** Focus on the example and tell Sts they will hear ten questions, and each time they must respond with a short answer.

Play the audio, pausing after each question to elicit a response from the whole class.

🔊 **1.25**
1 Is Sydney the capital of Australia? (*pause*) No, it isn't.
2 Are you English? (*pause*) No, I'm not.
3 Is Asterix French? (*pause*) Yes, he is.
4 Are the Simpsons English? (*pause*) No, they aren't.
5 Is sushi Chinese? (*pause*) No, it isn't.
6 Are Zara and Mango from Italy? (*pause*) No, they aren't.
7 Is Glasgow in Scotland? (*pause*) Yes, it is.
8 Are Honda and Suzuki Japanese? (*pause*) Yes, they are.
9 Is J.K. Rowling American? (*pause*) No, she isn't.
10 Is New York the capital of the United States? (*pause*) No, it isn't.

Now repeat the activity, eliciting responses from individual Sts.

 Play the audio again and ask Sts for the correct answers where appropriate, e.g. *'Is Sydney the capital of Australia?' 'No, it isn't. The capital of Australia is Canberra.'*

e Focus on the instructions and tell Sts to write similar questions to those they heard in **d**, beginning with *Is…?* or *Are…?*. Give them some more examples if necessary, and then set a time limit for Sts, in pairs, to write three questions.

Monitor and check what they are writing. Then put two pairs together and get them to answer each other's questions.

Get feedback from a few pairs.

4 SPEAKING

a Put Sts in pairs, **A** and **B**, and tell them to go to **Communication Where are they from?**, **A** on *p.102*, **B** on *p.108*.

Go through the instructions with them carefully, and focus on the two example questions (*Where's X from?* and *Where in (country)?*). Tell Sts they have to ask these questions for each of their three people and write the answers in the chart.

Sit **A** and **B** face-to-face. **A** asks his / her questions about person 1 to **B** and writes the information in the chart.

B now asks **A** about person 2, and they then take turns to ask and answer.

When they have finished, get them to compare charts, and then get feedback from some pairs.

Tell Sts to go back to the main lesson **1B**.

b Focus on the instructions and give Sts time to choose a different country from **Vocabulary Bank Countries** and then think of a city there.

Get Sts to ask you the questions first.

! The answer to *Where are you from?* is usually *I'm from (town)* when you're in your own country, and *I'm from (country)* or *I'm (nationality)* followed by the town when you're abroad.

Get Sts to stand up and ask five other Sts the questions.

Finally, ask a few Sts where they are from.

 In a multilingual class, get Sts to use their real towns and countries / nationalities.

5 VOCABULARY numbers 21–100

a 🔊 **1.26** This exercise revises numbers 1–20, which Sts did in **1A**. Focus on the illustration and elicit how to say it (*three plus one is…*). Then point out the speech bubble and elicit the number (*four*).

Tell Sts they are going to hear ten sums and they must only write the answers.

Play the audio, pausing after each question to give Sts time to write the answer.

Check answers by playing each sum again, pausing and getting individual Sts to answer.

See numbers in **bold** in script 1.26

🔊 **1.26**
1 What's three plus one? (*pause*) **four**
2 What's nine plus two? (*pause*) **eleven**
3 What's thirteen plus three? (*pause*) **sixteen**
4 What's eight plus five? (*pause*) **thirteen**
5 What's seven plus five? (*pause*) **twelve**
6 What's six plus four? (*pause*) **ten**
7 What's ten plus four? (*pause*) **fourteen**
8 What's five plus three? (*pause*) **eight**
9 What's eight plus three plus seven? (*pause*) **eighteen**
10 What's eleven plus seven plus two? (*pause*) **twenty**

b Tell Sts to go to **Vocabulary Bank** Days and numbers on *p.148* and get them to do **Part 3**.

Focus on **3 Numbers 21–100** and get Sts to do **a** individually or in pairs.

🔊 **1.27** Now do **b**. Play the audio for Sts to listen and check.

Check answers and write the numbers on the board.

30	35	40	43	50	59	60	67	70	72	80	88	90
94	100											

🔊 **1.27**
3 Numbers 21–100
twenty-one, thirty, thirty-five, forty, forty-three, fifty, fifty-nine, sixty, sixty-seven, seventy, seventy-two, eighty, eighty-eight, ninety, ninety-four, a hundred

Focus on the **Pronunciation** box and go through it with the class. Point out that *13, 14*, etc. are stressed on the second syllable, and *30, 40*, etc. are stressed on the first syllable. Sts will practise this difference in the next part of the lesson. Point out that with compound numbers e.g. *twenty-one, thirty-five, forty-three*, etc., the main stress is on the second number e.g. *twenty-<u>one</u>, thirty-<u>five</u>, forty-<u>three</u>*.

 Play the audio again or say the numbers yourself, pausing after each number for Sts to repeat.

Finally, focus on **Activation**. Get Sts to cover the words with a piece of paper and say the numbers.

Tell Sts to go back to the main lesson **1B**.

 A numbers game which Sts always enjoy is *Buzz*. You may want to play it now or at any other time when you want to revise numbers.
Get Sts to sit or stand in a circle and count out loud. When they come to a number which contains three (e.g. *13*) or a multiple of three (e.g. *three, six, nine*, etc.), they have to say *'Buzz'* instead of the number.
If a student makes a mistake, either saying the number instead of *'Buzz'*, or simply saying the wrong number, he / she is 'out', and the next player begins again from number one.
Carry on until there is only one student left, who is the winner, or until the group have got to 30 without making a mistake.
You can also play *Buzz* with seven as the 'wild' number, and go up to 50.

c 🔊 **1.28** Play the audio and get Sts to write the numbers they hear.

Check answers by eliciting the numbers onto the board.

> 25 33 47 50 66 78 81 99

🔊 **1.28**

> twenty-five thirty-three forty-seven fifty sixty-six
> seventy-eight eighty-one ninety-nine

d Sts work individually and choose ten numbers from 21 to 100, which they write on a piece of paper.

Put Sts in pairs and get them to dictate their numbers to their partner, who writes them down.

When they have swapped roles, they can compare pieces of paper to check for mistakes.

6 PRONUNCIATION & LISTENING word stress

Pronunciation notes

As Sts have seen in the **Vocabulary Bank**, *13*, *14*, etc. are stressed on the second syllable, and *30*, *40*, etc. are stressed on the first syllable. However, *13 / 30*, *14 / 40*, etc. can sound very similar and are often confused. Native speakers sometimes need to clarify which number they mean, by saying, e.g. *'one three'* or *'three oh'* to make it clear whether they are saying *13* or *30*.

a 🔊 **1.29** Play the audio and get Sts to repeat the numbers.

Ask What's the difference between the numbers in a and b?

The numbers in *a*, e.g. *13*, *14*, etc., are stressed on the second syllable, and the numbers in *b*, e.g. *30*, *40*, etc., are stressed on the first syllable.

Point out to Sts that this means that the pairs of numbers can be easily confused and this can be a problem, even for native speakers, particularly for example in a noisy environment like a restaurant or café.

🔊 **1.29**

See numbers in Student's Book on *p.9*

b 🔊 **1.30** Tell Sts that this time they will hear seven conversations, and in each conversation they will hear just <u>one</u> number from each pair in **a**.

Play the audio twice and Sts circle *a* or *b*.

Check answers.

EXTRA SUPPORT Read through the script and decide if you need to pre-teach any new lexis before Sts listen.

> **1** a 13 **2** b 40 **3** a 15 **4** b 60 **5** a 17 **6** b 80 **7** b 90

🔊 **1.30**

(script in Student's Book on *p.118*)

1 Announcer The train waiting on platform thirteen is the nine forty-eight Great Western train to Oxford, calling at Slough, Reading, Didcot Parkway, and Oxford.
  A That's our train. Platform thirteen. Come on.
  B OK. Let's go.
2 A Excuse me! How far is it to Dublin?
  B It's about forty kilometres.
  A Thanks a lot.
3 A Just one more set. Come on.
  B Fifteen–love.
  A Fantastic serve!
4 A Will all passengers on flight B-A two three four to Budapest please go to gate sixty immediately.
  B Gate sixty. Is that our flight?
  C No, it's to Budapest, not Bucharest.
5 A How much is that?
  B Two pizzas and a Coke. That's seventeen pounds.
6 A What's your address?
  B It's eighty Park Road.
  A Sorry? What number?
  B Eighty, eight oh. Park Road.
7 A OK, can you be quiet, please? Open your books on page ninety.
  B What page is it?
  C Page ninety.

EXTRA SUPPORT If there's time, you could get Sts to listen again with the script on *p.118*, so they can see exactly what they understood / didn't understand. Translate / Explain any new words or phrases.

EXTRA CHALLENGE Ask Sts what each conversation is about.

c Draw this bingo card on the board for Sts to copy.

In pairs, Sts complete their bingo card with six numbers from **a**. They must only choose one from each pair, e.g. either *13* or *30*, but not both.

Call out random numbers, choosing from the pairs of numbers in **a**. Keep a note of the numbers you call out.

If Sts have one of the numbers you call out on their card, they should cross it off. Keep calling until one pair has crossed off all the numbers, at which point they should call out *'Bingo!'*

Check the winning pair's card. If it's correct, they have won. If it isn't, continue the game. Once there is a winner, you can play again if there is time.

What's your email?

G possessive adjectives: *my*, *your*, etc.
V classroom language
P /əʊ/, /uː/, /ɑː/, the alphabet, sentence stress

Lesson plan

The context for this lesson is the classroom, and signing up for an English course. The lesson starts with a focus on classroom language, which helps Sts to understand and respond to common classroom instructions, and to ask the teacher in English for information and clarification. Sts then learn the pronunciation of the alphabet and practise it with common abbreviations. Next, Sts listen to a Skype interview with a student and a teacher at a language school in England, and learn how to give personal information and practise spelling. This leads into the grammar focus of possessive adjectives. The different elements of the lesson are brought together in the final activities, where Sts do a communication activity discovering what some actors' and singers' real names are, and a writing focus where they complete an application form for a visa.

More materials
For teachers
Photocopiables
Grammar possessive adjectives: *my*, *your*, etc. *p.170*
Vocabulary Classroom language *p.259* (instructions *p.253*)
Communicative Personal information *p.216*
(instructions *p.204*)
For students
Workbook 1C
Online Practice 1C

OPTIONAL LEAD-IN (BOOKS CLOSED)

Point to a few things in the classroom (from Vocabulary **a**) and ask Sts what they are. Write the words on the board, and model and drill pronunciation.

1 VOCABULARY classroom language

a Books open. Focus on the illustration and get Sts to match the words and pictures.

b ◗) **1.31** Play the audio for Sts to listen and check. Check answers.

◗) 1.31
4 a board
9 a chair
3 a computer
5 a desk
1 a door
2 a picture
8 a table
6 a wall
7 a window

Now play it again to drill the pronunciation of the words. Give further practice of any words your Sts find difficult to pronounce.

c Focus on the two small illustrations. Model and drill the two questions *What's this?* (for a singular object near you) and *What's that?* (for a singular object far from you). Demonstrate the meaning by touching your chair and asking *What's this?* Then point to the door and ask *What's that?*.

Put Sts in pairs and get them to point to objects and ask and answer the questions.

d Focus on the illustration in **a** again and the speech bubbles A–C. Tell Sts that sentences 1–3 are what the people are saying, and give them time to match them.

e ◗) **1.32** Play the audio for Sts to listen and check. Check answers.

1 C	2 A	3 B

◗) 1.32
1 C What page is it?
2 A Sorry I'm late.
3 B Look at the board, please.

f Tell Sts to go to **Vocabulary Bank** Classroom language on *p.150*. **The teacher says** section helps Sts recognize and respond to common instructions used in the classroom. Get Sts to do **a** individually or in pairs.

◗) **1.33** Now do **b**. Play the audio for Sts to listen and check.

Check answers. Make sure the meaning of each phrase is clear by miming or getting Sts to mime.

◗) 1.33
Classroom language
7 Open your books, please.
11 Go to page eighty-four.
13 Do exercise **a**.
5 Read the text.
1 Look at the board.
12 Close the door.
2 Work in pairs.
10 Answer the questions.
9 Listen and repeat.
6 Stand up.
3 Sit down.
8 Turn off your phone.
4 Please stop talking!

Focus on the **Please** box and go through it with the class.

In **You say** Sts learn phrases they themselves may need to use in class. Get Sts to do **c** individually or in pairs.

◗) **1.34** Now do **d**. Play the audio for Sts to listen and check.

Check answers. Make sure Sts know what all the phrases mean.

19 Sorry, can you repeat that, please?
14 Sorry I'm late.
18 I don't understand.
15 Can I have a copy, please?
22 How do you spell it?
17 I don't know.
21 How do you say *gato* in English?
20 Can you help me, please?
16 What page is it?

Either use the audio to drill the pronunciation of the sentences and questions, or model and drill them yourself. Encourage Sts to use the right rhythm.

Now focus on the instructions for **e**. Get Sts to cover the sentences and questions with a piece of paper, leaving the pictures visible.

Finally, focus on **Activation**. Tell Sts from now on you want them to try to use the phrases from this lesson. It's a good idea to have a poster on the wall with this classroom language for Sts to refer to.

Tell Sts to go back to the main lesson **1C**.

EXTRA SUPPORT If you think Sts need more practice, you may want to give them the **Vocabulary** photocopiable activity at this point.

g **1.35** Tell Sts they are going to hear some instructions and they must act out what they hear.

Play the audio and get Sts to follow the classroom instructions.

1.35
Stand up.
Sit down.
Open your books.
Go to page twelve.
Look at exercise one b.
Close your books.
Listen and repeat 'Nice to meet you.'
Answer the question 'Where are you from?'

2 PRONUNCIATION /əʊ/, /uː/, /ɑː/, the alphabet

Pronunciation notes

Remind Sts that the two dots in the symbols /uː/ and /ɑː/ mean that it's a long sound.

Remind Sts that /əʊ/ is a diphthong, i.e. two sounds together, /ə/ and /ʊ/, if you think this will help them.

a **1.36** Focus on the three sound pictures (*phone*, *boot*, *car*).

Now focus on the example words in the row next to each sound picture, e.g. *close* (verb), *go*, and *Poland*. Elicit / Explain that the pink letters are the same sound as the picture word they're next to. Demonstrate for Sts, e.g. say *phone*, *close*, *go*, etc.

Play the audio for Sts just to listen.

1.36
See words and sounds in Student's Book on *p.10*

Now play the audio again for Sts to listen and repeat.

EXTRA SUPPORT If these sounds are difficult for your Sts, it will help to show them the mouth position. You could model this yourself or use the Sound Bank videos on the *Teacher's Resource Centre*.

b **1.37** Focus on the alphabet. Explain that it's important to know how to say the English alphabet because you often need to spell names, surnames, town names, email addresses, passwords, etc. (especially when you're talking on the phone).

Play the audio for Sts to repeat the letters in groups of three.

1.37
See alphabet in Student's Book on *p.10*

c **1.38** Focus on the chart. Explain that the letters are in columns according to the vowel sound of each letter. Elicit the seven picture words and sounds (Sts have seen them all before).

Then show Sts how the letters in each column have the same vowel sound, e.g. *train*, A, H, J; *tree*, B, E, etc.

Put Sts in pairs. Get them to go through the alphabet, stopping at the letters that are missing from the chart, and writing them in the correct column. Do the first one with them (*C*). Write it on the board and ask Sts how to say it and which column it goes in (*tree*). Give Sts a time limit, e.g. three minutes, to complete the chart.

Play the audio once for Sts to listen and check answers (you may want to copy the complete chart onto the board).

1.38

train /eɪ/	A H J K
tree /iː/	B C D E G P T V
egg /e/	F L M N S X Z
bike /aɪ/	I Y
phone /əʊ/	O
boot /uː/	Q U W
car /ɑː/	R

Now play the audio again, pausing after each sound for Sts to repeat the group of letters.

d **1.39** Focus on the group of letters and explain that these letters are often confused. Play the audio for Sts just to listen to the different sounds.

1.39
See letters in Student's Book on *p.10*

e **1.40** Tell Sts that now they are going to hear just one letter from each group. They will hear the letter twice. Play the audio and tell Sts to circle the letter they hear. Check answers.

1.40
1 E, E   2 J, J   3 Q, Q   4 C, C   5 B, B   6 M, M   7 V, V   8 Y, Y

f Focus on the phrases and tell Sts that they are all things that we normally refer to just using abbreviations (the **bold** letters). Point out the example (*a PC*). Put Sts in pairs and get them to practise saying the abbreviations. Make sure they understand all the phrases.

Check answers.

 Play *Hangman*. Think of a word Sts know, preferably of at least eight letters, e.g. NATIONALITY. Write a dash on the board for each letter of the word:

— — — — — — — — — — —

Sts call out letters one at a time. If the letter is in the word (e.g. *A*), fill it in each time it occurs, e.g.
__ A __ __ __ __ __ A __ __ __ __. Only accept correctly pronounced letters. If the letter is <u>not</u> in the word, draw the first line of this picture on the board:

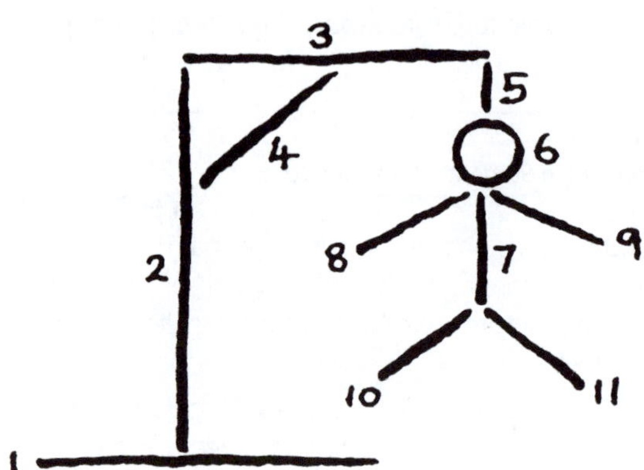

Write any wrongly guessed letters under the picture so that Sts don't repeat them. The object of the game is to guess the word before the man is 'hanged'. Sts can make guesses at any time, but each wrong guess is 'punished' by another line being drawn.
The student who correctly guesses the word comes to the board and chooses a new word.
Sts can also play in pairs / groups, drawing on a piece of paper.

3 LISTENING & SPEAKING understanding personal information

a 🔊 **1.41** Focus on the task and the photo of Micaela, a language student, and Mark, the man on the laptop screen, who is a teacher at a language school.

Now focus on the language school enrolment form. Explain (in Sts' L1 if necessary) that Micaela wants to study English at a language school in England. Tell Sts that they are going to listen to her having an interview with a teacher called Mark on Skype, and they must complete the form with her information.

Go through the different headings on the form and make sure Sts understand them. Explain the difference between *first name* and *surname*, using the names of famous people who you think Sts will know, e.g. *Brad Pitt*, showing that *Brad* is his first name and *Pitt* his surname (or family name). Sts may also not know *age* and *postcode*.

Play the audio once for Sts just to listen. Then play it again, pausing to give Sts time to complete the gaps. Play again if necessary.

 This is the first quite long listening that Sts have had. Reassure them by telling them just to relax and listen the first time, without trying to complete the form, but just trying to follow the conversation. Then tell them to try to complete some of the form, and play the audio as many times as you think they need, pausing where necessary, e.g. after the phone numbers.

Give Sts time to compare with a partner, and then check answers.

 Read through the script and decide if you need to pre-teach any new lexis before Sts listen.

1 Vazquez **2** 20 **3** Argentina **4** Buenos Aires **5** (Florida) 165 **6** C1005AAC **7** 11 15 8934 5568 **8** (54) 11 6023 5442

🔊 **1.41**
(script in Student's Book on *p.118*)

T = teacher, M = Micaela
T Hello? Hello? Can you hear me?
M Hi, yes, fine. I can hear you.
T Good! I'm Mark, from English House Language School.
M Hi, Mark.
T OK, can I check your details first?
M Yes, of course.
T What's your first name?
M Micaela.
T How do you spell it?
M M-I-C-A-E-L-A.
T M-I-C-A-E-L-A – is that right?
M Yes, that's right.
T And what's your surname?
M Vazquez.
T Vasquez. Is that V-A-S…?
M No, it's V-A-Z-Q-U-E-Z.
T V-A-Z-Q-U-E-Z. OK. And how old are you?
M I'm 20.
T Where are you from?
M I'm from Argentina.
T Where in Argentina?
M From Buenos Aires.
T What's your address?
M It's Florida one six five.
T Florida's the street? Number one six five?
M Yes.
T What's your postcode?
M Sorry?
T You know, the postcode.
M Ah yes. It's C-one zero zero five A-A-C.
T C-one zero zero five A-A-C. Great. What's your email address?
M It's m dot vazquez at mail dot com.
T And what's your phone number?
M My mobile or my home phone, my landline?
T Both – mobile and landline.
M My mobile is one one, one five, eight nine three four, five five six eight.
T One one, one five, eight nine three four, five five six eight. Great. And your landline?
M Five four, one one, six zero two three, five four four two.
T Five four, one one, six zero two three, five four four two.
M That's right.
T OK, that's great. So, what do you do, Micaela?
M I'm at university. I'm a medical student…

 If there's time, you could get Sts to listen again with the script on *p.118*, so they can see exactly what they understood / didn't understand. Translate / Explain any new words or phrases.

b 🔊 **1.42** Now focus on the teacher's questions and give Sts a couple of minutes to complete them. Point out that the first one (*What's*) has been done for them.

Play the audio for Sts to listen and check. Play it again, pausing if necessary.

Check answers and elicit the meaning of *How old are you?*

❗ The question *How old are you?* and the answer *I'm 20* are with the verb *be*. In your Sts' L1, a different verb may be used, e.g. *have*.

2 What's **3** How **4** How **5** from **6** What's **7** What's
8 email **9** number

◆) 1.42
1 What's your first name?
2 What's your surname?
3 How do you spell it?
4 How old are you?
5 Where are you from?
6 What's your address?
7 What's your postcode?
8 What's your email address?
9 What's your phone number?

EXTRA IDEA Get Sts to close their books. Play the audio
again, pausing after each question and get Sts to answer
about themselves.

c Focus on the **Sentence stress** box and go through it
with the class. Remind Sts that getting the rhythm right
when they speak will help them to understand and be
understood.

Play the audio, pausing after each question for Sts to
repeat the questions. Encourage them to copy the
rhythm.

EXTRA SUPPORT Play the audio, pausing after each question
for Sts to underline the stressed words. Check answers.

1 What's your first name?
2 What's your surname?
3 How do you spell it?
4 How old are you?
5 Where are you from?
6 What's your address?
7 What's your postcode?
8 What's your email address?
9 What's your phone number?

Then play the audio again for Sts to repeat the questions,
copying the rhythm.

d Focus on the **Saying emails** box and go through it with
the class.

EXTRA CHALLENGE Teach *underscore* (_) and *hyphen* (-), and
mention *double* for letters in spelling, e.g. *Ella*.

Put Sts in pairs, **A** and **B**, and get them to sit facing each
other. Explain that they're going to role-play the Skype
interview and ask and answer the questions in **b**. **A** is the
teacher, and **B** is a new student. **A** is going to interview **B**.
Tell **A** to start the interview: *Hello. What's your first name?*,
etc. Remind Sts to write down the answers.

! Tell Sts they can invent their ages, addresses, and phone
numbers if they prefer.

EXTRA CHALLENGE Get **B** to listen and answer the questions
with his / her book closed.

Get Sts to swap roles.

Get some quick feedback by asking a few Sts about their
partners, e.g. *What's his address? What's her email address?*

4 GRAMMAR possessive adjectives: *my*, *your*, etc.

a Focus on the two questions and answers, and get Sts to
complete the gaps.
Check answers.

1 you **2** I **3** your **4** My

b Tell Sts to go to **Grammar Bank 1C** on *p.124*.

Grammar notes

In some languages the possessive adjective agrees with
the following noun, i.e. it can be masculine, feminine, or
plural, depending on the gender and number of the noun
that comes after. In English, nouns don't have gender,
so possessive adjectives don't change, and the use of,
e.g. *his / her / their*, simply depends on whether we are
talking about something belonging or related to a man, a
woman, or two or more people.
Remind Sts that *your* is used for singular and plural.

◆) 1.43 Focus on the example sentences and play the
audio for Sts to listen and repeat. Then go through the
rules with the class.

Then focus on the ***it's or its?*** box and go through it with
the class.

Now focus on the exercises for **1C** on *p.125*. Sts do the
exercises individually or in pairs.

Check answers, getting Sts to read the full sentences.

a
1 Their **2** Her **3** Our **4** its **5** your **6** His **7** My
8 your **9** Her **10** Our
b
1 Her **2** their **3** your **4** she **5** He **6** his **7** your
8 Our **9** My **10** She

Tell Sts to go back to the main lesson **1C**.

EXTRA SUPPORT If you think Sts need more practice, you
may want to give them the **Grammar** photocopiable
activity at this point.

c **◆) 1.44** Focus on the examples and tell Sts they are
going to hear a sentence, e.g. *I'm Matt*, and they must
change it using a possessive adjective and the word *name*
(*My name's Matt*).

Play the audio, pausing after each sentence, and elicit a
response from the whole class.

◆) 1.44
1 I'm Matt. (*pause*) My name's Matt.
2 You're Sally. (*pause*) Your name's Sally.
3 We're Mike and Mia. (*pause*) Our names are Mike and Mia.
4 He's Ben. (*pause*) His name's Ben.
5 They're William and Harry. (*pause*) Their names are William and
   Harry.
6 She's Carla. (*pause*) Her name's Carla.

Now repeat the activity, eliciting responses from
individual Sts.

EXTRA SUPPORT The first time you could pause the audio
and give Sts time to write the transformed sentences. Then
repeat, getting Sts to cover what they wrote and do the
transformations orally.

d 🔊 **1.45** Focus on the photos and ask Sts if they know the people. Make sure they understand the meaning of *real* (= actually true, in this case names, e.g. on their passport or ID).

Ask the question to the class and for each photo, elicit with a show of hands who thinks they are their real names.

Play the audio for Sts to listen and check.

Check answers.

🔊 **1.45**
(script in Student's Book on *p.118*)
Snoop Dogg isn't his real name. His real name is Calvin Cordozar Broadus. He's American.
Shakira is her real name. Her full name is Shakira Isabel Mebarak Ripoll. She's from Colombia.

---

e Put Sts in pairs, **A** and **B**, and tell them to go to **Communication What's his / her real name?**, **A** on *p.102*, **B** on *p.108*.

Go through the instructions with them carefully. Explain / Elicit the meaning of *actor* (= a man in a film), *actress* (= a woman in a film), and *singer* (= a person whose job is singing). Tell Sts that nowadays the word *actor* is often used for both men and women. Then drill the question *What's his real name?* or *What's her real name?*.

Give Sts a minute to put crosses next to the names they think aren't real. Then sit **A** and **B** face-to-face. **A** asks his / her questions to **B** and writes the information in the chart.

B now asks **A** his / her questions.

At the end of the activity, get Sts to compare charts to check they have spelled the real names correctly.

Tell Sts to go back to the main lesson **1C**.

5 WRITING completing a form

This is the first time Sts are sent to the Writing section at the back of the Student's Book. Here Sts will find model texts, with exercises and language notes, and then a writing task. We suggest that you go through the model and do the exercise(s) in class, but set the actual writing task for homework.

Tell Sts to go to **Writing Completing a form** on *p.113*.

a Focus on the **Capital letters** box and go through it with the class. Tell them to highlight any rules which are different from their L1 (e.g. nationalities and languages are not written with a capital letter in several languages.).

b Focus on the application form for a visa. Go through the different sections with Sts. Highlight and check the meaning and pronunciation of:

- *Mr* for a man, *Mrs* for a married woman, and *Ms* /məz/ for a woman (giving no indication about marital status).
- *gender*, for the sex of the person (male or female).
- *married*, *single*, *divorced*, *separated*.
- *birth*.

  Give Sts a few minutes to complete the form. Remind them to check that they use capital letters correctly.

  Go round checking Sts are completing the form correctly. Then elicit answers from individual Sts for each section.

EXTRA IDEA If you want to give extra practice with personal information questions, get Sts to use the form to interview each other.

c Focus on the paragraph and get Sts to copy it out again, using capital letters where necessary.

Check answers by eliciting from Sts the words which need capital letters and writing the paragraph on the board.

My name's **M**arek. **I**'m from **G**dansk in **P**oland, and **I** speak **P**olish, **G**erman, and a little **E**nglish. **M**y teacher is **A**merican. **H**er name's **K**ate. **M**y **E**nglish classes are on **T**uesdays and **T**hursdays.

EXTRA SUPPORT Quickly revise how to say the alphabet in English before Sts try to correct the paragraph.

d As this writing task is very short, you may like to get Sts to do it in class. Get them to write their own paragraphs on a piece of paper, check for capital letters, and then swap the paragraph with another student.

Practical English Arriving in London

Function	checking in
Vocabulary	in a hotel

Lesson plan

This is the first in a series of six Practical English lessons (one every other File) which teach Sts functional language to help them 'survive' in English in travel and social situations. All the content for these lessons is on video. There is also an audio version, if you are unable to show the video in class. There is a storyline based on two characters, Rob Walker, a British journalist who works for a magazine called *London 24seven*, and Jenny Zielinski, who works in the New York office of the same magazine and is on a work trip to London. Sts meet them for the first time in this lesson, when Jenny arrives in the UK and checks into a hotel. The main focus of this lesson is on hotel vocabulary and checking into a hotel. You might want to point out to Sts that in the You say section of the lessons, they will be watching or listening and then repeating what the people say. If the speaker is Jenny, they will be listening to an American accent, but they do not need to copy the accent when they repeat her phrases. You can find the video on the *Teacher's Resource Centre*, *Classroom Presentation Tool*, *Class DVD*, and an audio-only version on the *Class Audio CDs*. Sts can find the video and extra activities on *Online Practice*.

More materials
For teachers
Teacher's Resource Centre
Video Practical English Episode 1
Quick Test 1
File 1 Test
For students
Workbook Practical English 1
Can you remember? 1
Online Practice Practical English 1
Check your progress

OPTIONAL LEAD-IN (BOOKS CLOSED)

Introduce this lesson (in Sts' L1 if you prefer) by giving the information in the lesson plan.

1 ▶ VOCABULARY in a hotel

a Books open. Focus on the symbols. Give Sts, in pairs, a few minutes to match the words and symbols.

b 🔊 1.46 Play the video / audio for Sts to check.

Check answers. Check Sts understand *ground floor*, and drill the pronunciation of *first*, *second*, and *third*. You may also want to teach that for other ordinals, you normally add *th*, e.g. *fourth*.

🔊 **1.46**

1 Reception   6 the lift   2 a single room   4 a double room
3 the bar   5 the ground floor

Focus Sts' attention on the phonetics next to each word. Now play the video / audio again, pausing after each word for Sts to repeat.

c Tell Sts to cover the words and look at the symbols. They could either test themselves or a partner.

2 ▶ INTRODUCTION

a 🔊 1.47 Focus on the two photos and elicit what Sts can see. Tell them that the man is Rob and the woman is Jenny, and that they are the main characters in these lessons.

Focus on sentences 1–6 and go through them with Sts, eliciting / explaining new words, e.g. *lives*, *works*, *magazine*, etc. Then play the video / audio once the whole way through for Sts just to watch or listen.

Then play it again for Sts to mark the sentences *T* (true) or *F* (false). Make it clear that they don't need to correct the false sentences yet.

Get Sts to compare with a partner, and then check answers.

1 T 2 T 3 F 4 F 5 T 6 F

🔊 **1.47**

Rob Hi. My name's Rob Walker.
I live here in London, I work in London, and I write about London!
I work for a magazine called *London 24seven*.
I write about life in London – the people, the theatre, the restaurants…It's fun!
I love London. It's a great city.
Jenny Hi. My name's Jenny Zielinski.
I'm from New York – the number one city in the world.
I'm the assistant editor of a magazine, *New York 24seven*. I'm the *new* assistant editor.
But this week, I'm on a business trip to London.
This is my first time in the UK.
It's very exciting!

b Play the video / audio again, so Sts can watch or listen again and correct the false sentences.

Get Sts to compare with a partner, and then check answers.

3 The name of his magazine is *London 24seven*.
4 Jenny is **American**.
6 It's her **first** time in the UK.

EXTRA SUPPORT If there's time and you are using the video, you could get Sts to watch again with subtitles / showing the script, so they can see exactly what they understood / didn't understand. Translate / Explain any new words or phrases.

3 ▶ CHECKING IN

a 🔊 1.48 Focus on the photo and ask Sts *Who is the person?* (the receptionist in a hotel).

Now either tell Sts to close their books and write questions 1 and 2 on the board, or get Sts to focus on the two questions.

Play the video / audio once the whole way through and then check answers.

 Sts will be surprised to hear Jenny say *zee*, not *zed*. Explain that this is American English, and is the only letter of the alphabet that is different from British English.

> **1** Z-I-**E**-L-I-**N**-S-K-**I**   **2** 306

🔊 **1.48** 🔊 **1.49**

R = receptionist, J = Jenny

R Good evening, madam.
J Hello. I have a reservation. (*repeat*) My name's Jennifer Zielinski. (*repeat*)
R Can you spell that, please?
J Z-I-E-L-I-N-S-K-I. (*repeat*)
R For five nights?
J Yes, that's right. (*repeat*)
R Can I have your passport, please?
J Just a second… (*repeat*) Here you are. (*repeat*)
R Thank you. Can you sign here, please? Thank you. Here's your key. It's room three oh six, on the third floor. The lift is over there.
J The lift? Oh, the elevator. (*repeat*)
R Yes. Enjoy your stay, Ms Zielinski.
J Thank you. (*repeat*)

b Now focus on the conversation in the chart. Ask Sts *Who says the **You hear** sentences?* and elicit that it is the receptionist. Then ask *Who says the **You say** sentences?* and elicit that here it is Jenny. These phrases will be useful for Sts if they need to check into a hotel.

Give Sts a minute to read through the conversation and think what the missing words might be. Then play the video / audio again, and get Sts to complete the gaps. Play again if necessary.

Get Sts to compare with a partner, and then check answers.

> **1** spell   **2** please   **3** key   **4** lift

Go through the conversation line by line with Sts, helping them with any words or expressions they don't understand. You might want to highlight that we use *over there* to indicate something which is some distance away from the speakers.

Now focus on the information box about **British and American English** and **Greetings**, and go through it with the class.

Ask Sts which greeting they would use now if they met someone.

c 🔊 **1.49** Now focus on the **You say** phrases and tell Sts they're going to hear the conversation again. They should repeat the **You say** phrases when they hear the beep. Encourage Sts to copy the rhythm and intonation, but <u>not</u> to try to copy Jenny's American accent. Where Jenny pronounces *z* as /ziː/, Sts should pronounce it as /zed/.
Play the video / audio, pausing if necessary for Sts to repeat the phrases.

🔊 **1.49**
Same as script 1.48 with repeat pauses

d Put Sts in pairs, **A** and **B**. **A** is the receptionist. Get Sts to read the conversation aloud, and then swap roles.

e Put Sts in pairs, **A** and **B**. Tell Sts to read their instructions, and help them to understand exactly what they have to do.

A is the receptionist and has his / her book open. He / She reads the **You hear** part with the new information. Elicit that he / she needs to change *Good evening* to *Good morning*, *madam* to *sir* if **B** is a man, and *It's room 306 on the third floor* to *It's room 207 on the second floor*.

B has his / her book closed. He / She should quickly read the **You say** phrases again before starting. Remind Sts **B** that they should use their own first name and surname.

f Sts now role-play the conversation. **A** starts. Monitor and help.

When they have finished, they should swap roles.
You could get a few pairs to perform in front of the class.

g 🔊 **1.50** Focus on the **Can you…? Can I have…?** box and go through it with the class. Highlight that *Can I have…?* is one of the most common ways to ask for something in English (much more common than *Can you give me…?*).
Now play the video / audio for Sts to listen and repeat the *Can* phrases.

🔊 **1.50**
See phrases in Student's Book on *p.13*

h Tell Sts to imagine they are in a hotel and they want certain things from the receptionist. Focus on the four things and make sure Sts know what they mean.
Elicit the phrases from the class or individual Sts.

> Can I have my key, please? / Can I have the key to room X, please?
> Can I have my passport, please?
> Can I have a map of London, please?
> Can I have a pen, please?

EXTRA IDEA Focus on how Jenny says *Here you are* as a response to *Can I have your passport, please?* Get Sts to practise in pairs, asking each other for the four things with *Can I have…, please?*.

4 ▶ JENNY TALKS TO ROB

a 🔊 **1.51** Focus on the photo and elicit that Jenny is in the hotel bar, and then she talks on the phone to Rob.

Focus on the instructions and on sentences 1–6. Go through them with Sts and make sure they understand them.

Now play the video / audio once the whole way through, and get Sts to mark the sentences *T* (true) or *F* (false). Make it clear that they don't need to correct the false sentences yet.

Get Sts to compare with a partner, and then check answers.

> **1** F   **2** T   **3** F   **4** F   **5** T   **6** F

🔊 **1.51**

W = waitress, J = Jenny, R = Rob
W Is your tea OK?
J   Yes, thank you…It's very quiet this evening.
W Yes, very relaxing! Are you on holiday?
J   No, I'm here on business.
W Where are you from?
J   I'm from New York. What about you?
W I'm from Budapest, in Hungary.
J   Really? Oh, sorry.
W No problem.
***
J   Hello?
R Is that Jennifer?
J   Yes…
R This is Rob. Rob Walker…from *London 24seven*?
J   Oh, Rob, yes, of course. Hi.
R Hi. How are you?
J   Oh, I'm fine, thanks. A little tired, that's all.
R I can meet you at the hotel tomorrow morning. Is nine OK for you?
J   That's perfect.
R Great. OK, see you tomorrow at nine.
J   Thanks. See you then. Bye.
W Would you like another tea?
J   No, thanks. It's time for bed.
W Good night, and enjoy your stay.
J   Good night.

b Play the video / audio again, so Sts can watch or listen a second time and correct the false sentences.

Get Sts to compare with a partner, and then check answers.

> 1 Jenny has **tea**.
> 3 The waitress is **Hungarian**.
> 4 **Rob Walker** phones **Jenny**.
> 6 Their meeting is at **9.00**.

EXTRA SUPPORT If there's time and you are using the video, you could get Sts to watch again with subtitles / showing the script, so they can see exactly what they understood / didn't understand. Translate / Explain any new words or phrases.

c 🔊 **1.52** Focus on the ***Would you like…?*** box and go through it with the class. Highlight that in English it is not polite to respond to an offer with simply *Yes* or *No*. We always use *Yes, please* or *No, thanks*.

Now tell Sts they must listen and repeat the *Would you like…?* phrases and responses.

Play the video / audio, pausing to give Sts time to repeat.

🔊 **1.52**
See script in Student's Book on *p.13*

d Focus on the list of drinks and make sure Sts know what they are.

Put Sts in pairs and get them to practise offering and responding to each other.

e Focus on the **Social English** phrases and go through them with the class.

In pairs, get Sts to decide who says them.

f 🔊 **1.53** Play the video / audio for Sts to watch or listen to the six phrases and check their answers to **e**.

Check answers. If you know your Sts' L1, you could get them to translate the phrases. Highlight that *This is (Rob Walker)* is what we use on the phone to say who we are.

> **1** J   **2** J   **3** w   **4** R   **5** J   **6** J

🔊 **1.53**
See Social English phrases in Student's Book on *p.13*

Now play the video / audio again, pausing after each phrase for Sts to watch or listen and repeat.

g Focus on the instructions and make sure Sts understand what they have to do. Point out that the first one (4) has been done for them.

Get Sts to compare with a partner, and then check answers.

> **B** 6   **C** 1   **D** 2   **E** 3   **F** 5

Now put Sts in pairs and get them to practise the conversations.

Finally, focus on the **CAN YOU…?** questions and ask Sts if they feel confident they can now do these things. If they feel that they need more practice, tell them to go to *Online Practice* to watch the episode again and practise the language.

2A Are you tidy or untidy?

G singular and plural nouns
V things, *in*, *on*, *under*
P final *-s* and *-es*

Lesson plan

Two rooms, one very tidy and one very untidy, where the well-known authors Virginia Woolf and Ian Rankin wrote their books provide the context for the presentation of both vocabulary and grammar in the lesson. Sts begin by looking at photos of these rooms, which are full of objects, and then learn more words for everyday things. They then learn the grammar of singular and plural nouns, and focus on the pronunciation of the final *-s* or *-es* in plural nouns. There is then a second vocabulary focus, where Sts learn how to use *in*, *on*, and *under*, after which all the language from the lesson is practised in Speaking and Listening.

More materials

For teachers

Photocopiables
Grammar single and plural nouns *p.171*
Vocabulary Things *p.260* (instructions *p.253*)
Communicative Mystery objects *p.217*
(instructions *p.205*)

For students

Workbook 2A

Online Practice 2A

OPTIONAL LEAD-IN (BOOKS CLOSED)

Make sure you have five of the things taught in **Vocabulary Bank Things** (*p.151*) in your bag, e.g. a phone, a purse or wallet, etc. Pre-teach some of the vocabulary from the lesson, first with the bag itself, by asking Sts *What's this?* and eliciting *It's a bag*, and continuing with the things in your bag.

Write the words for the things on the board, and model and drill pronunciation.

1 VOCABULARY things

a Books open. Focus on the photos on *p.14* and find out if Sts know Virginia Woolf and Ian Rankin. You might want to tell them that Virginia Woolf began writing as a young girl and published her first novel, *The Voyage Out*, in 1915. She committed suicide in 1941, at the age of 59. Ian Rankin is famous for his detective novels, especially the Inspector Rebus series. The books have been translated into 22 languages and are bestsellers around the world.

Now focus on the question and make sure Sts understand *tidy* (= with everything in the right place) and *untidy*. Model and drill the pronunciation of the two words.

Elicit a few answers from the class. You could tell the class whether you are tidy or not.

b Focus on the instructions and put Sts in pairs.

When time is up, elicit Sts' answers and write them on the board.

See which pair got the most words.

Virginia Woolf
1 door **2** lamp **3** file **4** glasses **5** chair
Ian Rankin
6 laptop **7** window **8** photo **9** table **10** newspaper

c Tell Sts to go to **Vocabulary Bank Things** on *p.151* and get them to do **a** individually or in pairs.

Vocabulary notes

You may want to highlight that:
- an *identity card* is often abbreviated to an *ID card*
- a *purse* is normally used by a woman, and a *wallet* by a man

◗) 2.1 Now do **b**. Play the audio for Sts to listen and check.
Check answers.

◗) 2.1
Things
15 a bag
9 a charger
1 a coin
21 a credit card
5 a diary
23 a dictionary
2 a file
4 glasses
22 headphones
13 an identity card
11 a key
29 a lamp
3 a laptop
17 a magazine
14 a newspaper
30 a notebook
26 a pen
16 a pencil
12 a phone
8 a photo
20 a piece of paper
24 a purse
19 scissors
28 sunglasses
25 a tablet
27 a ticket
7 a tissue
10 an umbrella
6 a wallet
18 a watch

Then either use the audio to drill the pronunciation of the words, or model and drill them yourself. Give further practice of any words your Sts find difficult to pronounce.

Focus on the **Plural nouns** box and go through it with the class.

Now focus on **Activation**. Model and drill the two questions, *What is it?* (for singular objects) and *What are they?* (for plural objects). Stress that *What are they?* is only for the four plural objects, *glasses*, *headphones*, *scissors*, and *sunglasses*. Demonstrate by holding up an object, e.g. a pen, and ask *What is it?* to elicit *It's a pen*. Then do the same with a pair of glasses or scissors, etc.

In pairs, get Sts to cover the words with a piece of paper, look at the photos, and ask the appropriate question.

Tell Sts to go back to the main lesson **2A**.

 If you think Sts need more practice, you may want to give them the **Vocabulary** photocopiable activity at this point.

2 GRAMMAR singular and plural nouns

a Focus on the chart and get Sts to complete it in pairs. Point out that the first one (*an umbrella*) has been done for them.

Check answers.

> (two) umbrellas   a watch   a diary

Now ask Sts if they can guess why we use *an* (not *a*) before *umbrella*.

> Because it begins with a vowel sound, not a consonant sound.

b Tell Sts to go to **Grammar Bank 2A** on *p.126*.

Grammar notes
Singular nouns
We usually use singular nouns for things with *a / an* (the indefinite article).

Articles are easy for some nationalities and more difficult for others, depending on Sts' L1. Here the focus is just on the indefinite article. Some nationalities may not have an indefinite article, and others may confuse the number one with the indefinite article as it may be the same word in their L1.

Plural nouns
The system in English of making regular nouns plural is very straightforward, simply adding an *s*.

es (/ɪz/) is added to some nouns when it would be impossible to pronounce the word by adding just an *s*, e.g. *watches*. A very small number of English words have an irregular plural form, e.g. *child – children*.

🔊 **2.2** Focus on the example sentences and play the audio for Sts to listen and repeat. Then go through the rules with the class.

Focus on the information box about **the** and go through it with the class.

❗ Articles are very easy for some nationalities and more difficult for others, depending on Sts' L1. If articles are a problem for your Sts, give more examples to highlight the meaning of *the*.

Then go through the rules for regular and irregular plurals with the class.

Highlight particularly the pronunciation of -*es* (/ɪz/) in *watches* and *boxes*.

Now focus on the exercises for **2A** on *p.127*. Sts do the exercises individually or in pairs.

Check answers, getting Sts to read the full sentences in **b**.

> **a**
> **1 a** window, windows   **2 a** key, keys   **3 an** identity card, identity cards   **4 a** country, countries   **5 a** watch, watches   **6 an** exercise, exercises   **7 a** person, people   **8 an** email, emails   **9 a** box, boxes   **10 a** woman, women
> **b**
> **1** They're children.   **2** It's a purse.   **3** They're men.   **4** It's an umbrella.   **5** They're sunglasses.   **6** They're scissors.   **7** It's a charger.   **8** They're diaries.   **9** It's a coin.   **10** It's an egg.

Tell Sts to go back to the main lesson **2A**.

 If you think Sts need more practice, you may want to give them the **Grammar** photocopiable activity at this point.

3 PRONUNCIATION final -*s* and -*es*

Pronunciation notes
When plural nouns end in *s*, the *s* is pronounced either as /s/ or as /z/ depending on the previous sound. The difference is small and difficult for Sts at this level to hear or produce (they will tend to pronounce all endings as /s/), and you simply want to point it out. Sometimes this difference can produce misunderstanding, e.g. *eyes* /aɪz/ and *ice* /aɪs/. The full rules are:

1 -*s* is pronounced /s/ after these unvoiced* sounds: /k/, /p/, /f/, /t/, e.g. *books, maps, cats*.

2 -*s* is pronounced /z/ after all other (voiced*) endings, e.g. *phones*, *keys*, *photos*. This is by far the biggest group.

*Voiced and unvoiced consonants
Voiced consonant sounds are made by vibrating the vocal chords, e.g. /b/, /l/, /m/, /v/, etc. Unvoiced consonant sounds are made without vibration in the throat, e.g. /p/, /k/, /t/, /s/, etc.

You can demonstrate this to Sts by getting them to hold their hands against their throats. For voiced sounds, they should feel a vibration in their throat, but not for unvoiced sounds.

However, a common error, which is easier to help Sts with, is the tendency to add the /ɪz/ pronunciation to nouns which don't need it, e.g. *files* as /faɪlɪz/, etc. This rule, i.e. when to pronounce -*es* as /ɪz/, is the main focus of the exercises here.

a 🔊 **2.3** Focus on the chart. Elicit the two sound picture words (*snake* and *zebra*) and the sounds /s/ and /z/. If your Sts have problems hearing the difference between these two sounds, tell them and demonstrate that the /s/ is like the sound a snake makes, and the /z/ is like the sound made by a bee or a fly.

Play the audio for Sts just to listen to the sounds and example words.

🔊 **2.3**
See words and sounds in Student's Book on *p.15*

Now play the audio again for Sts to listen and repeat.

b 🔊 **2.4** Focus on the **Final -s or -es** box and go through it with the class.

Now ask Sts to circle the words in 1–8 where *-es* is pronounced /ɪz/.

Get them to compare their answers with a partner.

Play the audio for Sts to listen and check.

Check answers.

1 classes **4** boxes **5** pieces **7** pages

🔊 **2.4**
See words in Student's Book on *p.15*

Now play the audio again for Sts to listen and repeat.

c Focus on the instructions and get Sts to look at the photos of Virginia Woolf and Ian Rankin's rooms on *p.14* and write all the plural items they can see. Sts could do this individually or in pairs.

Check answers.

Virginia Woolf: chairs, doors, files, glasses
Ian Rankin: tables / desks, chairs, pieces of paper, photos, CDs

4 VOCABULARY & SPEAKING *in, on, under*

a Tell Sts to look at the photos and complete the gaps with *in*, *on*, or *under*.

Check answers.

1 on **2** in **3** under

b Put Sts in pairs, **A** and **B**, and tell them to go to **Communication in, on, under**, A on *p.103*, B on *p.108*.

Go through the instructions with Sts carefully, and focus on the example question (*Where's the charger?*). Elicit the question for a plural object, e.g. headphones (*Where are the headphones?*). Tell Sts they have to ask these questions for the objects in their list, and then they must draw the object in the correct place in the picture. Elicit / Explain the meaning of *draw*.

Sit **A** and **B** face-to-face if possible. **A** asks his / her first question about the charger to **B** and draws the item in picture 1. When **A** has finished asking about all his / her objects, Sts swap roles and **B** now asks **A** about the file.

When they have finished, get them to compare pictures.

Finally, elicit some sentences from the class about the objects in both pictures.

Picture 1
The charger is in the bag.   The glasses are on the book.
The keys are under the desk.   The laptop is on the chair.
The scissors are on the book.   The umbrella is under the chair.
The wallet is on the desk.

Picture 2
The file is under the desk.   The headphones are in the bag.   The magazine is under the bag.   The phone is on the chair.   The photo is on the desk.   The tissues are in the bag.   The watch is on the book.

Tell Sts to go back to the main lesson **2A**.

5 LISTENING listening for detail

a 🔊 **2.5** Focus on the task. Elicit / Explain that *a study* is another term for a room in a house where you study, read, or write. Make sure Sts understand that the first time they listen, they just need to number the places in the left-hand column that the three speakers talk about.

Play the audio for Sts to listen and complete the task.

Check answers.

1 on his desk **2** in her study **3** in her bag

🔊 **2.5**
(script in Student's Book on *p.118*)
1 On my desk I have my computer. I have some pens and pieces of paper. I have a lamp, and a photo of my family. Oh, and a phone. It's very tidy.
2 In my study I have a desk, a table, and two chairs. I have a lot of books and a big dictionary on the desk – it isn't very tidy! And I have a map of Europe on the wall.
3 I have a lot of things in my bag. I have my phone. I have the charger for my phone. I have my sunglasses, tissues. And I have my house keys and my purse.

b Play the audio again, and this time, tell Sts to write the things each person has. Point out that the first item (*a computer*) has been done for them. Play the audio again if necessary.

Check answers.

Speaker 1
a computer, pens, pieces of paper, a lamp, a photo, a phone
Speaker 2
a desk, a table, two chairs, books, a dictionary, a map
Speaker 3
a phone, a charger, sunglasses, tissues, keys, a purse

c In pairs, Sts tell each other what they have in their bag, on their desk, or where they work or study.

Get some feedback on what things Sts have, and who has a tidy desk or study.

G adjectives: *bad*, *good*, etc.
V colours, adjectives, modifiers: *very / really*, *quite*
P long and short vowel sounds

Lesson plan

In this lesson iconic aspects of the USA are used to introduce common adjectives and their grammatical position, and Sts learn to give simple descriptions of things. Sts begin with a vocabulary focus on common adjectives. The grammar of adjectives is presented through a quiz about American icons, which includes common adjective / noun phrases such as *The White House* and *New York*, which should be familiar to Sts in English or in their own language. After the grammar practice, Sts go on to a pronunciation focus on long and short vowel sounds, which also serves to recycle the adjectives. Sts then do a picture-difference activity, before reading an article about the differences between British and American English.

More materials
For teachers
Photocopiables
Grammar adjectives *p.172*
Vocabulary Opposites crossword *p.261*
(instructions *p.253*)
Communicative Can you name…? *p.218*
(instructions *p.205*)
For students
Workbook 2B
Online Practice 2B

1 VOCABULARY colours, adjectives

a Books open. Focus on the question. Sts need to add the missing vowels.

Get Sts to compare with a partner, and then write the answer on the board.

red, white, blue

b 🔊 **2.6** Individually or in pairs, Sts complete the colours. Play the audio for Sts to listen and check.

Check answers by eliciting the missing letters onto the board. Model and drill pronunciation. Highlight especially the pronunciation of *orange* /ˈɒrɪndʒ/.

black yellow grey orange brown
pink green purple silver gold

🔊 **2.6**
black yellow grey orange brown
pink green purple silver gold

c Focus on the instructions, and model and drill the two questions.

Put Sts in pairs and get them to ask each other about things in the classroom.

d Tell Sts to go to **Vocabulary Bank Adjectives** on *p.152*.

> **Vocabulary notes**
> Three of the adjectives here have two meanings: *old*, *right*, and *short*. Make sure Sts are clear about the different meanings and their opposites.

Focus on the pictures and tell Sts they have to match the numbered pictures to the pairs of adjectives. Get Sts to do **a** individually or in pairs.

🔊 **2.7** Now do **b**. Play the audio for Sts to listen and check.
Check answers.

🔊 **2.7**
Adjectives
19 beautiful ugly
2 big small
7 cheap expensive
4 clean dirty
5 easy difficult
9 fast slow
6 full empty
1 good bad
10 high low
17 hot cold
20 light dark
11 long short
14 old new
16 old young
15 rich poor
13 right left
12 right wrong
3 safe dangerous
8 the same different
18 strong weak
21 tall short

Then either use the audio to drill the pronunciation of the adjectives, or model and drill them yourself. Give further practice of any words your Sts find difficult to pronounce.

Focus on the instructions for **c**. Put Sts in pairs and get them to test each other. **A** (book open) says an adjective, e.g. *full*, and **B** (book closed) answers *empty*. They then swap roles.

Focus on the **Modifiers** box and go through it with Sts.

Get Sts to do **Activation**, checking that they know the names and places before they start.

Check answers.

Possible answers

Mount Everest is very high and cold.
Bill Gates is American and very rich.
The *Mona Lisa* is beautiful, old, and quite small.
The Pyramids are very old and very big.
Africa is very hot and quite poor.

Finally, focus on the **Opinion adjectives** box and go through it with the class. Model and drill the adjectives.

Tell Sts to go back to the main lesson **2B**.

EXTRA SUPPORT If you think Sts need more practice, you may want to give them the **Vocabulary** photocopiable activity at this point.

2 GRAMMAR adjectives

a Focus on the photos in *American Icons* and the **Adjectives** and **Nouns** in the circles. Then focus on the example (*American football*) and make sure Sts know what they have to do.

Put Sts in pairs and set a time limit, e.g. two or three minutes, for Sts to label the photos.

Check answers.

2 yellow taxis   **3** fast food   **4** French fries   **5** White House
6 blue jeans   **7** hot dog   **8** New York

b Focus on the instructions and give Sts time to circle the correct word or phrase in 1 and 2.

Check answers. Elicit / Explain that adjectives go before a noun, and adjectives don't change before a plural noun.

1 hot dog   **2** yellow

c Tell Sts to go to **Grammar Bank 2B** on *p.126*.

Grammar notes

The grammar of adjectives in English is simple.

There is only *one* possible form, which never changes.

When an adjective is with a noun in a phrase, there is only *one* possible position: *before* the noun, e.g. *a new car*, *a big house*.

However, Sts sometimes get confused because when the adjective goes with a noun, the order is, e.g. *a fast car*, but if it is in a question with *be*, it goes after the subject, e.g. *Is your car fast?*

2.8 Focus on the example sentences and play the audio for Sts to listen and repeat. Then go through the rules with the class.

Now focus on the exercises for **2B** on *p.127*. Sts do the exercises individually or in pairs.

Check answers, getting Sts to read the full sentences.

a
1 It's a very big house.
2 Is Louis French?
3 It's an expensive watch.
4 Is it an easy exercise?
5 Is your girlfriend Spanish?
6 These questions are very difficult.
7 Are they cheap tickets?
8 My new glasses are very good.

b
1 It's a very hot day.
2 Is your teacher Australian?
3 That car isn't very fast.
4 It's a bad idea.
5 Are you good students?
6 English is quite easy.
7 My brother is really strong.
8 This is a slow train.

Tell Sts to go back to the main lesson **2B**.

EXTRA SUPPORT If you think Sts need more practice, you may want to give them the **Grammar** photocopiable activity at this point.

d Get Sts to close their books and try to remember the phrases in *American Icons*. You could do this as a whole-class activity or get Sts to do it in pairs.

If Sts worked in pairs, check answers.

3 PRONUNCIATION long and short vowel sounds

Pronunciation notes

Many Sts will find it difficult to hear the difference between some or all long and short vowel sounds, as they may not have these sounds in their L1. You can help Sts to hear the difference by exaggerating the long sounds.

You can also use the videos with the **Sound Bank** to show Sts the correct mouth position, or get Sts to watch them at home.

a **2.9** Focus on the eight sound pictures.
Play the audio for Sts just to listen.

2.9
See words and sounds in Student's Book on *p.17*

Now play the audio again for Sts to listen and repeat. Elicit that /iː/, /ɑː/, /ɔː/ and /uː/ are long sounds. Remind Sts that the two dots in the phonetic symbol mean that it is a long sound.

EXTRA SUPPORT If these sounds are difficult for your Sts, it will help to show them the mouth position. You could model this yourself or use the Sound Bank videos on the *Teacher's Resource Centre.*

b **2.10** Focus on the instructions. Tell Sts they are going to hear two adjectives for each sound, and they must write them in the chart.

Play the audio, pausing after each pair to give Sts time to write.

Get Sts to compare with a partner, and then play the audio again.

Check answers.

2.10

fish /ɪ/	rich, big
tree /iː/	easy, cheap
cat /æ/	black, bad
car /ɑː/	fast, dark
clock /ɒ/	hot, wrong
horse /ɔː/	small, short
bull /ʊ/	full, good
boot /uː/	blue, new

Then play the audio again, pausing after each group for Sts to repeat.

c Focus on the two groups of words and the example, and explain the activity. Remind Sts to use the article *a / an* with singular nouns.

Put Sts in pairs and give them time to write the phrases.

 You could make **c** into a race with a time limit of, for example, three minutes.

d ◗ **2.11** Play the audio for Sts to listen and check.

Check answers and find out if any pairs have made nine correct phrases.

◗ **2.11**

a big city   a black bag   cheap jeans   dark glasses   a good book
a grey day   new boots   an old photo   a short story

Then play the audio again to drill the pronunciation of the phrases.

 Get Sts to make adjective + noun phrases about things in the classroom, e.g. *a dirty board, big windows, a brown bag*, etc.

4 SPEAKING

a Focus on the instructions, and then give Sts time to think of eight things they have.

 You could get Sts to write the eight things they have.

Put Sts in pairs and get them to tell each other about their eight things.

Get some feedback from individual Sts.

 Before getting feedback, ask Sts if they can remember the eight things their partner has. Get Sts to tell each other *You have…*.

b Put Sts in pairs, **A** and **B**, and tell them to go to **Communication The same or different?**, **A** on *p.103*, **B** on *p.109*.

Go through the instructions with them carefully.

Sit **A** and **B** face-to-face. **A** describes the odd pictures and **B** describes the even pictures. **A** starts by describing picture 1, and **B** must say if his / her picture is the same or different. Then **B** describes picture 2, and **A** responds.

When Sts have found the eight pictures where there are differences, tell them to compare pictures to see if they have correctly identified them.

Different: Pictures 1, 3, 4, 5, 7, 9, 11, 12
The same: Pictures 2, 6, 8, 10

Tell Sts to go back to the main lesson **2B**.

5 READING   identifying paragraph headings

a Focus on the title of the article and elicit what it is about (the differences between the two languages).

Give Sts time to read the article and complete the headings. Point out that the first one (*Vocabulary*) has been done for them.

Get Sts to compare with a partner.

 Before Sts read the article the first time, check whether you need to pre-teach any vocabulary.

b ◗ **2.12** Play the audio for Sts to listen to the article and check answers to **a**.

Check answers.

2 Spelling   **3** Grammar   **4** Pronunciation

◗ **2.12**
British and American English – the same, but different
British and American people speak the same language, English, but with some small differences.
1 Vocabulary
Some words are different in American English, for example, they say *ZIP code*, not *postcode*; *vacation*, not *holiday*; and *cell phone*, not *mobile phone*. Some words have different meanings, for example, in British English a *purse* is a thing where women have their money and credit cards. In American English a *purse* is a woman's bag.
2 Spelling
Colour, *favour*, and other words that end in *o-u-r* in British English end in *o-r* in American English. *Centre*, *theatre*, and other words that end in *t-r-e* in British English, end in *t-e-r* in American English.
3 Grammar
There are some small differences, especially prepositions. For example, Americans say *See you Friday*, but British people say *See you on Friday*.
4 Pronunciation
This is the really important difference between American and British English. American accents and British accents are very different. When an American starts speaking, British people know he or she is American, and vice versa.

 You could ask the class what nationality they think the speaker is. With a show of hands find out who thinks the speaker is American (The speaker is American.).

c Give Sts time to mark sentences 1–6 *T* (true) or *F* (false).

Check answers. Elicit why the *F* answers are false.

1 F (The differences are small.)
2 F (In American English they are *vacation* and *ZIP code*.)
3 T
4 F (It's the American spelling. British spelling is *kilometre*.)
5 T
6 F (It's easy.)

 Get Sts to read the article again to check their answers, and then check answers as a class.

 Get Sts to cover the article. Then write the following words and phrases on the board: CELL PHONE, CENTER, COLOR, PURSE, SEE YOU FRIDAY, VACATION, ZIP CODE. Ask Sts what they are in British English.

USA	UK
cell phone	mobile phone
center	centre
color	colour
purse	handbag
See you Friday.	See you on Friday.
vacation	holiday
ZIP code	postcode

Deal with any other new vocabulary. Model and drill the pronunciation of any tricky words.

d Do this as a whole-class activity. Sts may remember *elevator* and *z* (/zed/) from **Practical English 1**). Other common American words include *movie*, *cookie*, *apartment*, *soccer*, etc.

G imperatives, *let's*
V feelings: *hungry*, *thirsty*, etc.
P linking

Lesson plan

In this lesson, Sts begin by learning adjectives to describe states and feelings, e.g. *hungry*, *happy*. They then listen to a series of conversations between a couple with a baby, who are in a car going on holiday. The husband becomes increasingly irritated, and the child tired, hungry, etc. as the journey goes on. This serves as a context to present more imperatives (Sts have already learned some in Classroom language) and phrases to make suggestions beginning with *Let's…*. Following this is a speaking activity with Sts role-playing different situations and asking each other what's wrong. There is then a pronunciation focus on connected speech, which is aimed at helping Sts to understand native speakers, and the lesson ends with a video listening about safe car journeys.

More materials
For teachers
Photocopiables
Grammar imperatives, *let's p.173*
Communicative Dominoes *p.219* (instructions *p.205*)
Teacher's Resource Centre
Video Have a safe journey!
For students
Workbook 2C
Online Practice 2C

Mime being hot and cold, and elicit *I'm hot* and *I'm cold*, and write them on the board. Model and drill pronunciation.

1 VOCABULARY feelings

a Books open. Give Sts a time limit to match the adjectives and pictures. Point out that the first one (*worried*) has been done for them.

b 🔊 **2.13** Play the audio for Sts to listen and check. Check answers.

🔊 **2.13**
5 I'm angry.
11 I'm bored.
9 I'm cold.
12 I'm frightened.
2 I'm happy.
4 I'm hot.
6 I'm hungry.
10 I'm sad.
8 I'm stressed.
3 I'm thirsty.
7 I'm tired.
1 I'm worried.

When Sts have finished matching, go through the **Collocation** box together.

Vocabulary notes
In English, feelings are expressed using the verb *be* and an adjective. In some other languages, they are expressed using the verb *have* + a noun, and this causes Sts to make mistakes like *I have hot*, etc. For this reason it is important to highlight the structure here as well as the adjectives themselves.

Play the audio again, pausing after each phrase for Sts to listen and repeat. Model and drill any phrases which are difficult for your Sts, e.g. *I'm thirsty*. Make sure Sts can hear and pronounce the difference between *angry* /ˈæŋgri/ and *hungry* /ˈhʌŋgri/.

Then give further practice by calling out the numbers of some pictures for Sts to tell you how the person feels using the verb *be*, e.g.

T *Number 5*

Sts *She's angry.*

T *Number 2*, etc.

c Focus on the instructions and the example sentences. Demonstrate the activity by telling Sts how you feel, using the phrases in **a**. Remind Sts of the modifiers *very* and *quite*.

In pairs, Sts cover the words, look at the pictures, and make true sentences about themselves.

Get some quick feedback, asking the class about a few of the adjectives, e.g. *Who's thirsty?*, and getting a show of hands.

2 LISTENING & READING inferring mood

a 🔊 **2.14** Set the scene by going through the instructions and telling Sts to cover the conversations on *p.19* and only look at the pictures.

Play the audio and tell Sts to listen and look at the pictures.

In pairs, Sts tell each other how the people feel in each picture. Point out the example (*angry*).

<u>Don't</u> check answers at this stage.

EXTRA SUPPORT Read through the script and decide if you need to pre-teach any new lexis before Sts read and listen.

🔊 **2.14**
See story in Student's Book on *p.19*

b Now tell Sts to uncover the conversations. Play the audio again for Sts to listen and read at the same time. The pictures and sound effects should help them to understand the conversations.

Check answers to **a**.

Picture 1: *Lisa's angry / stressed.*
Picture 2: John's thirsty, Alfie's hungry.
Picture 3: Lisa's cold and frightened, John's hot.
Picture 4: Lisa and Alfie are tired.

Go through the conversations and deal with any new vocabulary.

c ◉ **2.15** Focus on the instructions and play the audio for Sts to listen to the end of the story. Play the audio again if necessary.

Check whether it is a happy ending by getting a show of hands.

Yes. A police officer stops John because he is driving too fast, but the police officer isn't angry with them because of Alfie, and they go to their hotel.

◉ **2.15**
(script in Student's Book on *p.118*)

L = Lisa, J = John, P = policewoman
L   The Highland Hotel's twenty miles from here. Let's go there.
J   Twenty miles? No problem.
L   John! Slow down!
J   Oh no!…Here she comes.
P   Good evening, sir, madam. Turn off the engine, please, sir. Thank you.
J   What's the problem, officer?
P   The problem? Well, sir, seventy miles an hour is the problem. That's very, very fast. The limit on this road is fifty miles an hour. Can I see your driving licence?
J   Seventy? Oh. Er, I'm very sorry, officer.
P   Ah, what a beautiful baby! What's his name?
L   Alfie. He's *very* tired, officer. And it's twenty miles to our hotel.
P   Well…OK…go to your hotel. But please slow down, sir.
J   Yes – thank you, officer.
P   Goodbye, sir, madam. Goodbye, Alfie!

EXTRA SUPPORT   If there's time, you could get Sts to listen again to both parts of the audio with the scripts in the main lesson and on *p.118*, so they can see exactly what they understood / didn't understand. Translate / Explain any new words or phrases.

EXTRA IDEA   You could ask Sts if they're more similar to John or Lisa on car journeys.

3 GRAMMAR imperatives, *let's*

a Tell Sts to look at the highlighted phrases in **2b** again and to complete the chart. Point out that the first one (*Turn*) has been done for them.

Check answers.

	Imperatives	Suggestions
➕	*Turn* right. **Be** careful! **Look** for a hotel.	**Let's** stop at a café. **Let's** go there.
➖	**Don't** turn left! **Don't** drive fast! **Don't** worry.	Let's **not** stop.

b Tell Sts to go to **Grammar Bank 2C** on *p.126*.

Grammar notes
Imperatives
Emphasize the simplicity of imperatives in English. There are only two forms, e.g. *Stop. / Don't stop.*

Emphasize too that an imperative can sound abrupt in English if you are asking somebody to do something, e.g. *Close the door (please). I'm cold.* Here it would be much more normal to use a polite request with *Can…*, e.g. *Can you close the door, please?*

Let's (= *Let us*) + infinitive is used to make suggestions which include the speaker.

A positive suggestion is made by using *Let's* + infinitive, e.g. *Let's go to the cinema.*

A negative is made with *Let's not*, e.g. *Let's not eat here.*

◉ **2.16** Focus on the example sentences and play the audio for Sts to listen and repeat. Then go through the rules with the class.

Then focus on the **Can you…?** box and go through it with the class.

Now focus on the exercises for **2C** on *p.127*. Sts do the exercises individually or in pairs.

Check answers, getting Sts to read the full sentences.

a
1 Read   2 don't speak   3 Go   4 Don't watch   5 Have
6 Be   7 Take   8 Don't be
b
1 Let's go   2 Let's turn off   3 Let's do   4 Let's not take
5 Let's stop   6 Let's not go, Let's watch

Tell Sts to go back to the main lesson **2C**.

EXTRA SUPPORT   If you think Sts need more practice, you may want to give them the **Grammar** photocopiable activity at this point.

c Tell Sts to look at the nine signs and to write a positive ➕ or negative ➖ sentence for each, using the verb phrases from the list. Point out that the first two have been done for them.

Get Sts to compare with a partner, and then check answers.

3 Don't eat or drink here.
4 Turn off your phone.
5 Don't take photos.
6 Don't go in here.
7 Cross the road now.
8 Be careful.
9 Don't listen to music here.

d Get Sts to cover the list of phrases and look at the signs.

In pairs, Sts tell each other the phrases.

Get some feedback from the class, by calling out a number and getting Sts to tell you the meaning.

EXTRA CHALLENGE   Ask Sts where they might see these signs, e.g. *Don't smoke here* in a station, *Turn off your phone* in the classroom, *Don't take photos* in a museum, etc.

4 SPEAKING

Put Sts in pairs, **A** and **B**, and tell them to go to
Communication What's the matter?, **A** on *p.103*,
B on *p.109*.

Carefully go through the instructions and example
conversation in **a** with the class, explaining and drilling the
question *What's the matter?*, and explain the expression
cheer up (= be happy). Then focus on **b** and **c**, and explain
that Sts are going to have similar conversations using
prompts 1–4 and responding with a phrase, e.g. *Thanks,
OK, Good idea*, etc.

Demonstrate the activity with a good student.

Then sit **A** and **B** face-to-face if possible. **A** asks **B** *What's
the matter?*, **B** responds with his / her first prompt, and
they have a mini conversation. They then have three more
conversations, using **B**'s other prompts.

A and **B** then swap roles, and **B** asks *What's the matter?*.
When they have finished, focus on instruction **d**. Sts
should try to do all eight conversations without looking at
their books.

 Write the eight adjectives (*bored, cold*, etc.)
on the board to remind Sts how to start.

Tell Sts to go back to the main lesson **2C**.

5 PRONUNCIATION linking

a 🔊 **2.17** Focus on the **Connected speech** box and go
through it with the class. Explain that in English, when
people speak fast they don't pronounce each word
separately. They tend to run them together and this can
make it difficult for Sts to hear what has been said.

Tell Sts they will hear six short sentences and they must
write them down.

Play the audio, pausing after each sentence to give Sts
time to write. Play again if necessary.

Check answers by writing the sentences on the board.

🔊 **2.17**
1 Turn off your phone.
2 Let's eat in this café.
3 Take a book with you.
4 Let's open the windows.
5 Let's stop at a hotel.
6 Don't open the door.

---

b In pairs, Sts practise saying the six sentences. Encourage
them to try to say them fast and link the words like on the
audio.

6 ▶ VIDEO LISTENING understanding specific
advice

This is the first of six video listenings, which are
incorporated into the Student's Book. If you are unable
to show the video in class, remind students that they can
find the video on *Online Practice* and ask them to watch
the video and do the activities for homework.

a Tell Sts they are going to watch a programme about car
journeys. Make sure they know the meaning of the title,
Have a safe journey!, and *a tip* (= a small piece of advice).

Give Sts time to read tips 1–10 and point out that the first
one (*Plan*) has been done for them. Elicit / Explain any
words they may not know, e.g. *seat belt*.

Play the video for Sts to watch. Then play it again, pausing
after each tip to give Sts time to complete them.

Get Sts to compare with a partner, and then check
answers.

 Read through the script and decide if you
need to pre-teach any new lexis before Sts watch or listen.

2 car **3** traffic **4** map **5** water **6** tablets **7** Check
8 petrol **9** fifteen **10** phone

Have a safe journey!
Here are ten top tips to make your car journey safe.
Tip one: Plan your journey. Look at a map and plan where to stop on
the way.
Tip two: Check your car. Is it ready for a long journey? Do it yourself
or take it to a garage.
Tip three: Listen to traffic information on the radio, or check on the
internet, before you start your journey.
Tip four: Take a map with you in the car, or have a map app on your
phone – satnav (or GPS) isn't always right.
Tip five: Take bottles of water. People are often thirsty on long car
journeys.
Tip six: If you have children in the car, take books, games, and tablets
with you. Then the children can watch videos or read. When children
are quiet, the driver is less distracted.
Tip seven: Check that all the passengers in the car have their seat
belt on.
Tip eight: Check that you have petrol. Don't wait until your petrol
tank is nearly empty before you look for a petrol station.
Tip nine: After driving for two hours, stop for fifteen minutes. Have a
snack, and get some fresh air. If you're very tired, have a coffee or a
drink with caffeine.
Finally, tip ten. This is very, very important. Don't use your phone.
Phoning and texting are very dangerous because you don't
concentrate on the road.
Have a safe journey!

---

b Play the video again. Sts in pairs decide on their top
three tips.

Get some feedback from various pairs.

You could also ask Sts if they have any tips of their own.

 If there's time, you could get Sts to watch
again with subtitles / showing the script, so they can see
exactly what they understood / didn't understand.
Translate / Explain any new words or phrases.

1&2 Revise and Check

There are two pages of revision and consolidation after every two Files. These exercises can be done individually or in pairs, in class or at home, depending on the needs of your Sts and the class time available.

The first page revises the **grammar**, **vocabulary**, and **pronunciation** of the two Files. The exercises add up to 50 (grammar = 15, vocabulary = 25, pronunciation = 10), so you can use the first page as a mini-test on Files 1 and 2. The **pronunciation** section sends Sts to the Sound Bank on *pp.166–167*. Explain that this is a reference section of the book, where they can check the symbols and see common sound–spelling patterns for each of the sounds. Highlight the Sound Bank videos showing the mouth position for each sound. If you don't want to use these in class, tell Sts to look at them at home and to practise making the sounds and saying the words.

The second page presents Sts with a series of skills-based challenges. First, there is a **reading** text which is of a slightly higher level than those in the File, but which revises grammar and vocabulary Sts have already learned. The **listening** is some unscripted street interviews, where people are asked questions related to the topics in the Files. Sts can either watch the interviews on video or listen to them on audio. You can find these on the *Teacher's Resource Centre*, *Classroom Presentation Tool*, *Class DVD*, and *Class Audio CDs* (audio only). Alternatively, you could set these sections / activities as homework. Sts can find the video on *Online Practice*. Finally, there is a **speaking** challenge which assesses Sts' ability to use the language of the Files orally. You could get Sts to do these activities in pairs, or Sts can tick the boxes if they feel confident that they can do them.

More materials

For teachers

Teacher's Resource Centre

Video Can you understand these people? 1&2

Quick Test 2

File 2 Test

For students

Online Practice Check your progress

GRAMMAR

1 c **2** a **3** c **4** b **5** a **6** b **7** c **8** a **9** b **10** b
11 c **12** a **13** c **14** b **15** a

VOCABULARY

a
1 from **2** to **3** in **4** at **5** off

b
1 Read **2** Work **3** Stand **4** Open **5** Answer

c
1 file (the others are numbers)
2 Chinese (the others are countries)
3 France (the others are nationalities / languages)
4 Ireland (the others are continents)
5 sixteen (the others are multiples of ten)
6 Italy (the others are days of the week)
7 purse (the others are always used in the plural)
8 school (the others are part of a classroom)
9 wallet (the others are things you read)
10 happy (the others are negative adjectives)

d
1 bad **2** cheap **3** clean **4** low **5** right

PRONUNCIATION

c
1 email /iː/ **2** fast /ɑː/ **3** page /dʒ/ **4** sit /ɪ/ tissues /ʃ/

d
1 address **2** Italy **3** expensive **4** sunglasses **5** thirteen

CAN YOU understand this text?

a It's for tourists / visitors to New York.
b **1** F **2** T **3** T **4** F **5** F **6** T

CAN YOU understand these people?

1 b **2** c **3** c, a **4** c

2.18

1 Mallini
I = interviewer, M = Mallini
I What's your name?
M Mallini.
I How do you spell it?
M M-A-L-L-I-N-I.

2 Olga
I = interviewer, O = Olga
I Where are you from?
O Originally I'm from Russia.
I And where in Russia?
O Moscow.

3 Mairi
I = interviewer, M = Mairi
I What's your name?
M My name's Mairi.
I How do you spell it?
M M-A-I-R-I.
I Where are you from?
M I'm from Edinburgh.
I Where's that?
M That's in Scotland.

4 Jake
I = interviewer, J = Jake
I Are you tidy or untidy?
J I'm very tidy.
I What's on your desk?
J On my desk I have all of my pencils and my computer.

Britain: the good and the bad

G present simple ⊞ and ⊟
V verb phrases: *cook dinner, do homework,* etc.
P third person *-s*

Lesson plan

Different aspects of life in Britain provide the context for Sts to meet the present simple for the first time. They begin by learning a group of common verb phrases, and then, in a short text where a journalist writes what she likes about Britain, they see how the verb forms change for positive and negative forms and in the third person singular (question forms are presented separately in **3B**). Sts then practise the pronunciation of verb + *-s* or *-es*, as well as the vocabulary and grammar, talking about themselves and about a partner. The lesson ends with Reading and Speaking. Sts read a text adapted from a British newspaper, in which foreigners who live in Britain say what they like or don't like about it, and Sts compare what they think about their country.

More materials
For teachers
Photocopiables
Grammar present simple ⊞ and ⊟ *p.174*
Vocabulary Verb phrases *p.262* (instructions *p.254*)
Communicative I work… He works… *p.220* (instructions *p.205*)
For students
Workbook 3A
Online Practice 3A

OPTIONAL LEAD-IN (BOOKS CLOSED)
Write DRINK EAT DRIVE READ on the board. Ask Sts for words that can go after these verbs. Elicit ideas from the class and write them on the board.

1 VOCABULARY verb phrases

a ◗ **3.1** Books open. Give Sts time to look at the verb phrases.

Tell them they are going to hear a sound effect for each verb phrase and they must listen and number them.

Play the audio for Sts to listen and complete the task.

Play it again, pausing after each sound effect to check the answer. Model and drill the pronunciation of the phrases.

1 speak German   **2** drink mineral water   **3** watch TV   **4** play the guitar   **5** like animals

◗ **3.1**
(sound effects of the following)
1 *Guten Tag. Wie geht's?*
2 *noise of bottle being unscrewed, a glass of water being poured…*
3 *sound of opening of TV news programme with music*
4 *someone playing a classical guitar*
5 *someone opening the front door, dogs barking, cats meowing…*

b Tell Sts to go to **Vocabulary Bank Verb phrases** on *p.153* and get them to do **a** individually or in pairs. Many of these verbs may already be familiar to them

Vocabulary notes
You could point out that *have* can be used for possessions, but also with both food and drink (*have a sandwich, have a coffee*) and is more common when we talk about specific meals, e.g. *have breakfast / lunch. Eat*, e.g. *eat fast food*, can only be used for food.
You might also want to make sure Sts are clear about the meaning of *take* (*an umbrella*). Give a clear example like *'Take an umbrella with you. It's raining.'* Sts may think that this verb means *carry* (e.g. *Can you carry my bag for me? It's very heavy.*).

◗ **3.2** Now do **b**. Play the audio for Sts to listen and check.
Check answers.

◗ **3.2**
Verb phrases
19 cook dinner
20 do exercise
14 do housework
24 do homework
17 drink mineral water
23 drive a car
18 eat vegetables
9 go to the cinema
3 have a garden
8 like animals
11 listen to music
6 live in a flat
22 need a new phone
15 play the guitar
12 play tennis
7 read a book
16 say sorry
5 speak German
4 study history
13 take an umbrella
1 want a coffee
10 watch TV
21 wear glasses
2 work in an office

Either use the audio to drill the pronunciation of the phrases, or model and drill them yourself. Give further practice of words and phrases your Sts find difficult to pronounce.

Finally, focus on **Activation**. Get Sts to cover the verbs and use the photos to test themselves or their partner.

Tell Sts to go back to the main lesson **3A**.

EXTRA SUPPORT If you think Sts need more practice, you may want to give them the **Vocabulary** photocopiable activity at this point.

c 🔊 **3.3** Focus on the example and tell Sts they will hear the second part of some verb phrases and they must say the whole verb phrase.

Play the audio, pausing after each one, and elicit a response from the whole class.

🔊 **3.3**
1 TV (*pause*) watch TV
2 the guitar (*pause*) play the guitar
3 mineral water (*pause*) drink mineral water
4 to music (*pause*) listen to music
5 glasses (*pause*) wear glasses
6 a garden (*pause*) have a garden
7 vegetables (*pause*) eat vegetables
8 to the cinema (*pause*) go to the cinema
9 history (*pause*) study history
10 exercise (*pause*) do exercise

Now repeat the activity, eliciting responses from individual Sts.

EXTRA CHALLENGE In pairs, Sts do a similar activity to the listening. **A** (book open) says the second part of a verb phrase from the **Vocabulary Bank**, e.g. *dinner*, and **B** (book closed) has to guess the whole phrase, e.g. *cook dinner*.

2 GRAMMAR present simple ⊞ and ⊟

a Ask Sts *What do you think of when you hear the word 'Britain'?* to elicit some ideas and write them on the board.

Focus on the instructions and the words / phrases in the list, and help Sts with vocabulary if necessary, e.g. *the BBC*, *freedom*. Elicit / Explain what a *journalist* is. Point out that the first one (*multiculturalism*) has been done for them.

Give Sts time to read the article and complete the task.

b 🔊 **3.4** Play the audio for Sts to listen and check.

Check answers.

> **2** the language **3** gardens **4** the freedom **5** the BBC
> **6** pubs **7** the weather **8** Indian food

🔊 **3.4**
My name's Carola. I'm a journalist. I like…
multiculturalism. People from all over the world live in the UK, and they live together happily. Usually.

the language. English is international. I speak English. You speak English. I don't have communication problems.

gardens. My garden's small, but I have flowers and vegetables in it. When the sun's out I sit in the garden and I feel really happy.

the freedom. I wear what I want. I say what I want. I do what I want.

the BBC. I listen to the radio in the morning and I watch TV in the evening. A lot of programmes are interesting, funny, or educational. Sometimes all three.

pubs. We drink there, and we eat there, too – the food now is very good.

the weather. It's cold, but not very cold. It's hot, but not very hot. It rains, but it doesn't rain every day.

Indian food. My boyfriend cooks fantastic curries, and the UK is great for Indian restaurants!

Finally, deal with any new vocabulary. Model and drill pronunciation.

EXTRA CHALLENGE Tell Sts to cover the article and, in pairs, try to remember what Carola likes.

c Focus on the instructions, and get Sts to answer the questions in pairs.

Check answers.

> **1** They end with -*s* because they are third person singular (*he*, *she*, *it*).
> **2** ⊟ I don't have, it doesn't rain.
> We use *don't* to make negatives with *I*, *you*, *we*, and *they*.
> We use *doesn't* to make negatives with *he*, *she*, and *it*.

EXTRA SUPPORT If you have a monolingual class, don't be afraid of using your Sts' L1 to talk about the grammar here. At this level, it is unrealistic to expect Sts to talk about grammar in English.

d Tell Sts to go to **Grammar Bank 3A** on *p.128*.

> ### Grammar notes
>
> Emphasize to Sts the relative simplicity of the present simple. There is only one different verb ending in the present simple (third person singular verbs add an -*s* or -*es*). All other forms are the same as the infinitive. For this reason, the use of the pronoun (*I*, *you*, etc.) is not optional as it is in many languages. It is essential as it identifies which person is being referred to.
>
> In the negative, highlight the use of *don't* and *doesn't*, which are put before the infinitive. These contracted forms (of *do not* and *does not*) are almost always used in spoken English and in informal writing.
>
> Highlight that *goes* /gəʊz/ and *does* /dʌz/ both end with -*oes*, but are pronounced differently.

🔊 **3.5** Focus on the example sentences and play the audio for Sts to listen and repeat. Then go through the rules with the class.

Focus on the information box **Be careful with some *he* / *she* / *it* forms** and go through it with the class.

Now focus on the exercises for **3A** on *p.129*. Sts do the exercises individually or in pairs.

Check answers. Get Sts to read the sentences out loud and help them with the rhythm of ⊞ and ⊟ sentences, e.g. *We <u>live</u> in a <u>flat</u>. We <u>don't</u> <u>study</u> <u>French</u>.*

> **a**
> 1 She goes to the cinema.
> 2 He lives in a flat.
> 3 They have two children.
> 4 I don't like cold weather.
> 5 The supermarket closes at 5.30.
> 6 My sister doesn't study French.
> 7 I do housework.
> 8 My son wants a guitar.
> 9 My friend doesn't work on Saturdays.
> 10 Our lessons finish at 5.00.
>
> **b**
> 1 doesn't work **2** reads **3** speak **4** don't play **5** wears
> 6 listen **7** don't eat **8** has

Tell Sts to go back to the main lesson **3A**.

EXTRA SUPPORT If you think Sts need more practice, you may want to give them the **Grammar** photocopiable activity at this point.

3 PRONUNCIATION third person -s

Pronunciation notes

The pronunciation rules for third person singular -s and -es endings are exactly the same as those for plural nouns (see **2A**).

As with the plurals, if Sts want to know when the final s is pronounced /s/ and when it is pronounced /z/, explain that it is pronounced /s/ after verbs ending with these unvoiced sounds: /k/, /p/, /f/, /t/, e.g. *works*, *stops*, *laughs*, *sits*. After all other voiced endings, the s is pronounced /z/. See the **Voiced and unvoiced consonants** box on *p.31*.

Sts will have problems distinguishing between, and producing, the /s/ and the /z/ sounds, and will tend to pronounce all s endings as /s/. Remind them that the /s/ is like the sound made by a snake, and the /z/ is like the sound made by a bee or a fly.

a Sts read the rule in the **Final -s or -es** box and then, in pairs, they answer the question.

Check answers. Model and drill the three words.

> books /bʊks/
> keys /kiːz/
> watches /wɒtʃɪz/

b 🔊 **3.6** Play the audio for Sts just to listen to the three sounds and sentences.

🔊 **3.6**
See sounds and sentences in Student's Book on *p.22*

Now play the audio again for Sts to listen and repeat. If Sts are having difficulties producing the /s/ and /z/ endings, tell them that the difference is small and reassure them that it will come with practice. The most important thing at this stage is to make the /ɪz/ sound in the right place, e.g. *watches*, and not to make it in the wrong place, e.g. *lives* (NOT /lɪvɪz/).

Play the audio again if necessary.

Give Sts time to practise saying the sentences in pairs.

 If these sounds are difficult for your Sts, it will help to show them the mouth position. You could model this yourself or use the Sound Bank videos on the *Teacher's Resource Centre.*

c 🔊 **3.7** Focus on the instructions and the example, and tell Sts that they must listen to the first sentence and then change it using the new subject given, e.g. *he*, *she*, *it*.

Play the audio, pausing after each sentence, and elicit a response from the whole class.

🔊 **3.7**
1 I live in a flat. She (*pause*) She lives in a flat.
2 I need a new phone. He (*pause*) He needs a new phone.
3 They work in an office. She (*pause*) She works in an office.
4 We wear glasses. He (*pause*) He wears glasses.
5 They finish at eight. It (*pause*) It finishes at eight.
6 I want a coffee. She (*pause*) She wants a coffee.
7 They have two children. He (*pause*) He has two children.
8 We do homework. She (*pause*) She does homework.
9 They study French. He (*pause*) He studies French.
10 They go shopping. She (*pause*) She goes shopping.

Now repeat the activity, eliciting responses from individual Sts.

d Focus on the instructions and the two example sentences. Highlight the use of *don't* to make a negative in the second sentence. Then tell Sts to go to the **Vocabulary Bank Verb phrases** on *p.153* and demonstrate the activity by making true sentences about yourself.

Give Sts time to think about their six sentences.

 You could get Sts to write the six sentences.

In pairs, Sts tell each other their sentences. Tell Sts to put a tick or a cross next to the pictures that apply to their partner, so that they don't forget the information.

e Get Sts to change partners. Sts now tell their new partner about their first partner, using the third person singular.

 Write the example on *p.23* of the Student's Book on the board to help Sts: EVA PLAYS TENNIS. SHE DOESN'T WEAR GLASSES…

Get some feedback from individual Sts, both about themselves and about their partners.

Tell Sts to go back to the main lesson **3A**.

4 READING identifying attitude

a Focus on the title and explain / elicit the meaning of *foreigner* (= a person from another country). Model and drill pronunciation.

Now focus on the instructions and make sure Sts understand what they have to do. Tell them that this is a real (adapted) article from a British newspaper. It is very motivating for Sts to realize that they can actually understand a newspaper article even at elementary level.

Give Sts time to read the article and complete the task.

Check answers.

 Before Sts read the article the first time, check whether you need to pre-teach any vocabulary.

> **Erdal** ✗ British people don't work like that. They only want to finish work and go home.
> **Khalal** ✗ I don't like the weather. And I don't like the food.
> **Camille** ✓ The British are friendly.
> **Shurooq** ✓ In the UK women have a lot of freedom. I like the weather here. I love days when it rains, or it's cold. The people are also nice and friendly.
> **Michelle** ✓ My favourite thing about Britain is the Scotch eggs. Everybody says that British food is awful, but I love it… The shops are great too…
> **Lian Tang** ✓ Because I like the culture, the art, the history. I also love the beautiful scenery…
> ✗ I don't like…the weather and the food.

b Tell Sts they are going to read the article again and must complete each gap in 1–7 with a name.

Give Sts time to read the article again and complete the task.

Then get them to compare with a partner, and check answers.

Ask Sts if they have been to the UK and if so, find out if they agree with anything they read in the article.

c Do this as a whole-class activity.

Either explain / demonstrate meaning, getting Sts to check in their dictionaries, or translating into Sts' L1.

Deal with any other new vocabulary. Model and drill the pronunciation of any tricky words.

5 SPEAKING

a Focus on the two headings and the sentence beginnings under each one. Elicit / Explain the meaning of *favourite* (= the one that you like more than any other), and model and drill pronunciation /ˈfeɪvərɪt/.

Tell Sts to complete the sentences under each heading, using their own words. Monitor and help.

b Focus on the instructions and go through the **Useful words** box, making sure Sts understand the meaning of *why* and *because* /bɪˈkɒz/. Model and drill the pronunciation.

Now read the example. Put Sts in pairs and get them to compare sentences. Monitor and help, encouraging Sts to pay attention to the use of *because*.

Get some feedback from individual Sts.

EXTRA SUPPORT You could do this as a whole-class activity.

G present simple [?]
V jobs: *journalist*, *doctor*, etc.
P /ɜː/ and /ə/

Lesson plan

The topic of this lesson is jobs and work. Sts begin by reading an interview which presents questions in the present simple in both second and third person singular, (*Do you…? Does he…?*). Then Sts learn the vocabulary for common jobs, and how to say what they do. There is a pronunciation focus on the /ɜː/ and /ə/ sounds. Sts then listen to a radio programme, where competitors try to guess first a man's job, and then his wife's job. Sts then practise by asking each other present simple questions about imaginary jobs, and the lesson finishes with Sts asking questions in the third person singular to guess someone's job.

More materials

For teachers

Photocopiables
Grammar present simple [+] , [–] and [?] *p.175*
Vocabulary Jobs *p.263* (instructions *p.254*)
Communicative Present simple questionnaire *p.221* (instructions *p.206*)

For students

Workbook 3B

Online Practice 3B

OPTIONAL LEAD-IN (BOOKS CLOSED)

Write the following sentences on the board. Make them true for you.

1 I'M A TEACHER.
2 I WORK IN (THE NAME OF YOUR SCHOOL).
3 I WORK (…) HOURS A DAY.
4 I LIKE MY JOB VERY MUCH.

Elicit the difference between *job* and *work* (*job* is a noun; *work* is a verb) and focus on the use of *a* before *teacher*.

1 GRAMMAR present simple [?]

a Books open. Focus on the photo of Jess and Carl, and the question.

Now tell Sts to read the interview quickly to find the answer. Remind Sts that they need to find out what Carl's job is, not Jess's.

Check the answer.

He's a police officer.

b Focus on the title and elicit the meaning of *night* and *day*.

Tell Sts they are going to read the interview and this time they need to complete it with the questions the interviewer asks.

Focus on the example (*What do you do, Jess?*) and elicit / explain that this question is the same as *What's your job?*.

Point out the **Glossary**. Give Sts time to read the questions from the list, the interview, and then complete 2–5.

c 🔊 **3.8** Play the audio for Sts to listen and check. Check answers.

2 Do you work long hours?
3 What does your husband do?
4 Does he have free weekends?
5 Do you have time together?

🔊 **3.8**

I = interviewer, J = Jess

I What do you do, Jess?
J I work in an office. I'm an administrator.
I Do you work long hours?
J No, I don't. I work normal hours, from nine to five, Monday to Friday.
I What does your husband do?
J He's a police officer. He works at night, from eight p.m. to six in the morning.
I Does he have free weekends?
J No, he doesn't. Well, he has two free days, but they're Wednesday and Thursday. He works Saturday and Sunday – they're busy nights for police officers.
I Do you have time together?
J Not really, except when we're on vacation. I'm in bed when he comes home, he's in bed when I leave home in the morning. We don't eat together. That's awful. Sometimes I don't cook, I just have cookies for dinner.
I Can you think of any good things about your different hours?
J Yes, we earn more money because Carl does a lot of overtime.
I Do you have any suggestions for couples like you?
J Have a whiteboard in your hall or your kitchen and write down all the housework. Then tick things when you do them. That way, the dogs don't eat twice!

---

d Get Sts to cover the interview and just look at the five questions in **b**. In pairs or as a whole-class activity, get Sts to answer them.

Deal with any new vocabulary in the interview. Model and drill pronunciation, e.g. *administrator*.

e Do this as a whole-class activity.

f Focus on the instructions and give Sts time to check who the questions in **b** are about.

Check answers.

1 What do you do, Jess?, Do you work long hours?
2 Does he have free weekends?, What does your husband do?
3 Do you have time together?

Now ask *What's different when the question is about Jess and about Carl?*

About Jess: Do you…?   About Carl: Does he…?

g Tell Sts to go to **Grammar Bank 3B** on *p.128*.

3.9 Focus on the example sentences and play the audio for Sts to listen and repeat. Then go through the rules with the class.

Focus on the **do and does** box and go through it with Sts.

Now focus on the exercises for **3B** on *p.129*. Sts do the exercises individually or in pairs.

Check answers, getting Sts to read the full sentences.

a
1 Do   **2** Do   **3** Does   **4** Does   **5** Do   **6** Does   **7** Does
8 Does   **9** Do   **10** Does
b
1 **Does he like** tennis?
2 **Does she speak** German?
3 **Do you eat** pizzas?
4 **Do they cook** lasagne?
5 **Does she live** in a house?
6 **Do you want** an iPhone?
7 **Does he drive** fast?
8 **Does she drink** it with milk?
9 **Do you have** boys or girls?
10 **Do you listen** to music on your phone?

Tell Sts to go back to the main lesson **3B**.

EXTRA SUPPORT If you think Sts need more practice, you may want to give them the **Grammar** photocopiable activity at this point.

2 VOCABULARY jobs

a Focus on the jobs in the list and point out to Sts that they have seen all these jobs before.

Individually or in pairs, Sts complete sentences 1–5 with a job from the list.

Check answers and write the words on the board.

1 police officer   **2** actor   **3** teacher   **4** receptionist
5 administrator

Model and drill the pronunciation, and underline the stress.

b Tell Sts to go to **Vocabulary Bank Jobs** on *p.154* and get them to do **a** individually or in pairs.

Focus on the **a / an + jobs** box and go through it with the class.

3.10 Now do **b**. Play the audio for Sts to listen and check.

Check answers.

3.10
Jobs
28   an accountant
26   an actor
 2   an administrator
 1   an architect
 6   a builder
 7   a chef
27   a cleaner
 4   a dentist
17   a doctor
 8   an engineer
11   a factory worker
22   a flight attendant
13   a footballer
30   a guide
19   a hairdresser
10   a journalist
12   a lawyer
14   a manager
16   a model
18   a musician
 5   a nurse
21   a pilot
23   a police officer
24   a receptionist
15   a shop assistant
 9   a soldier
29   a taxi driver
25   a teacher
 3   a vet
20   a waiter / a waitress

Either use the audio to drill the pronunciation of the phrases, or model and drill them yourself. Point out that in compound nouns (e.g. *factory worker*, *flight attendant*), the main stress is on the first word. Give further practice of any words and phrases your Sts find difficult to pronounce.

3.11 Focus on the flow chart in **c** and go through the possible answers to the question *What do you do?*. Play the audio for Sts to listen and repeat the sentences.

3.11
See flow chart in Student's Book on *p.154*

Play again if necessary.

Highlight the use of the prepositions *for*, *in*, *at*, and the article *a / an*.

Then give Sts time to decide how to say what they do in English, and go round helping with any jobs they don't know how to express. <u>Don't</u> ask Sts at this stage what they do as they will be asking each other in **c** in the main lesson.

Now focus on **Activation**. In pairs, get Sts to cover the words with a piece of paper, look at the photos, and try to remember the jobs. They could test each other – **A** says a number, and **B** says the job.

Tell Sts to go back to the main lesson **3B**.

EXTRA SUPPORT If you think Sts need more practice, you may want to give them the **Vocabulary** photocopiable activity at this point.

c Focus on the two questions and give Sts time to decide how to say in English what their parents do.

Get Sts to stand up and ask at least three other Sts the two questions.

Monitor and help, encouraging Sts to answer in a full sentence.

Get feedback from as many Sts as possible.

EXTRA SUPPORT Elicit the two questions that Sts need to ask (*What do you do? What do your parents do?*) and write them on the board to help Sts.

3 PRONUNCIATION /ɜː/ and /ə/

Pronunciation notes

Remind Sts that the two dots in /ɜː/ mean that this sound is long. It is a longer version of the /ə/ sound. Also remind them that they have met the /ə/ sound before, on *p.8* of **1B**, and that it is the most common vowel sound in English.

You may want to tell Sts that the most common *wor-* words which have the /ɜː/ sound, and which Sts often mispronounce, are *work*, *word*, and *world*. You could also remind them that when *er* and *or* are <u>unstressed</u>, e.g. at the end of many job words, they are pronounced /ə/ (the schwa).

a 🔊 **3.12** Focus on the new sound picture, *bird*, and on *computer*.

Play the audio for Sts just to listen to the two sounds and example words.

🔊 **3.12**
See sounds and words in Student's Book on *p.25*

Now play the audio again for Sts to listen and repeat.
Finally, focus on the /ɜː/ **and** /ə/ box and go through it with the class.

EXTRA SUPPORT If these sounds are difficult for your Sts, it will help to show them the mouth position. You could model this yourself or use the Sound Bank videos on the *Teacher's Resource Centre*.

b 🔊 **3.13** Play the audio for Sts just to listen to the six sentences.

🔊 **3.13**
See sentences in Student's Book on *p.25*

Now play the audio again, pausing after each sentence for Sts to repeat.
Put Sts in pairs and get them to practise saying the sentences.
Get a few Sts to say them aloud to the class.

4 LISTENING understanding specific information

a 🔊 **3.14** Tell Sts they're going to listen to a game show called *His job, her job*, where a team of three people ask a man, Alex, and then his wife, Sue, questions for two minutes, and then have to guess their jobs.

Focus on the questions in the chart. Go through them, and elicit / explain any new words, e.g. *outside / inside*, *with the public*, *qualifications*, etc.

EXTRA SUPPORT Read through the scripts and decide if you need to pre-teach any new lexis before Sts listen.

Tell Sts that they will hear the contestants asking Alex questions first and they must underline the questions in the chart. Point out that the first one (*work in an office?*) has been done for them.

EXTRA SUPPORT Tell Sts that the contestants ask Alex a total of nine questions.

Play the audio for Sts to listen and underline the questions. Play the audio again if necessary, pausing after each question, and then check answers.

EXTRA IDEA You might want to pause the audio after the announcer says *Let's have your first question for Alex* and ask Sts what David, Kate, and Lorna do.
You could also ask how long they have to ask Alex and Sue about their jobs.

David is a teacher, Kate is unemployed, and Lorna is a writer. They have one minute to ask about Alex's job, and one minute to ask about Sue's.

Alex's questions about his job
Do you work in an office?
Do you work in the evening?
Do you make things?
Do you wear a uniform or special clothes?
Do you drive?
Do you work in a team?
Do you have special qualifications?
Do you speak foreign languages?
Do you travel?

🔊 **3.14**

(script in Student's Book on *p.118*)

A = announcer, P = presenter, D = David, K = Kate, L = Lorna, AI = Alex,
S = Sue

Part 1

A   And now on Radio 4, *His job, her job.*
P   Good evening and welcome again to the jobs quiz *His job, her job*.
    And our team tonight are David, a teacher…
D   Hello.
P   Kate, who's unemployed…
K   Hi.
P   …and Lorna, who's a writer.
L   Good evening.
P   And our first couple tonight are…
AI Alex.
P   And?
S   Sue.
P   Welcome to the programme, Alex and Sue. OK team, you have
    one minute to ask Alex questions about his job and then one
    minute to ask Sue about her job, starting now. Let's have your first
    question for Alex.
D   Hi, Alex. Do you work in an office?
AI No, I don't.
L   Do you work in the evening?
AI It depends. Yes, sometimes.
K   Do you make things?
AI No, I don't.
L   Do you wear a uniform or special clothes?
AI Er, yes – I wear special clothes.
K   Do you drive in your job?
AI No, I don't.
L   Do you work in a team?
AI Yes, I do. With ten other people.
K   Do you have special qualifications?
AI Qualifications? No, I don't.
D   Do you speak foreign languages?
AI No, only English.
P   You only have time for one more question, team…
D   Er, do you travel?
AI Yes, I do. At weekends. Well, not every weekend…
P   Your time's up.

b Focus on the instructions and tell Sts that now they have
to focus on Alex's answers. Elicit that he can only answer
yes, *no*, or *it depends*. Explain / Elicit the meaning of *it
depends* and drill pronunciation. Point out that the first
one has been done for them.

Play the audio again for Sts to listen and put a tick, a cross,
or a *D* in Alex's column.

Check Alex's answers about his job and elicit / explain the
meaning of *sometimes* (= not all the time).

Alex's answers about his job
Do you work in an office? ✗
Do you work in the evening? *D*
Do you make things? ✗
Do you wear a uniform or special clothes? ✓
Do you drive? ✗
Do you work in a team? ✓
Do you have special qualifications? ✗
Do you speak foreign languages? ✗
Do you travel? ✓

c 🔊 **3.15** Sts now do the same for Sue. Tell Sts that they will
hear the contestants asking Sue questions and they must
underline the questions they hear. You might want to
suggest that Sts underline her questions using a different
colour if they can.

Play the audio for Sts to listen and underline the
questions. Play the audio again if necessary, pausing after
each question, and then check answers.

EXTRA SUPPORT Tell Sts that the contestants ask Sue a total
of seven questions.

Sue's questions about her job
Do you work outside?
Do you work at the weekend?
Do you work with the public?
Do you have good holidays?
Do you work at night?
Do you earn a lot of money?
Do you like your job?

🔊 **3.15**

(script in Student's Book on *p.119*)

Part 2

P   Now team, you have a minute to ask Sue about her job.
K   Hello, Sue. Do you work outside?
S   It depends. Outside and inside.
L   Do you work at the weekend?
S   Yes, I do.
D   Do you work with the public?
S   No, I don't.
K   Do you have good holidays?
S   No, I don't. I never have any holidays.
K   Do you work at night?
S   Sometimes. It depends.
L   Do you earn a lot of money?
S   No, nothing! I don't have a salary.
D   Do you like your job?
S   Yes, I do! I love it.
P   That's time. OK, team…

Now play the audio again for Sts to listen and put a tick, a
cross, or a *D* in Sue's column.

Check Sue's answers about her job.

Sue's answers about her job
Do you work outside? *D*
Do you work at the weekend? ✓
Do you work with the public? ✗
Do you have good holidays? ✗
Do you work at night? *D*
Do you earn a lot of money? ✗
Do you like your job? ✓

d Focus on the instructions and two examples. You might
want to point out to Sts the position of *sometimes* before
the verb.

Put Sts in pairs and get them to make sentences about
Alex and Sue's jobs.

EXTRA SUPPORT Give Sts time to write their sentences.

Elicit the sentences about Alex from the class.

Alex
…doesn't work in an office.
…sometimes works in the evening.
…works in a team.
…doesn't have special qualifications.
…doesn't speak foreign languages.
…travels at weekends.
…doesn't drive in his job.
…doesn't make things.
…wears special clothes.

Now give Sts 30 seconds to guess his job. Write the different ideas on the board.

Get feedback, but <u>don't</u> tell Sts if they're right or wrong.

Now elicit the sentences about Sue from the class.

Sue
…sometimes works outside.
…sometimes works at night.
…works at the weekend.
…doesn't work with the public.
…doesn't have any holidays.
…doesn't earn a lot of money / doesn't have a salary.
…loves her job.

Now give Sts 30 seconds to guess her job.

Get feedback, but <u>don't</u> tell Sts if they're right or wrong.

e 🔊 **3.16** Play the end of the show on the audio. Pause after they ask *Are you a footballer, Alex?* and ask Sts what they think, before letting them hear his job.

Then continue the audio until *So, Sue, what do you do?* and ask Sts what they think, before letting them hear Sue's job.

Ask the class with a show of hands who had guessed correctly for each job.

Alex is a footballer. Sue is a full-time mother.

🔊 **3.16**

P OK, team. So, what's Alex's job?
K OK, so he wears special clothes, he works with ten other people, he sometimes travels… Are you a footballer, Alex?
Al Yes, I am.
P Very good! And Sue?
D Let's see. She works outside and inside. She works at the weekend. She doesn't earn any money. She doesn't have holidays. But she likes her job! We give up. We can't think of any jobs with those conditions!
P So, Sue, what do you do?
S I'm a mum. A full-time mother!

EXTRA SUPPORT If there's time, you could get Sts to listen again to the audio with scripts 3.14 and 3.15 on *pp.118–119*, so they can see exactly what they understood / didn't understand. Translate / Explain any new words or phrases.

5 SPEAKING

a Tell Sts they are now going to play the same game, *His job, her job*, but as individuals, not couples. Put Sts in groups of four. Tell them to go to **Vocabulary Bank Jobs** on *p.154* and each choose a job.

When they are ready, tell them they have two minutes to ask each person the questions in the chart in **4b**. Get Sts to make notes of the answers to help them to guess the jobs.

When the time is up, tell Sts to guess the jobs.

Find out how many Sts guessed correctly.

b Tell Sts to go to **Vocabulary Bank Jobs** on *p.154* again, and this time, think of someone they know who has one of the jobs.

In the same groups, Sts first tell the others if they are thinking about a man or a woman. Then Sts take it in turns to ask questions from the chart in the third person singular to find out what this person's job is.

EXTRA SUPPORT Demonstrate the activity by getting Sts to ask you the questions first.

Get Sts to make notes of their partners' answers to help them guess the jobs when time is up.

Get some feedback from various groups.

Love me, love my dog

G word order in questions
V question words
P sentence stress

Lesson plan

This lesson starts with a listening in which two characters, Becca and Dave, meet for the first time. This provides a context for asking a lot of questions to try to get to know somebody. Sts go on to look at the grammar of word order in questions, especially those beginning with question words. There is then a vocabulary stage, where Sts revise and expand their knowledge of questions words, and then in Pronunciation they practise the rhythm of questions. Sts have a Speaking activity where they practise asking each other a variety of questions, and the lesson ends with Writing as they learn to write a personal profile.

More materials
For teachers
Photocopiables
Grammar word order in questions *p.176*
Communicative Famous people *p.222*
(instructions *p.206*)
For students
Workbook 3C
Online Practice 3C

OPTIONAL LEAD-IN (BOOKS CLOSED)

Ask the class who has a dog (either their own or a family pet). Then ask Sts who have a dog what kind of dog it is and who usually takes it for a walk.

1 LISTENING identifying who's who

a ◆ **3.17** Books open. Focus on the instructions and the first illustration. Give Sts time to read the four names, and make sure they understand what they have to do. Point out that the first one (*Becca is the woman*) has been done for them.

Play the audio for Sts to listen and match the names to the people or the dogs.

Check answers.

EXTRA SUPPORT Read through the scripts and decide if you need to pre-teach any new lexis before Sts listen.

Barry is her dog. Dave is the man. Dolly is his dog.

Now ask Sts if they know any more information about the dogs.

Barry is a Labrador; he's two years old.
Dolly is a fox terrier; she's two years old.

◆ **3.17**
(script in Student's Book on *p.119*)

B = Becca, D = Dave
B He's beautiful. Is he a fox terrier? Sorry, he or she?
D She. Yes, she's a fox terrier. Her name's Dolly. And your dog?
B He's a Labrador.
D What's his name?
B Barry. Barry, come here!
D Dolly. Here. Stop it.
B I think Barry likes her.
D Yes! Sorry, I'm Dave. What's your name?
B Becca. Hi.
D Nice to meet you, Becca! How old is Barry?
B Er…He's, er, two. And Dolly?
D Er…The same. Hey, Dolly! Come back!

b ◆ **3.18** Focus on the second illustration and establish that Becca and Dave go to a café. Tell Sts to cover the conversation with a piece of paper and listen to the conversation to find out what happens in the end.

Play the audio for Sts to listen and complete the task.

Check the answer.

Dave invites Becca to lunch.

◆ **3.18**
D It's really hot. Would you like a drink? Or an ice cream?
B Yes, why not? Let's go to the café.
D What kind of ice cream do you want?
B Er, a Magnum if they have it.
D Here you are. One Magnum.
B Thanks, Dave.
D Where do you live?
B Very near here, in Park Road. And you?
D I live quite near, in Queen's Road. What do you do, Becca?
B I'm a journalist.
D Really? How interesting! Do you work for a newspaper?
B No, for TV. What about you?
D I'm a teacher. I'm on holiday now.
B Me too. Oh! My ice cream.
D Dolly! Bad dog! I'm really sorry.
B That's OK.
D Do you want another ice cream?
B No, thanks.
D Are you sure? I'm really sorry. Look, let's have lunch one day. Are you free on Saturday?
B Oh, well, OK, then. Yes. Thanks very much.

c Tell Sts to uncover the conversation, and give them a few minutes to read it.

EXTRA CHALLENGE Tell Sts, in pairs, to try to guess the missing words before they listen.

Play the audio again for Sts to complete the questions (or check their guesses). Play again if necessary.

Check answers.

2 What…want? **3** Where…live? **4** What…do **5** work
6 What **7** want

d 🔊 **3.19** Focus on the **Showing interest** box and go through it with the class.

Tell Sts they are going to hear three sentences from Becca and Dave's conversation, and they must only repeat each phrase that shows interest.

Play the audio for Sts to listen and repeat the phrases.

🔊 **3.19**
1 **B** I'm a journalist.
   D Really? (*pause*) How interesting! (*pause*)
2 **D** Do you work for a newspaper?
   B No, for TV. What about you? (*pause*)
3 **D** I'm on holiday now.
   B Me too. (*pause*)

Now repeat the activity, eliciting responses from individual Sts.

Tell Sts that they will be using these phrases later, in the Speaking activity.

e Put Sts in pairs and get them to read the conversation in **c**. If there's time, get them to swap roles.

f 🔊 **3.20** Focus on the instructions and give Sts some time to read the six sentences.

Play the audio for Sts to listen and complete the task. Play again if necessary.

Get Sts to compare with a partner, and then check answers.

1 D **2** B **3** D **4** D **5** B **6** D

🔊 **3.20**
(script in Student's Book on *p.119*)
B Hi. It's me. Becca.
D Hi. It's the first floor.
B Hi, Dave. Very nice flat.
D Do you like it? It has a big kitchen.
B Mmm. Nice smell. Er, where's Dolly?
D She isn't here. Er, Becca, I need to tell you something. Dolly isn't my dog. She's my friend's dog. I sometimes help and take her for a walk.
B You don't have a dog?
D No. Er…I don't like dogs very much. And my flat's quite small. I'm so sorry. I know you love dogs.
B Don't worry! Barry isn't my dog either! He's my sister's dog. I like dogs, but…in fact…I have two cats. How do you feel about cats?
D I love cats – in fact, I prefer cats to dogs! Come and sit down. It's nearly ready.
B What's for lunch?
D Spaghetti carbonara – and then chocolate ice cream. Home-made!
B All for me this time!

 If there's time, you could get Sts to listen again to the three parts of the audio with the scripts in the main lesson and on *p.119*, so they can see exactly what they understood / didn't understand. Translate / Explain any new words or phrases.

g Focus on the question and make sure Sts understand it.

Do this as a whole-class activity and elicit opinions. Say what you think, too. You could also ask Sts if they prefer cats or dogs.

2 GRAMMAR word order in questions

a Focus on the instructions, and tell Sts to try to put the words in the correct order to make questions.

b 🔊 **3.21** Play the audio for Sts to listen and check. Check answers.

🔊 **3.21**
1 How old is Barry?
2 What's his name?
3 Do you like it?
4 How do you feel about cats?

---

c Tell Sts to go to **Grammar Bank 3C** on *p.128*.

> **Grammar notes**
>
> Word order in English is less flexible than in many other languages, and this is especially true of questions. Sts often have problems remembering the position of the auxiliaries *do* and *does* in present simple questions. The acronyms **ASI** (auxiliary, subject, infinitive) and **QuASI** (question word, auxiliary, subject, infinitive) will help your Sts remember to use the correct word order in questions. Use the acronyms as a quick way of reminding them if they make mistakes.

Focus on the example sentences and play both audio 🔊 **3.22** and 🔊 **3.23** for Sts to listen and repeat. Then go through the rules with the class.

Now focus on the exercises for **3C** on *p.129*. Sts do the exercises individually or in pairs.

Check answers, getting Sts to read the full sentences.

a
1 How many children do you have?
2 Is your job interesting?
3 What colour is his car?
4 Where does your brother work?
5 Do you work with computers?
6 What kind of magazines do you read?
7 What does he do at the weekend?
8 Are you stressed in your job?
9 Where does your sister live?
10 How do you say that in English?
b
1 does…do **2** does she work **3** Does…like **4** does…do
5 Is he **6** Does…do **7** do you do

Tell Sts to go back to the main lesson **3C**.

 If you think Sts need more practice, you may want to give them the **Grammar** photocopiable activity at this point.

3 VOCABULARY question words

a Focus on the question words and phrases, and questions
1–8. Point out that the first one (*What*) has been done
for them.

Give Sts time to complete the questions.

b 🔊 **3.24** Play the audio for Sts to listen and check.
Check answers.

See words in **bold** in script 3.24

🔊 **3.24**

1 **What** phone do you have?
   I have a Samsung.
2 **How many** brothers and sisters do you have?
   I have two sisters.
3 **Which** do you prefer, cats or dogs?
   Cats, I think.
4 **Where** do you work?
   In a restaurant in the city centre.
5 **When** do you have language classes?
   On Mondays and Wednesdays.
6 **What kind of** music do you like?
   I like pop and reggae.
7 **Who**'s your favourite actor?
   Benedict Cumberbatch.
8 **Why** do you like him?
   Because he's a fantastic actor.

Now either put Sts in pairs to answer questions 1–3 or do
it as a whole-class activity.

If Sts worked in pairs, check answers.

1 /h/
2 /w/
3 We use *What…?* when there's a large number of possibilities.
   We use *Which…?* when there's a small number, often two.

4 PRONUNCIATION sentence stress

Pronunciation notes

Sts have already seen how within a word one syllable is
stressed more strongly than the others. They also need
to be aware that within a sentence, some words are
stressed more strongly than others. Stressed words are
usually 'information' words, i.e. nouns, adjectives, verbs.
Unstressed words are usually shorter words such as
pronouns, articles, prepositions, and auxiliary verbs.

This mixture of stressed and unstressed words is what
gives English its rhythm.

a 🔊 **3.25** Tell Sts that in sentences we stress the important
words and that the words in big bold print in the four
questions are important words and are stressed.

Play the audio for Sts just to listen to the four questions.

🔊 **3.25**
See questions in Student's Book on *p.27*

Now play the audio again for Sts to listen and repeat,
copying the rhythm.

b Now put Sts in pairs, **A** and **B**. **A** asks the questions in **3a**
and **B** gives his / her own answers.

  Point out that in the first question they
might need to change *work* to *study*.

  Tell the Sts **B** to close their books, and
get the Sts **A** to ask the questions in a different order.

Monitor and help as necessary. Then get Sts to swap roles.

Get some feedback from the class.

5 SPEAKING

a Focus on the instructions with the class. Then focus on the
prompts. Elicit that in the first, second , and third group
they need to add *do you* between the question word or
phrase and the verb, and in the fourth group, they need to
add *is / 's* after *Who* or *What*.

Then elicit the questions from the first and second groups,
e.g. *Where do you live? Where do you work? What kind of
films do you like?*, etc.

b Focus on the instructions. You could model the example
conversation with a strong student. Remind Sts of the
ways of showing interest that they saw earlier in the
lesson, e.g. *How interesting!*

Put Sts in pairs, **A** and **B**, preferably with a student they
don't usually work with. Sts interview each other.

! If you have an odd number of Sts in the class, have one
group of three. Choose strong Sts who will have time to do
the interview three times.

Get some feedback from the class.

EXTRA CHALLENGE Encourage the Sts who are asking the
questions to ask extra questions if they can, e.g.
A *What car do you have?*
B *I have a Mini.*
A *What colour is it? / Do you like it?*, etc. (extra questions)

Encourage the Sts who are answering the questions to give
extra information, e.g.
A *Where do you work?*
B *I work in a shop. I'm a…*

Round off the activity by asking various pairs what they have
in common.

6 WRITING a personal profile

Tell Sts to go to **Writing A personal profile** on *p.113*.

a Focus on Fiona's profile and give Sts time to read it.

Go through the different sections with Sts. Highlight and
check the meaning and pronunciation of:
– *occupation* (= what they do, e.g. their job)
– *interests* (= hobbies)

Tell Sts to cover the profile and ask them questions about
Fiona, e.g. *Where is she from? What does she do? What
languages does she speak? What kind of music does she
like?*, etc.

Then ask Sts if they have similar interests to Fiona.

b Focus on the ***and, but, or*** box and go through it with the
class.

Get Sts to do the writing in class or set it for homework.

c Remind Sts to check their profiles for mistakes, e.g. with
capital letters or spelling, and the use of *and*, *but*, and *or*.

2 Practical English Coffee to take away

Function buying a coffee
Vocabulary telling the time

Lesson plan

In this lesson Sts learn to tell the time and how to buy a coffee (or other drink) in a coffee shop or bar. The Rob and Jenny story develops. They meet at the hotel, and go to buy a takeaway coffee. They then go to the office and Jenny meets Karen, the administrator, and Daniel, the boss.

More materials
For teachers
Photocopiables
Vocabulary Practical English 2 Time *p.264* (instructions *p.254*)
Teacher's Resource Centre
Video Practical English Episode 2
Quick Test 3
File 3 Test
For students
Workbook Practical English 2
Can you remember? 1–3
Online Practice Practical English 2
Check your progress

OPTIONAL LEAD-IN (BOOKS CLOSED)

Before starting Episode 2, elicit what Sts can remember about Episode 1. Ask them *Who's Rob? Where does he work / live? Who's Jenny? Where is she from?*, etc.

Alternatively, you could play the last scene of Episode 1.

1 ▶ VOCABULARY telling the time

a Books open. Focus on the clock and the question. Elicit the answer *It's nine o'clock* and write it on the board. You may want to point out here that we often just say, e.g. *The meeting is at nine* (rather than *at nine o'clock*), but if someone asks you the time, it's more common to answer *It's nine o'clock.*

Note: there is no difference in exactness between *It's nine* and *It's nine o'clock*. If you want to emphasize an exact time, you need to add the word *exactly*, e.g. *It's exactly nine o'clock.*

b Tell Sts to go to **Vocabulary Bank Time** on *p.157* and get them to do **Part 1**.

Focus on **1 Telling the time** and get Sts to do **a** individually or in pairs.

◗)) **3.26** Now focus on **b**. Play the audio for Sts to listen and check.

Check answers. You may also want to point out that British people often leave out the *a* before *quarter past* and *quarter to*, e.g. *It's (a) quarter to ten.*

◗)) **3.26**
Time, 1 Telling the time
3 It's quarter past six.
5 It's six o'clock.
1 It's quarter to seven.
8 It's ten past six.
7 It's five to seven.
4 It's twenty-five to seven.
2 It's half past six.
9 It's three minutes past six.
6 It's twenty past six.

Vocabulary notes
Highlight:

- that from 12 o'clock to half past (the right-hand side of the clock) all the times are expressed with *past*, and that from half past to 12 o'clock (the left-hand side) all the times are expressed with *to*.
- the pronunciation of *half* /hɑːf/ (highlighting the silent *l*) and *quarter* /ˈkwɔːtə/.
- the origin of *o'clock* (originally 'of the clock').

EXTRA SUPPORT Play the audio again and get Sts to repeat the times.

Now focus on the **Time** box and go through it with the class.

Finally, focus on the instructions for **Activation**. Get Sts to cover the phrases with a piece of paper and, in pairs, to point at the clocks and ask and say the times.

EXTRA SUPPORT If you think Sts need more practice, you may want to give them the **Vocabulary** photocopiable activity at this point.

c Put Sts in pairs, **A** and **B**, and tell them to go to **Communication What's the time?**, **A** on *p.104*, **B** on *p.109*.

Sit **A** and **B** face-to-face if possible. Go through the instructions with them carefully, and drill the question *What's the time?* (or *What time is it?*).

At the end of the activity, get Sts to compare their clocks to make sure they have drawn the right times.

Finally, elicit the time on some of the clocks from the class.

Tell Sts to go back to the main lesson.

2 ▶ ROB AND JENNY MEET

a ◗)) **3.27** Focus on the photo and elicit who the people are and where they are (*Rob and Jenny in the hotel*).

Then focus on the instructions and the question. Play the video / audio once the whole way through.

Check the answer.

They go for a coffee.

R = Rob, J = Jenny
R   Erm…Jennifer?
J   Rob?
R   Yes, hello. Nice to meet you, Jennifer.
J   Call me Jenny. Good to meet you, too.
R   Welcome to London. Am I late?
J   Erm…just a little.
R   What time is it?
J   Nine fifteen.
R   I'm really sorry. The traffic is terrible today.
J   No problem.
R   How are you? How's the hotel?
J   The hotel's very nice. But breakfast isn't great. I'd like a good cup of coffee. Not hotel coffee – *real* coffee.
R   OK, let's get a coffee.
J   Do I have time? I have a meeting at nine thirty.
R   With Daniel?
J   Yes.
R   Don't worry. We have lots of time – the office is very near. So, Jenny, where do you live in New York?

b Focus on questions 1–4 and go through them with Sts, eliciting / explaining new words, e.g. *late*.

Now play the video / audio again for Sts to watch or listen and complete the task.

Get Sts to compare with a partner, and then check answers.

> 1   Because the traffic is terrible.
> 2   Because the hotel coffee isn't great.
> 3   Because she has a meeting with Daniel.
> 4   Because they have lots of time. The office is very near.

EXTRA SUPPORT   If there's time and you are using the video, you could get Sts to watch again with subtitles / showing the script, so they can see exactly what they understood / didn't understand. Translate / Explain any new words or phrases.

3 ▶ BUYING A COFFEE

a Focus on the photo and ask where Rob and Jenny are (*in a coffee shop*). Then focus on the menu and check Sts understand all the items on it. You may want to point out that in coffee shops in the UK they now use the Italian words for different types of coffee, e.g. *latte*, *cappuccino*, etc.

Explain that *regular* means normal size, and that *large* is another word for *big*.

Elicit / Explain that although the prices are just numbers, as the coffee bar is in the UK the prices are in pounds and pence (*3.00* = three pounds, *2.80* = two (pounds) eighty). Saying prices is practised in more detail in **Practical English 3**.

EXTRA IDEA   You could get Sts to practise in pairs like this:
A *How much is a single espresso?*
B *Two (pounds) forty-five. How much is a regular cappuccino?*, etc.

b 🔊 **3.28** Focus on the task and on questions 1–3. Elicit / Explain that question 3, *How much is it?*, means *What is the price?*

Now either tell Sts to close their books and write the three questions on the board, or get Sts to focus on the questions.

Play the video / audio once the whole way through. Then play it again if necessary.

Get Sts to compare with a partner, and then check answers.

> 1   Jenny has a double espresso and Rob has a large latte.
> 2   Jenny doesn't have anything. Rob has a brownie and a croissant.
> 3   £12.45

🔊 **3.28** 🔊 **3.29**
B = barista, R = Rob, J = Jenny
B   Can I help you?
R   What would you like, Jenny? (*repeat*)
J   An espresso, please. (*repeat*)
B   Single or double?
J   Double. (*repeat*)
R   Can I have a latte, please? (*repeat*)
B   Regular or large?
R   Large. (*repeat*)
B   To have here or take away?
R   To take away. (*repeat*)
B   Anything else?
J   No, thanks. (*repeat*)
R   A brownie for me, please…and a croissant… (*repeat*)
B   OK.
R   How much is that? (*repeat*)
B   That's twelve forty-five, please.
R   Sorry, how much? (*repeat*)
B   Twelve forty-five. Thank you. And your change.
R   Thanks. (*repeat*)

c Focus on the conversation in the chart. Elicit who says the **You hear** phrases (the barista) and who says the **You say** phrases (the customer, or here Rob and Jenny). These phrases will be useful for Sts if they need to order food or a drink. Point out the **Glossary** on the page. *Barista* is an imported Italian word.

Give Sts a minute to read through the conversation and to think about what the missing words might be. Then play the video / audio again, and get Sts to complete the gaps. Play again if necessary.

Get Sts to compare with a partner, and then check answers.

> 1 help   2 Single   3 Regular   4 here   5 change

Go through the conversation line by line with Sts, helping them with any words or expressions they don't understand. Remind Sts that *What would you like?* is a common way of offering a drink to someone, and *Can I have…?* is a common way of asking for what you want.

Highlight that to ask for a (total) price we can say either *How much is it?* or *How much is that?*.

d ◗ **3.29** Now focus on the **You say** phrases and tell
Sts they're going to watch or listen to the conversation
again. They should repeat the **You say** phrases when they
hear the beep. Encourage them to copy the rhythm and
intonation.

Play the video / audio, pausing if necessary for Sts to
repeat the phrases.

◗ **3.29**
Same as script 3.28 with repeat pauses

e Put Sts in groups of three, **A**, **B**, and **C**. **A** is the barista. Get
Sts to read the conversation aloud and then swap roles.

f Now assign a role to each student in their groups and
focus on the instructions.

A keeps his / her book open and is the barista. **B** and **C**
both close their books. **B** invites **C** to have a drink and
something to eat.

Elicit that **A** begins with *Can I help you?* and **B** then asks **C**
What would you like?.

Sts now role-play the conversation. When they have
finished, they swap roles.

You could get a few groups to perform in front of the
class.

4 ◗ FIRST DAY IN THE OFFICE

a ◗ **3.30** Focus on the photo and ask Sts some questions,
e.g. *Where is Jenny now? Who do you think the other people
are?* (You may want to teach / revise *maybe* and *I think* to
encourage speculation.).

Go through questions 1–6.

Now play the video / audio once for Sts just to watch or
listen.

Then play it again, pausing for Sts to answer the questions.
Play it again if necessary.

Get Sts to compare with a partner, and then check
answers.

1 She is an administrator.
2 In Poland.
3 In Manhattan.
4 Yes, a sister in Brooklyn.
5 Tea, coffee, or water.
6 Twelve o'clock.

◗ **3.30**
R = Rob, J = Jenny, K = Karen, D = Daniel
R Here we are. This is the office. And this is Karen.
J Hello, Karen.
R Karen, this is Jennifer Zielinski from the New York office.
K Hello, Jennifer.
J Nice to meet you.
R Karen is our administrator. We all depend on her.
K Don't listen to Rob.
R But it's true!
K Is this your first time in the UK, Jennifer?
J Yes, it is. But it isn't my first time in Europe. I have family in Poland.
K Really? And where do you live in New York?
J In Manhattan. Do you know New York?
K Yes. My sister lives in Brooklyn.
J I have family in Brooklyn, too. Where does your sister live?
D Jennifer!
J Daniel?
D How nice to meet you, at last. Would you like something to drink?
   Tea, coffee, water?
J Oh no, I'm fine, thanks.
D Great. Oh, Karen. What time is my next meeting?
K At twelve o'clock.
D That's good – we have time. OK, come into my office, Jennifer.
J Thank you.
D Talk to you later, Rob.
R Yeah. Sure.

EXTRA SUPPORT   If there's time and you are using the video,
you could get Sts to watch again with subtitles / showing
the script, so they can see exactly what they understood /
didn't understand. Translate / Explain any new words or
phrases.

b Focus on the **Social English** phrases and go through
them with the class.

In pairs, get Sts to decide who says them.

c ◗ **3.31** Play the video / audio for Sts to watch or listen to
the four phrases and check their answers to **b**.

Check answers. If you know your Sts' L1, you could get
them to translate the phrases.

1 R **2** K **3** D **4** D

◗ **3.31**
See Social English phrases in Student's Book on *p.29*

Now play the video / audio again, pausing after each
phrase for Sts to watch or listen and repeat.

d Focus on the instructions and make sure Sts understand
what they have to do.

Get Sts to compare with a partner, and then check
answers.

A 3 **B** 4 **C** 2 **D** 1

Now put Sts in pairs and get them to practise the
conversations.

Finally, focus on the **CAN YOU...?** questions and ask Sts
if they feel confident they can now do these things. If
they feel that they need more practice, tell them to go to
Online Practice to watch the episode again and practise
the language.

Family photos

G possessive *'s, Whose…?*
V family: *sister, aunt*, etc.
P /ʌ/, the letter *o*

Lesson plan

The main context for this lesson is pictures of people in the public eye who have been photographed with a member of their family or partner who is not well known. This provides a natural context for presenting the grammar of the possessive *'s* (e.g. *Who is he? He's Brad Pitt's brother.*) and the question word *Whose…?*. Sts then learn the vocabulary of family members, which leads into a focus on the /ʌ/ sound, and the most common pronunciations of the letter *o*. The lesson ends with Sts listening to a woman showing her friend photos of members of her family, which Sts then do themselves.

More materials
For teachers
Photocopiables
Grammar possessive *'s, Whose…? p.177*
Vocabulary The family *p.265* (instructions *p.254*)
Communicative Everyday objects *p.223*
(instructions *p.206*)
For students
Workbook   4A
Online Practice   4A

OPTIONAL LEAD-IN (BOOKS CLOSED)   Draw a simple family tree on the board, preferably of your family, or a well-known family, showing two generations: mother / father + children, e.g.

ALAN = MARIAN
ROBERT   ME   SUSAN

Ask *Who's Alan?* to elicit *He's your father*, and do the same with the other names to elicit *mother / brother / sister*. Use Alan and Marian to teach *husband* and *wife*.

Get Sts to spell the words to you and write them on the board. Model and drill pronunciation.

1 GRAMMAR possessive *'s, Whose…?*

a Books open. Ask Sts *Do you read magazines like* Hello! *or* OK!? *What kind of people are in them?* (Famous people and their families).

Focus on the title of the article and the photo. Ask the question about Doug to the class, but <u>don't</u> confirm any ideas yet. Then ask if they think it's good or bad to have a famous person in the family and elicit opinions.

b Give Sts time to read the article and see if they still think their guess in **a** is correct or if they have changed their minds. Get them to answer the second questions as well.

Check answers. You could ask Sts how they guessed whilst reading the article. Also find out if Sts know any information about Brad Pitt.

> His brother is the actor Brad Pitt.
> Yes, he does.

Deal with any new vocabulary.

c Focus on the instructions. Tell Sts to think about the other person's age and appearance.

Now focus on the photos and give Sts time, in pairs, to read sentences 1–5 and choose *a* or *b* for each one. Remind them of the expressions *I think…* and *Maybe…*

d 🔊 **4.1**   Play the audio for Sts to listen and check.

Check answers by eliciting full sentences and elicit / explain that *'s = of*, i.e. *of Carey Mulligan*. Ask Sts if they know the people. Some Sts may know that in fact Carey Mulligan's husband is famous in his own right (he is Marcus Mumford, lead singer of the band Mumford & Sons), and Maggie Gyllenhaal, Jake's sister, is also a well-known actress.

🔊 **4.1**
1 He's Carey Mulligan's husband.
2 She's Meryl Streep's daughter.
3 She's Jake Gyllenhaal's sister.
4 He's Morgan Freeman's son.
5 He's Mary-Kate Olsen's husband.

e Tell Sts to go to **Grammar Bank 4A** on *p.130*.

> **Grammar notes**
>
> Elementary Sts tend not to have too many problems with the possessive *s* being used in English with things / places, e.g. *Harry's bar*, and with people, e.g. *Jane's brother*. However, they may be less clear about <u>not</u> using it in phrases like *The end of the film* or in compound noun phrases like *bus stop* (if this is an *of* construction in their L1).
>
> **Names that end in *s***
>
> *James's* or *James'*? After names ending in *s*, you can add either *'s* or just an apostrophe. We teach the first form because it is more common and follows the basic rule. The pronunciation is /ɪz/, e.g. /dʒeɪmzɪz/.

🔊 **4.2**   Focus on the example sentences and play the audio for Sts to listen and repeat. Then go through the rules with the class.

Focus on the *'s* and **Whose / Who's** box and go through it with the class.

Now focus on the exercises for **4A** on *p.131*. Sts do the exercises individually or in pairs. With **a**, go through the instructions with Sts first, to make sure they understand exactly what they have to do.

Check answers. For **a**, ask Sts for the answers, and then write the sentences on the board, so they can see where they have to put the apostrophes. Elicit each time whether the *'s* is the contraction of *is* or the possessive *s*.

a

1 They're Hillary's cars.   **2** It's Hillary's purse.   **3** They're Bill's magazines.   **4** It's Hillary's watch.   **5** They're Bill's glasses.

b

1 my mother's birthday   **2** her parents' house
3 the end of the day   **4** my sister's friends
5 The door of the classroom   **6** the students' desks

c

1 Whose   **2** Whose   **3** Who's   **4** Who's   **5** Whose   **6** Who's

Tell Sts to go back to the main lesson **4A**.

EXTRA SUPPORT If you think Sts need more practice, you may want to give them the **Grammar** photocopiable activity at this point.

f Ask Sts to focus on the things from the photos. Model and drill their pronunciation. Then tell Sts that they belong to the famous people in **c**.

Focus Sts' attention on the speech bubbles. Give Sts, in pairs, a few minutes to practise asking and answering the questions.

Check answers.

It's Jake Gyllenhaal's watch.
It's Carey Mulligan's bag.
They're Meryl Streep's glasses.
It's Mary-Kate Olsen's ring.

EXTRA IDEA Try to find some photos of famous people's relatives who your Sts will know. You could find these on the internet or in celebrity magazines. Ask who the people are.

2 VOCABULARY family

a Tell Sts to go to **Vocabulary Bank The family** on *p.155*.

Vocabulary notes

Highlight that in English, unlike in some other languages, we don't use the masculine word in the plural to refer to masculine and feminine family members, i.e. *brothers* only refers to males. For this reason, we normally ask, e.g. *Do you have any brothers and sisters?*.

Focus on the instructions for **a** and the first family tree. Make sure that Sts realize that they have to number the people in relation to Richard.

Ask Sts *Who is Gary?* and elicit *He's Richard's father*. Then show them where to find the word *father* and point out that number *1* is in the box next to *Gary*.

Give Sts, in pairs, five minutes to write the numbers on the two family trees.

! Tell Sts they will need to use one of the words (*cousin*) twice.

<u>Don't</u> check answers at this stage.

Focus on **b**. Give Sts time to complete gaps 1–5. <u>Don't</u> check answers at this stage.

4.3   Now do **c**. Play the audio for Sts to listen and check answers to **a** and **b**.

Check answers.

4.3
The family
a   **7** John is Richard's grandfather.
   8 Jennifer is Richard's grandmother.
   2 Carol is Richard's mother.

1 Gary is Richard's father.
9 Sue is Richard's aunt.
10 Nick is Richard's uncle.
4 Kate is Richard's sister.
3 Steven is Richard's brother.
13 Hugh is Richard's cousin.
13 Sarah is Richard's cousin.
14 Emma is Richard's wife.
5 Chloe is Richard's daughter.
6 Jake is Richard's son.
12 Ruby is Richard's niece.
11 Oliver is Richard's nephew.
b **1** my father and my mother (*pause*) my **parents**
   2 my wife's mother and father (*pause*) my **parents-in-law**
   3 my grandfather and my grandmother (*pause*) my **grandparents**
   4 my son and my daughter (*pause*) my **children**
   5 a husband and wife (*pause*) a **couple**

Then either use the audio to drill the pronunciation of the sentences, or model and drill them yourself. Give further practice of any words your Sts find difficult to pronounce, e.g. *cousin, daughter, niece,* and *nephew*.

EXTRA SUPPORT You might want to get Sts just to repeat the family words.

Focus on the **More family words** box and go through it with the class.

EXTRA CHALLENGE You may also want to teach *half-brother / -sister* (someone who has the same mother as you but a different father, or the same father but a different mother).

Focus on **Activation**. Demonstrate by asking individual Sts, e.g. *Who's Jennifer?* (*She's Richard's grandmother.*). Then get Sts to continue in pairs, covering the words in **a** and **b**.

Tell Sts to go back to the main lesson **4A**.

EXTRA SUPPORT If you think Sts need more practice, you may want to give them the **Vocabulary** photocopiable activity at this point.

b Focus on the questions and point out that the first one (*grandmother*) has been done for them.

Give Sts two minutes to answer them in pairs.

Check answers.

2 uncle   **3** niece   **4** cousin   **5** brother-in-law   **6** nephew

3 PRONUNCIATION /ʌ/, the letter o

Pronunciation notes
The /ʌ/ sound

The most common spelling of this short sound is *u* between consonants, e.g. *up, husband, sun*, etc. However, *o* can also make this sound as in the family words *mother, brother*, etc., and also *ou*, e.g. *young*.

The letter o

Following on from the /ʌ/ sound, this exercise focuses on the two most common pronunciations of the letter *o*, /ɒ/ (e.g. *clock*) and /əʊ/ (e.g. *phone*), and two less common ones, /ʌ/ (e.g. *up*) and /uː/ (e.g. *boot*).

Highlight that *clock* and *up* are short sounds, *boot* is a long sound, and *phone* is a diphthong. For these sounds, you may want to help Sts by using the videos showing mouth positions, or by demonstrating the positions yourself.

a 🔊 **4.4** Focus on the sound picture (*up*) and play the audio for Sts just to listen to the sound and example words.

🔊 **4.4**
See sound and words in Student's Book on *p.31*

Now play the audio again for Sts to listen and repeat.

EXTRA SUPPORT If this sound is difficult for your Sts, it will help to show them the mouth position. You could model this yourself or use the Sound Bank videos on the *Teacher's Resource Centre*.

b Focus on the **Remember!** box and go through it with the class. This exercise focuses on the two most common pronunciations of the letter o, /ɒ/ (e.g. *not*) and /əʊ/ (e.g. *photo*), and two less common ones, /ʌ/ (e.g. *mother*) and /uː/ (e.g. *two*).

Focus on the sound pictures and elicit the four words and sounds, e.g. *clock* /ɒ/, *phone* /əʊ/, etc. Point out the four examples.

Give Sts two or three minutes to put the 11 words into the correct columns according to the pronunciation of the pink *o*. Encourage Sts to say the words out loud to themselves to help decide where to put them.

! Two of the words, i.e. *doctor* and *London*, have a second *o* in them, which is not pink. This is the schwa sound.

EXTRA SUPPORT To help Sts you could tell them how many words go into each column (excluding the example): /ɒ/ has four, /əʊ/ has three, /ʌ/ has three, and /uː/ has one.

c 🔊 **4.5** Get Sts to compare with a partner.
Play the audio for Sts to listen and check.
Elicit the answers onto the board.

🔊 **4.5**

clock /ɒ/	doctor, job, model, Scotland, strong
phone /əʊ/	don't, go, home, no
up /ʌ/	come, London, money, one
boot /uː/	do, who

Play the audio again, pausing after each word or column for Sts to listen and repeat.

d Model the example conversations with a strong student or two.

Get Sts to practise the conversations in pairs.

Then get a few pairs to read out loud for the class.

4 LISTENING & SPEAKING identifying the main / supporting information

a 🔊 **4.6** Focus on the instructions and on the photos on Grace's phone. Now focus on the chart and tell Sts they need to listen to find out who Mark, Celia, and Miriam are in relation to Grace. Point out that the first one for Mark has been done for them (*He's Grace's boyfriend*).
Play the audio once or twice.
Check answers.

EXTRA SUPPORT Read through the script and decide if you need to pre-teach any new lexis before Sts listen.

Celia is Grace's sister. Miriam is Grace's sister-in-law.

🔊 **4.6**
(script in Student's Book on *p.119*)
A = Anna, G = Grace
A Who's that?
G That's my boyfriend, Mark.
A He's good-looking. How old is he?
G Twenty-six.
A What does he do?
G He's a medical student. He finishes this year – I hope!
A Where does he study?
G At University College London.
A Does he like it?
G Yes, he loves it. And this is my sister Celia and her kids.
A Ah. She looks like you.
G Yes, she does.
A How old is she?
G She's thirty-five.
A How old are the children?
G Carlos, the little one, is two, and Daniel, the older one's, er, six, I think. They live in Chile, so I don't see them very often.
A Is that another sister?
G No, she's my sister-in-law, Miriam. She's married to my brother Tim.
A What does Tim do?
G He's a lawyer, and Miriam's a teacher.
A How old are their children?
G Alex is four and Helen's thirteen months now.
A They look lovely!…So how about you and Mark? When's the wedding?
G Wedding! No, thanks! I'm too young!

---

b Focus on the instructions. Play the audio again, pausing after each person has been described, to give Sts time to write. Play again if necessary.

Get Sts to compare with a partner, and then check answers.

Mark: He is good-looking. He's 26. He's a medical student at University College London. He loves it.
Celia: She looks like Grace. She's 35. She has two sons. Carlos is two; Daniel is six. They live in Chile.
Miriam: She is married to Tim, Grace's brother. Tim is a lawyer; Miriam is a teacher. Their children are Helen, 13 months old, and Alex, four.

EXTRA SUPPORT If there's time, you could get Sts to listen again with the script on *p.119*, so they can see exactly what they understood / didn't understand. Translate / Explain any new words or phrases.

c Focus on the instructions and the examples. If Sts have, e.g. their phones or tablets with them, ask them to show each other photos of friends or people in their family. They must ask each other three questions about each person. If not, they could write the names of some of their relatives and friends on a piece of paper. They swap pieces of paper, and then **A** asks **B** three questions about each person.

They then swap roles.

EXTRA SUPPORT Demonstrate by bringing in some photos of your family / friends. If possible, blow them up or project them onto the board, and then elicit questions from Sts.

G prepositions of time (*at, in, on*) and place (*at, in, to*)
V daily routine: *get up, get dressed*, etc.
P linking

Lesson plan

This lesson is based on the daily routine of two real people with busy lives (Marjan Jahangiri is a professor of cardiac surgery in London, and the article about her appeared in *The Sunday Times*. Her son, Darius, is in his last year of secondary school.). Sts begin by learning verb phrases to talk about daily routines. There is then a pronunciation focus on linking, which will help Sts to understand spoken English. Sts then read about Marjan's day and listen to an interview with her son, and decide whose day they think is more tiring. This is followed by a grammar focus on prepositions of time and place, which are commonly used when we describe a typical day. The lesson ends with a Speaking activity where Sts ask each other about their typical weekdays, and they then write a description of their favourite day of the week.

! This lesson also revises telling the time. This was taught at the beginning of **Practical English Episode 2** on *p.52*. If you did not do this lesson, you will need to do this section first instead of the **Optional lead-in**.

More materials

For teachers

Photocopiables

Grammar prepositions of time and place (*in, on, at, to*) *p.178*
Vocabulary A day in the life of a fitness instructor *p.266* (instructions *p.254*)
Communicative Prepositions questionnaire *p.224* (instructions *p.207*)

For students

Workbook 4B

Online Practice 4B

OPTIONAL LEAD-IN (BOOKS CLOSED) Revise telling the time. Draw a clock on the board and then draw different hands and ask Sts *What time is it?*.

Ask Sts *What time does this class start?* and elicit the answer *It starts at (X)*. Highlight that we use the preposition *at* when we say what time something happens.

1 VOCABULARY daily routine

a ◖ **4.7** Books open. Focus on the phrases and give Sts time to look at them.

Play the audio (sound effects), pausing after each one for Sts to guess which one it is. Point out that the first one (*wake up*) has been done for them.

Check answers. Model and drill the pronunciation of the phrases.

2 have a shower	**3** get dressed	**4** have a coffee / tea
5 have breakfast	**6** go to work / school	

◖ **4.7**
(sound effects of the following)
1 *alarm clock ringing, groans, noises of someone waking up*
2 *somebody having a shower*
3 *somebody opening wardrobe, taking out shirt on hanger, putting it on*
4 *pouring a coffee, drinking*
5 *pouring cereal and milk, eating breakfast, etc.*
6 *banging front door, walking down drive, getting into car, car driving off*

b Focus on the task and example. Demonstrate it yourself by using phrases 1–6 in **a** to tell the class your typical morning.

Then put Sts in pairs and get them to do the same.

Get feedback from some pairs to find out if they do things in the same order.

c Tell Sts to go to **Vocabulary Bank** **Daily routine** on *p.156*.

Vocabulary notes

Make sure Sts know the difference between *go to work* (= leave the house), *get to work* (= arrive at work), *go home* (= leave school / work and go to your house), and *get home* (= arrive home).

Focus on the names *Busy Belinda* and *Chilled Charlie*, and get Sts to guess from the pictures what *busy* and *chilled* mean. Model and drill pronunciation (/ˈbɪzi/ and /tʃɪld/). Then get Sts to do **a** individually or in pairs.

◖ **4.8** Now do **b**. Tell Sts that they will hear the answers in the order that Belinda and Charlie do the things, not in the order of the verbs. Play the audio for Sts to listen and check.

Check answers.

◖ **4.8**
Daily routine
Busy Belinda
1 wake up at seven o'clock
2 have a shower
3 get dressed
4 put on make-up
5 have a coffee
6 go to work by bus
7 get to work
8 start work at eight thirty
9 have lunch at work
10 finish work at six thirty
11 go shopping
12 get home late
13 do the housework
14 have pizza for dinner
15 check emails
16 go to bed

Chilled Charlie
17 get up at eight o'clock
18 have a shave
19 take the dog for a walk
20 have breakfast
21 walk to work
22 go home early

23 go to Italian classes
24 see friends
25 make dinner
26 relax
27 have a bath
28 sleep for eight hours

Then either use the audio to drill the pronunciation of each verb / phrase, or model and drill them yourself. Give further practice of any words or phrases your Sts find difficult to pronounce.

Focus on the *have* box and go through it with the class.

Finally, focus on **Activation** and tell Sts they are now going to tell each other about Belinda and Charlie, and they must make full sentences, e.g. *She wakes up at seven o'clock*. Put Sts in pairs, **A** and **B**. Sts **A** should cover the verb phrases about Belinda and look at the pictures to see if they can remember the expressions. Sts **B** can look at the verb phrases and help if necessary. Sts then swap roles, and Sts **B** do the same with Charlie.

Tell Sts to go back to the main lesson **4B**.

 Ask Sts if they are more like Busy Belinda or Chilled Charlie and why.

 If you think Sts need more practice, you may want to give them the **Vocabulary** photocopiable activity at this point.

2 PRONUNCIATION linking

a 🔊 **4.9** Focus on the **Connected speech** box and remind Sts about linking in spoken English (They saw it in **2C**). Tell Sts they are going to hear five sentences, each read at natural speed. Point out that for each sentence they can see how many words there are.

Tell them the first time you play the audio they should just listen. Play the audio once.

🔊 **4.9**
1 He wakes up at eight.
2 She works in an office.
3 She has a coffee at eleven.
4 He has a lot of homework.
5 She has an interesting day.

Now play it again, pausing for Sts to write the five sentences. Play again if necessary.

Get Sts to compare with a partner, and then check answers by eliciting the sentences onto the board.

See sentences in script 4.9

b 🔊 **4.10** This exercise practises sentence stress and rhythm. Focus on the sentences and tell Sts that the words in bigger **bold** print are the words that are stressed.

Play the audio, pausing after each sentence for Sts to listen and repeat, copying the rhythm.

🔊 **4.10**
See sentences in Student's Book on *p.32*

In pairs, Sts practise the sentences, paying attention to linking and rhythm.

Get a few Sts to read some of the sentences aloud.

3 READING & LISTENING inferring feelings, understanding specific information

a Focus on the title of the article, *Busy lives Mother…and son*, and the photos. Read the introduction about Marjan together and make sure Sts understand it all. Tell Sts they will now read about a typical (working) day in Marjan's life and then listen to an interview with Darius about a day in his life. Model and drill Marjan's name /ˈmɑːdʒæn/.

Focus on the adjectives in the list and make sure Sts can remember what they mean.

Go through the **Glossary** and model and drill the pronunciation of the words and phrases, and make sure Sts understand their meaning.

Set Sts a time limit and tell them that all they have to do is find out how they think Marjan feels at the end of the day.

When the time limit is up, get feedback.

 Before Sts read the article the first time, check whether you need to pre-teach any vocabulary.

Suggested answer
Marjan probably feels (very) tired, but happy.

b Tell Sts they need to read the article again and then answer questions 1–8. Make sure Sts can remember what a 9–5 job is (They saw it in **3B**).

Put Sts in pairs and tell them to read the article, then cover it and answer the questions with their partner.

Check answers.

1 Between 6.00 and 6.30 a.m.
2 She has meetings and lectures. She does operations.
3 At her desk
4 She has dinner with her son. She does research. She watches the news on TV. She plays the piano. Sometimes she does operations.
5 No. She works long hours, sometimes during the night, and she often works at weekends.
6 She sees her son a lot, but not her husband.
7 She plays the piano every day, late at night. She also goes to the hairdresser.
8 Yes, she loves it.

Deal with any other new vocabulary. Model and drill the pronunciation of any tricky words.

 Write the following phrases from the article on the board and elicit the verbs:
AWAY / AT HOME
RESEARCH
TO THE HAIRDRESSER
A BREAK / A MEETING
THE PIANO
ON THE PHONE
TIME WITH SOMEONE

be away / at home
do research
go to the hairdresser
have a break / a meeting
play the piano
speak on the phone
spend time with someone

c 🔊 **4.11** Focus on the photo of Darius and read the instructions. Point out the **Glossary** and go through it with the class. Model and drill the pronunciation of the words, especially *choir* /ˈkwaɪə/.

Give Sts a couple of minutes to read the information about Darius's day. Tell them to think about what the missing words / phrases could be. Point out that the first one (*7.30*) has been done for them.

Play the audio once for Sts just to listen. Then play it again for Sts to complete the gaps, pausing if necessary to give them time to write. Play again if necessary.

Get Sts to compare with a partner, and then check answers.

  Read through the script and decide if you need to pre-teach any new lexis before Sts listen.

> **2** gets   **3** four…five   **4** school   **5** 1.45   **6** go home
> **7** sings   **8** Thursdays   **9** plays   **10** has…shower
> **11** two…three   **12** 10.30

🔊 **4.11**
(script in Student's Book on *p.119*)
I = interviewer, D = Darius
I What time do you get up in the morning?
D I get up at about half past seven.
I How do you feel when you get up?
D I know half past seven isn't that early, but it's early for me and I usually feel tired and in a bit of a bad mood.
I Do you have breakfast?
D Absolutely. I have cereal and milk, and some bread with honey or jam. I love honey!
I Do you walk to school?
D No, it's quite far away. I go to school by Tube. I usually get to school about twenty past eight. I like to be early.
I What time does your first lesson start?
D It starts at nine. I have four or sometimes five lessons before lunch.
I Where do you have lunch?
D I usually have lunch at school at about one o'clock. I know people usually say that school food is terrible, but actually at my school the food is really good.
I And after lunch?
D We start lessons again at one forty-five. I usually have two or three lessons in the afternoon.
I What time does school finish?
D At four fifteen. But I don't go home then. I stay at school to do extra things – I study in the library or play music.
I What kind of music?
D Well, I sing in the school choir on Tuesdays, and on Thursdays, I play percussion in the orchestra. I love music – it's my main hobby.
I So what time do you usually get home?
D At about six o'clock.
I What's the first thing you do?
D I have a shower, and then I have dinner. And then, of course, homework.
I How much homework do you have?
D Two or three hours. It's my last year at school and I have my A levels this summer. I need to get really good marks to get into university.
I Do you watch TV in the evening?
D No, never. I don't have time. When I finish my homework I practise the piano and then I go to bed.
I What time do you go to bed?
D At about half past ten. I'm usually so tired I go to sleep straight away. All I really do these days is study, eat, and sleep.
I So no social media or anything like that?
D Well…I do spend a bit of time on Facebook. But not much, I promise!

  If there's time, you could get Sts to listen again with the script on *p.119*, so they can see exactly what they understood / didn't understand. Translate / Explain any new words or phrases.

d Finally, put Sts in pairs or small groups to discuss the questions. Make sure they know the meaning of the phrase *to have something in common* (= to be like somebody in a certain way or to have the same interests as somebody).

Elicit some feedback.

> Marjan and Darius both have long days and work hard. They both like what they do.
> Marjan is probably more tired. She has less time to relax, and has more responsibility.

  Ask the class if they think busy people are usually happy. Encourage them to try to say why (even if they make mistakes).

4 GRAMMAR prepositions of time and place

a Focus on the instructions and give Sts time to complete the sentences about Darius's day with a preposition.

b 🔊 **4.12** Play the audio for Sts to listen and check. Check answers.

> **1** at   **2** to   **3** at   **4** in   **5** on

🔊 **4.12**
1 I get up at half past seven.
2 I usually go to school by Tube.
3 I have lunch at school.
4 I usually have two or three lessons in the afternoon.
5 I sing in the school choir on Tuesdays.

c Tell Sts to go to **Grammar Bank 4B** on *p.130*.

Grammar notes

There are three main prepositions of time: *at, in, on*.

There are simple rules for *in* and *on*. The rules for *at* require a little bit more effort to remember because these include the exceptions *at night* and *at the weekend*.

Some uses are not yet practised (*in* + months and year, *on* + dates) because Sts do not have this lexis yet, but they are focused on later when Sts learn dates in **6B**.

Under prepositions of place, Sts focus on *at* or *in*, and *to*. The main aim is for Sts to be clear that *at* and *in* are used for position whereas *to* is used for movement. Sts also learn that *in / at* are often alternatives when talking about place, e.g. *I was in a restaurant / at a restaurant last night*. Sometimes there is a subtle difference between the two prepositions in this context, but it is not necessary to go into this at this level.

Focus on the example sentences and play both audio 🔊 **4.13** and 🔊 **4.14** for Sts to listen and repeat. Then go through the rules with the class.

Now focus on the exercises for **4B** on *p.131*. Sts do the exercises individually or in pairs.

 You may want to focus on the rules for prepositions of time, and then do **a**, followed by the rules for prepositions of place and **b**.

Check answers, getting Sts to read the full sentences for **b**.

a
1 in **2** on **3** in **4** at **5** at **6** on **7** at **8** in **9** in
b
1 at **2** to **3** in **4** at **5** to **6** in **7** in **8** at **9** in
10 at

Tell Sts to go back to the main lesson **4B**.

 If you think Sts need more practice, you may want to give them the **Grammar** photocopiable activity at this point.

d ◀) **4.15** Tell Sts they are going to hear some time phrases and they must repeat the time phrase with a preposition. Focus on the example.

Play the audio, pausing after each time phrase for Sts to listen and repeat with the correct preposition.

◀) **4.15**
1 the weekend (*pause*) at the weekend
2 the morning (*pause*) in the morning
3 seven o'clock (*pause*) at seven o'clock
4 Sunday (*pause*) on Sunday
5 night (*pause*) at night
6 the evening (*pause*) in the evening
7 midnight (*pause*) at midnight
8 the summer (*pause*) in the summer
9 Tuesday morning (*pause*) on Tuesday morning
10 Christmas (*pause*) at Christmas

Now repeat the activity, eliciting responses from individual Sts.

5 SPEAKING & WRITING an article

a Put Sts in pairs and tell them they are going to interview their partner. Stress that they are going to talk about a typical weekday (Monday to Friday).

Focus on the questions and elicit that Sts need to add *do you* each time there is a /.

Demonstrate the activity by getting Sts to ask you two or three questions. Remind Sts of the typical rhythm of questions, and encourage them not to stress *do you*, e.g. *What time do you get up?*.

b Put Sts in pairs and get them to ask and answer the questions. Monitor and help, correcting especially any mistakes with the time and prepositions.

In their pairs, Sts decide what they have in common.

Get feedback from various pairs.

c Tell Sts to go to **Writing An article** on *p.114*.

The aim here is to give Sts practice describing habitual actions. Sts learn to recognize and use common connectors and common sequencers.

Focus on the title and elicit the meaning and pronunciation of *favourite*.

Now focus on **a** and give Sts time to read the article and answer questions 1–4.

Get Sts to compare with a partner, and then check answers.

1 Saturday, because it's the first day of the weekend.
2 I stay in bed until about 10.30. Then I usually go shopping with a friend.
3 I often have lunch at my mother's house, with her and my brother. After lunch I sometimes study from about 4.00 to 6.00.
4 I usually go out with my friends. We often go to the cinema, and after that, we have a pizza or *tapas*.

 Ask a few Sts *Is Cristina's Saturday like yours?*

Now do **b** and go through the ***after*** and ***then*** box with the class. Highlight that:

- *after* and *before* are prepositions and opposites. They are used with a noun or a verb phrase: *I always have a cup of coffee after lunch.*
- *then* is used with a verb phrase. It can go at the beginning or in the middle of a sentence: *I have a bath. Then I go to bed. I have a bath and then I go to bed.*
- *after that* is an alternative to *then*. However, highlight that you can't use *after* to connect two clauses, e.g. NOT ~~I get up, and after I have breakfast~~.

With a partner, Sts check they know the highlighted words in the article, and then they complete the six sentences.

Check answers.

1 Then **2** After **3** before **4** During, from, to **5** that
6 until

Focus on the task in **c** and the instructions. Elicit / Explain that the article has four paragraphs and each one describes one main idea. Give Sts a few minutes to make some notes for each paragraph.

In **d**, Sts write their article. They can do this in class if there is time or for homework. Monitor and help Sts, encouraging them to use the highlighted words from the article.

In **e**, Sts spend a few minutes checking their article and the use of the highlighted words.

Now do **f** and get Sts to exchange articles. They read each other's articles and try to find something in common.

Elicit some feedback from various pairs.

G position of adverbs, expressions of frequency
V months, adverbs and expressions of frequency: *minute, hour*, etc.
P the letter *h*

Lesson plan

The topic of this lesson is lifestyle choices which may determine whether you have a longer or shorter life. Sts begin by learning the vocabulary for months and adverbs and expressions of frequency. A study carried out recently which investigates why American teenagers may not live as long as their parents provides the context for Sts to learn the word order for adverbs and expressions of frequency. Pronunciation focuses on the letter *h*. In the second half of the lesson, Sts read about the so-called 'Blue Zones', five places in the world which have a very high proportion of centenarians, and about the lifestyles in two of them, which they compare to their own country. The lesson ends with a video listening about a third one, Okinawa, in Japan.

More materials

For teachers

Photocopiables
Grammar adverbs and expressions of frequency *p.179*
Communicative How often? Board game *p.225*
(instructions *p.207*)

Teacher's Resource Centre
Video The island of Okinawa

For students
Workbook 4C
Online Practice 4C

OPTIONAL LEAD-IN (BOOKS CLOSED) Write on the board HOW CAN I LIVE TO BE 100? Invite suggestions from the class and write them on the board, e.g. *Don't smoke, Do exercise every day*, etc.

1 VOCABULARY months, adverbs and expressions of frequency

a 4.16 Books open. Focus on the months. In pairs, Sts complete the words.

Play the audio for Sts to listen and check.

Elicit the months onto the board.

See letters in **bold** in script 4.16

4.16
January February March April May June July August September October November December

b Play the audio again for Sts to listen and repeat. Give further practice of any months your Sts find difficult to pronounce.

Now ask the class which five months are stressed on the second syllable.

July, September, October, November, December

c Tell the class the month of your birthday and write on the board MY BIRTHDAY IS IN…

Now tell Sts in turn to say their birthday month in the same way, and find out if there is a month in which many Sts have their birthdays. Make sure they only say the month and not the date.

EXTRA IDEA Get Sts to do this as a mingle and ask each other *When's your birthday?* Find out if any Sts found someone born in the same month as them.

d Tell Sts to go to **Vocabulary Bank Time** on *p.157* and get them to do **Parts 2** and **3**.

Vocabulary notes
Highlight that *once* and *twice* are irregular forms. For all other numbers, we use a number + *times*, e.g. *five times, ten times*.

Focus on **2 Expressions of frequency** and get Sts to do **a** individually or in pairs. Make sure Sts are clear about the meaning and pronunciation of *How often…?* (which is used when you want to ask someone about the frequency with which they do an activity) and *every*.

4.17 Now do **b**. Play the audio for Sts to listen and check.

Check answers.

4.17
2 Expressions of frequency
1 every day   2 every week   3 every month   4 every year
5 once a week   6 twice a week   7 three times a week   8 four times a year

Now either use the audio to drill the pronunciation of the phrases, or model and drill them yourself. Give further practice of any words your Sts find difficult to pronounce.

Focus on the instructions for **Activation**. Get Sts to cover the left-hand column with a piece of paper, leaving the rest visible to see if they can remember the expressions.

Focus on **3 Adverbs of frequency** and get Sts to do **a** individually or in pairs.

Vocabulary notes
If Sts don't have an exact equivalent in their L1, you may want to point out that these words don't have an exact meaning in terms of frequency – the meaning depends on the activity, e.g. in *I often have fruit for breakfast, often* probably means three times a week, whereas in *I often travel abroad for work, often* may mean once a month.

4.18 Now do **b**. Play the audio for Sts to listen and check.

Check answers.

See letters in **bold** in script 4.18

4.18

3 Adverbs of frequency

1b I always get up at seven o'clock during the week. **I start work at eight o'clock every day.**

2a I often go to the cinema after work. **About seven or eight times a month.**

3c I usually finish work at six o'clock. **But on Fridays we stop at three o'clock.**

4f I sometimes meet a friend for lunch. **About once or twice a month.**

5e I hardly ever go to the theatre. **Only once or twice a year.**

6d I never have coffee. **I don't like it.**

Then either use the audio to drill the pronunciation of the sentences, or model and drill them yourself. Give further practice of any words your Sts find difficult to pronounce.

Focus on the meaning of the six highlighted adverbs.

4.19 Focus on **c** and play the audio for Sts to listen and repeat the adverbs. Give further practice of any adverbs your Sts find difficult to pronounce.

4.19

See highlighted adverbs of frequency in Student's Book on *p.157*

Focus on the ***normally*** box and go through it with the class.

Finally, focus on the instructions for **Activation**. Get Sts to cover sentences 1–6 with a piece of paper, leaving a–f visible to see if they can remember the sentences and especially the adverb of frequency.

Tell Sts to go back to the main lesson **4C**.

2 GRAMMAR position of adverbs, expressions of frequency

a Focus on the photo. Ask Sts how old they think the girl is, and elicit the meaning of *teenagers* (= young people between the ages of 13 and 19).

Focus on the text. You may want to pre-teach *a screen* (= the flat, square part of a television or computer, where you see pictures or words) and *sugary* (= containing a lot of sugar).

Read the introduction together and make sure Sts understand the phrase *unhealthy lifestyles*. Elicit the opposite of *unhealthy*.

Set a time limit for Sts to read the rest of the text.

Ask the class which situations they think are probably similar in their country and elicit opinions.

b Get Sts to read the text again, focusing on the position of the highlighted words, which all express frequency. They then circle the correct word in rules 1 and 2.

Check answers.

1 before a main verb, **after** the verb *be*   **2 at the end** of a phrase or sentence

c Tell Sts to go to **Grammar Bank 4C** on *p.130*.

Grammar notes

The normal position for adverbs of frequency is before the main verb, but after *be*. However, *sometimes* and *usually* can be used at the beginning of a sentence or clause for emphasis, e.g. *Sometimes I wake up really early…*

Similarly, the normal position for expressions of frequency is at the end of a sentence or verb phrase, but they are sometimes placed at the beginning for emphasis, e.g. *Every day I check my emails first thing in the morning*.

4.20 Focus on the example sentences and play the audio for Sts to listen and repeat. Then go through the rules with the class.

Now focus on the exercises for **4C** on *p.131*. Sts do the exercises individually or in pairs.

Check answers, getting Sts to read the full sentences.

a
1 I always walk to work.
2 Do you usually wear glasses?
3 I'm hardly ever bored.
4 She sometimes does housework.
5 We hardly ever go to the cinema.
6 Why are you always late?
7 My girlfriend is never stressed.
8 Does it often rain in December?

b
1 I am never late for class.
2 We hardly ever eat fast food.
3 What time do you usually finish work?
4 My parents don't often go out at night.
5 My brother is always hungry at lunchtime.
6 We don't always do our homework.
7 Do you usually drive to work?
8 Our teacher is hardly ever angry.

Tell Sts to go back to the main lesson **4C**.

EXTRA SUPPORT If you think Sts need more practice, you may want to give them the **Grammar** photocopiable activity at this point.

d Tell Sts that they will now find out if they are going to live a short or long life, by answering a questionnaire. Tell them to go to **Communication Short life, long life?** on *p.104*.

Go through the instructions with Sts carefully. Put them in pairs. Give Sts **A** time to interview Sts **B** and to circle their partner's answers.

Now the pairs swap roles, and Sts **B** interview Sts **A** and circle their answers.

When they have finished, they should calculate their partner's score and tell him / her the result.

Get feedback from the class, finding out who is going to live the longest.

Tell Sts to go back to the main lesson **4C**.

3 PRONUNCIATION the letter *h*

Pronunciation notes

How difficult this sound is will depend on your Sts' L1 and you should spend more or less time here accordingly.

The main problem with the letter *h* is that in many languages it is silent at the beginning of a word. Highlight that in English it is almost always pronounced like the /h/ in *hotel* and *How*. There are very few exceptions. The only one which is relevant at this level is *hour*, but don't focus on this until after Sts have done **b**.

a 🔊 **4.21** Focus on the sound picture (*house*) and sound /h/.

Play the audio for Sts just to listen to the sound and example words.

🔊 **4.21**
See sound and words in Student's Book on *p.34*

Now play the audio again for Sts to listen and repeat.

b 🔊 **4.22** In pairs, Sts read the sentences aloud and try to find in which word the letter *h* is not pronounced.

Play the audio for Sts to listen and check.

Check the answer.

In the word *hour* the *h* is not pronounced.

🔊 **4.22**
See sentences in Student's Book on *p.34*

Now, in their pairs, Sts practise saying the sentences.

c Focus on the task and make sure Sts understand all the lexis in the verb phrases.

Demonstrate the activity first by making true sentences about yourself.

Sts should write true sentences about themselves, using the verb phrases and an adverb or expression of frequency.

EXTRA SUPPORT Elicit adverbs and expressions of frequency and write them on the board for Sts to refer to.

They then say their sentences to a partner.

EXTRA CHALLENGE Get Sts to make sentences orally with a partner, without writing them down first.

Get feedback, asking two or three pairs if they were similar or different.

4 READING & SPEAKING retelling the main information from a short text

a Focus on the photos and the title. Elicit / Explain the meaning of *secret* (= something you do not or must not tell other people).

Get Sts to read the text or read it aloud. Ask Sts to predict anything that they think the places might have in common. Elicit possible answers (e.g. their lifestyle, the weather, etc.). You might want to pre-teach *diet* (here meaning *daily food*).

Do the questions as a whole-class activity.

The 'Blue Zones' are five places where many people live for a long time.
Alexis is 102 and María is 97.

If you think your Sts might be interested, you could tell them that 'Blue Zones' were first identified in 2004 by *National Geographic* and a team of longevity researchers.

EXTRA IDEA If you have a world map in the class, get Sts to find the five 'Blue Zones'.

b Put Sts in pairs, **A** and **B**, and tell them to go to **Communication, A Ikaria** on *p.104*, **B Nicoya** on *p.110*.

Go through the instructions carefully. Make sure Sts understand the word(s) in the **Glossary**. You may want to point out that *beans* can also refer to the green variety.

Sit **A** and **B** face-to-face if possible. When they have finished reading their articles and have answered the questions, Sts **B** starts by describing life in Nicoya to Sts **A**. Tell them to try to use their own words.

When Sts **B** have finished, they swap roles.

Sts then decide what the two places have in common.

Check answers. You could ask Sts if they would like to live in either Ikaria or Nicoya.

EXTRA SUPPORT Before Sts read their article, check whether you need to pre-teach any vocabulary.

People in both places spend a lot of time outside. They are very active; they walk everywhere. They eat beans. They don't eat much meat.

Tell Sts to go back to the main lesson **4C**.

c Tell Sts to work with a partner and write words or phrases they can remember from their articles related to the two categories. Point out the two examples.

Check answers.

food and drink: potatoes, green vegetables, fish, sugar, herbal tea, red wine, rice, sweet potatoes, egg, cheese, meat, fruit (marañón), water
physical exercise: do exercise, work in their gardens, go to a gym, walk everywhere, ride horses

Deal with any other new vocabulary. Model and drill the pronunciation of any tricky words.

5 ▶ VIDEO LISTENING comparing and contrasting

a Now tell Sts they are going to watch a documentary about a third Blue Zone, the island of Okinawa in Japan. Focus on the task and go through 1–8 with Sts. Elicit / Explain any new vocabulary, e.g. *seaweed*.

Play the video for Sts to watch or listen and mark each statement *T* (true) or *F* (false). Remind them that they don't need to correct the *F* sentences at this stage.

Check answers.

 Read through the script and decide if you need to pre-teach any new lexis before Sts watch or listen.

1 F 2 T 3 T 4 F 5 T 6 F 7 F 8 F

The island of Okinawa

Okinawa is an island about four hundred miles south of Japan. Its a beautiful island, with wonderful beaches and clear blue water. It also has more centenarians – people who are a hundred years old or more – than anywhere else in the world. What's more, they seem to age more slowly than other people. According to scientists, people there who are actually seventy often have the bodies of fifty-year-olds. Many of them are very healthy all through their lives.
What's their secret? Most people think it's because of their healthy lifestyle. They don't have big meals – they have a cultural habit called *hara hachi*, which means they always stop eating before they're full. They usually just have fish and vegetables, especially sweet potatoes, and they eat a lot of seaweed, which is one of the healthiest foods that there is.
But diet isn't the only reason why they live so long. The Okinawans are very active, and they often work in their gardens until they're eighty or more. Many of them also do *t'ai chi* or martial arts, every day. They have a good social life. They visit friends or family, and a lot of them belong to community centres. Some play the traditional Okinawan guitar, an instrument similar to a banjo.
The old people of Okinawa are very positive and happy with their lives. They aren't stressed, because they're never in a hurry. Their spiritual lives are important to them, especially the women, and many of them meditate every day.
In Okinawa, people say you're a child until you are fifty-five. And when you reach ninety-seven, your local town holds a special ceremony called *kajimaya* to celebrate the fact that now it's time to be young again, to be free of all responsibilities and to simply enjoy life.

b Now play the video again for Sts to correct the *F* sentences in **a**.

Get Sts to compare answers with a partner, and then check answers.

1 The island of Okinawa is **south** of Japan.
4 They **eat fish**.
6 They do **t'ai chi or martial arts** every day.
7 They are **never** in a hurry.
8 When they reach **97**, they have a ceremony called *kajimaya*.

 If there's time, you could get Sts to watch again with subtitles / showing the script, so they can see exactly what they understood / didn't understand. Translate / Explain any new words or phrases.

c In pairs or small groups, Sts discuss the questions. Check the answer to the first question.

A healthy diet, a lot of exercise, a good social life

Elicit some answers to the other questions from the class.

 Put Sts in pairs to answer the questions and then get feedback from various pairs.

For instructions on how to use these pages, see *p.39*.

More materials
For teachers
Teacher's Resource Centre
Video Can you understand these people? 3&4
Quick Test 4
File 4 Test
For students
Online Practice Check your progress

GRAMMAR

1 b 2 a 3 c 4 a 5 b 6 c 7 b 8 a 9 b 10 c
11 c 12 b 13 b 14 a 15 c

VOCABULARY

a
1 On 2 at 3 up 4 in 5 to
b
1 get 2 take 3 have 4 do 5 go 6 play 7 listen
8 see 9 read 10 wear
c
1 niece (the others are male relatives)
2 husband (the others are female relatives)
3 factory (the others are jobs)
4 early (the others are adverbs of frequency)
5 Monday (the others are months)
d
1 Where 2 What 3 Who 4 How many 5 Why

PRONUNCIATION

c
1 brother /ʌ/ 2 nephew /f/ 3 teacher /ə/ 4 which /w/
5 work /ɜː/
d
1 because 2 dentist 3 unemployed 4 policeman
5 grandmother

CAN YOU understand this text?

a
He wakes up at 1.00 p.m. His work starts in the evening. He
arrives in secret at the club. He finishes work at 4.00 a.m.
b
1 T 2 F 3 T 4 T 5 T 6 F 7 T

▶ CAN YOU understand these people?

1 c 2 a 3 c 4 a 5 b

🔊 **4.23**

1 Talitha
I = interviewer, T = Talitha
I What do you do?
T I work in Marketing.
I How many hours a week do you work?
T I work for thirty-seven hours a week.

2 Joelle
I = interviewer, J = Joelle
I Do you have a big family?
J No, I have a small family. One sister and parents.
I How old is your sister?
J My sister is thirteen.

3 Sophie
I = interviewer, S = Sophie
I What time do you get up in the morning?
S Usually around half past seven.
I What about at weekends?
S Much later. Probably half past nine, ten o'clock.

4 Brian
I = interviewer, B = Brian
I How often do you do sport or exercise?
B I tend to do sports three or four times a week.
I What do you do?
B Gym three times and then I normally do some yoga.

5 Tom
I = interviewer, T = Tom
I Do you like about New York?
T New York? The variety. The people. Change.
I What don't you like?
T What don't I like? No, not much.

5A Vote for me!

G *can / can't*
V verb phrases: *buy a newspaper*, etc.
P sentence stress

Lesson plan

This lesson is based on TV shows like *The X Factor*, where amateur musicians compete in the hope of winning and becoming famous. The lesson starts with the introduction of more verb phrases. Then a picture story of a contestant waiting for her first audition (based on a real participant's blog) introduces Sts to sentences with *can*. *Can* is a very versatile verb in English and is used to express ability, possibility, permission, and to make requests. Sts will have met *can* for requests and permission in Practical English 1, and should already be familiar with the verb. The use of *can* for ability, presented here, along with the other uses, may be expressed by a different verb in your Sts' L1. In the second half of the lesson, special attention is given to the pronunciation of *can* and *can't* when stressed and unstressed. Sts then practise orally with a questionnaire.

More materials
For teachers
Photocopiables
Grammar can / can't *p.180*
Vocabulary More verb phrases *p.267* (instructions *p.255*)
Communicative What can you do? *p.226* (instructions *p.207*)
For students
Workbook 5A
Online Practice 5A

OPTIONAL LEAD-IN (BOOKS CLOSED)

Revise the uses of *can* that Sts have already met. Write on the board:

WHAT DO YOU SAY BEGINNING WITH *CAN* IF…?

1 YOU WANT A PHOTOCOPY
2 YOU'RE IN A CAFÉ AND YOU WANT A COKE
3 YOU WANT ANOTHER PERSON TO SIGN SOMETHING
4 YOU WANT ANOTHER PERSON TO OPEN THE WINDOW

Give Sts a few minutes to discuss in pairs. Check answers.

1 Can I have a photocopy, please?
2 Can I have a Coke, please?
3 Can you sign this, please?
4 Can you open the window, please?

Elicit / Explain that we often use *Can I have…?* to ask for something and *Can you…?* to ask another person to do something. Tell Sts that in this lesson they will learn other uses of *can*.

1 VOCABULARY verb phrases

a Books open. Ask Sts to match the verbs in blue to the words / phrases in green.
Check answers.

go to the gym, play the guitar, do exercise, watch TV, have a coffee, listen to music

b Tell Sts to go to **Vocabulary Bank More verb phrases** on *p.158* and get them to do **a** individually or in pairs. Many of these verbs may already be familiar to them.

Vocabulary notes

Highlight that it is more useful to remember complete phrases, e.g. *meet a friend* (instead of just *meet*).

Sts sometimes confuse *forget* and *leave* when talking about something they didn't bring with them. You may want to explain that with *leave* we always say the place where we left something, but not with *forget*, e.g. *Don't forget your bag. Don't leave your bag in class.*

◆)) 5.1 Now do **b**. Play the audio for Sts to listen and check.
Check answers.

◆)) 5.1
More verb phrases
3 buy a newspaper
2 call a taxi
1 dance the tango
24 draw a picture
7 find a parking space
8 forget somebody's name
11 give somebody flowers
14 hear a noise
16 help somebody
6 leave your bag on a train
19 look for your keys
20 meet a friend
21 paint a picture
9 remember somebody's name
23 run a race
25 see a film
18 send a text message
13 sing a song
4 swim in the sea
15 take a photo
12 talk to a friend
10 tell somebody a secret
5 try to do something difficult
17 use the internet
22 wait for a bus

Now either use the audio to drill the pronunciation of the phrases, or model and drill them yourself. Give further practice of any words or phrases your Sts find difficult to pronounce.

Focus on **Activation**. Get Sts to cover the verbs and use the photos to test themselves or their partner. Encourage them to say the complete phrase, i.e. verb + collocate.

Tell Sts to go back to the main lesson **5A**.

EXTRA SUPPORT If you think Sts need more practice, you may want to give them the **Vocabulary** photocopiable activity at this point.

2 LISTENING focusing on practical information

a Do this as a whole-class activity. You could also tell Sts if you watch this kind of programme and why (not).

b ◗)) **5.2** Focus on the picture story and go through the instructions with Sts. Elicit / Explain the meaning of *audition* (= a short performance by an actor, a singer, etc., so that somebody can decide if they are suitable to be in a play, a concert, etc.).

You might want to pre-teach some vocabulary, e.g. *nervous* and *It's your turn* (= the time when you can or should do something).

Now tell Sts to look at the pictures and read the questions.

Play the audio for Sts to listen and answer the questions. If necessary, play the audio again, pausing after each question has been answered, and elicit the answer from the class.

Get Sts to compare with a partner, and then check answers.

EXTRA SUPPORT Read through the script and decide if you need to pre-teach any new lexis before Sts listen.

> **1** She needs ID.   **2** Her passport   **3** She waits with Amy.
> **4** Three   **5** Good luck, Amy! You can do it!   **6** She leaves it with her friend.   **7** *One Day*   **8** It isn't on.   **9** Oh no! I can't remember the first line.

◗)) **5.2**
(script in Student's Book on *p.119*)
A = Amy, G = guard, O = organizer, F = friend, J = judge
A Half past twelve. In a long queue outside the Conference Centre in Manchester.
G Remember, you need ID. You can't come in if you don't have ID.
A Here's my passport.
G Thanks. Amy Jones. Yes, that's you! OK, come in. Next, please!
A Twelve forty-five. In the waiting area with three hundred and fifty other singers!
O1 OK, Amy, sit here and wait until we call your name.
A Thanks.
O1 Are you here for the audition, too?
F No, I'm not. I'm Amy's friend. Can I wait with her?
O1 Yeah, sure.
F Thanks.
A Let's sit here. I'm so nervous…
O2 Mike Smith, Pat Jones, Tony Cash, come with me. This way.
A Good luck!
A Four o'clock. Three hours later! My turn at last!
O2 Amy Jones, Naomi Williams, Justin Elliot? Can you come with me, please? It's your turn now.
A Oh help! It's my turn.
F Good luck, Amy! You can do it!
A Excuse me. Can my friend come with me?
O2 No, she can't. She can wait there. And you can't take your bag into the audition. Leave it with your friend.
A OK.
A Quarter past four. In the audition, with three judges. Really nervous!
J Amy…Jones? What's your song?
A *One Day*.
J We can't hear you. Is the microphone on?
A Sorry…Sorry. Can you hear me now?
J Yes, that's fine.
A My song's *One Day*.
J Can you start, please?
A Oh no! I can't remember the first line.
J Take your time.
A I'm OK now!

c ◗)) **5.3** Tell Sts that they are going to hear Amy and two other contestants sing. They will then vote to see which of the three they want to win a place in the show.

Play the audio and pause it after each singer has finished. Ask Sts in pairs to give each singer a score out of ten.

◗)) **5.3**
Amy
Extract of audition song 1
Justin
Extract of audition song 2
Naomi
Extract of audition song 3

Now ask Sts to vote (with a show of hands) for their favourite. Write the scores on the board.

d ◗)) **5.4** Focus on the questions and play the audio.

Elicit what the judges said about each person and write it on the board.

Check answers, and see how many Sts agreed with the judges.

> The judges think Amy is very good, Justin is terrible – he can't sing – and Naomi has a good voice, but doesn't have feeling. They want to see Amy on the show next week.
> Amy feels very happy.

◗)) **5.4**
J = judge, A = Amy
J1 Justin, Naomi, Amy, come and stand here. OK Amy. Very nervous at the beginning! But in the end, very good!
J2 Yes, a great performance. Well done.
J1 Justin. In a word…terrible!
J2 Justin, I'm sorry. You're good-looking, you move well, but you can't sing!
J1 Naomi. Quite good. You have a nice voice.
J2 Naomi, you have a good voice, but I can't hear the feeling.
J1 OK. Justin and Naomi – thank you very much, but no, thank you. Amy, congratulations! See you on the show next week.
A Fantastic! That's great. Thank you.

EXTRA SUPPORT If there's time, you could get Sts to listen again to 5.2 with the script on *p.119*, so they can see exactly what they understood / didn't understand. Translate / Explain any new words or phrases.

3 GRAMMAR *can / can't*

a Tell Sts to look at four sentences taken from Amy's story. Get them to match each one to its meaning and then to compare answers in pairs.

Check answers.

> **1** d   **2** a   **3** c   **4** b

b Tell Sts to go to **Grammar Bank 5A** on *p.132*.

Grammar notes

Can is the first modal verb that Sts are introduced to. Modal verbs, unlike normal verbs, do not add *s* in third person singular (*he / she can*, NOT ~~he / she cans~~).
Questions are made by inverting the verb and subject, not with *do / does*, e.g. *Can you come?* NOT ~~Do you can come?~~
Negatives are formed by adding *n't* (*not*), not with *don't / doesn't*, e.g. *I can't swim* NOT ~~I don't can swim.~~

The normal form of a second verb after a modal verb is the infinitive without *to*. This can be hard to remember for many Sts who are used to thinking of the infinitive as with *to* (*to be or not to be…*), and adding *to* after *can* is a common error.

Although other languages may have an equivalent verb to *can* (= be possible / permitted), they probably do not use this same verb to also talk about ability (*I can sing*, *I can play the piano*), and would express this with an equivalent of *know how to*.

5.5 Focus on the example sentences and play the audio for Sts to listen and repeat. Then go through the rules with the class.

Now focus on the exercises for **5A** on *p.133*. Sts do the exercises individually or in pairs.

Check answers, getting Sts to read the full sentences.

a
1 can speak   **2** Can…help   **3** can't see   **4** Can…close
5 Can…repeat   **6** can't park   **7** can't swim   **8** Can…use
b
1 She can meet me after work.
2 Can you open the door, please?
3 My boyfriend can't ski.
4 Can I use your car?
5 You can't take photos here.

Tell Sts to go back to the main lesson **5A**.

EXTRA SUPPORT   If you think Sts need more practice, you may want to give them the **Grammar** photocopiable activity at this point.

4 PRONUNCIATION   sentence stress

Pronunciation notes

There are two main pronunciation problems related to *can / can't*:

Can is usually unstressed = /kən/ in positive sentences like *I can sing*. Your Sts may find this difficult to hear and to say. If they stress *can*, the listener may think they are saying a negative sentence.

The negative *can't* is always stressed. Not stressing it can cause a communication problem (the listener may understand *can*, not *can't*). The pronunciation of this word varies among different groups of native English speakers. The standard pronunciation is /kɑːnt/, but there are regional variations. The important thing for Sts is to make sure that they stress /kɑːnt/ quite strongly.

a **5.6** Focus on the conversations, which give examples of positive, negative, and question forms of *can / can't*. Remind Sts that the bigger words in the conversations are stressed, and the underlining shows stress within a word.
Play the audio for Sts to listen to the three conversations.

5.6
See conversations in Student's Book on *p.39*

Now play the audio again, pausing after each sentence for Sts to try to copy the rhythm.

! If your own pronunciation of *can / can't* is different from what is on the audio, you may want to model the conversations yourself.

Get Sts to practise the conversations in pairs. Encourage them to stress the bigger words more strongly and say the other words more quickly and lightly.

b **5.7** This exercise gives Sts practice in distinguishing between positive and negative *can* statements.

Focus on the instructions. Play the audio for Sts to hear the sentences. Elicit that *can* is unstressed and has a short sound, but *can't* is stressed and has a long sound.

5.7
See sentences in Student's Book on *p.39*

c **5.8** Focus on the instructions. Play the audio at least twice.

Get Sts to compare with a partner, and then check answers by playing the audio again, stopping after each sentence, and asking Sts if it's positive or negative.

1 b   **2** a   **3** a   **4** b   **5** b   **6** a

5.8
1 I can't sing.
2 She can dance very well.
3 He can cook.
4 I can't come to the meeting.
5 You can't park here.
6 I can drive.

EXTRA CHALLENGE   As a follow-up, get Sts, in pairs, to write four *can* sentences each (two positive and two negative, in jumbled order). They take turns to say their sentences to each other as clearly as possible and decide if their partner has said a positive or negative sentence, e.g.
A *I can't cook.* **B** *Negative.*

5 SPEAKING

a Focus on the instructions and make sure Sts understand what they have to do. Point out what the numbers 1, 2, and 3 represent.

Focus on the title and elicit / explain the meaning of *talent* (= a natural ability to do something very well).

Read the introduction together and explain any vocabulary Sts might not know.

Put Sts in pairs and get them to interview each other. Remind them to mark their partner's answers in the questionnaire, not their own.

b Now tell Sts to look at the answers their partner gave them and say what their talent is. Sts tell each other of any competitions or TV shows they can enter.

c Put Sts in new pairs and tell them to look at their questionnaires and tell their new partner what they found out from their first partner.

Get some feedback from various pairs.

G present continuous: *be* + verb + *-ing*
V noise: verbs and verb phrases: *make a noise*, etc.
P /ŋ/

Lesson plan

The first part of this lesson is based on a UK online forum about noisy family members and neighbours. Sts begin by learning new verbs and verb phrases and talk about noise problems in their families or with their neighbours. Then the present continuous (used for what is happening now or for temporary actions / situations) is presented through conversations between family members and noisy neighbours. Pronunciation focuses on the /ŋ/ sound, used in all present continuous endings, and Sts then do a 'spot the differences' Speaking activity, where they practise the new grammar. The lesson ends with Sts listening to six conversations and guessing what the people are doing.

More materials
For teachers
Photocopiables
Grammar present continuous: *be* + verb + *-ing* p.181
Communicative Guess what I'm doing! p.227
(instructions *p.207*)
For students
Workbook 5B
Online Practice 5B

OPTIONAL LEAD-IN (BOOKS CLOSED)

Do something which makes a noise, e.g. put some music on very loudly, bang the desk, etc., and elicit / teach the word *noise*. Then elicit / teach the verb we use with *noise*, *make a noise*, and the adjective *noisy*.

Now elicit / teach the word *neighbours* (= people who live in the flats / houses near you). Model and drill pronunciation /ˈneɪbəz/. Then give Sts in pairs a few moments to think of three things noisy neighbours do.

Get feedback and write Sts' ideas on the board.

1 VOCABULARY & SPEAKING noise: verbs and verb phrases

a Books open. Focus on the instructions and, if you didn't do the **Optional lead-in**, teach / elicit the words *neighbours* and *noisy*. Model and drill pronunciation.

Now focus on the questions.

Get Sts to interview you first. Give as much (simple) information as you can to model the way you want Sts to answer the questions.

Sts interview each other in pairs or groups of three. Monitor and help with any new vocabulary they need.

Get some feedback about their family members and neighbours.

b 🔊 **5.9** Focus on the instructions and the forum, and give Sts a few minutes to read the kinds of noises that family members and noisy neighbours make. Get them to try to guess the meaning of the new verbs and verb phrases.

Tell Sts they will hear eight sounds, each representing one of the problems, and they must write 1–8 as they hear them. Play the audio once the whole way through.

🔊 **5.9**
(sound effects of noisy neighbours / family)
1 *couple next door arguing*
2 *neighbours' dog barking*
3 *baby in the flat upstairs, crying*
4 *TV on very loud*
5 *builders making a lot of noise*
6 *people next door having noisy parties*
7 *learner practising the piano*
8 *teenager playing loud music*

Then play the audio again, pausing after each sound effect to elicit the answer. Make sure Sts understand the meaning of the new verbs and verb phrases. Model and drill pronunciation.

1 The couple next door argue a lot.
2 The neighbours' dog barks all day – and all night!
3 The baby in the flat upstairs cries all the time.
4 The old people in the flat next door have the TV on very loud – and their living room is next to my bedroom!
5 The people next door have builders who make a lot of noise.
6 The people next door often have noisy parties until 3.00 a.m.
7 My sister practises the piano for hours.
8 My son plays loud music in his room – awful music, too.

When you check *My sister practises the piano for hours*, elicit the names of some instruments that can be particularly irritating e.g. *violin*, *drums* (these will then be used later in the lesson). When you check *My son plays loud music*, elicit / explain that *play* here means putting on music on a device, e.g. a music system or tablet – he is not actually making the music himself.

c Focus on the three questions and go through them.

Get Sts to interview you first. Give as much (simple) information as you can to model the way you want Sts to answer the questions.

Sts interview each other in pairs or groups of three. Monitor and help with any new vocabulary they need.

Get some feedback.

2 GRAMMAR present continuous

a ◖🔊 **5.10** Ask Sts to look at the picture of the houses and elicit ideas why Max and his mother are unhappy.

Tell Sts to cover the conversations in **b** with a piece of paper and listen to the audio.

Play the audio once and check answers.

> Max is unhappy because he can't study. His family are making a lot of noise.
> His mother is unhappy because of the noise from the neighbours', and their dog.

◖🔊 **5.10**

M = Max, L = Lucy, I = Isabel, P = Paul
1 **M** Hey, Lucy. I'm trying to study, and you're making an awful noise.
  L It isn't a noise, it's Beethoven. I'm practising – I have a school concert tomorrow. You can study downstairs.
  M I can't, Jake's playing a video game.
  L What about the kitchen?
  M No, Mum's cooking dinner, and she's listening to the radio. It's impossible to work in this house!
2 **I** Paul! Come here.
  P Yes, dear? What's the matter?
  I What's happening next door? Why's their dog barking? I can't hear the radio.
  P They're having a party in the garden.
  I Not again! Can you go and talk to them?
  P Yes, good idea. It's their second party in three weeks!

> **EXTRA SUPPORT** Pause the audio after each conversation and elicit the problem.

b Now get Sts to uncover the conversations and focus on the verbs in the list. Give Sts a few minutes to read the conversations and the list.

> **EXTRA CHALLENGE** Get Sts to complete the gaps first and then listen and check their answers.

Then play the audio once or twice more for Sts to complete the gaps.

Check answers.

> **1** trying **2** making **3** practising **4** playing **5** cooking
> **6** listening **7** happening **8** barking **9** having

> **EXTRA IDEA** Get Sts, in pairs, to read the conversations out loud.

c ◖🔊 **5.11** Focus on the question and elicit a few ideas.
Play the audio for Sts to listen and find out what happens.
Check the answer.

> The neighbours invite him to the party and offer him a drink.

◖🔊 **5.11**
(script in Student's Book on *p.119*)
W = woman, P = Paul
W Oh, hello Paul. Jack, it's Paul, from next door. Come in! We're having a party. It's my birthday.
P Oh! Er, Happy Birthday!
W Thanks. Would you like a drink?
P Actually, I want to talk to you about the noise.
W Sorry?
P The NOISE. It's very noisy.
W Yes. We're having a great time! Do you want a beer? Or a glass of wine?
P Oh, well, yes, OK. A beer, please.
W Here you are. Come and meet our friends. Hey, everyone, say hello to Paul. He's our neighbour.
All Hello, Paul.
P Hello.
W Do you want to dance, Paul?

d Ask Sts to read the two sentences and question, and complete them.

Check answers.

> ⊞ They**'re / are** having a party next door.
> ⏃ **Are** they playing music?
> ⊟ No, they **aren't** playing music. They're talking.

e Ask Sts to read the rule and circle the correct option.

Check the answer. Elicit / Teach that we use this form of the verb (present continuous) for something that's happening now, at the moment of speaking. Give a few more examples, e.g. *We're having a class. I'm talking to you and you're listening.*

> now

f Tell Sts to go to **Grammar Bank 5B** on *p.132*.

> ### Grammar notes
>
> Sts don't usually find the form of the present continuous difficult (*be* + *-ing* form of the verb), but they may have problems using it correctly, especially if they do not have an equivalent form in their L1. A common mistake is to use the present simple, not continuous, for things which are happening now / around now, or for temporary situations, e.g. *Hello. What do you do here? I work at home this week.*
>
> The present continuous is contrasted with the present simple in the next lesson (**5C**).
>
> The use of the present continuous to express future arrangements is presented in *English File* Pre-intermediate.
>
> #### Spelling rules for the *-ing* form
>
> In the *-ing* form, remind Sts that verbs ending in *y* don't change the *y* for an *i* as they do in third person singular (e.g. *study – studying* NOT ~~*studing*~~). Highlight also that there are a few exceptions to the rule about dropping the final *e* before adding *-ing*. These are *be*, and verbs ending in *-ee*, e.g. *see* and *agree*.

◖🔊 **5.12** Focus on the example sentences and play the audio for Sts to listen and repeat. Then go through the rules with the class.

Now focus on the exercises for **5B** on *p.133*. Sts do the exercises individually or in pairs.

Check answers, getting Sts to read the full sentences.

a
1 What's she doing? She's crying.
2 What are they doing? They're watching TV.
3 What's he doing? He's playing basketball.
4 What are they doing? They're singing.
5 What's it doing? It's eating.
b
1 'm staying   2 are…doing   3 'm looking for   4 'm looking
5 Are…living   6 's…doing   7 Is…studying   8 's working
9 isn't enjoying   10 's looking for

Tell Sts to go back to the main lesson **5B**.

EXTRA SUPPORT   If you think Sts need more practice, you may want to give them the **Grammar** photocopiable activity at this point.

g ◗) **5.13**   Focus on the task and example. Explain that if Sts don't know if it's a man or a woman, they should use *Somebody*. Point out that the first one (*Somebody's cooking*) has been done for them.

Now tell Sts to close their books and listen to eight sounds. They have to decide what they think is happening and write a sentence for each sound.

Play the audio once the whole way through for Sts just to listen. Then play it again, pausing after each sound effect, and give Sts, in pairs, time to write a sentence. Emphasize that they should write full sentences, not just the *-ing* form, e.g. *It's raining*.

Elicit answers, accepting all appropriate sentences. Get Sts to write their sentences on the board or to spell the verbs.

2 Somebody's sending messages / texting.
3 Somebody's having a shower and singing.
4 It's raining.
5 Somebody's eating spaghetti.
6 Somebody's making a coffee.
7 Somebody's crying.
8 Somebody's doing the housework.

◗) **5.13**
(sound effects of the following)
1 *a person cooking*
2 *someone sending and receiving WhatsApp messages*
3 *someone having a shower and singing*
4 *rain*
5 *someone eating pasta noisily*
6 *a coffee machine grinding, clunking, hot water pouring…*
7 *someone crying*
8 *sounds of hoovering, dusting, wiping surfaces…*

3 PRONUNCIATION & SPEAKING /ŋ/

a ◗) **5.14**   Focus on the sound picture and elicit the word and sound (*singer* /ŋ/).

Now focus on the example words next to the sound picture, e.g. *singing*. Remind Sts that the pink letters are the same sound as the picture word.

Play the audio for Sts to listen to the sound and example words.

◗) **5.14**
See sound and words in Student's Book on *p.41*

Now play the audio again for Sts to listen and repeat. Correct pronunciation and give further practice if necessary.

EXTRA SUPPORT   If this sound is difficult for your Sts, it will help to show them the mouth position. You could model this yourself or use the the Sound Bank videos on the *Teacher's Resource Centre*.

b Focus on the instructions and the example.

Put Sts in pairs and tell them to look at the houses on *pp.40–41* and ask and answer questions about the people.

c Put Sts in pairs, **A** and **B**, and tell them to go to **Communication Spot the differences**, **A** on *p.105*, **B** on *p.110*.

Go through the instructions with them carefully. Highlight that when we describe a picture, we use the present continuous for actions which are happening in the picture.

Sit **A** and **B** face-to-face if possible. **A** describes what is happening in flats 1–4 and the garden on the left. **B** must say if there are any differences.

B now describes what is happening in flats 5–8 and the garden on the right. **A** tells his / her partner if there are any differences.

When they have found all eight differences, tell them to compare pictures to see if they have correctly identified the differences.

Check by getting pairs to explain the differences, e.g.

A *In my picture the woman in flat 2 is painting the walls.*

B *In my picture she's reading.*

The garden on the left: In A two dogs are barking; in B there are no dogs.
Flat 2: In A the woman is painting the wall; in B she is reading.
Flat 3: In A the boy is playing the violin; in B he is playing the piano.
Flat 4: In A the couple are watching TV; in B they are listening to the radio.
Flat 6: In A the man is cooking; in B he is doing housework.
Flat 7: In A the boy is listening to music; in B he is studying / doing his homework.
Flat 8: In A the baby is crying; in B the baby is sleeping.
The garden on the right: In A the garden is empty; in B some people are having a party.

4 LISTENING working out a situation from context

a 🔊 **5.15** Write WHAT'S THE WOMAN DOING? on the board and tell Sts that they need to listen to a conversation and answer this question.

Play the audio once the whole way through.

Check the answer.

She's checking in at a hotel.

🔊 **5.15**
(script in Student's Book on *p.119*)
A Good afternoon. How can I help you?
B Hello. I have a reservation for two nights.
A Your name?
B Carter.
A Carter. Here we are. Can you sign here, please?…Here's your key card. You're in room two hundred and twelve, on the second floor.

b Tell Sts they will listen again and this time they must write down the words which helped them guess the answer.

Get Sts to compare with a partner, and then check answers.

reservation, two nights, sign here, key card, room 212, second floor

c 🔊 **5.16** Tell Sts that they need to listen to five more conversations and say what the people are doing.

Play the audio once the whole way through. If necessary, play the audio again, pausing after each conversation to elicit the answer.

Check answers.

1 He's buying a coffee.
2 He's looking for his car keys.
3 They're waiting for a train.
4 She's taking a photo.
5 He's having a job interview. / She's interviewing a man for a job.

🔊 **5.16**
(script in Student's Book on *p.120*)
1 A Can I help you?
  B Yes, I'd like a latte, please.
  A Regular or large?
  B Large, please.
  A To have here or take away?
  B To have here.
  A That's three pounds forty, please.
  B Here you are. Three pounds forty.
2 A Where are my car keys? I can't find them anywhere.
  B I don't know. In your jacket pocket?
  A No, they aren't there.
  B How about on the hall table?
  A No.
  B Are you sure you don't have them?
  A Absolutely sure.
  B Look in the living room.
3 A Oh no, it's twenty minutes late.
  B Is there a waiting room somewhere? It's really cold here on the platform.
  A No, I don't think so.
  B What's the time now?
  A Six fifteen. We can take the six twenty, but it's a slow train.
  B No, let's wait, then.
4 OK, come on everyone, out here. Right, stand together under the tree. OK! Are you ready? Carole, I can't see you. Can you stand next to Jim? OK, ready? Say cheese!
5 A …So, Mr Bartlett, do you have any questions you'd like to ask?
  B Er, yes. On the website it says the hours are from ten to six. What about the weekends?
  A The hours are ten to six at the weekends too, but you get paid overtime on Sundays. Saturday counts as a normal day. But if you work on a Saturday, you have a weekday free. The contract says clearly five days a week, with possibilities of overtime.
  B Oh, right.

d Tell Sts they will listen again and this time they must write down two words or phrases which helped them guess each answer.

Get Sts to compare with a partner, and then check answers.

Possible answers
1 latte, regular or large, here or take away, £3.40
2 Where are my car keys?, I can't find them, Look in the living room.
3 a waiting room, the platform, a slow train
4 stand together, Are you ready?, Say cheese!
5 the hours, overtime, work, the contract

5C A city for all seasons

- **G** present simple or present continuous?
- **V** the weather and seasons
- **P** places in London

Lesson plan

The main context of this lesson is London – first its weather, and then some unusual tourist attractions. Many Sts who have not visited the UK have the idea that in London it rains a lot, and some even think that it's still a foggy city. Here they learn the real facts about its climate. Sts begin by learning basic vocabulary to talk about the weather, and listen to a travel guide describing typical London weather. The Grammar (present simple or present continuous) is then presented through some messages between friends in different places around the world. Sts then read an online guide which recommends what to do in London in different seasons. Pronunciation helps Sts pronounce and understand famous place names in London, and the lesson finishes with writing, which deals with how to write posts about your holiday on a social networking site.

More materials
For teachers
Photocopiables
Grammar present simple or present continuous? *p.182*
Vocabulary The weather *p.268* (instructions *p.255*)
Communicative It's Friday evening *p.228* (instructions *p.208*)
For students
Workbook 5C
Online Practice 5C

OPTIONAL LEAD-IN (BOOKS CLOSED)

Write LONDON on the board and teach / elicit the correct pronunciation (/ˈlʌndən/).

Tell Sts, in pairs, to write down three things they associate with London, e.g. *red buses, Trafalgar Square, the River Thames, Big Ben, Oxford Street, Camden Market,* etc.

Write their suggestions on the board.

Ask Sts *Have any of you visited London? Which of these did you see?* and get feedback.

1 VOCABULARY & LISTENING the weather and seasons

a Books open. Focus on the task and elicit / explain the meaning of *weather forecast*. Model and drill pronunciation. Check the meaning of *temperature* and model and drill pronunciation.

Give Sts time to answer the questions.

Check answers and elicit opinions in answer to *Do you think it's typical weather for London?*

1 21 (degrees), ten (degrees)
2 It's probably summer – it could be any month from May to September.
3 It's typical weather during this period. British weather is very changeable.

b Tell Sts to go to **Vocabulary Bank The weather and dates** on *p.159* and get them to do **Part 1**.

Vocabulary notes

Sts may find the question *What's the weather like?* confusing. Emphasize that the question means *How is the weather?*. In this question *like* is a preposition, not a verb. The weather in English is usually expressed by *It's* + adjective, e.g. *It's windy*. However with *rain* and *snow*, although the adjectives *rainy* and *snowy* exist, we use the verbs in the present continuous e.g. *It's raining*.

Focus on **1 The weather** and the chart in **a**.

Get Sts to complete the chart individually or in pairs.

🔊 **5.17** Now do **b**. Play the audio for Sts to listen and check.

Check answers.

🔊 **5.17**

The weather and the dates, 1 The weather
1 It's sunny.
2 It's hot.
3 It's cloudy.
4 It's raining.
5 It's windy.
6 It's foggy.
7 It's cold.
8 It's snowing.

Either use the audio to drill the pronunciation of the phrases, or model and drill them yourself. Give further practice of any words your Sts find difficult to pronounce.

Now focus on the **Other adjectives for weather** and **Nouns and adjectives** box and go through it with the class.

Now focus on **c** and get Sts, in pairs, to practise asking about the weather, using the pictures in the chart.

🔊 **5.18** Focus on the pictures and words for the seasons in **d** and get Sts to match them.

Play the audio to check answers and drill pronunciation.

🔊 **5.18**

1 The weather
3 spring
1 summer
4 autumn
2 winter

Finally, focus on **Activation** and elicit answers from the class.

Tell Sts to go back to the main lesson **5C**.

EXTRA SUPPORT If you think Sts need more practice, you may want to give them the **Vocabulary** photocopiable activity at this point.

c ◗ **5.19** Focus on the instructions. If you didn't do the **Optional lead-in**, ask Sts if they have been to London, and if so, what the weather was like.

Give Sts some time to read the five sentences. Elicit / Teach the word *degrees* (= a measurement of temperature), e.g. *22°C*.

Play the audio once the whole way through for Sts to mark the sentences *T* (true) or *F* (false).

Get Sts to compare their answers with a partner.

Tell Sts they are going to listen to the travel guide again and this time they must correct the false sentences.

Now play the audio again, pausing after each paragraph for Sts to correct the false ones. Play again if necessary.

Check answers. Ask Sts if they were surprised by any of the information.

 Read through the script and decide if you need to pre-teach any new lexis before Sts listen.

1 F (It isn't usually very hot or very cold.)
2 T
3 F (It hardly ever snows.)
4 T
5 F (Today the air is clean and it's hardly ever foggy.)

◗ **5.19**
(script in Student's Book on *p.120*)
The best thing about the weather in London is that it's never extreme. It isn't usually very hot or very cold. In the summer, it's sometimes sunny and sometimes cloudy, with temperatures of about twenty-two degrees. And of course, it sometimes rains.
In winter the temperature is usually between zero and ten degrees. It can be windy and cold, but it hardly ever snows.
In spring and in autumn the weather is very changeable – you can have all the four seasons in one day! It can be sunny in the morning, cloudy at lunchtime, raining in the afternoon, and then cold and windy in the evening. I always tell tourists to take their sunglasses and their umbrellas when they go out!
But one thing you don't often see these days in London is fog. A lot of tourists come to London and say, 'Where's the fog? London is always foggy in films!' Well, it's true that, in the past, that is, until the 1950s, London was a very foggy city because the air was really dirty. But today the air is clean and it's hardly ever foggy.

 If there's time, you could get Sts to listen again with the script on *p.120*, so they can see exactly what they understood / didn't understand. Translate / Explain any new words or phrases.

d Get Sts, in pairs, to discuss the question, or do it as a whole-class activity.

If Sts worked in pairs, elicit some answers from the class.

2 GRAMMAR present simple or present continuous?

a Focus on the photos and messages. Tell Sts to read the messages and answer the questions.
Check answers.

Tim is sad because he loves snow, but he lives in Valencia and it never snows there.
Jane is sad because she is on holiday in Cancún, Mexico, but it's raining.

b Tell Sts to read the messages again and focus on the highlighted verbs. In pairs, they should answer the two questions.
Check answers.

We use the present simple to talk about things that are normally true.
We use the present continuous to talk about things that are happening now / at the moment.

 Draw two columns on the board, one for the present simple and the other the present continuous. Go through the messages with the class. After each highlighted verb, elicit whether it is the present simple or present continuous and write it in the correct column. Then ask Sts the two questions.

c Tell Sts to go to **Grammar Bank 5C** on *p.132*.

Grammar notes
There is a clear difference in use between the present simple and present continuous:
The present simple is used for habitual actions (things which are always true or which happen every day).
The present continuous is used for temporary actions, things happening now / at this moment, or around now.
The use of these two forms can cause problems either because Sts don't have the present continuous in their L1, or because English is 'stricter' about using it when talking about now.
If you know your Sts' L1, contrast it with English to anticipate or correct errors.
Stative verbs, e.g. *want*, *like*, *need*, *have* (= possess), and *know*, are not normally used in the present continuous.

◗ **5.20** Focus on the example sentences and play the audio for Sts to listen and repeat. Then go through the rules and the information box with the class.
Focus on the **What do you do? or What are you doing?** box and go through it with the class.
Now focus on the exercises for **5C** on *p.133*. Sts do the exercises individually or in pairs.
Check answers, getting Sts to read the full sentences.

a
1 He's playing   2 Do your parents live, have   3 do you go, needs   4 is sleeping, doesn't usually sleep
b
1 are…doing, 'm waiting   2 Do…like, don't eat   3 are having, have   4 does…do, works

Tell Sts to go back to the main lesson **5C**.

 If you think Sts need more practice, you may want to give them the **Grammar** photocopiable activity at this point.

d Put Sts in pairs, **A** and **B**, and tell them to go to **Communication What do you do? What are you doing now?**, **A** on *p.105*, **B** on *p.111*.

Sit **A** and **B** face-to-face if possible. **A** asks **B** his / her questions and **B** answers. Stress that **B** needs to listen carefully as to which form **A** uses in the question, and to use this form in his / her answer.

When **A** has asked all his / her questions, they swap roles.

Get some feedback from the class.

Tell Sts to go back to the main lesson **5C**.

3 READING & SPEAKING finding specific information

a Focus on the online guide and the photos, and if some of your Sts have been to London, ask them if they recognize any of the places.

Focus on the task and make sure Sts understand what they have to do.

Now go through the *Where can you…?* questions. Elicit / Teach any lexis you think Sts might not know.

Set a time limit, e.g. five minutes, for Sts to read the guide to find the answers.

Get them to compare with a partner, and then check answers.

EXTRA SUPPORT Before Sts read the guide the first time, check whether you need to pre-teach any vocabulary.

> **1** TW **2** OAT **3** TW **4** V&A **5** LM **6** OAT **7** LM
> **8** V&A

b Tell Sts to read the guide again and complete the nouns or noun phrases used with adjectives 1–7. Point out that the first one has been done for them (see text 1 about the London Marathon).

Check answers.

> **2** places (text 1) **3** weather (text 1) **4** place, café (text 2, text 4) **5** buildings (text 3) **6** museums (text 4)
> **7** collections (text 4)

Deal with any other new vocabulary. Model and drill the pronunciation of any tricky words.

c In pairs, Sts discuss the questions. If you are from a different town than your Sts, you might want to tell them about your town first.

Get some feedback from various pairs.

4 PRONUNCIATION places in London

a 🔊 **5.21** Focus on the instructions and the place names. Tell Sts that it can be very useful to be able to pronounce them correctly, for example if they want to ask for directions, get a taxi, or buy a bus or underground ticket.

Play the audio for Sts just to listen.

🔊 **5.21**
See place names in Student's Book on *p.43*

Then play the audio again, pausing after each place to give Sts time to underline the stress.

Check answers, getting Sts to say the words out loud. Highlight the pronunciation of *Leicester* /ˈlestə/ and *Parliament* /ˈpɑːləmənt/.

> Buckingham Palace   Wembley Stadium   the Tower of London
> Leicester Square   Piccadilly Circus   the Houses of Parliament
> Trafalgar Square   St Paul's Cathedral   Westminster Abbey
> Covent Garden

b Now play the audio again and get Sts to repeat the places.

Ask Sts what they know about the places, and what you can see and do there.

Suggestions

Buckingham Palace: It is where the monarch stays when in London. You can visit 19 rooms.
Wembley Stadium: The new stadium opened in 2007. You can see concerts and various sports events, such as football, rugby, etc.
The Tower of London: It's a UNESCO World Heritage Site. You can see the monarch's crown jewels.
Leicester Square: It's a public square for pedestrians. There are a lot of cinemas and restaurants around the square.
Piccadilly Circus: It's particularly known for its video display and neon signs, as well as a statue in the centre, mistakenly, believed to be of Eros.
the Houses of Parliament: Big Ben is the nickname of the clock. You can see debates or take a tour.
Trafalgar Square: It's a public square. Nelson's Column is at its centre, and the National Gallery is on one side.
St Paul's Cathedral: Building started in 1675 and finished in 1710. You can visit the cathedral and enjoy the wonderful architecture.
Westminster Abbey: It's a very large church used for royal weddings and funerals. Many famous people are buried there.
Covent Garden: It was London's old fruit and vegetable market. Now it is full of shops, restaurants, bars, and street entertainers.

c Focus on the instructions and point out the questions each person asks. Make sure Sts understand them, e.g. *Is it far?*.

Put Sts in pairs and get them to role-play a short conversation with a partner.

Make sure they swap roles.

Get a few pairs to perform in front of the class.

5 WRITING posting on social media

a Focus on the questions and elicit the meaning of *social media* (= communication with people who share your interests, using a website or other service on the internet).

Then elicit answers from the class (or get Sts to answer the question in pairs and then get feedback from the class). Elicit the names of websites which are popular in your Sts' country.

b Tell Sts to go to **Writing Posting on social media** on *p.115*.

Focus on the instructions in **a**. Give Sts a few minutes to read posts 1–5 and match them to photos A–E.

Check answers.

> **1** E **2** B **3** C **4** D **5** A

Now focus on **b** and tell Sts to imagine that they are either in their country or in a different country. Point out that they must write four posts of about 30 words each.

Sts could do **c** in class or for homework. Remind them of the word count.

Focus on **d** and remind Sts to read through their writing and check it for mistakes before they give it in.

3 Practical English In a clothes shop

Function buying clothes
Vocabulary clothes

Lesson plan

In this third Practical English lesson, Sts learn some basic clothes vocabulary and some key phrases for buying clothes in English. The story develops: Jenny spills Rob's coffee over his shirt, so he has to buy a new one. While he is looking for a new shirt, Jenny gets a call from somebody called Eddie. Rob comes out of the shop and hears the end of her conversation, and wonders who Eddie is. When Jenny sees the shirt he has chosen, she insists he goes back to change it.

More materials
For teachers
Teacher's Resource Centre
Video Practical English Episode 3
Quick Test 5
File 5 Test
For students
Workbook Practical English 3
Can you remember? 1–5
Online Practice Practical English 3
Check your progress

OPTIONAL LEAD-IN (BOOKS CLOSED)
Before starting Episode 3, elicit what Sts can remember about Episode 2. Ask them *Who's Rob? Where does he work / live? Who's Jenny? Where is she from?*, etc.

Alternatively, you could play the last scene of Episode 2.

1 ▶ VOCABULARY clothes

a Books open. Focus on the task and get Sts to match the words and photos.

Get Sts to compare with a partner.

b ◀ **5.22** Play the video / audio for Sts to watch or listen and check.

Check answers.

◀ **5.22**
7 a jacket
1 jeans
5 a shirt
2 a T-shirt
6 a skirt
3 shoes
4 a sweater
8 trousers

Focus Sts' attention on the phonetics next to each word. Now play the video / audio again, pausing after each word for Sts to repeat.

Ask Sts why they think it's *a jacket, a shirt, a T-shirt, a skirt, a sweater* (with article) but *jeans, shoes, trousers* (no article), and elicit that it's because the latter are plural.

c Tell Sts to cover the words, look at the photos, and test each other in pairs.

2 ▶ MEETING IN THE STREET

a ◀ **5.23** Focus on the photos and elicit what is happening.

Focus on the question and then play the video / audio once the whole way through for Sts to see if their guesses were correct and to see what problem Rob has.

Check the answer.

Rob spills the coffee down his shirt.

◀ **5.23**
R = Rob, J = Jenny
R Hey, Jenny!
J Oh, hi, Rob. Is that coffee for me?
R Yes. A double espresso.
J Oh wow, thanks. That's really nice of you.
R No problem. Do you have a meeting with Daniel?
J Yes, *another* meeting. And you?
R I'm going to the office, too. I have an interview in twenty minutes.
J Oh really? With who?
R A theatre director.
J Sounds interesting.
R What time is your meeting with Daniel?
J At half past nine.
R Ugh!
J Oh no. Are you OK? I'm so sorry!
R I'm fine!
J I'm really sorry. You can't do an interview in that shirt.
R Don't worry, there's a clothes shop over there. I can buy a new one.
J OK. I can help you choose one. Oh, that's my phone. Sorry, I need to answer this. See you in there.
R OK.

b Focus on sentences 1–7 and give Sts time to read them and think about what the missing words might be.

Then play the video / audio again, pausing if necessary for Sts to complete the gaps.

Get them to compare with a partner. Play the video / audio again if necessary.

Check answers.

1 double espresso **2** Daniel **3** 20 **4** half **5** shirt **6** shop
7 phone

EXTRA SUPPORT If there's time and you are using the video, you could get Sts to watch again with subtitles / showing the script, so they can see exactly what they understood / didn't understand. Translate / Explain any new words or phrases.

c 🔊 **5.24** Focus on the **Apologizing** box and go through it with the class. Elicit that *I'm so sorry / I'm really sorry* are stronger than *I'm sorry*. Point out that the three responses are interchangeable.

Play the video / audio once for Sts to watch or listen to the phrases.

🔊 **5.24**
See script in Student's Book on *p.44*

Now play it again, pausing after each apology and response for Sts to repeat.

d Put Sts in pairs. Get them to cover the box (or close their books). Tell them to pretend to knock each other's book or pen off the table, and then apologize.

3 ▶ BUYING CLOTHES

a 🔊 **5.25** Focus on the photo and ask Sts some questions, e.g. *Where is Rob? Who is he talking to?*, etc.

Now focus on the **Saying prices** and **Sizes** box and go through it with Sts.

Either tell Sts to close their books and write the three questions on the board, or get Sts to focus on the questions.

Play the video / audio once the whole way through and then check answers.

1 Medium **2** Yes, he does. **3** £44.99	

🔊 **5.25** 🔊 **5.26**
S = shop assistant, R = Rob
S Can I help you?
R Yes, what size is this shirt? (*repeat*)
S Let's see. It's a small. What size do you need?
R A medium. (*repeat*)
S This is a medium.
R Thanks. (*repeat*) Where can I try it on? (*repeat*)
S The changing rooms are over there.
R Thank you. (*repeat*)
S How is it?
R It's fine. (*repeat*) How much is it? (*repeat*)
S It's forty-four pounds ninety-nine.

b Focus on the conversation in the chart. Elicit who says the **You hear** phrases (the shop assistant) and who says the **You say** phrases (the customer, here Rob). These phrases will be useful for Sts if they want to buy clothes.

Give Sts a minute to read through the conversation and think what the missing words might be. Then play the video / audio again, and get Sts to complete the gaps. Play again if necessary.

Get Sts to compare with a partner, and then check answers.

1 help **2** size **3** medium **4** rooms **5** How	

Go through the conversation line by line with Sts, helping them with any words or expressions they don't understand. You may want to highlight the meaning of the phrasal verb *try on*.

c 🔊 **5.26** Now focus on the **You say** phrases and tell Sts they're going to hear the conversation again. They should repeat the **You say** phrases when they hear the beep. Encourage them to copy the rhythm and intonation.

Play the video / audio, pausing if necessary for Sts to repeat the phrases.

🔊 **5.26**
Same as script 5.25 with repeat pauses

d Focus on the information box and make sure Sts understand it. The meaning of *this / these* (for things within reach) and *that / those* (for things out of our reach, or far away) is easier to demonstrate than it is to explain. They can be determiners (*this book*) or pronouns (*What's this?*).

Now put Sts in pairs, **A** and **B**. **A** is the shop assistant. Get Sts to read the conversation aloud, and then swap roles.

e Focus on the photos of clothes at the bottom of the page. Elicit what they are and how much they are.

Tell Sts they are now going to do a role-play. **A** is the shop assistant and **B** the customer. **A** keeps his / her book open and **B** should quickly choose what he / she wants to buy (i.e. a T-shirt, a jacket, or jeans) before closing his / her book.

Ask some individual **B**s *What do you want to buy?* and elicit their first sentences, e.g. *What size is this T-shirt / jacket?* or *What size are these jeans?*.

Sts now role-play the conversation. Monitor and help.

Then get Sts to swap roles.

You could get a few pairs to perform in front of the class.

4 ▶ JENNY'S ON THE PHONE

a 🔊 **5.27** Focus on the photo and ask Sts *What do you think of Rob's shirt?*.

Focus on sentences 1–6 and give Sts time to read them. Then play the video / audio once the whole way through for Sts to mark the sentences *T* (true) or *F* (false). Play again if necessary.

Get Sts to compare with a partner, and then check answers. Make it clear that they don't need to correct the false sentences yet.

1 T **2** F **3** T **4** T **5** F **6** F	

◀)) 5.27

E = Eddie, J = Jenny, R = Rob

E So, Jenny, what do you think of London?
J I love it, Eddie! It's so cool!
E What about the people in the office?
J They're really nice. And they're very polite!
E What are you doing right now? You aren't in the office. I can hear traffic.
J Right now? I am standing outside a men's clothing store.
E You're what?
J I'm waiting for Rob…
E Who's Rob? Do you have a new boyfriend already?
J Don't be silly. He's just a guy from the office. He's buying a new shirt.
E Wait a minute. So you're waiting for a guy named Rob outside a men's clothing store…?
J Stop it. I don't have time to explain it all now. Oh, here he is now. I have to go.
E OK. Have fun!
J Bye Eddie. Love you.
R So, what do you think?
J You cannot be serious!
R What's wrong? You don't like my new shirt?
J No way! You can't wear that to an interview! Come on, let's go back into the store and change it.
R OK.

b Play the video / audio again, so Sts can watch or listen and correct the false sentences.

Get Sts to compare with a partner, and then check answers.

> 2 F (She says 'I love it!')
> 5 F (He says 'Do you have a new boyfriend already?')
> 6 F (She says 'You can't wear that…')

EXTRA SUPPORT If there's time and you are using the video, you could get Sts to watch again with subtitles / showing the script, so they can see exactly what they understood / didn't understand. Translate / Explain any new words or phrases.

c Focus on the **Social English** phrases and go through them with the class.

Then focus on the **British and American English** box about *shop* and *store*.

In pairs, get Sts to decide who says the phrases.

d ◀)) 5.28 Play the video / audio for Sts to watch or listen to the seven phrases and check their answers to **c**.

Check answers. If you know your Sts' L1, you could get them to translate the phrases.

> 1 J   2 J   3 E   4 J   5 E   6 R   7 J

◀)) 5.28

See Social English phrases in Student's Book on *p.45*

Now play the video / audio again, pausing after each phrase, for Sts to watch or listen and repeat.

e Focus on the instructions and make sure Sts understand what they have to do.

Get Sts to compare with a partner, and then check answers.

> **A** 6   **B** 2   **C** 1   **D** 5   **E** 3   **F** 7   **G** 4

Now put Sts in pairs and get them to practise the conversations.

Finally, focus on the **CAN YOU…?** questions and ask Sts if they feel confident they can now do these things. If they feel that they need more practice, tell them to go to *Online Practice* to watch the episode again and practise the language.

G object pronouns: *me, you, him*, etc.
V words in a story
P /aɪ/, /ɪ/, and /iː/

Lesson plan

The aim of this lesson, apart from its grammar and lexical objectives, is to encourage Sts to begin reading, as this is a great way to consolidate and expand their knowledge of English. Sts are advised to read 'Graded Readers' (easy to read books which have been simplified according to level). Sts first look at people's different reading habits and in Communication they talk about their own general reading habits. Then object pronouns (*me, you, him*, etc.) are presented through Part 1 of a traditional North African story. In the second part of the lesson Sts read and listen to Part 2 of the story, and then listen to the last part, getting more practice with pronouns and possessive adjectives. This is followed by Vocabulary, where the focus is on learning words through reading. Sts then look at three sounds (/aɪ/, /ɪ/, and /iː/) in Pronunciation, which will enable them to do the speaking better. Finally, Sts retell the story, each in the role of one of the two main characters.

More materials
For teachers
Photocopiables
Grammar object pronouns: *me, you, him*, etc. *p.183*
Communicative The pronoun game *p.229*
(instructions *p.208*)
For students
Workbook 6A
Online Practice 6A

OPTIONAL LEAD-IN (BOOKS CLOSED)
Write THINGS PEOPLE READ on the board and elicit words from the class, e.g. *books, magazines, Kindles, iPads, websites*, etc. Get Sts to spell the words and drill the pronunciation.

1 SPEAKING

a Books open. Focus on the questions and make sure Sts understand *on screen* (= on a computer, laptop, tablet, etc.).

First, answer the questions yourself, and then elicit answers from the class. You could get a show of hands to see if the majority prefer reading on paper or on screen.

b Tell Sts to go to **Communication** Reading in English on *p.105*.

Focus on the questions and make sure all the vocabulary is clear to Sts, e.g. *subtitles* (= words at the bottom of a film or TV programme that tell you what people are saying), etc.

Set a time limit for Sts to interview each other.

Get some feedback from various pairs.

Finally, focus on the **Reading in English** box and go through it with the class. Point out that many graded readers come with audio and some are available as e-books, so that they can listen and read at the same time to help them with understanding and pronunciation.

Tell Sts to go back to the main lesson **6A**.

EXTRA IDEA If you have a school library, get Sts to take a book out and start reading. Put up a chart in your classroom, so that Sts can write down the name of the book they're reading, and you can keep track of how many they read. If your school doesn't have a library, you could create a class library by getting each student to buy one Graded Reader (either a Starter (A1) or Stage 1 (A2/B1)) – they are relatively inexpensive. They then swap books with each other.

2 READING

a 🔊 **6.1** Sts are going to read and listen to a traditional story called *The Glass Bottle*.

Focus on questions 1–5 and highlight the pronunciation of the names (*Hassan* /hæsæn/ and *Walid* /wæliːd/) and the meaning of *valuable* (= worth a lot of money).

Now focus on **Part 1** and play the audio once the whole way through for Sts to read and listen to the story.

Then put Sts in pairs and give them some time to answer the questions.

Check answers.

EXTRA SUPPORT Before Sts read the story the first time, check whether you need to pre-teach any vocabulary, but <u>not</u> the words in **b**.

1 Hassan and Walid are brothers. They live in a small house in the desert.
2 They're very poor, and they don't have anything. Every day is the same.
3 Hassan works, but Walid doesn't.
4 She has a ring. She doesn't want to sell it because it was her husband's ring.
5 Because he wants to help his mother.

🔊 **6.1**
See Part 1 of *The Glass Bottle* in Student's Book on *p.46*

b Now focus on the words in the list and get Sts to match them to the pictures.

Check answers and model and drill pronunciation.

1 a desert   2 mountains   3 a field   4 the sky

Deal with any other new vocabulary. Model and drill the pronunciation of any tricky words.

c Give Sts time to read **Part 1** again.

Now get Sts to cover the text and either elicit from the class who and what they can see in the picture on this page, or get them to describe it in pairs and get feedback. Then tell Sts that they will find out the rest of the story later.

3 GRAMMAR object pronouns

a Focus on the highlighted words in **Part 1** and the example. Explain that the highlighted words are object pronouns, and we use them (like subject pronouns *he, she,* etc.) because we don't want to repeat a name or a noun.

Then give Sts a few minutes in pairs to write the relevant name or noun.

Check answers.

> it = the ring
> him = Hassan and Walid's father
> her = Hassan and Walid's mother

b Tell Sts to go to **Grammar Bank 6A** on *p.134*.

Grammar notes

Sts will be familiar with some examples of object pronouns in phrases like *I love you* or *Excuse me*.

The main problems they may have will be with word order and mixing up subject and object pronouns, e.g. *I spoke to she*.

You could point out that the object pronoun *me* is used instead of the subject pronoun *I* to answer the question *Who?*, e.g. **A** *Who wants a cup of coffee?* **B** *Me!* (NOT *I*).

6.2 Focus on the example sentences and play the audio for Sts to listen and repeat. Then go through the rules with the class.

Focus on the **Object pronouns after prepositions** box and go through it with the class.

Now focus on the exercises for **6A** on *p.135*. Sts do the exercises individually or in pairs.

Check answers, getting Sts to read the full sentences.

> **a 1** it **2** him **3** them **4** us **5** her **6** them
> **b 1** She, it, her, us **2** They, me, them, I **3** him, her, she, him
> **4** He, them, them, they, me **5** he, them, it

Tell Sts to go back to the main lesson **6A**.

 If you think Sts need more practice, you may want to give them the **Grammar** photocopiable activity at this point.

c **6.3** Focus on the example and tell Sts they are going to hear ten sentences and each time they must repeat the sentence changing the object (name, person, or thing) to a pronoun.

Play the audio, pausing after each sentence, and elicit a response from the whole class.

6.3

1 I like Anna. (*pause*) I like her.
2 I know your husband. (*pause*) I know him.
3 Can you help Jane and me? (*pause*) Can you help us?
4 I want to speak to David and Sally. (*pause*) I want to speak to them.
5 I love this song. (*pause*) I love it.
6 I live near Catherine and Richard. (*pause*) I live near them.
7 Wait for my brother and me! (*pause*) Wait for us!
8 I don't like these shoes. (*pause*) I don't like them.
9 Do you work with Suzanna? (*pause*) Do you work with her?
10 I see Jack every day. (*pause*) I see him every day.

Now repeat the activity, eliciting responses from individual Sts.

 When you play the audio the first time, stop it after each pause. Elicit the object, e.g. in 1 *Anna*, then elicit the object pronoun, e.g. *her*, and finally elicit the whole sentence, e.g. *I like her*. Repeat with the other sentences. Then play the audio again for Sts to produce the sentences with object pronouns more quickly.

4 READING & LISTENING retelling a story

a **6.4** Before Sts read and listen to **Part 2**, elicit the main details of **Part 1** by asking them questions, e.g. *What are the brothers' names? Where do they live? Are they rich?*, etc.

Now ask Sts what they think happens next and elicit ideas.

Give Sts time to read questions 1–8, making sure they understand *palace* (Sts saw Buckingham Palace in **5C**) and *plan* (= something you have decided to do and how you are going to do it).

Now focus on **Part 2** and play the audio once the whole way through for Sts to read and listen to the story.

Then put Sts in pairs and give them some time to answer the questions.

Check answers.

 Read through the scripts and decide if you need to pre-teach any new lexis before Sts listen.

> **1** He walks through the mountains.
> **2** The prince welcomes him and gives him food, drink, and a bed.
> **3** The windows have no glass.
> **4** His empty water bottle.
> **5** Because he doesn't know what glass is.
> **6** A box (with 100 gold coins).
> **7** Because now they can buy food and clothes.
> **8** Walid wants to give the prince his mother's ring, and get 1,000 gold coins.

6.4

See Part 2 of *The Glass Bottle* in Student's Book on *p.47*

Deal with any other new vocabulary. Model and drill the pronunciation of any tricky words.

 Go through the story line by line with Sts, eliciting guesses for the meaning of any vocabulary that they don't know.

b Before Sts read **Part 2** again, go through the **Pronouns and possessive adjectives** box with the class.

Now tell Sts to re-read Part 2 and, in pairs, decide what or who the highlighted pronouns and possessive adjectives refer to. Point out that the first one has been done for them.

Check answers.

> **2** Hassan **3** Hassan's **4** the glass bottle **5** the prince
> **6** the prince **7** the box **8** Hassan and Walid's **9** Hassan
> **10** Hassan, Walid, and their mother **11** Walid **12** his / their mother's

c **6.5** Do this as a whole-class activity and elicit ideas.

Play the audio for Sts to listen to **Part 3** to find out what happens.

Check the answer.

> Walid goes to the palace. He gives the prince the silver ring. The prince gives him a box, but when he gets home and opens it, inside is the glass bottle.

◀) 6.5
(script in Student's Book on *p.120*)
Part 3
Walid walks for five days through the mountains. The sun shines, and at night it's very cold. Then, one evening, he finds the palace. The prince welcomes him and gives him food and drink, and a comfortable bed. But Walid can't sleep. He's thinking about the one thousand gold coins.

The next morning he says to the prince, 'I want to say thank you to you. Please have this silver ring. It's my mother's.'

The prince is very happy. 'This is a beautiful ring,' he says. 'Thank you. Let me give you something in return.'

He gives Walid a box. 'Don't open this until you get home,' he says. 'Be careful with it. It's very, very valuable.'

Walid runs through the mountains, and after three days he arrives home.

'Where's my silver ring?' shouts his mother.

'Don't worry about your ring!' says Walid. 'Look at this!'

Hassan and their mother watch as he opens the box. Inside he finds…the glass bottle.

 You could ask Sts what they think the moral of the story is, and elicit some ideas.

Possible morals
Don't ask for more than you need.
Different things are important to different people.
Be happy when you have enough.

 If there's time, you could get Sts to listen again with the scripts in the main lesson and on *p.120*, so they can see exactly what they understood / didn't understand. Translate / Explain any new words or phrases.

5 VOCABULARY words in a story

a Focus on the task and make sure Sts understand the four column headings. Point out the two examples.

Give Sts time to put the words in the correct columns.

b ◀) **6.6** Play the audio for Sts to listen and check.

Check answers.

◀) 6.6
adjectives comfortable, strange, surprised, valuable
verbs arrive, decide, leave, sell
nouns desert, mountain, palace, village
prepositions inside, into, through, towards

Either use the audio to drill the pronunciation of the words, or model and drill them yourself. Give further practice of any words your Sts find difficult to pronounce.

6 PRONUNCIATION /aɪ/, /ɪ/, and /iː/

Pronunciation notes

This pronunciation exercise focuses on a small but significant difference between two similar but very common sounds /ɪ/, /iː/ as well as /aɪ/, all of which occur in subject and object pronouns. Depending on their L1, Sts may find the difference between /ɪ/ and /iː/ very difficult to hear and to produce. It is important to encourage elementary Sts when they do these kinds of pronunciation exercises. Reassure them that this difference is small and that with time and practice they will be able to differentiate and make these sounds.

a ◀) **6.7** Focus on the sound pictures and the words (*bike*, *fish*, and *tree*). Tell Sts that these sounds can seem quite similar, but one difference is that *fish* is a short sound and *tree* is a long sound, and *bike* is a diphthong (= has two vowel sounds). Remind / Elicit from Sts that the symbols which have two dots are always long sounds.

Tell Sts to match each group of words to one of the sound pictures. Remind them that it is easier if they say the words aloud.

Play the audio for Sts to listen and check. Encourage Sts to see the sound–spelling relationship, i.e. that the *fish* sound here is always the letter *i*, usually between consonants; the *tree* sound here is always *e*, *ee*, or *ea*.

Check answers.

1 fish /ɪ/ **2** tree /iː/ **3** bike /aɪ/

◀) 6.7
fish /ɪ/ him, it, his, ring, sit, kiss
tree /iː/ he, she, me, meet, read, leave
bike /aɪ/ my, I, buy, sky, nice, high

 If these sounds are difficult for your Sts, it will help to show them the mouth position. You could model this yourself or use the Sound Bank videos on the *Teacher's Resource Centre*.

b ◀) **6.8** This exercise gives Sts practice in distinguishing between the sounds.

Play the audio for Sts just to listen.

◀) 6.8
See list of words in Student's Book on *p.47*

c ◀) **6.9** Focus on the instructions. Play the audio at least twice.

Get Sts to compare with a partner, and then check answers by playing the audio again, stopping after each pair of words.

1 b **2** b **3** a **4** a **5** b **6** a

◀) 6.9
1 his **2** my **3** it **4** leave **5** keys **6** we

d Put Sts in pairs to practise saying sentences 1–5.

 Read each sentence and get Sts to listen and repeat. Then put Sts in pairs and get them to practise saying the sentences.

7 SPEAKING

Focus on the task and make sure Sts understand what they have to do.

Tell Sts to close their books and put them in pairs, **A** and **B**. Sts **B** role is harder, as Sts have only listened to this part of the story, rather than reading it. For this reason it's a good idea for stronger Sts to take the **B** role.

Give Sts time to prepare their stories.

Sts **A** start. Monitor and help.

When Sts **A** have finished, Sts **B** should start telling their story.

G *like* + (verb + *-ing*)
V the date, ordinal numbers
P /ð/ and /θ/, saying the date

Lesson plan

The main vocabulary focus in this lesson is how to say the date, and the lesson starts with Sts revising the months, and then learning ordinal numbers. This is followed by a Listening on identifying ordinal numbers. Sts then read an online forum where readers answer questions about their favourite month, day of the week, and time of the day. Sts then focus on the grammar, *like*, *love*, etc. + the *-ing* form, and talk about what free-time activities they like and dislike. The lesson ends with Sts interviewing each other about their favourite or least favourite month / day / week, and then writing about their own favourite times.

More materials
For teachers
Photocopiables
Grammar *like* + (verb + *-ing*) p.184
Vocabulary Dates p.269 (instructions p.255)
Communicative Likes and dislikes p.230
(instructions p.208)
For students
Workbook 6B
Online Practice 6B

OPTIONAL LEAD-IN (BOOKS CLOSED)

Write the question WHAT'S THE DATE TODAY? on the board. Elicit / Teach the answer and write it on the board like this, e.g. *6th April 2019*. Elicit / Teach that *th* indicates an ordinal number (here *sixth*). Sts will practise this in more detail in Vocabulary. You may want to explain that the date can also be written *6 April 2019* (without *th*).

Draw a face and a speech bubble on the board and write in the bubble: ***The*** *sixth* **of** *April twenty nineteen*. Explain that this is the way the date is said in English.
Highlight the use of *the* /ðə/ and *of* /əv/, and model and drill pronunciation.

1 VOCABULARY & PRONUNCIATION

the date, /ð/ and /θ/

a Books open. Focus on the task and do it as a whole-class activity. If you have more than 12 Sts, go back to *January* with the 13th and start again. Give further practice of any months your Sts find difficult to pronounce.

EXTRA SUPPORT Write the first letter of each month on the board and elicit them from the whole class.

b Tell Sts to go to **Vocabulary Bank The weather and dates** on *p.159* and get them to do **Part 2**.

Vocabulary notes
Although the date can be said in two ways, e.g. *the sixth of April* or *April the sixth*, we have focused on the former, which is more common, as it is easier for Sts just to learn one form.

Focus on **2 Ordinal numbers and the date** and look at **a** which introduces ordinal numbers. Focus on the first four, and show Sts how the last two letters of the word (*st*, *nd*, *rd*, and *th*) are written after the numeral to make it an ordinal number.

Get Sts to complete the missing numbers and words, and then compare with a partner.

◉ 6.10 Now do **b**. Play the audio for Sts to listen and check.

Check answers.

sixth
seventh
8th
9th
tenth
eleventh
12th
thirteenth
fourteenth
20th
twenty-first
22nd
twenty-third
24th
thirtieth
31st

◉ 6.10
1 Ordinal numbers and the date
first, second, third, fourth, fifth, sixth, seventh, eighth, ninth, tenth, eleventh, twelfth, thirteenth, fourteenth, twentieth, twenty-first, twenty-second, twenty-third, twenty-fourth, thirtieth, thirty-first

Now either use the audio to drill the pronunciation of the numbers, or model and drill them yourself. Give further practice of any numbers your Sts find difficult to pronounce. When Sts go back to the main lesson, there will be further practice of the more tricky ordinal numbers.

In **c** Sts focus on the way dates are written and spoken. Focus on the **Writing and saying the date** box and go through the **We write** and **We say** section. Highlight that the words *the* and *of* are said, but not written.

Then go through the **Prepositions with months and dates** section and stress that we use *in* followed by a month and *on* followed by a day of the week or a date.

Finally, go through the **Saying years** section.

Now focus on **Activation** and get Sts to tell you what the date is today and tomorrow.

Tell Sts to go back to the main lesson **6B**.

EXTRA SUPPORT If you think Sts need more practice, you may want to give them the **Vocabulary** photocopiable activity at this point.

c 🔊 **6.11** Focus on the two sound pictures, *mother* /ð/ and *thumb* /θ/.

Play the audio for Sts just to listen to the two sounds and example words.

🔊 **6.11**
See sounds and words in Student's Book on *p.48*

Encourage Sts to try to approximate the *th* sound as far as possible and to hear the difference between the voiced sound /ð/ and the unvoiced sound /θ/ although they may find this quite difficult. Now play the audio again for Sts to listen and repeat.

EXTRA SUPPORT If these sounds are difficult for your Sts, it will help to show them the mouth position. You could model this yourself or use the Sound Bank videos on the *Teacher's Resource Centre*.

d 🔊 **6.12** Before playing the audio, focus on the **Ordinal numbers** box and go through it with the class.

Now play the audio, pausing after each ordinal number for Sts to listen and repeat.

🔊 **6.12**
See ordinal numbers in Student's Book on *p.48*

Then give Sts a few minutes to practise saying the ordinal numbers on their own.

e 🔊 **6.13** Give Sts a few minutes in pairs to try saying the dates.

Play the audio for Sts to listen and check.

🔊 **6.13**
the first of March   the second of November   the third of May
the fourth of June   the fifth of January   the sixth of July
the twelfth of September   the seventeenth of October
the twentieth of August   the twenty-third of February
the twenty-eighth of April   the thirty-first of December

EXTRA CHALLENGE First, elicit the answers from the class and then play the audio for Sts to listen and check.

f Now play the audio again for Sts to listen and repeat each date. Make sure they copy the rhythm and stress the ordinal number and month.

EXTRA IDEA Get Sts to mingle and ask *When's your birthday?*. They did this in **4C** with months, but not saying the actual date. Get feedback by asking if anyone found someone with exactly or nearly the same birthday.

g Elicit / Teach the meaning of *a public holiday* (= a day which is holiday for everybody, e.g. 25th December). Do these questions as a whole-class activity if Sts are from the same place. If they are from different countries, do it in pairs and get feedback.

2 LISTENING making connections

a 🔊 **6.14** Tell Sts that they are going to listen to five conversations and they need to circle the ordinal number they hear.

EXTRA SUPPORT Elicit all the ordinal numbers in the chart before Sts listen.

Play the audio, pausing after each conversation to give Sts time to circle their answer.

Check answers.

EXTRA SUPPORT Read through the script and decide if you need to pre-teach any new lexis before Sts listen.

1 21st **2** 30th **3** 5th **4** 53rd **5** 6th

🔊 **6.14**
(script in Student's Book on *p.120*)
1 A Hi, Kim. Listen, do you want come to the theatre in London this Saturday?
   B Saturday? I can't – it's my brother's twenty-first birthday! We're having a big party at my parents' house.
   A Oh, that sounds great! Have a wonderful time – and say 'Happy Birthday' from me!
2 A Are you in the office next week?
   B No, I'm on holiday.
   A Where are you going?
   B Australia!
   A Lucky you! When do you get back?
   B On the thirtieth.
   A Wow! That's a long holiday.
   B Yeah, three weeks! I can't wait.
3 A You drink a lot of coffee!
   B Yes, this is my fifth this morning.
   A It's not good for you, you know.
   B I know, but I can't wake up without it.
4 A Where's the restaurant?
   B It's not far. It's on the corner of Park Avenue and fifty-third.
   A Great. See you there at 7.30.
5 A Good morning. I'm here to see Lynn Mody. My name's Graham Davies.
   B Just a moment, sir, I'll give her a ring…Is that Lynn? There's a Mr Davies here to see you…That's fine, sir. Could you sign in here? Great. You can go straight up. She's on the sixth floor. The lifts are just over there.
   A Many thanks.

b Now tell Sts they are going to listen to each conversation again and this time they need to match the ordinal number they hear to one of the things in the list.

Play the audio again, pausing after each conversation.

Get Sts to compare with a partner, and then check answers.

1 21st: a birthday   **2** 30th: a date   **3** 5th: a drink   **4** 53rd: a street   **5** 6th: a floor

 If there's time, you could get Sts to listen again with the script on *p.120*, so they can see exactly what they understood / didn't understand. Translate / Explain any new words or phrases.

3 READING

a Focus on the first part of the text – the introduction on the forum. Elicit / Teach the meaning of *the happiest* and *the most depressing*. If you are teaching in the southern hemisphere, highlight that the psychologist is talking about the UK, where the months referred to (January and June) fall in different seasons.

Set a time limit for Sts to read the introduction and answer the two questions.

Get Sts to compare with a partner, and then check answers. (Sts will focus on superlatives in **10A**; this is just a preview). Then get Sts to tell you the reasons for this.

 Before Sts read the article, check whether you need to pre-teach any vocabulary, but not the adjectives in **c**.

The third Friday in June is the happiest day of the year. This is because it's summer, it's warm, the evenings are light, and it's the day before a weekend.
The third Monday in January is the most depressing day of the year. The reasons are because it's winter, the weather is grey and cold, the days are dark, and Monday is the first day of the working week.

Ask Sts if they think these dates / times might also be the most depressing / happiest in their country, and if not, which are (they will almost certainly not be the same dates for people who live in the southern hemisphere).

b Now focus on the comments. Elicit / Explain that the happy face emojis go with comments about people's favourite months, days, and times, and the sad face ones with people's least favourite.

Focus on the months, days, and times in the list, and give Sts time to complete the comments with them.

Get Sts to compare with a partner, and then check answers.

1 June   **2** December   **3** October   **4** February   **5** Monday
6 Saturday   **7** Sunday   **8** Friday   **9** 9.00 a.m.   **10** 7.45 p.m.
11 6.30 a.m.   **12** 5.30 p.m.

 Before Sts start, elicit from the class the answer to gap 1.

c Tell Sts to look at the highlighted adjectives, and in pairs use the context to work out if they are positive or negative.

Positive light, fun, festive, favourite
Negative sad, cold, least favourite, tired, dirty

Check Sts understand *depressing* (= makes you feel very unhappy) and *festive* (= typical of a special event or celebration).

Deal with any other new vocabulary. Model and drill the pronunciation of any tricky words.

4 GRAMMAR *like* + (verb + *-ing*)

a Focus on the faces and the five verb phrases. Give Sts a minute to complete the chart in pairs.

Check answers by quickly drawing each emoticon on the board and eliciting the phrases. Explain that *don't mind* is a 'neutral' answer, e.g. *I don't mind cooking* = I don't especially like cooking, but it isn't a problem for me.

😃	I love
🙂	I like
😐	I don't mind
🙁	I don't like
😠	I hate

b Tell Sts to complete sentences 1–5 from the forum comments.

Check answers.

1 celebrating   **2** sitting   **3** working   **4** thinking   **5** getting

Now read the question together and elicit the answer.

The form of a verb after *love*, *like*, etc. is the *-ing* form, the same form that is used after *be* in the present continuous.

c Tell Sts to go to **Grammar Bank 6B** on *p.134*.

🔊 **6.15** Focus on the example sentences and play the audio for Sts to listen and repeat. Then go through the rules with the class.

Now focus on the exercises for **6B** on *p.135*. Sts do **a** individually or in pairs.

Check answers. When you check the *-ing* forms also check that Sts remember the meaning of the verbs.

a

verb + *-ing*	verb ending in *e*	double consonant
cooking	dancing	getting
eating	having	running
sleeping	writing	stopping
studying		swimming

Sts now do **b**. Remind them that they have to add *-ing* to the verbs, e.g. *working*, to make the sentences.

Check answers, getting Sts to read the full sentences.

b
1 He loves going to the cinema.
2 He likes taking the dog for a walk.
3 He likes listening to music.
4 He doesn't mind doing housework.
5 He doesn't mind working in an office.
6 He doesn't like watching football on TV.
7 He doesn't like reading novels.
8 He hates having lunch with his parents.
9 He hates wearing a tie.

Tell Sts to go back to the main lesson **6B**.

EXTRA SUPPORT If you think Sts need more practice, you may want to give them the **Grammar** photocopiable activity at this point.

d Focus on the task and make sure Sts understand all the verb phrases.

Put Sts in pairs and get them to tell each other what they *love*, *like*, etc.

EXTRA SUPPORT Draw the smiley faces from **4a** on the board and elicit the verbs, *love*, *like*, etc. Give Sts time to write a few sentences before putting them in pairs to tell their partner about themselves.

Find out if any pairs felt the same about some of the verb phrases.

5 SPEAKING & WRITING

a Focus on the questions and point out the example.

Now give Sts time to think about their answers.

Put Sts in pairs and get them to interview each other. Monitor and help while Sts are interviewing each other. Make sure they swap roles.

Then get Sts to discuss in their pairs if they are similar or different.

Finally, get some feedback from various pairs.

b Using their answers in **a**, Sts now write their own positive comments (beginning 'My favourite…') and negative comments (beginning 'My least favourite…') for each of the three sections of the forum.

If you want Sts to add photos and drawings, you might like to set the task as homework.

G revision: *be* or *do*?
V music
P /j/, giving opinions

Lesson plan

This lesson, the last of the first half of the book, uses the topic of music to revise the uses of *be* and *do*. First, Sts focus on the vocabulary of musical instruments and musicians. Sts then interview each other with a music questionnaire to find out about their partner's musical tastes and habits. After revising the grammar, there is a pronunciation focus on the /j/ sound, including the 'hidden' /j/, e.g. in *music*, and Sts also look at the stress on words when giving opinions. Sts then listen to a programme about busking in London. The lesson finishes with a visit to the Writing section to learn how to write an informal email.

More materials
For teachers
Photocopiables
Grammar *be* or *do*? p.185
Communicative Tell me about you p.231
(instructions p.208)
Teacher's Resource Centre
Video A London busker
For students
Workbook 6C
Online Practice 6C

OPTIONAL LEAD-IN (BOOKS CLOSED)

Write on the board the names of some musicians who are popular in your Sts' country. Then elicit the musical instrument they play and write it next to each name.

1 VOCABULARY music

a Books open. Focus on the list of musical instruments. Tell Sts to first match the word to the photo and then write the word next to the correct number in the **instruments** column. Point out that the first one (*accordion*) has been done for them.

! Don't ask Sts if they play a musical instrument yet as they will be doing this later in the lesson.

b 🔊 **6.16** Play the audio for Sts to listen and check.

Check answers. Give further practice of words your Sts find difficult to pronounce.

🔊 **6.16**
1 accordion   2 bass   3 violin   4 guitar   5 piano
6 drums   7 keyboard   8 trumpet   9 saxophone

EXTRA SUPPORT Write the words on the board for the next activity.

c 🔊 **6.17** Play the audio for Sts to listen and complete the **musicians** column.

EXTRA CHALLENGE Get Sts to guess the words for musicians before they listen. Then play the audio for them to listen and check.

Check answers, eliciting the words onto the board. Elicit from Sts how the words for musicians are formed (we usually add *-ist* to a musical instrument to make the musician, e.g. *violin > violinist*; we sometimes add *-er*, e.g. *drum > drummer*; with a few instruments we say *instrument + player*, e.g. *keyboard > keyboard player*).

🔊 **6.17**
1 accordion – ac<u>cord</u>ionist
2 bass – bass <u>play</u>er
3 violin – vio<u>lin</u>ist
4 guitar – gui<u>tar</u>ist
5 piano – <u>pi</u>anist
6 drums – <u>drum</u>mer
7 keyboard – <u>key</u>board player
8 trumpet – <u>trum</u>peter
9 saxophone – sa<u>xoph</u>onist

EXTRA SUPPORT Leave the words on the board for the next activity.

d Play the audio again and tell Sts to underline the stressed syllables in the words for musicians.

Check answers, by underlining the stress in the words on the board. Give further practice of words your Sts find difficult to pronounce.

See underlining in script 6.17

Now get Sts to compare the words in both columns and ask them when the stress is different.

piano / *pianist* and <u>saxophone</u> / <u>saxophonist</u> have different stress.

e 🔊 **6.18** Tell Sts they are going to hear nine short pieces of instrumental music and they must say the name of the instrument being played and the musician. Get them to cover the chart or close their books.

Play the audio, pausing after each extract to elicit the words.

1 piano – pianist   **2** saxophone – saxophonist   **3** accordion – accordionist   **4** drums – drummer   **5** keyboard – keyboard player   **6** bass – bass player   **7** violin – violinist   **8** trumpet – trumpeter   **9** guitar – guitarist

f Do this as a whole-class activity. You could demonstrate the activity by telling the class if you play an instrument and how well you play it.

2 GRAMMAR revision: *be* or *do*?

a Get Sts to read the five sentences and circle the correct options.

Get Sts to compare with a partner, and then check answers.

1 do you   2 I don't   3 isn't   4 Do you   5 is

b Tell Sts to go to **Grammar Bank 6C** on *p.134*.

Grammar notes

In this first half of the book Sts have learned to use the verb *be*, the present simple, and the present continuous. For many Sts the use of *do* and *does* in questions and negatives in the present simple takes some getting used to, and as a result there is sometimes a tendency to overuse them. Sts sometimes forget that *be*, both as a main verb and as an auxiliary, does not form questions and negatives in the same way, but simply by inverting the subject and verb or adding *not*.

Focus on the example sentences and play both audio 🔊 **6.19** and 🔊 **6.20** for Sts to listen and repeat. Then go through the rules with the class.

Now focus on the exercises for **6C** on *p.135*. Sts do the exercises individually or in pairs.

Check answers, getting Sts to read the full sentences.

a

Are you…?	Do you…?
hungry	have a car
listening to me	know those people
stressed	like classical music
tired	live in the city centre
waiting for a friend	speak Russian

b

1 's, 's   2 Do, don't   3 Does, doesn't   4 are, 'm   5 Does, 's
6 Are, 're   7 is, doesn't   8 Are, 'm

Tell Sts to go back to the main lesson **6C**.

EXTRA SUPPORT If you think Sts need more practice, you may want to give them the **Grammar** photocopiable activity at this point.

c 🔊 **6.21** Focus on the instructions and the examples in the speech bubbles. Explain to Sts that they are going to hear a sentence and they must turn it into a question.

Play the audio, pausing after each sentence, and elicit a response from the whole class.

🔊 **6.21**
1 She's British. (*pause*) Is she British?
2 He plays the piano. (*pause*) Does he play the piano?
3 You like music. (*pause*) Do you like music?
4 Anna's having a shower. (*pause*) Is Anna having a shower?
5 You're tired. (*pause*) Are you tired?
6 She lives near here. (*pause*) Does she live near here?
7 I'm late. (*pause*) Am I late?
8 The train arrives at six o'clock. (*pause*) Does the train arrive at six o'clock?

Now repeat the activity, eliciting responses from individual Sts.

3 SPEAKING

Focus on the *My music* questionnaire and go through it with Sts, making sure they know the different types of music in **1**. You might want to elicit / explain the difference between a *concert* (= a public performance of music) and a *gig* (= a public performance of music by musicians playing popular music or jazz). Model and drill their pronunciation, /ˈkɒnsət/ and /ɡɪɡ/. Make sure Sts understand and can pronounce *download* /daʊnˈləʊd/ and *lyrics* /ˈlɪrɪks/.

Monitor and help with vocabulary whilst Sts think about their answers.

Now put Sts in pairs and get them to interview each other. Encourage them to ask for and give more information where possible. You could demonstrate by asking individual Sts some of the questions.

Monitor and correct.

When time is up, focus on the question *Do you have similar musical tastes and habits?* and elicit some answers.

4 PRONUNCIATION /j/, giving opinions

Pronunciation notes

/j/

y at the beginning of a word is always pronounced /j/, e.g. *yes*.

Some words containing *u* or *ew* also have a 'hidden' /j/ sound, e.g. *music*, *student*, *new*, etc.

Sts must be careful with this phonetic symbol because it is not the same as the letter *j*.

Giving opinions

When we give our opinion, we give extra stress to the 'opinion' word, e.g. *He's **fantastic***.

a 🔊 **6.22** Play the audio for Sts just to listen to the two sounds and example words.

🔊 **6.22**
See sounds and words in Student's Book on *p.51*

Focus on the **Hidden /j/ sound** box and go through with the class.

Now play the audio again for Sts to listen and repeat.

EXTRA SUPPORT If these sounds are difficult for your Sts, it will help to show them the mouth position. You could model this yourself or use the Sound Bank videos on the *Teacher's Resource Centre*.

b 🔊 **6.23** Focus on the task. Point out that Sts will hear phrases and not sentences.

Play the audio, pausing after each phrase to give Sts time to write it down.

Check answers.

🔊 **6.23**
1 a beautiful tune
2 a young musician
3 music students
4 your yoga teacher
5 the New Year

In pairs, get Sts to practise saying the phrases.

c 🔊 **6.24** Focus on the sentences and remind Sts that the words in bigger font are stressed and the underlining shows the extra stress. Point out that the words in blue here are the 'opinion' words and that we give them extra stress.

Play the audio once for Sts just to listen to the sentences and rhythm.

🔊 **6.24**
See sentences in Student's Book on *p.51*

Now play the audio again, pausing after each sentence for Sts to listen and repeat.

In pairs, get Sts to practise saying the sentences.

d Focus on the instructions and give Sts time to write the names of two male musicians, two female, and two bands – one that they love and one that they hate.

Tell Sts they are going to ask their partner's opinion of the musicians and bands they have written down. Model and drill the question *What do you think of…?*

Demonstrate the activity by asking Sts their opinion of a male musician, a female musician, and a band that you either love or hate, and elicit responses. Remind Sts that they will need to use an object pronoun in their answer after the verb (e.g. *I like him*, *her*, or *them*.) or a subject pronoun after *I think* (e.g. *I think he's / she's / they're great.*).

Put Sts in pairs and get them to ask and answer the questions. Encourage them to add sentences like those in **c** to give their opinions and to ask for and give more information where possible. Monitor, checking Sts are using the right pronouns and adding extra stress correctly.

Find out from various pairs if they have the same taste in music.

5 ▶ VIDEO LISTENING understanding specific information

a Read the definition of *busker* together and model and drill pronunciation.

Now do the questions as a whole-class activity.

b Now tell Sts they are going to watch a documentary about busking in London, and about a professional busker called Charlotte Campbell.

Focus on the question and play the video for Sts to watch or listen.

Get Sts to compare with a partner, and then check the answer.

EXTRA SUPPORT Read through the script and decide if you need to pre-teach any new lexis before Sts watch. You may want to check that Sts know what *Waterloo* (= a major London train station) and *the London Eye* are (= a popular tourist attraction on the South Bank).

Yes, Charlotte likes her job.

A London busker

This is Charlotte Campbell. She's twenty-five and she's a busker. Charlotte plays the guitar and sings on the South Bank in London. Today, she's busking near the London Eye.
'On a typical day when I'm going busking, I get the train to Waterloo and I walk to the London Eye. I start at about eleven o'clock and I play until one. Then I take a lunch break. And sometimes I stay until six or seven p.m. but in the winter when it gets dark I go home a little earlier.'
You can find buskers everywhere – in the streets, in shopping centres, outside bars and restaurants and in the parks of most British cities. In London, you can also listen to music while you're on the London Underground. Buskers play or sing all kinds of different music – opera, jazz, pop and folk.
'I like music that's on the radio, Ed Sheeran and things like that, and some older music from the 60s, like the Beatles.'
But busking isn't always easy. London is a busy city and there are lots of buskers, which means you can't just play music wherever you like.
'You need to get a permit to busk in London, and pass an audition, but when you do, there's a really nice community and busking in London becomes easy.'
So buskers like Charlotte have to choose an area of London to sing and play in. They share this area with other buskers and sometimes they have to wait for the other buskers to finish.
Charlotte lives in Brixton, in South London. In her flat, she writes her own songs and practises.
'I love writing songs. I love writing my own music.'
For Charlotte, there are good and bad things about life as a busker.
'I like meeting new people and sharing my music with a new audience. I don't like it when it gets cold.'

EXTRA IDEA Ask Sts what musicians apart from Charlotte they saw busking.

Two saxophonists, a drummer, and an opera singer

c Focus on 1–6 and go through them with Sts.

Now play the video again for Sts to mark the sentences *T* (true) or *F* (false).

Get Sts to compare with a partner, and then check answers.

> **1** F (She takes a lunch break at 1.00, and she sometimes plays until 6.00 or 7.00 p.m.)
> **2** F (Buskers play all kinds of different music – opera, jazz, pop, and folk.)
> **3** T
> **4** T
> **5** F (She writes her own songs.)
> **6** T

Elicit why the *F* sentences are false.

 If there's time, you could get Sts to watch again with subtitles / showing the script, so they can see exactly what they understood / didn't understand. Translate / Explain any new words or phrases.

d Finally, focus on the questions and do them as a whole-class activity.

 When Charlotte sings her song *Streets of London* at the end of the video, you could get Sts to write down some of the lyrics as they listen:

Ba-baa, ba-baa, there's music on the streets of London
Ba-baa, ba-baa, there's music in my heart
Ba-baa, ba-baa, there's music on the streets of London
That's where we are, that's where we are.

Ah-hoo, yeah I get lonely
Ah-hoo, yeah I get cold
Ah-hoo, I get tired, oh so tired
But I'll never sell my soul.

Ah-hoo, from Piccadilly
Ah-hoo, to Leicester Square
Oh I gave my heart to London
And you'll always find me there.

6 WRITING an informal email

Here Sts consolidate the language they have learned so far through writing about themselves, and learn the conventions for writing an informal email. Sts will learn how to write a more formal email in **10B**.

Tell Sts to go to **Writing An informal email** on *p.115*.

a Focus on the title and elicit / explain the meaning of *informal* (= friendly). Elicit / Teach the opposite *formal* and explain that this is more serious, e.g. a business letter / email.

Focus on the information box at the bottom of the page and make sure Sts understand the meaning of *penfriend*.

Then focus on the beginning of the email. Elicit / Teach the meaning of the headings *From*, *To*, and *Subject*.

Give Sts time to read the email. Tell them <u>not</u> to worry about the spelling mistakes.

Elicit who Sts think Stefan is.

> Stefan is Carmen's penfriend. She is writing to him to practise her English.

b Tell Sts to cover the email or close their books and elicit the information Carmen gives about herself in each paragraph.

Check answers.

> **Personal information:** She's 19. She's from Madrid. She's a receptionist at a hotel. She's studying English for her job.
> **Family:** She lives with her parents and her brother and sister. Her father is an architect and her mother works in a clothes shop. Her brother and sister are at school.
> **Free time:** She doesn't have much free time. She usually goes shopping on her day off. In the evening she likes seeing friends or listening to music.

c Individually or in pairs, Sts correct the six spelling mistakes.

Check answers, by eliciting the words onto the board.

> **1** studying   **2** because   **3** architect   **4** usually   **5** shopping   **6** friends

d Focus on the instructions and go through the **Informal emails** box with the class. Tell Sts that you can also begin an email with *Dear*, but *Hi* is more informal. Contractions are common in informal language. Finally, focus on the end of the email. Elicit / Teach the meaning of *Please write soon* and *Best wishes*, and tell Sts they are useful expressions to put at the end of an email to a friend.

Sts now make notes for their own email.

e Using their notes from **d**, Sts now write their email. Either give Sts at least 15 minutes to write the email in class, or set it for homework.

❗ Tell Sts to set their email out in paragraphs like in the model email.

f If Sts do the writing in class, give them time to check their emails for mistakes. They could then swap them with a partner and read each other's emails, before you collect them in.

 If you know any good websites for Sts to find their own penfriends, now would be an ideal moment to tell Sts about them.

For instructions on how to use these pages see *p.39*.

More materials
For teachers
Teacher's Resource Centre
Video Can you understand these people? 5&6
Quick Test 6
File 6 Test
Progress Test Files 1–6
For students
Online Practice Check your progress

GRAMMAR

1 a **2** c **3** b **4** b **5** a **6** c **7** a **8** b **9** b **10** c
11 a **12** b **13** c **14** a **15** c

VOCABULARY

a
1 hear **2** play **3** forget **4** buy **5** tell **6** have **7** take
8 run **9** call **10** dance
b
1 at **2** on **3** for **4** to **5** for **6** in **7** on
c
1 fog (the others are weather adjectives)
2 cold (the others are verbs)
3 season (the others are seasons)
4 seven (the others are ordinal numbers)
5 twenty-second (the others are numbers)
6 ring (the others are parts of a country)
7 drummer (the others are musical instruments)
8 concert (the others are musicians)

PRONUNCIATION

c
1 c**oo**k /ʊ/ **2** sitti**ng** /ŋ/ **3** ten**th** /θ/ **4** **th**ere /ð/
5 v**i**olin /aɪ/
d
1 <u>neigh</u>bour **2** re<u>mem</u>ber **3** <u>fif</u>tieth **4** <u>sa</u>xophone
5 <u>pi</u>anist

CAN YOU understand this text?

b 1 a **2** c **3** b **4** c

▶ CAN YOU understand these people?

1 a **2** c **3** c **4** b **5** b

🔊 **6.25**

1 Duncan
I = interviewer, D = Duncan
I Can you play a musical instrument?
D I can. I can play the violin.
I How well do you play it?
D Not very.

2 Myles
I = interviewer, M = Myles
I Do you have noisy neighbours?
M Um, I'm lucky, um, I don't. But I think I'm the noisy neighbour, so...
I What do you do?
M I play the guitar.

3 Tiffany
I = interviewer, T= Tiffany
I What's your favourite month of the year? Why?
T My favourite month is December because it gets colder, and I like snow and cold weather. And I like Christmas time.

4 Stephen
I = interviewer, S = Stephen
I What kind of music do you like?
S A lot of kinds of music. Um, I typically listen to electronic dance, and um, indie rock. I listen to the new folk, they call it. But I like opera and a lot of jazz. The list could go on.
I What kind of music don't you like?
S I don't like country music.
I Do you have a favourite band or singer?
S Sure. Right now, my favourite band is Wye Oak from Brooklyn.

5 Dasha
I = interviewer, D = Dasha
I What kind of books do you like?
D Um, I read like all sorts of books, from history books to like, novels, and all sorts of books really.
I What are you reading at the moment?
D Er, at the moment I'm reading a history of modern France.

Selfies

G past simple of *be: was / were*
V word formation: *write › writer*
P sentence stress

Lesson plan

This lesson uses the context of self-portraits and selfies to introduce and practise the past simple of the verb *be* (*was / were*). The Grammar is presented through an audio guide talking about Vincent van Gogh. Pronunciation gets Sts to focus on sentence stress in past simple sentences and questions with *was* and *were*. The Reading picks up the topic of self-portraits of famous people and then moves onto word formation, e.g. *music – musician*. In Speaking, Sts discuss whether or not they take selfies, and talk about selfies and photos on their phones.

More materials
For teachers
Photocopiables
Grammar past simple of *be: was / were p.186*
Communicative Where were you? *p.232*
(instructions *p.209*)
For students
Workbook 7A
Online Practice 7A

OPTIONAL LEAD-IN (BOOKS CLOSED)

Start to draw a picture of yourself on the board. Ask Sts who they think it is, and keep adding details until they realize that it's you. Teach the word *self-portrait* and ask Sts if they think it looks like you.

1 GRAMMAR past simple of *be*

a Books open. Focus on the title and elicit / teach the meaning of *selfie* (= a photo that you take of yourself). Ask Sts if they like taking selfies to elicit *yes / no* answers. Sts will be discussing this in more details in Speaking.

If you haven't done the **Optional lead-in**, elicit / teach the meaning of *portrait* (= a painting of a person). Model and drill pronunciation /ˈpɔːtrət/. Now elicit the meaning of *self-portrait*.

Now focus on the portrait and the three questions. Put Sts in pairs to discuss them.

Elicit some ideas, but <u>don't</u> tell Sts if they are right or not.

b ◗ **7.1** Play the audio for Sts to listen and check. Tell Sts to just listen for the answers to questions 1 and 2 in **a**.

Check answers. Elicit opinions for question 3. You could tell Sts what you think of his paintings.

1 Vincent van Gogh **2** He is 35 years old.

◗ **7.1**
(script in Student's Book on *p.120*)
This painting is a self-portrait by the Dutch painter Vincent van Gogh.

Van Gogh was born in the Netherlands on the thirtieth of March eighteen fifty-three. His parents weren't poor – his father was a church minister, and his mother was an artist. Van Gogh's first job was in his uncle's company, selling paintings, but later he was a teacher in England, and finally a painter. We only really know what he looked like because of his many self-portraits. Only three photographs of him exist, and they are all from when he was young. This portrait is from his time in Arles in the south of France, in eighteen eighty-eight, when he was thirty-five. He was very poor, but he was happy because of the beautiful light and colours there. This portrait was a present for his friend, the painter Paul Gauguin. Gauguin and van Gogh were together in Arles for a month. Van Gogh was not strong mentally, and the relationship between them was difficult. After a big fight, van Gogh cut off his ear, and was in a mental hospital for some time. He died on the twenty-ninth of July eighteen ninety. He was only thirty-seven years old. His paintings weren't popular during his lifetime and he was never rich or famous. But today people think that Vincent van Gogh is one of the greatest painters in the world, and his paintings, like *Sunflowers*, and *The Starry Night*, sell for millions of pounds.

EXTRA IDEA If you have an interactive whiteboard connected to the internet, you could show Sts some of van Gogh's paintings, especially *Sunflowers* and *The Starry Night* as they are mentioned in the audio.

c Focus on questions 1–8. Give Sts time to read all the questions and options and make sure they understand all the lexis, e.g. *a present, complicated, died, unpopular*.

Play the audio again for Sts to listen and complete the task.

Get Sts to compare with a partner, and then check answers.

1 b **2** c **3** a **4** c **5** c **6** b **7** b **8** a

d Give Sts time to complete the chart with the highlighted verbs.

Check answers, and model and drill pronunciation, /wəz/, /wə/, /ˈwɒznt/, /wɜːnt/.

was were wasn't weren't

e Tell Sts to go to **Grammar Bank 7A** on *p.136*.

Grammar notes
was is the past of *am* and *is*, and *were* of *are*.
was and *were* are used to talk about both recent and distant completed actions in the past, e.g. *I was tired this morning. Caesar was a Roman Emperor.*
was and *were* are used exactly like *is* and *are*, i.e. they are inverted to make questions (*he was › was he?*) and *not* (*n't*) is added to make negatives (*wasn't, weren't*).
We use the passive construction *was born* to talk about the time and place of our birth.

◀)) 7.2 Focus on the example sentences and play the audio for Sts to listen and repeat. Then go through the rules with the class.

Now focus on the exercises for **7A** on *p.137*. Sts do the exercises individually or in pairs.

Check answers, getting Sts to read the full sentences.

a
1 She was **2** were you **3** I was **4** Was it **5** It wasn't
6 They weren't **7** We were **8** They were **9** We weren't
10 I wasn't

b
1 were **2** Was **3** wasn't **4** was **5** Were **6** were **7** was
8 was **9** Were **10** weren't **11** was **12** was

Tell Sts to go back to the main lesson **7A**.

EXTRA SUPPORT If you think Sts need more practice, you may want to give them the **Grammar** photocopiable activity at this point.

2 PRONUNCIATION sentence stress

Pronunciation notes

was and *were* have two different pronunciations depending on whether they are stressed or not (i.e. they can have either a strong or weak pronunciation).

was and *were* tend to have a weak pronunciation in positive sentences and questions: *I was /wəz/ born in 1990. They were /wə/ famous. Was /wəz/ it expensive?* The vowel sound in both words, as in most weak forms, is the schwa.

was / wasn't and *were / weren't* have a strong pronunciation in short answers and negative sentences: *Yes, I was /wɒz/, No, I wasn't /ˈwɒznt/, Yes, we were /wɜː/, No, we weren't /wɜːnt/.*

As pronunciation of strong and weak forms tends to occur quite naturally when there is good sentence stress and rhythm, it is best to concentrate your efforts on this (as in **2a**).

a ◀)) 7.3 Focus on the sentences and remind Sts that the words in larger font are stressed and that the underlining shows the stress within a word.

Play the audio once for Sts just to listen.

◀)) 7.3
See sentences in Student's Book on *p.54*

Now play it again, pausing after each sentence for Sts to listen and repeat, copying the rhythm. Give further practice as necessary.

b ◀)) 7.4 Tell Sts they are going to hear some sentences and questions in the present simple and they must say them in the past simple. Focus on the example, and highlight that the rhythm of the past simple sentence is the same as the present simple sentence, e.g. *I'm at **home**, I was at **home***.

Play the audio, pausing after each sentence / question, and elicit the past simple version from the whole class.

◀)) 7.4
1 I'm at home. (*pause*) I was at home.
2 He's American. (*pause*) He was American.
3 They aren't famous. (*pause*) They weren't famous.
4 It's very cheap. (*pause*) It was very cheap.
5 Where are they? (*pause*) Where were they?
6 Is she an actress? (*pause*) Was she an actress?
7 You're right. (*pause*) You were right.
8 What's his name? (*pause*) What was his name?
9 She isn't happy. (*pause*) She wasn't happy.
10 Are they tired? (*pause*) Were they tired?

Now repeat the activity, eliciting responses from individual Sts.

3 READING understanding the order of life events

a Focus on the self-portraits and photos on *p.55* and ask Sts if they know any of the three people (They may know one or two, e.g. the singer Adele). Elicit anything they know, and tell them they are going to find out more about them when they read the texts.

Now ask the question to the class to elicit some opinions.

b Focus on the biographies and the events for each person and tell Sts that they need to number the events in the correct order.

Give Sts time to read the biographies and number the events.

Get Sts to compare with a partner, and then check answers.

EXTRA SUPPORT Before Sts read the biographies the first time, check whether you need to pre-teach any vocabulary.

Kurt Vonnegut
1 He was a soldier.
2 *Slaughterhouse-Five* was a bestseller.
3 He was a painter.

Billy Dee Williams
1 He was an art student.
2 He was in his first film.
3 He was very successful as an actor.

Adele
1 She wasn't very interested in schoolwork.
2 She was a student with singer Jessie J.
3 *19* was a bestseller.

Deal with any other new vocabulary. Model and drill the pronunciation of any tricky words.

c Give Sts time to read the biographies again.

Put Sts in pairs and get them to cover the biographies or close their books. Together they see how much they can remember about each person.

Elicit from the class as much information as possible about each person.

EXTRA SUPPORT Put Sts in small groups of three. Each student sees how much they can remember about one of the biographies whilst the other two Sts look at the biography and help if necessary.

d Do this as a whole-class activity. You could also tell the class which of the self-portraits you like the most and why.

EXTRA IDEA Ask the class if they know any other famous self-portraits and if they like them.

4 VOCABULARY word formation

a Give Sts a few minutes to find the words in the biographies, or get them to guess first and then check with the texts.

Check answers, modelling the pronunciation and getting Sts to underline the stress.

> 1 writer   2 actor   3 singer   4 painter

Focus on the **Word building** box about professions and go through it with the class. Point out that to make the word for a person (e.g. *writer*) you add the letters *-(e)r* or *-or* to a verb and *-ist* or *-ian* to a noun. You might also want to point out that sometimes with nouns you have to make more changes, e.g. *science – scientist* (the *ce* disappears and a *t* is added).

b Tell Sts to first look at the group of words and decide if they are verbs or nouns. Then they should write the words for the jobs.

Get Sts to compare answers with a partner.

EXTRA SUPPORT You could first ask Sts to tell you whether group 1 is verbs or nouns (They are verbs). Then give Sts some time to add the correct ending. Then do the same for group 2.

c 🔊 **7.5** Play the audio for Sts to listen and check answers to **b**. Pause the audio after each word and get Sts to spell the endings to you. Write the answers on the board.

> 1 verbs; composer, dancer, director, inventor
> 2 nouns; artist, novelist, politician, scientist

🔊 **7.5**
1 composer, dancer, director, inventor
2 artist, novelist, politician, scientist

Now play the audio again and this time Sts should underline the stress.

Check answers by underlining the stress in the words on the board.

> 1 composer, dancer, director, inventor
> 2 artist, novelist, politician, scientist

Finally, in pairs, Sts practise saying the words. If you think they need more practice, you could play the audio again for them to listen and repeat the words.

EXTRA IDEA Test Sts' memory by getting them to cover the words in **a** and **b** and then saying the noun / verb as a prompt, e.g.
T   *art*
Sts   *artist*.

EXTRA CHALLENGE Elicit a famous name(s) for each of the professions in **a** and **b** (preferably a dead person). Elicit a full sentence for one, e.g. *(X) was a famous writer.*

d Focus on the words *Alive* and *Dead* in the circles. Elicit / Teach that they are opposites. Get Sts to write four names of famous people in each circle.

Put Sts in pairs and get them to ask and answer questions about the names using either *Who is / Who's...?* or *Who was...?* depending on whether the person is alive or dead.

EXTRA SUPPORT Demonstrate the activity by copying the circles on the board and writing the names of two people in each, and eliciting the questions from Sts.

5 SPEAKING

If you haven't already focused on the title of the lesson, focus on the initial question and elicit the meaning of *selfie*. Point out the two possible answers, *Yes* and *No*. If you have some selfies on your phone, you could show the class.

Put Sts in pairs and get them to ask each other the questions. Encourage them to take their phones out and show their partner some of their selfies or other photos.

EXTRA SUPPORT Give Sts time to think about their answers before putting them in pairs. Monitor and help.

Get some feedback from various pairs. With a show of hands, find out how many Sts take selfies.

G past simple: regular verbs
V past time expressions: *three years ago, last week,* etc.
P *-ed* endings

Lesson plan

Past simple regular verbs are introduced in this lesson. The context is provided by two true stories of people having a problem with a flight. The lesson begins with a Reading about someone needing to change the surname on their ticket, and then Sts listen to a story about a couple having a problem when they arrive at the airport. These are used to present the past simple of regular verbs. Then there is a focus on the pronunciation of *-ed* endings. Vocabulary introduces past time expressions, and Grammar, Vocabulary and Pronunciation are put together in the final Speaking activity.

More materials
For teachers
Photocopiables
Grammar past simple: regular verbs *p.187*
Communicative Are we in Australia? *p.233*
(instructions *p.209*)
For students
Workbook 7B
Online Practice 7B

OPTIONAL LEAD-IN (BOOKS CLOSED)

Ask Sts *Do you have a passport, an ID card, or both? What information is in it?*

Write ideas on the board, e.g.:

FIRST NAME   MIDDLE NAME(S)
SURNAME   NATIONALITY
DATE OF BIRTH   PLACE OF BIRTH

Explain that the first part of the lesson is about somebody who wanted to change something in their passport.

1 READING & LISTENING predicting the order of events from existing knowledge

a Books open. Tell Sts that they are going to read and listen to two true stories. Focus on the task and make sure Sts know what *a flight* is. Model and drill pronunciation.

Now go through questions 1–3 and check Sts know *to fly*, *to book a ticket*, and *a booking*.

Give Sts time to read the beginning of the story and answer the questions.

Get Sts to compare with a partner, and then check answers for 1 and 2. Elicit / Explain that *stepfather* = a man who has married your mother, but who is not your father.

EXTRA SUPPORT Before Sts read the story, check whether you need to pre-teach any vocabulary.

1 They wanted to fly to Ibiza from Manchester.
2 India's stepfather

Finally, elicit some ideas for question 3.

b Now tell Sts they are going to read the second part of the story and they have to put it in order. Point out that the first paragraph (*B*) has been numbered for them.

Give Sts time to order the rest of the paragraphs.

Get Sts to compare with a partner, and then check answers.

2 D **3** E **4** C **5** A **6** F

Deal with any other new vocabulary. Model and drill the pronunciation of any tricky words.

c Do this as a whole-class activity and elicit different opinions.

d Focus on the task and give Sts time to order the sentences. Point out that the first one (*C*) has been done for them.

Get Sts to compare with a partner.

e 🔊 **7.6** Tell Sts they are now going to hear the first part of the story, not just the sentences in **d**, and they must listen and check their answers.

Play the audio and then check answers.

EXTRA SUPPORT Read through the scripts and decide if you need to pre-teach any new lexis before Sts listen.

2 F **3** B **4** E **5** D **6** G **7** A

🔊 **7.6**
(script in Student's Book on *p.120*)
Kevin and his partner Jeanette live in Birmingham, England. Last year they decided to go on a winter holiday to Trinidad in the Caribbean, and they looked for flights online. They were very happy to find cheap flights – only eight hundred pounds return for the two of them. Kevin booked the flights and they started to plan their holiday.
On the day of their flight they arrived at Birmingham Airport and parked their car in the long-stay car park. Then they walked into the terminal building and tried to check in their bags. The check-in assistant looked at their boarding passes and asked where they wanted to go. 'Trinidad,' they replied. 'We're going there on holiday.' The check-in assistant looked surprised.

f 🔊 **7.7** Before Sts listen to the rest of the story, ask them what they think might be the problem. Elicit some ideas.

Play the audio for Sts to hear the end of the story.

Check the answer.

They booked their flights from the wrong airport – Birmingham, Alabama, in the United States, instead of Birmingham, England.

(script in Student's Book on *p.120*)

C = check-in assistant, J = Jeanette, K = Kevin
C Where do you want to go?
J Trinidad. We're going there on holiday.
C I'm sorry, but there are no flights from here to Trinidad.
K No flights? But we booked last month!
C Let me check your booking. Oh, I see. I'm really sorry, but your booking isn't from this Birmingham. It's from Birmingham Alabama, in the United States.
J No, it can't be.
C I'm very sorry, but it is. Look, it says BHM – that's the code for Birmingham Airport in the States. You can't fly from here.
J I don't believe it. Kevin, did you check the airport when you booked?
K Yeah. It was Birmingham. I didn't check which Birmingham.
J You idiot!
C I'm very sorry, but you can't fly today.

EXTRA SUPPORT If there's time, you could get Sts to listen again with the scripts on *p.120*, so they can see exactly what they understood / didn't understand. Translate / Explain any new words or phrases.

g Make sure Sts understand the question.

Do this as a whole-class activity. First, elicit some opinions for the first story about Adam and India, and then elicit some opinions about Kevin and Jeanette's story. Ask Sts if they know anyone who had a problem when they booked flights online.

2 GRAMMAR past simple: regular verbs

a Tell Sts to read **1b** again and find the four past tense verbs. Make sure they know the meaning of *reply*.

Elicit the answers onto the board.

> **1** asked   **2** decided   **3** replied   **4** didn't want

b 7.8 Now tell Sts to look at the question taken from the second story.

Play the audio for Sts to listen and complete the gap. Check the answer.

> did

7.8
J I don't believe it. Kevin, did you check the airport when you booked?
K Yeah. It was Birmingham.

c Tell Sts to go to **Grammar Bank 7B** on *p.136*.

Grammar notes

It is important to emphasize that the past simple is used for completed actions in the past, both distant and recent and which happened once or more than once. The form of regular past simple verbs is very easy. The main problem Sts have is the pronunciation, and remembering to use the infinitive, not the -*ed* form, after *did / didn't*.

7.9 Focus on the example sentences and play the audio for Sts to listen and repeat. Then go through the rules with the class. You may want to point out here that the *e* is not normally pronounced in -*ed* endings unless there is a *t* or a *d* before it. This will be focused on more fully in **Pronunciation**.

Now focus on the exercises for **7B** on *p.137*. Sts do the exercises individually or in pairs.

Check answers, getting Sts to read the full sentences. Correct any mispronunciation of the -*ed* ending. Get Sts to spell the verbs to you and write them on the board.

> **a**
> **1** I studied English
> **2** Did you listen to the news
> **3** He didn't cook
> **4** Did she play sport
> **5** They worked late
> **6** She travelled a lot
> **7** Jack worked in New York
> **8** I called my parents
> **9** We didn't live in France
> **10** Anna asked a lot of questions
> **b**
> **1** didn't call   **2** Did…cry   **3** played   **4** didn't listen
> **5** Did…dance   **6** booked

Tell Sts to go back to the main lesson **7B**.

EXTRA SUPPORT If you think Sts need more practice, you may want to give them the **Grammar** photocopiable activity at this point.

d Focus on the instructions and questionnaire, and explain the activity. Sts need to find a person who did each of the activities in the questionnaire yesterday. Elicit that Sts need to make the sentences into questions by adding *Did you…* and then putting the verb in the infinitive, e.g. *Did you watch football on TV yesterday?*

Tell Sts they are going to move around the classroom asking questions in the past simple to find out if people did the activities mentioned. If someone says *yes*, they should write that person's name on the line on the left.

Focus on the speech bubbles and demonstrate the activity by asking the first question until someone says *yes* and then mime that you are writing down their name.

EXTRA SUPPORT Before starting the activity, you could get Sts to ask you all the questions first, making sure they don't say, e.g. *Did you watched football on TV yesterday?*. Give simple answers that they can understand.
With a large class, divide Sts into two separate groups.

Get Sts to stand up and move around the class asking questions. Stop the activity when someone gets a name for each statement or when you think Sts have had enough practice, and get some feedback from the class.

3 PRONUNCIATION -*ed* endings

Pronunciation notes

The regular past simple ending (-*ed*) can be pronounced in three different ways:

1 -*ed* is pronounced /t/ after verbs ending in these unvoiced sounds*: /k/, /p/, /f/, /s/, /ʃ/, /tʃ/, e.g. *cooked, booked, laughed, missed, relaxed, stopped, washed, watched*.

2 After voiced endings* (all other consonant sounds except /d/ and /t/) -*ed* is pronounced /d/, e.g. *arrived, called, changed, showed*. This is the biggest group. Verbs which ends with consonant + *y*, e.g. *study, carry*, also belong to this group because the sound added is /d/.

3 After verbs ending in /d/ or /t/ the pronunciation of -ed is /ɪd/, e.g. *wanted, chatted, needed, decided*. This group is very small.

In practice, the difference between 1 and 2 is very small and can only be appreciated when a verb is said in isolation or is followed by a word beginning with a vowel (e.g. *I liked it*).

However, the difference between 3 and the other two is significant (it is an extra syllable) and many Sts tend to pronounce all past simple verbs in this way, e.g. /ˈlaɪkɪd/, /ˈstʊpɪd/, etc.

Voiced and unvoiced consonants

- Voiced consonant sounds are made by vibrating the vocal chords, e.g. /b/, /l/, /m/, /v/, etc. Unvoiced consonant sounds are made without vibration in the throat, e.g. /p/, /k/, /t/, /s/, etc.
- You can demonstrate this to Sts by getting them to hold their hands against their throats. For voiced sounds they should feel a vibration in their throat, but not for unvoiced sounds.

a ◖ **7.10** Focus on the **Past simple regular verbs** box and go through it with the class. Elicit / Explain that there are three different ways of pronouncing -ed. Two are similar (/d/ and /t/), but the third /ɪd/ is very different.

Focus on the phonetics which show the three different pronunciations of -ed (/d/, /t/, and /ɪd/). Then look at the sentences for each pronunciation and play the audio once. Tell Sts to listen and concentrate on how the -ed is pronounced.

◖ **7.10**
See chart in Student's Book on *p.57*

Now play the audio again, pausing after each sentence for Sts to listen and repeat.

Ask Sts the question *In which group do you pronounce the 'e' in -ed?* (group 3).

Tell Sts to look at the spelling of the verbs in group 3, and see what letters come before the -ed (*d* or *t*). Explain / Demonstrate that it would be impossible to pronounce another /d/ or /t/ after a *d* or a *t*. For that reason an extra syllable is added, which is why the pronunciation here is /ɪd/. Emphasize that this group of verbs is very small.

Highlight that the most important rule to remember is <u>not</u> to pronounce the *e* in -ed (unless it comes after a *t* or *d*).

b ◖ **7.11** Tell Sts to look at the verbs in the list and circle the ones which have the /ɪd/ sound in the past simple. Remind Sts that an exercise like this is easier if they say the verbs aloud.

Play the audio for Sts to listen and check.

Check answers.

ended, painted, started

◖ **7.11**
See list of verbs in Student's Book on *p.57*

EXTRA CHALLENGE Get Sts to look at all the verbs again and then to try and put them in the appropriate columns in **a**.

c ◖ **7.12** Focus on the speech bubble and explain to Sts that they are going to hear some verb phrases and they must make either a positive sentence or a negative one depending on what they really did yesterday.

Play the audio, pausing after each verb phrase. Elicit sentences from a few Sts before moving on to the next phrase.

◖ **7.12**
1 play tennis
2 travel by train
3 cook lunch
4 wait for a bus
5 play the guitar
6 study English
7 watch TV
8 listen to music

4 VOCABULARY & SPEAKING past time
expressions

a Write a true sentence about yourself in the past with a regular verb, e.g. *I started teaching English in 1999*. Then write underneath it *I started teaching English (x) years ago*, and elicit the meaning of *ago*. Model and drill pronunciation.

Focus on the past time expressions, and explain that Sts must number them from the most recent (*five minutes ago*) to the most distant (*in 2017*). Give Sts time to do the activity and get them to check their order with a partner.

b ◖ **7.13** Go through the **Past time expressions** box with the class and highlight that in time expressions with *last* (e.g. *last week*) the definite article *the* is not used. Also explain that we say *last night* NOT ~~yesterday night~~.

Play the audio for Sts to listen and check.

Check answers.

◖ **7.13**
1   five minutes ago
2   last night
3   yesterday morning
4   the day before yesterday
5   three days ago
6   last week
7   last month
8   last summer
9   a year ago
10 in 2017

Now play the audio again for Sts to listen and repeat.

c Focus on the instructions and the sentences. Make sure Sts understand the question *When was the last time?*.

Give Sts time to write a time expression for each activity.

d Tell Sts they will now tell each other when they did each activity. Focus on the example.

Put Sts in pairs and set a time limit.

Monitor and help. Make sure Sts swap roles.

Get some feedback by getting individual Sts to tell you an activity they did and asking a few extra questions.

G past simple: irregular verbs
V *go, have, get*
P sentence stress

Lesson plan

The topic of this lesson is New Year's Eve. Three blogs about memorable New Year's Eves (good and bad!) provide the context for the introduction of past simple irregular verbs. The vocabulary focus is common collocations of the key verbs *go*, *have*, and *get* (e.g. *go out*, *get home*, etc.). Then Sts listen to a fourth person talking about a memorable New Year's Eve in Brazil. Sts then work on the stress pattern in *Wh-* questions in the past simple, which prepares them for the final Speaking and Writing activity, where Sts ask each other about a memorable New Year's Eve and then write about it.

More materials
For teachers
Photocopiables
Grammar past simple: irregular verbs *p.188*
Vocabulary *go, have, get p.270* (instructions *p.255*)
Communicative Born on 31st December *p.234* (instructions *p.209*)
For students
Workbook 7C
Online Practice 7C

OPTIONAL LEAD-IN (BOOKS CLOSED)

Write on the board 31ST DECEMBER, 1ST JANUARY. Ask Sts if they know what these days are called in English, and elicit *New Year's Eve* and *New Year's Day*.

Ask Sts what they usually do on New Year's Eve.

1 READING

a Books open. Focus on the photos and the questions. If you didn't do the **Optional lead-in**, elicit when New Year's Eve is (31st December). Elicit answers to the second question. If you don't come from the same country as your Sts, tell them if New Year's Eve is an important occasion in your country.

b Focus on the task and make sure Sts understand the three options.

You may want to pre-teach the past of *go* (*went*), *midnight*, and *a lift* to help Sts understand the stories.

Give Sts time to read all three stories.

Check answers.

EXTRA SUPPORT Before Sts read the stories the first time, check whether you need to pre-teach any vocabulary.

Jenny had a great evening. Andy had an OK evening. Mina had a terrible evening.

c Focus on the task and the six sentences. You might want to check Sts know the meaning of *alone*.

Give Sts time to read the stories again and complete the six sentences with an initial.
Check answers.

1 J **2** A **3** M **4** A **5** M **6** J

Deal with any other new vocabulary. Model and drill the pronunciation of any tricky words.

d If your Sts come from the same country, do this as a whole-class activity. If your Sts come from different countries, put them in pairs or small groups to discuss the questions.

EXTRA SUPPORT If Sts come from different countries, give them time to make notes about New Year's Eve celebrations in their country. Monitor and help with vocabulary.

Get some feedback from various pairs / groups. If you don't come from the same country as your Sts, tell them how people celebrate New Year's Eve in your country.

2 GRAMMAR past simple: irregular verbs

a Focus on the 15 infinitives and check Sts remember their meaning. Then put Sts in pairs and give them a few minutes to find the past simple forms in the stories. Point out that the first one (*bought*) has been done for them. Encourage Sts to use the phonetics to help them.

b 🔊 **7.14** Write the infinitives on the board. Play the audio, pausing after each verb to check answers. Get Sts to spell the verbs to you and write the past simples on the board next to the infinitives.

See verbs in **bold** in script 7.14

🔊 **7.14**

buy	bought
can	could
come	came
drink	drank
feel	felt
find	found
get	got
go	went
have	had
know	knew
put on	put on
say	said
take	took
think	thought
wear	wore

Focus on the phonetics and tell Sts to listen to the pronunciation. Play the audio again, pausing after each infinitive and past tense for Sts to repeat them. Give more practice as necessary, getting Sts to repeat after you or after the audio.

EXTRA CHALLENGE Focus on the phonetics and elicit the pronunciation of the verbs before playing the audio.

Get Sts to cover the past simple verb and see if they can remember it, uncovering them one by one to check their answers.

c Tell Sts to go to **Grammar Bank 7C** on *p.136*.

Grammar notes

The vast majority of verbs in the past are regular. However, a small number of verbs (several of which are very common) are irregular in the past simple. These verbs don't add *-ed* in the past, they change their form. This change can be just one or two letters, e.g. *wear › wore*, or can be a completely new word, e.g. *go › went*. Some verbs don't change their form, e.g. *cost*, *put*, etc. The verb *read* is spelled the same, but pronounced differently.

Irregular verbs are only irregular in the affirmative. In questions and negatives, as with regular verbs, the infinitive is used after *did / didn't*.

There is a list of the most common irregular verbs on *p.165* of the Student's Book.

◗) 7.15 Focus on the example sentences and play the audio for Sts to listen and repeat. Then go through the rules with the class.

Focus on the **can / could** box and go through it with the class.

Now focus on the exercises for **7C** on *p.137*. Sts do the exercises individually or in pairs.

❗ Monitor while Sts are doing the exercises. If you see they are having problems with word order in **c**, remind them of **QuASI** and **ASI** (see *p.50* of this book).

Check answers, getting Sts to read the full sentences.

> **a**
> **1** She didn't wear a red dress. She wore a blue dress.
> **2** I didn't come home early. I came home late.
> **3** We didn't go by train. We went by bus.
> **4** He didn't say hello. He said goodbye.
> **5** You didn't have a sandwich. You had a salad.
> **6** He didn't know her surname. He knew her first name.
>
> **b**
> **1** had **2** took **3** were **4** went **5** could **6** had **7** got
> **8** felt **9** were
>
> **c**
> **1** did you wear **2** did she buy **3** did you get home

Tell Sts to go back to the main lesson **7C**.

EXTRA SUPPORT If you think Sts need more practice, you may want to give them the **Grammar** photocopiable activity at this point.

3 VOCABULARY *go, have, get*

a Focus on the three verbs in the heading and elicit the past simple (*went*, *had*, *got*).

Give Sts a moment to decide which verb goes in each gap.

Check answers.

> **1** went **2** had **3** got **4** had **5** went **6** got

b Tell Sts to go to **Vocabulary Bank** *go, have, get* on *p.160* and get them to do **a** individually or in pairs.

Vocabulary notes

You may want to tell Sts that *get* is one of the most common verbs in English partly because it has many different meanings. The most common are *buy* (as in *get a newspaper*), receive (as in *get an email*), arrive (as in *get home*) and take (as in *get a taxi*).

Remind Sts that *go home* = go to your house, *get home* = arrive at your house.

◗) 7.16 Now do **b**. Play the audio for Sts to listen and check.

Check answers.

◗) 7.16

go
8 go by bus
1 go for a walk
5 go home
10 go out
9 go shopping
2 go to a restaurant
11 go to bed
7 go to church
3 go to the beach
6 go back
4 go on holiday

have
15 have a car
12 have long hair
18 have breakfast
14 have a drink
13 have a good time
16 have a sandwich
17 have a shower

get
20 get a newspaper
23 get a taxi
19 get an email
21 get dressed
25 get home
22 get to the airport
24 get up

Then either use the audio to drill the pronunciation of the phrases, or model and drill them yourself. Give further practice of any words or phrases your Sts find difficult to pronounce

Focus on **c**. Get Sts to cover the verb phrases and use the photos to test themselves or each other. Encourage them to say the complete phrase.

For **Activation**, put Sts in pairs and get them to take it in turns to say five things they did the previous day and five the previous week. All the sentences should include *went*, *had*, or *got*. Get some feedback.

Tell Sts to go back to the main lesson **7C**.

EXTRA SUPPORT If you think Sts need more practice, you may want to give them the **Vocabulary** photocopiable activity at this point.

4 LISTENING understanding extra information

a ◉ **7.17** Focus on the photo and the task. Elicit / Teach the meaning and pronunciation of *memorable* /ˈmemərəbl/ (= easy to remember because it is special). Tell Sts to close their books, relax and listen, and just focus on where Denisa was at midnight.

Play the audio once, and elicit the answer.

  Read through the script and decide if you need to pre-teach any new lexis before Sts listen.

> Denisa was on the beach in Rio de Janeiro, in Brazil.

◉ **7.17**

(script in Student's Book on *p.120*)

F = friend, D = Denisa

F What was your best ever New Year's Eve? One you always remember?

D Oh, definitely twenty fourteen, when I was in Rio.

F Who were you with?

D I was with my boyfriend Marcelo, who's Brazilian.

F Why was it so special?

D Well, Brazil has special traditions for New Year's Eve, and they were all new for me. For example, it's a Brazilian tradition to wear white clothes for New Year's Eve because white is a symbol of peace, so I wore a beautiful white dress, which Marcelo's mother bought me. I have a photo somewhere on my phone. Yes, here, look!

F How lovely. So what did you do?

D Er, let me think. Well, first we had a typical New Year's Eve dinner with Marcelo's family. And then, I suppose it was about ten, we got a bus to Copacabana.

F What was the atmosphere like there?

D Oh, it was amazing! The streets were already full of people. We went to a show at a place near the beach. It was great, and we danced samba.

F Wow. Were you there at midnight?

D No, no. When we saw it was nearly midnight, we went to the beach, and the typical countdown started, you know – ten, nine, eight…Happy New Year! Everywhere we heard the sound of people opening champagne, and we watched the wonderful fireworks.

F It sounds great. What did people do when the fireworks finished?

D Most people went to other parties, or they went home.

F And what about you?

D We decided to go to a different beach, a beach called Praia do Arpoador, and we had our first swim of the new year. It was magical.

b Focus on the people and things in 1–8, and make sure Sts understand them.

Give Sts time in pairs or individually to see what they can remember.

c Play the audio again for Sts to listen and check. Play it again if necessary, pausing after she mentions each person or thing.

Check answers.

> 1 **Marcelo** – is her Brazilian boyfriend.
> 2 She wore **white clothes** because it's a Brazilian tradition.
> 3 **Marcelo's mother** bought the dress.
> 4 They had a typical **dinner** with Marcelo's family.
> 5 They got a bus to **Copacabana**.
> 6 They went to **a show** at a place near the beach and danced samba.
> 7 When it was **nearly midnight**, they went to the beach and watched fireworks.
> 8 They had their first **swim** of the New Year **at** another beach called **Praia do Arpoador**.

  If there's time, you could get Sts to listen again with the script on *p.120*, so they can see exactly what they understood / didn't understand. Translate / Explain any new words or phrases.

d Do the questions as a whole-class activity. You could also tell Sts whether you would like to spend New Year's Eve in Rio, and if not where.

5 PRONUNCIATION sentence stress

a Go through the instructions and focus on the questions.

Give Sts time in pairs or individually to complete the questions.

Check answers.

> **1** was **2** were **3** were you **4** did you **5** did you **6** did you **7** did you **8** did you **9** was **10** did you **11** Did you

b ◉ **7.18** Play the audio once for Sts just to listen and focus on the rhythm.

◉ **7.18**

1 When was it?
2 Where were you?
3 Who were you with?
4 Where did you have dinner?
5 What did you wear?
6 What did you do before midnight?
7 What did you do at midnight?
8 What did you do after midnight?
9 How was the weather?
10 What time did you go to bed?
11 Did you have a good time?

Now play the audio again, pausing after each question for Sts to listen and repeat, trying to copy the rhythm.

6 SPEAKING & WRITING

a Give Sts a few minutes individually to think about their own answers to the questions in **5a**. Help with any new vocabulary they might need.

  If your Sts don't celebrate New Year's Eve, they could discuss and write about another important event, such as a wedding or a special night out.

b Put Sts in pairs. Get Sts **A** to give Sts **B** a complete 'interview' and then swap roles. Monitor the interviews, encouraging Sts to ask their questions with good sentence stress and rhythm. Help with any new vocabulary that Sts need and correct as necessary.

  Get Sts to interview you about a memorable New Year's Eve before they interview each other.

Get feedback, asking a few pairs whose night was more memorable / fun / interesting, etc.

c Sts now write an article similar to the ones they read in **1**. Tell them they need to answer all the questions in **5a** and they should look back at Mina's, Jenny's, and Andy's memorable New Year's Eves in **1** to help them.

Once Sts have finished, they should spend a few minutes checking their story, before handing it to another student to read or to you.

Practical English Getting lost

Function asking the way
Vocabulary directions

Lesson plan

In this lesson Sts get practice with directions. The focus is more on asking for and understanding directions than on giving them, as this is a difficult skill to perform at this level. Rob and Jenny have a free morning, and Rob plans to hire bikes and show Jenny some of London. But then Daniel calls and asks Rob to interview an artist at the Tate Modern. Jenny agrees to meet Rob at the gallery and ventures into London on her own and gets lost.

More materials
For teachers
Teacher's Resource Centre
Video Practical English Episode 4
Quick Test 7
File 7 Test
For students
Workbook Practical English 4
Can you remember? 1–7
Online Practice Practical English 4
Check your progress

OPTIONAL LEAD-IN (BOOKS CLOSED)

Before starting Episode 4, elicit what Sts can remember about Episode 3, e.g. ask them *What happens when Rob and Jenny meet in the street? What does Rob buy? Does Jenny like it? Who does Jenny talk to on the phone when Rob's in the shop?*, etc.

Alternatively, you could play the last scene of Episode 3.

1 ▶ A FREE MORNING

a ◀) **7.19** Books open. Focus on the photos and elicit what Sts think is happening. <u>Don't</u> tell them if they are right or not yet.

Now focus on the question and play the video / audio once the whole way through for Sts to check their ideas.

Check the answer.

> Rob and Jenny want to go sightseeing, but Daniel phones Rob and asks him to do an interview that morning.

◀) **7.19**

R = Rob, J = Jenny, D = Daniel
R So, Jenny, we have a free morning. What do you want to do?
J Well, you're the expert on London life! What do you suggest?
R Well, we can go cycling.
J I don't have a bike.
R We can rent bikes. It's easy.
J That's cool.
R OK, great. So we can cycle through the parks, and you can see a bit of London. Oh, hang on. Uh oh. It's Daniel. Daniel, hi!
D Hi, Rob. You need to do an interview this morning with an artist. He's at the Tate Modern.
R Can I do the interview on Monday?
D Sorry, he can only do this morning.
R OK, send me the details.
D Thank you very much, Rob.
R I'm sorry.
J That's OK, I understand. Work is work!
R But I can meet you later, outside the Tate Modern. It's on the South Bank.
J I can find it. I have a map, I can cycle there.
R Let's meet at twelve o'clock then.
J Great.

b Focus on sentences 1–6 and give Sts time to read them and think what the missing information might be.

Before Sts watch or listen again, focus on the **Glossary**. You could tell Sts that the official name is 'Tate Modern' but a lot of people call it 'the Tate Modern'. You could also tell Sts that the Tate Modern is London's most important gallery of modern art. It was created in 2000 from an old building, which used to be a power station. If they would like more information, see *www.tate.org.uk/visit/tate-modern*.

Play the video / audio again the whole way through, pausing if necessary for Sts to complete the gaps.

Get Sts to compare with a partner, and play again if necessary.

Check answers.

> **1** cycling **2** rent **3** Daniel, Rob **4** artist **5** Monday
> **6** twelve

EXTRA SUPPORT If there's time and you are using the video, you could get Sts to watch again with subtitles / showing the script, so they can see exactly what they understood / didn't understand. Translate / Explain any new words or phrases.

2 ▶ VOCABULARY directions

a Focus on the phrases and pictures and get Sts to match them.

Get Sts to compare with a partner.

b 🔊 **7.20** Play the video / audio for Sts to watch or listen and check.

Check answers.

🔊 **7.20**
3 on the corner
1 at the traffic lights
5 a bridge
7 opposite
2 turn left
4 turn right
9 go straight on
6 go past the church
8 at the end of the street

Play the video / audio again, pausing after each phrase for Sts to repeat. Give further practice of the phrases your Sts find difficult to pronounce.

Highlight that when *opposite* is used to describe the position of a building, it usually means 'facing on the other side of the road'. Get an example by asking Sts what there is opposite your school.

c Tell Sts to cover the phrases and use the pictures to test themselves or a partner.

3 ▶ ASKING THE WAY

a 🔊 **7.21** Focus on the instructions and the map. Make sure Sts can see where Jenny is.

Tell Sts that they are going to hear Jenny asking for directions and they need to listen to the directions and try to mark the Tate Modern on the map. Play the video / audio at least twice.

Get Sts to compare with a partner, and then check that they have marked the right building.

❗ The map in the Student's Book has been adapted and is impressionistic rather than strictly accurate.

It's B.

🔊 **7.21** 🔊 **7.22**
J = Jenny, P = passer-by
J Excuse me, please. (*repeat*) Where's the Tate Modern? (*repeat*)
P1 Sorry, I don't live here.
J Excuse me. Is the Tate Modern near here? (*repeat*)
P2 The Tate Modern? It's near here, but I don't know exactly where. Sorry.
J Thank you. (*repeat*)
J Excuse me. Can you tell me the way to the Tate Modern, please? (*repeat*)
P3 Yes, of course. Go straight on. Go past the church, then turn left at the traffic lights. And it's at the end of the street.
J Sorry, could you say that again, please? (*repeat*)
P3 Yes, go straight on. Go past the church, and then turn left at the traffic lights. And it's at the end of the street. You can't miss it!
J Thank you. (*repeat*)

Now check how many people she asks.

She asks three people.

b Now focus on the conversation in the chart. Elicit that **You say** is what Jenny says and the **You hear** phrases are said by three different people in the street, who she asks for directions. The **You say** phrases will be useful for Sts if they need to ask for directions.

Give Sts a minute to read through the conversation and think what the missing words might be. Then play the video / audio again, and get Sts to complete the gaps. Play again if necessary.

Get Sts to compare with a partner, and then check answers.

1 Sorry **2** where **3** past **4** left **5** miss

Go through the conversation line by line with Sts, helping them with any words or expressions they don't understand. Highlight that *Can you tell me the way to…, please?* is the typical question to ask for directions.

c 🔊 **7.22** Now focus on the **You say** phrases and tell Sts they're going to hear the conversation again. They should repeat the **You say** phrases when they hear the beep. Encourage them to copy the rhythm and intonation.

Play the video / audio, pausing if necessary for Sts to repeat the phrases.

🔊 **7.22**
Same as script 7.21 with repeat pauses

---

d Put Sts in pairs, **A** and **B**. **A** is Jenny and **B** plays the parts of all the passers-by. Get Sts to read the conversation aloud, and then swap roles.

Focus on the ***Can you…? or Could you…?*** box and go through it with the class.

e In pairs, Sts role-play asking for and giving simple directions using the map on *p.60*. Go through the instructions with Sts, making sure they starts where Jenny is on the map. Sts **A** starts saying *Excuse me. Where's…?*.

Monitor and help with any issues relating to directions. Make sure Sts swap roles.

EXTRA SUPPORT Demonstrate the activity by getting a confident student to ask you for directions to somewhere on the map.

EXTRA IDEA Give Sts clear directions from the school to a nearby restaurant, shop or landmark, and see if they can work out where it is.

4 ▶ JENNY AND ROB GO SIGHTSEEING

a ◗ **7.23** Focus on the photo and ask Sts some questions, e.g. *Where are Rob and Jenny? What's happening?*, etc.

Tell Sts that they are on the bank of the River Thames in central London, outside the Tate Modern.

Focus on sentences 1–6 and go through them with Sts. Tell Sts that the Millennium Bridge is a bridge over the Thames, which was built to celebrate the year 2000. Check Sts understand *gift shop*, *the top floor*, and *power station*.

Then play the video / audio for Sts to choose the correct option.

Get Sts to compare with a partner, and then check answers.

> **1** The Millennium **2** 100 **3** Shakespeare **4** can't
> **5** restaurant **6** power

◗ 7.23

R = Rob, J = Jenny, D = Daniel

R Sorry about the weather.

J Yeah… but what a view! It's a great bridge, too.

R It's the Millennium Bridge. It's not for cars, only for people. It was the first new bridge over the Thames in one hundred years.

J You sound like a tour guide!

R Sorry… I interviewed the architect last year. So what would you like to visit?

J What is there to see?

R Well, we could see the Tate Modern first as we're here, and then we could go to the Globe Theatre. Do you like Shakespeare?

J Not really. I studied too much Shakespeare in college. It's Daniel. Sorry. Hi, Daniel.

D Hi, Jennifer. How's your free day? Are you enjoying London?

J Absolutely. It's fantastic.

D Listen, I have some free time today. Would you like to meet for lunch?

J That's really nice of you, Daniel, but I'm sorry, I can't. I'm really far away from the office right now.

D That's OK. No problem. Maybe another time?

J Definitely. Bye.

R What did he want? Anything important?

J Not at all. Hey, let's go inside the Tate Modern now.

R Yes, of course. There's a great restaurant on the top floor. The view is fantastic. The Tate Modern was a power station until 1981. Did you know that?

J I didn't. Do you know anything else about the Tate Modern?

R Thank you for asking, I know a lot about it actually…

J Oh, great!

b Focus on the **Social English** phrases and go through them with the class.

In pairs, get Sts to decide who says them.

c ◗ **7.24** Play the video / audio for Sts to listen to the eight phrases and check.

Check answers. If you know your Sts' L1, you could get them to translate the phrases.

> **1** J **2** R **3** J **4** R **5** D **6** J **7** D **8** R

◗ 7.24

See Social English phrases in Student's Book on *p.61*

Now play the video / audio again, pausing after each phrase for Sts to watch or listen and repeat.

d Focus on the instructions and make sure Sts understand what they have to do.

Get Sts to compare with a partner, and then check answers.

> **A** 4 **B** 2 **C** 7 **D** 5 **E** 1 **F** 8 **G** 3 **H** 6

Now put Sts in pairs and get them to practise the conversations.

Finally, focus on the **CAN YOU…?** questions and ask Sts if they feel confident they can now do these things. If they feel that they need more practice, tell them to go to *Online Practice* to watch the episode again and practise the language.

G past simple: regular and irregular
V irregular verbs
P past simple verbs

Lesson plan

The aim of this lesson is to revise all forms of the past simple, regular and irregular, through the context of a murder story. The lesson begins with a description of the story, which introduces the characters and several new past forms of irregular verbs. A pronunciation focus then revises the pronunciation of irregular and regular past forms. Sts then hear more of the story, this time on audio, as part of a TV adaptation, when the inspector interviews the suspects. Sts decide who they think the murderer was before hearing what actually happened. This part of the lesson will work best if you can generate and maintain suspense, so that Sts want to find out who the murderer was. After the murder story, there is a grammar focus pulling together and revising the past simple. The lesson finishes with an extended Speaking activity where Sts role-play trying to break down the alibi of a robbery suspect.

More materials		
For teachers		
Photocopiables		
Grammar past simple: regular and irregular verbs *p.189*		
Communicative Past simple question time *p.236*		
(instructions *p.209*)		
For students		
Workbook 8A		
Online Practice 8A		

OPTIONAL LEAD-IN (BOOKS CLOSED)

Write DETECTIVE NOVELS AND TV SERIES on the board and elicit names from Sts.

Now ask Sts *What usually happens in these books or series?* (A murder), *How do the police or detectives find out who the murderer is?* (They question everyone and look for evidence.), etc.

Then get Sts, in pairs, to ask each other which of the novels or TV series they like.

Finally, tell Sts that they are going to read and listen to a murder mystery.

1 READING

a Books open. Focus on the photo of the house and ask Sts a few questions, e.g. *What is it? How old do you think it is? Where do you think it is?* and elicit ideas / suggestions. Elicit / Explain what a *country house* is.

Then focus on the task, explaining the meaning and pronunciation of *murder* /ˈmɜːdə/, *victim* /ˈvɪktɪm/, and *a suspect* /ˈsʌspekt/.

Focus on the photos of the victim and suspects, and give Sts a few minutes to read the information about the murder.

Focus on the speech bubbles and get Sts to cover the text and practise saying, in pairs, who everybody is in relation to Jeremy, e.g. *Who's Claudia?* (She's Jeremy's secretary). This will help Sts to remember who's who as they read / listen to the story, and also revises the use of the possessive *'s*.

EXTRA SUPPORT In their pairs, **A** covers the text and **B** looks at the text to help **A**. They then swap roles.

Ask a few comprehension questions, e.g. *On what day does the story take place?* (On 23rd June), *Who is the main character and murder victim?* (Jeremy Travers), *Why was 22nd June an important day for him?* (It was his birthday), *What did he do that night?* (He had dinner with his wife, his daughter, and two guests).

Ask Sts *Who do you think the murderer is?* and elicit ideas / suggestions.

b 🔊 **8.1** Now focus on the story, and tell Sts that they are going to read the story and listen to it at the same time.

Play the audio for Sts to read and listen. Then set a time limit and get Sts, in pairs, to re-read the story and mark sentences 1–7 *T* (true) or *F* (false). They must also correct the false ones.

Check answers, getting Sts to say why the *F* sentences are false.

EXTRA SUPPORT Before Sts read the story, check whether you need to pre-teach any vocabulary.

1 F (Somebody killed Jeremy between 11.45 p.m. and 8.00 a.m.)
2 F (The inspector questioned Amanda in the library.)
3 T
4 F (Amanda and Jeremy slept in different rooms.)
5 F (Somebody opened and closed Jeremy's door.)
6 F (Amanda got up at about 7.15.)
7 T

🔊 **8.1**
See story in Student's Book on *p.62*

Deal with any other new vocabulary, e.g. *moustache*, *library* (contrast it with *bookshop*), and *asleep*, but leave the new irregular verbs as Sts are about to focus on them. Model and drill the pronunciation of any tricky words.

2 PRONUNCIATION past simple verbs

a Focus Sts' attention on the instructions and on the highlighted irregular verbs in the story. Point out that the first three have been done for them.

In pairs, Sts write the infinitives – tell them that the context will help them to guess the ones they don't know.

b 🔊 **8.2** Play the audio for Sts to listen and check.

Check answers. Model and drill the pronunciation. Pay particular attention to *said* /sed/, which has an unexpected pronunciation, and *read* /red/, which is spelled but not pronounced like the infinitive.

🔊 **8.2**

1	be	was
2	be	were
3	come	came
4	say	said
5	speak	spoke
6	sit	sat
7	go	went
8	sleep	slept
9	see	saw
10	hear	heard
11	think	thought
12	read	read
13	get up	got up
14	have	had
15	take	took
16	find	found

Now play the audio again for Sts to listen and repeat.

c 🔊 **8.3** Remind Sts how regular past simple verbs end (*-ed*) – see **Pronunciation notes** in **7B** on *pp.96–97*. Get them to underline the nine regular past simple verbs in the story.

Play the audio for Sts to listen and check.

Check answers, getting Sts to say how they think the endings are pronounced.

> /d/ arrived, died, killed, followed, opened, closed
> /t/ looked, finished
> /ɪd/ hated

🔊 **8.3**

arrived	Inspector Granger arrived.
died	Mr Travers died.
killed	Somebody killed him.
looked	He looked at them.
followed	She followed him.
finished	We finished dinner.
opened	The door opened.
closed	The door closed.
hated	I hated him.

Tell Sts that the phrases they hear aren't exactly the same as the phrases in the story, so they must listen and repeat the phrases carefully. Now play the audio again for Sts to listen and repeat. Give Sts more practice if necessary.

 Get Sts to predict how the *-ed* is pronounced for each verb, /d/, /t/ or /ɪd/. Then play the audio for them to check.

3 LISTENING taking notes and comparing information

a 🔊 **8.4**, **8.5**, **8.6** Focus on the chart and elicit / explain the meaning of *motive*. Highlight that the names at the top are all the suspects in the murder mystery. Elicit from Sts that Amanda is Jeremy's wife, and point out to Sts that her answers to the inspector's questions have been written in the chart. Explain that Sts are now going to hear the inspector interview the other three suspects, Barbara, Gordon, and Claudia. Sts have to complete the chart.

Ask *Who's Barbara?* (Jeremy's daughter). Then play audio 🔊 **8.4** twice for Sts to complete the chart. Get Sts to compare their answers with a partner between each listening.

 Read through the scripts and decide if you need to pre-teach any new lexis before Sts listen.

🔊 **8.4**
(script in Student's Book on *pp.120–121*)

N = narrator, I = inspector, B = Barbara
N *Then the inspector questioned Barbara Travers.*
I What did you do after dinner yesterday evening?
B After dinner? I played cards with Gordon, and then I went to bed.
I What time was that?
B It was about half past eleven. I remember, I looked at my watch.
I Did you hear anything in your father's room?
B No. I didn't hear anything.
I Miss Travers, did you have any problems with your father?
B No, I didn't have any problems with him at all. Daddy was a wonderful man and…a wonderful father. I'm sorry, Inspector.
I Don't worry, Miss Travers. No more questions.

Ask *Who's Gordon?* (Jeremy's business partner). Then play audio 🔊 **8.5** twice for Sts to complete the chart. Again, get Sts to compare their answers with a partner between each listening.

🔊 **8.5**
(script in Student's Book on *p.121*)

N = narrator, I = inspector, G = Gordon
N *Next the inspector questioned Gordon Summers.*
I What did you do after dinner, Gordon?
G I played cards with Barbara. Then she went to bed.
I Did you go to bed then?
G No. I stayed in the living room and I had a glass of whisky. Then I went to bed.
I What time was that?
G I don't remember exactly. I didn't look at the time.
I Did you hear anything during the night?
G No, I didn't. I was very tired. I slept very well.
I You and Mr Travers were business partners, weren't you?
G Yes, that's right.
I And it's a very good business, I understand.
G Yes, Inspector, it is.
I And now it's your business.
G Listen, Inspector, I did not kill Jeremy. He was my partner and he was my friend.

Ask *Who's Claudia?* (Jeremy's secretary). Then play audio 🔊 **8.6** twice for Sts to complete the chart. Get Sts to compare their answers with a partner between each listening.

◁))) **8.6**
(script in Student's Book on *p.121*)

N = narrator, I = inspector, C = Claudia
N *Finally, the inspector questioned Claudia Pasquale.*
I What did you do yesterday evening, after dinner?
C I went to my room and I had a bath and I went to bed.
I What time was that?
C About eleven o'clock.
I Did you hear anything?
C Yes. I heard somebody go into Jeremy's room. It was about twelve o'clock.
I Who was it?
C It was Amanda, his wife.
I Are you sure? Did you see her?
C Well no, I didn't see her. But I'm sure it was Amanda.
I You were Mr Travers's secretary, Claudia.
C Yes, I was.
I Were you just his secretary?
C What do you mean?
I Were you in love with Mr Travers?
C No, I wasn't.
I The truth, please, Claudia.
C Very well, Inspector. Yes, I was in love with him and he said he was in love with me. He said he wanted to leave his wife – Amanda – and marry me. I was stupid. I believed him. But he didn't leave her. He used me, Inspector! I was very angry with him.
I Did you kill him?
C No, Inspector, I *loved* Jeremy.

b Now get Sts to compare charts in pairs.

Check answers. You could copy these onto the board.

Barbara
She played cards with Gordon.
11.30.
No.
No motive – she loved him.

Gordon
He played cards with Barbara. Then he stayed in the living room and had a glass of whisky.
He doesn't remember.
No.
He wanted the business for himself.

Claudia
She went to her room and had a bath.
About 11.00.
She heard somebody go into Jeremy's room at about 12.00. She thinks it was Amanda, but she didn't see her.
She was in love with Jeremy, but Jeremy didn't leave his wife, Amanda.

Tell Sts to look at their completed charts again and, in pairs, decide who they think the murderer is (they don't have to agree).

Write the names of the four suspects on the board, and get a show of hands for each suspect. Elicit a few reasons for each suspect.

c ◁))) **8.7** Play the audio for Sts to see if they were right. Pause the audio after Amanda says *Dinner everybody*, and ask comprehension questions, e.g. *What happened before dinner? What did Gordon tell Jeremy?*, etc., to make sure Sts are following the story.

Now play the last part. Repeat it from the beginning if Sts want to hear it again.

Elicit who the murderer is and why he / she killed Mr Travers.

The murderer was Gordon. He killed Jeremy because he wanted to marry Barbara. He says he was in love with her, but he probably wanted to marry her because her father was rich. Jeremy said that he couldn't. He said, 'If you marry Barbara, all my money goes to Claudia.'

◁))) **8.7**

N = narrator, I = inspector, J = Jeremy, A = Amanda
N *Before dinner, Gordon had a drink with Jeremy in the library.*
G Cheers, Jeremy. Happy Birthday.
J Ah, thanks, Gordon.
G Listen, Jeremy, I want to talk to you about Barbara.
J Barbara? What's the problem?
G It's not exactly a problem. I'm in love with her, and I want to marry her.
J Marry Barbara? Marry my daughter! Are you crazy? Never! You don't love Barbara. You only want her money!
G That's not true, Jeremy. I love her.
J Listen to me. If you marry Barbara, when I die all my money goes to Claudia.
G To Claudia? To your secretary?
J Yes.
G Is that your last word, Jeremy?
J Yes, it is.
A Dinner, everybody!
N *At midnight, Gordon was in the living room. He finished his whisky and went upstairs.*
J Who is it? Gordon? What are you...

EXTRA SUPPORT Finally, you could play the three interviews again and get Sts to listen and read the scripts on *pp.120–121*, so they can see exactly what they understood / didn't understand. Translate / Explain any new words or phrases.

4 GRAMMAR & VOCABULARY
past simple: regular and irregular

a Tell Sts to cover the story and look at the eight verbs in the list. They must first mark the verbs *regular* or *irregular* in the past simple, and then write the positive and negative form. Point out that the first one (*arrived, didn't arrive*) has been done for them.

regular	arrive, close, hate, kill
irregular	come, sit, sleep, speak

b ◗ **8.8** Play the audio for Sts to listen and check. Check answers.

◗ **8.8**

arrive	arrived	didn't arrive
close	closed	didn't close
come	came	didn't come
hate	hated	didn't hate
kill	killed	didn't kill
sit	sat	didn't sit
sleep	slept	didn't sleep
speak	spoke	didn't speak

c Tell Sts to go to **Grammar Bank 8A** on *p.138*.

Grammar notes

This **Grammar Bank** reference section is purely revision, and reminds Sts how to form the past tense with regular and irregular verbs using the auxiliaries *did / didn't*.

It also reminds Sts that *was / were* is the past of *be* and that questions are formed by inverting the subject and verb, and negatives are made by adding *not*, e.g. *wasn't*.

◗ **8.9** Focus on the example sentences and play the audio for Sts to listen and repeat. Then go through the rules with the class.

Now focus on the exercises for **8A** on *p.139*. Sts do the exercises individually or in pairs.

Check answers, getting Sts to read the full sentences.

a
1 was **2** were **3** were…doing **4** watched **5** had
6 weren't **7** went **8** did…go **9** Did…hear **10** didn't hear
b
1 slept **2** heard **3** couldn't **4** read **5** arrived **6** saw
7 sat **8** didn't want

Tell Sts to go back to the main lesson **8A**.

d Now tell Sts to go to **Irregular verbs** on *p.165*. Tell Sts that this is their reference list of irregular verbs. Explain that there are three columns, because irregular verbs also have irregular past participles, but that for the moment, they should just concentrate on the first two columns.

You could go through them one by one, eliciting / teaching the meaning of any new ones, and getting Sts to tick the ones they already know. Tell them to choose three new verbs to learn, and tell them they should try to learn at least three more new ones every week.

Tell Sts to go back to the main lesson **8A**.

5 SPEAKING

Put Sts into groups of four, and then into pairs. Assign two the role of **A** (police officers) and two the role of **B** (friends / suspects). If you have odd numbers, have extra **A**s (i.e. three police officers and two suspects).

Tell Sts to go to **Communication Police interview**, **A** on *p.106*, **B** on *p.111*.

Go through the instructions with Sts carefully. Then give at least five minutes for Sts **A** to look at the police interview form and prepare their questions. Tell them to think of more questions. At the same time, Sts **B** prepare their alibis by working out where they were the previous night.

When they are ready, re-divide the groups of four so that each **A** is with a different **B**. If possible, tell Sts **A** to take their suspects to different ends of the classroom to be interviewed. (It doesn't matter if they are near other police officers / suspects, they should just not be near their own 'partner'.)

Allow at least five minutes for the interviews, making sure the police officers take notes.

When the interviews are over, get the police officers (Sts **A**) to compare the two friends' (Sts **B**) alibis. If they are identical, Sts **B** are innocent. If there are any differences, they are guilty.

Find out, with a show of hands, how many 'suspects' were found guilty.

G *there is / there are, some / any* + plural nouns
V the house: *living room, sofa,* etc.
P /eə/ and /ɪə/

Lesson plan

This lesson links back to the murder story in **8A**. Many years later, an American couple who are looking for a house to rent are shown around Jeremy Travers's house by Barbara, his daughter, who is now quite elderly. It is only after they have decided to rent it that they discover the house has a dark secret: someone was murdered there. The lesson begins with a vocabulary focus on house and furniture lexis. Sts then listen to a conversation between Barbara and the young American couple as she shows them around the Travers family's old house, now for rent. Sts then hear how Kim is reluctant to rent the house, but she is talked into it by her husband, and finally how when they go to celebrate at the local pub, they hear the true story of the house. Sts then focus on the grammar in the conversations, and the use of *there is* and *there are*. The pronunciation focus is on /eə/ and /ɪə/, which prepares Sts for a Speaking activity in which Sts describe where they live. Finally, they go to the Writing section and write a description of their house or flat.

More materials
For teachers
Photocopiables
Grammar there is / there are, some / any + plural nouns *p.190*
Vocabulary Race around the house *p.271* (instructions *p.255*)
Communicative A place to rent *p.237* (instructions *p.210*)
For students
Workbook 8A
Online Practice 8A

OPTIONAL LEAD-IN (BOOKS CLOSED)

Write on the board:

IMAGINE THAT YOU WANT TO RENT A FLAT IN (Sts' city).

WHAT THINGS ARE IMPORTANT TO YOU? (e.g. location, rent, etc.)

HOW WOULD YOU LOOK FOR THE FLAT?

Put Sts in pairs to discuss the questions.

1 VOCABULARY the house

a Books open. Focus on the advertisement and elicit the meaning of *advertisement, to rent,* and *low price*. Model and drill the pronunciation of *advertisement* /əd'vɜːtɪsmənt/.

! You could elicit / tell Sts that the house is the same house as in **8A** (but more than 50 years later). Alternatively, you could say nothing, and wait for Sts to realize as the lesson develops.

Then focus on the questions and elicit responses.

Get ideas / feedback from a few Sts.

b Get Sts to cover the advertisement, and elicit what they can remember about the house.

Possible answer
It's in the country. It's very quiet. It has six bedrooms, four bathrooms, and a large garden. It's five miles from Oxford. It isn't expensive.

c Focus on the instructions and give Sts a few minutes to brainstorm with a partner.

Write all the words on the board and drill pronunciation.

d Tell Sts to go to **Vocabulary Bank The house** on *p.161*, and get them to do **1 Rooms**, **2 Parts of a house**, and **3 Things in a room** individually or in pairs.

Vocabulary notes
Highlight that:
- *a wardrobe* is in a bedroom and for keeping clothes, but *a cupboard* can be anywhere e.g. in kitchen or a living room, and you can keep anything in it.
- we us *a light* to refer to a ceiling light, and *lamp* for all other types, e.g. *a floor lamp, a table lamp*.

8.10 Now do **b**. Play the audio for Sts to listen to all three sections and check. Check answers.

8.10

The house

1 Rooms
4 a bathroom
2 a bedroom
9 a dining room
6 a garage
7 a garden
8 a hall
10 a kitchen
3 a living room
5 a study
1 a toilet

2 Parts of a house
12 a balcony
11 a ceiling
15 a floor
14 stairs
13 a wall

3 Things in a room
23 an armchair
25 a bath
19 a bed
27 a carpet
32 a cooker
30 a cupboard
33 a dishwasher
22 a fireplace
28 a fridge
18 a light
29 a microwave
21 a mirror
16 a plant
26 a shelf
24 a shower
20 a sofa
17 a wardrobe
31 a washing machine

Then either use the audio to drill the pronunciation of the words, or model and drill them yourself. Give further practice of any words Sts find difficult to pronounce.

Now focus on the **Central heating and air conditioning** box and go through it with the class.

In **Activation**, get Sts to cover the words and use the pictures to test themselves or a partner.

Tell Sts to go back to the main lesson **8B**.

 If you think Sts need more practice, you may want to give them the **Vocabulary** photocopiable activity at this point.

2 LISTENING using evidence to predict outcome

a ◉ **8.11** Focus on the photo and instructions. Elicit that the older woman is showing the young couple the house because they are thinking of renting it.

Now tell Sts to close their books or to cover the conversation and listen for the answer to *Which three rooms in the house do they go into?*. Stress that Sts should listen to find out which rooms they actually go into, not which ones they mention.

Play the audio once, and check answers.

 Read through the scripts and decide if you need to pre-teach any new lexis before Sts listen.

They go into the living room, the library, and the kitchen.

◉ **8.11**

K = Kim, L = Leo, B = Barbara
K   The garden's wonderful. I love it.
L   Is there a garage?
B   Oh yes, there's a big garage over there.
K   You lived in this house, is that right, Mrs…?
B   Miss Travers. But call me Barbara, dear. Yes, I lived here. A long time ago. Now I live in the village. Let's go inside the house… This is the living room. It's a lovely room – very light. And this is the library…
L   Wow! There's a library, Kim!
K   I love the furniture, the old sofa, the armchairs, the fireplace…
B   And this is the kitchen. It's very big, as you can see.
K   Is there a dishwasher?
B   No, there isn't. It's an old house, you see.
L   Never mind. I think it's lovely. Is there a bathroom downstairs?
B   Yes, there's one downstairs and there are three upstairs.
K   Are there any neighbours with children?
B   No, there aren't any neighbours near here. But there are some families with children in the village.
K   That's great. We have two children.
B   Very nice, dear. Now let's go upstairs…

Highlight that Leo pronounces *garage* in the American way /ɡəˈrɑːʒ/, whereas Barbara uses British pronunciation /ˈɡærɑːʒ/.

b Tell Sts to open their books or uncover the conversation, and focus on the gapped conversation. Point out that the first one (*garage*) has been done for them. Play the audio again for Sts to complete the gaps. Play again if necessary.

 You could give Sts time to read through the conversation and think about what the missing words could be before you play the audio.

Get Sts to compare with a partner, and then check answers.

2 living room **3** fireplace **4** kitchen **5** bathroom
6 downstairs **7** neighbours **8** upstairs

Go through the conversation, making sure Sts understand it. They should be able to understand the examples of *there is / are* from the context. Tell Sts that this structure will be focused on in **Grammar**. Elicit / Teach the meaning and pronunciation of *furniture* /ˈfɜːnɪtʃə/, and point out that it is singular, but has a plural meaning.

c ◉ **8.12** Tell Sts that Barbara and the Americans now go upstairs. Focus on the questions. Then play the audio twice.

Get Sts to compare with a partner, and then check answers.

She says the bedroom is cold.
It was Barbara's father's bedroom (Jeremy Travers).
Yes, they do.

◉ **8.12**
(script in Student's Book on *p.121*)
B   Let's go upstairs. Follow me…Be careful. The ceiling is very low here.
L   It's a very old house.
B   Yes, the house is three hundred years old. My family lived here for nearly
    eighty years. There are six bedrooms. This was my father's bedroom.
K   Is there central heating in the house?
B   Yes, there is. Why do you ask? Are you cold?
K   Yes, it's very cold in here.
L   That's because we're from California.
B   Let's go and see the other bedrooms.
L   Yes, of course.
***
L   Well, what do you think, Kim? I love it! Don't you?
K   I'm not sure. There's something about the house I don't like.
L   Kim, it's perfect for the kids. Think of the garden. And it's a real, authentic English country house. What do you say?
K   I suppose so. If you're sure.
L   I am sure! Miss…er, Barbara. We want it. We want to rent the house.
B   Excellent.
L   When can we move in?
B   As soon as you like.

Ask a few more comprehension questions, e.g. *How old is the house?* (300 years old), *What kind of heating is there?* (central heating), etc.

Finally, ask Sts if Kim and Leo decide to rent the house.

Yes, they do

d ◉ **8.13** Focus on the photo and ask *Where are Kim and Leo?* (In a pub, near the house they just rented). Go through the instructions and make sure Sts understand this is not a conversation, but extracts from a conversation.

Play the audio for Sts to listen and complete the gaps.

Get Sts to compare with a partner, and then check answers. Play the audio again if necessary. You could tell Sts that *cheers* is a word people say to each other as they lift up their glasses to drink.

1 house **2** wrong **3** thought **4** tell **5** what **6** horrible

🔊 8.13

1 Kim   Cheers. To our new house.
2 Leo   Is something wrong?
3 Barman   Some people thought that she was the one that did it.
4 Barman   Didn't she tell you?
5 Kim   Tell us what?
6 Kim   Oh, how horrible!

Focus on the question *What do you think they find out?* and elicit ideas from Sts, but <u>don't</u> tell them if they're right yet.

e 🔊 **8.14** Focus on the task and make sure Sts understand the question.

Play the audio at least twice for Sts to listen and answer the questions.

Get Sts to compare with a partner, and then check answers. Play the audio again if necessary.

They decide not to rent the house. They don't want to live in a house where somebody was murdered.

🔊 8.14

(script in Student's Book on *p.121*)

L = Leo, K = Kim, B = barman

L   Hello.
B   Good evening, sir, madam. What would you like to drink?
L   Do you have champagne?
B   Yes, sir.
L   Two glasses of champagne, please.
B   Here you are!
L   Cheers, Kim.
K   Cheers. To our new house.
B   You're Americans, aren't you?
L   Yes, that's right. We're from California.
K   But this afternoon we rented the big house near here.
B   Which house? The Travers family's house?
L   Yes.
B   Oh.
L   Is something wrong?
B   Who showed you the house?
K   Barbara. The old lady who lived there before.
B   Ah, Barbara. Old Mr Travers's daughter. Some people thought that she was the one that did it.
K   The one that did what? What happened?
B   Didn't she tell you?
L   Tell us what?
B   About the murder.
L & K   Murder?
B   Yes, Mr Travers was murdered in that house in 1965…in his bed.
K   Oh, how horrible!
B   The man who killed Mr Travers was Barbara's lover. The family never lived there again. They tried to sell the house, but nobody wanted to buy it. Not after a murder. That's why that house is always rented. Barbara never married, of course.
L   Kim?
K   Yes?
L   Are you thinking what I'm thinking?
K   Yes – I don't want to live in a house where somebody was murdered. Come on. Let's go.
B   Hey, hey, your champagne! You didn't drink your champagne… Ah, well…

Ask a few more comprehension questions, e.g. *Where are Kim and Leo from?* (California), *Why do the Travers family always rent out the house?* (Because nobody wants to buy it), *Does Kim finish her champagne?* (No).

Finally, ask Sts if they would rent a house where somebody was murdered.

3 GRAMMAR *there is / there are, some / any* + plural nouns

a Put Sts into groups of three and get them to practise the conversation in **2b**.

When they have finished, tell them to focus on the chart and complete it.

Check answers.

singular	plural
➕ There's a library.	There **are** some families…
➖ There **isn't** a dishwasher.	There aren't any neighbours.
❓ **Is there** a garage?	**Are there** any neighbours?

b Give Sts a moment to look at the question and discuss it in pairs.

Check answers.

Three is a specific number. *Some* means 'more than one', but isn't a specific number.

c Tell Sts to go to **Grammar Bank 8B** on *p.138*.

Grammar notes

there is / there are

Some Sts tend to always use *there is* for both singular and plural nouns because in their language there is only one form. They may also confuse *There is / are* and *It is / They are*.

some and *any*

Some and *any* are indefinite articles used here with plural countable nouns. For simplicity's sake, *some* is taught here as only being used in positive sentences, however (as will later be pointed out in **Grammar Bank 9A**), it can also be used in questions, and especially in requests, e.g. *Do you want some biscuits? Can we have some more chairs?*

Some and *any* with uncountable nouns is presented in **9A**.

🔊 **8.15** Focus on the example sentences and play the audio for Sts to listen and repeat. Then go through the rules with the class.

Focus on the **There is / There are** or **It is / They are?** box and go through it with the class.

Now focus on the exercises for **8B** on *p.139*. Sts do the exercises individually or in pairs.

Check answers, getting Sts to read the full sentences.

a

1 Are there **2** Is there **3** There are **4** There's **5** There are
6 Is there **7** There are **8** Is there **9** There's **10** Are there

b

1 There's a table in the kitchen.
2 Is there a fireplace in the living room?
3 There aren't any plants in my flat.
4 Are there any people in the garden?
5 There are some pictures in my bedroom.
6 There isn't a TV in the kitchen.
7 There's a computer in the study.
8 There aren't any cupboards in the dining room.
9 Is there a bath in the bathroom?
10 There isn't a light in the garage.

Tell Sts to go back to the main lesson **8B**.

 If you think Sts need more practice, you may want to give them the **Grammar** photocopiable activity at this point.

d Put Sts in pairs, **A** and **B**, and tell them to go to **Communication** *Is there…? Are there…?*, **A** on *p.106*, **B** on *p.111*.

Go through the instructions with them carefully, and focus on the two questions (*Is there a…?* and *Are there any…?*). Tell Sts they have to ask these questions for items 1–6. Point out the four possible answers, and tell Sts to give as much information as they can when answering.

Sit **A** and **B** face-to-face if possible. **A** asks his / her questions to **B**. Then they swap roles.

Get feedback from various pairs.

Tell Sts to go back to the main lesson **8B**.

4 PRONUNCIATION /eə/ and /ɪə/

a ◀)) **8.16** Focus on the two sound pictures chair /eə/ and ear /ɪə/.

Play the audio for Sts just to listen to the two sounds and example words.

◀)) **8.16**
See words and sounds in Student's Book on *p.65*

Now play the audio again for Sts to listen and repeat.

b Get Sts to look at the words in the list and to decide which sound they go with in the chart in **a**. Remind Sts to say the words aloud to themselves and then write them in the correct row.

c ◀)) **8.17** Play the audio for Sts to listen and check.
Check answers.

◀)) **8.17**
chair /eə/ there, careful, wear, they're, stairs, where
ear /ɪə/   here, beer, dear, near, we're, hear

Now play the audio again, pausing after each word for Sts to listen and repeat.

Ask Sts which three pairs of words are pronounced exactly the same.

there they're
here hear
wear where

 If these sounds are difficult for your Sts, it will help to show them the mouth position. You could model this yourself or use the Sound Bank videos on the *Teacher's Resource Centre*.

d ◀)) **8.18** Tell Sts they are going to hear six sentences or questions and they need to write them.

Play the audio, pausing after each one to give Sts time to write it down.

Check answers.

◀)) **8.18**
1 Here you are.
2 I can't hear you.
3 Where's the kitchen?
4 She always wears trousers.
5 Is there a washing machine?
6 They're from America.

5 SPEAKING

a Tell Sts that they are going to do a role-play between someone who wants to rent a house or flat and the person who owns it.

Put Sts into pairs, **A** and **B**. Tell Sts **A** they want to rent a place and must ask Sts **B** the questions in the book. Tell Sts **B** to imagine they want to rent out the house or flat that they live in to Sts **A**, and must answer **A**'s questions.

Now get Sts to interview each other. Monitor and help.

Make sure they swap roles.

b Focus on the instructions. To demonstrate, quickly sketch a basic plan of your living room on the board, and describe it to the class (you don't need to draw everything, just the main pieces of furniture).

Sts do the same in pairs. Monitor and help Sts with any other vocabulary they need.

6 **WRITING** describing your home

Tell Sts to go to **Writing Describing your home** on *p.116*.

a Focus on the task. Give Sts a few minutes to read the website.

Ask the class *Would you like to stay in the flat in Budapest? Why (not)?* and elicit some answers.

b Now tell Sts to read the description of the flat again and number the information in the correct order.

Check answers, making sure Sts understand all the lexis.

> **1** Where it is
> **2** What floor the flat is on
> **3** What rooms there are
> **4** Details about some of the rooms
> **5** What you can see from the flat
> **6** What places or services there are nearby
> **7** How far it is from the city centre

c Now tell Sts to look for the adjectives the writer used to describe 1–4.

Check answers.

> **1** quiet   **2** light, pretty, small   **3** great   **4** beautiful

d Focus on the information box about *so* and go through it with the class.

Tell Sts they are now going to advertise their house or flat on the website. First, they should make notes about their house / flat using the seven topics in **b**.

e When Sts have finished their notes, get them to write the full description.

f Sts read their descriptions, looking for mistakes, and then show it to another student.

Get some feedback from various pairs. Did they find anything that was the same in their descriptions?

8C Room 333

Lesson plan

This lesson is based on real information about a hotel in London that is said to be haunted. A BBC journalist stayed there and reported on what happened during the night, as did members of the England cricket team. An article about the hotel provides a context for Sts to practise *there was / there were* and prepositions of place and movement. The lesson begins with Sts reading the article and listening to two guests describing their experiences of staying in room 333, where the ghosts are said to appear – this provides the context for the grammar presentation of *there was / there were*. It then leads into a vocabulary focus on more prepositions of place and movement (Sts have already focused on simple ones, e.g. *in, on, under*, and *to*). Pronunciation focuses on silent letters in words like *ghost* and *guest*. Then Sts do a Speaking activity in which the Grammar and Vocabulary are practised. The lesson finishes with a video listening about Portchester Castle.

More materials
For teachers
Photocopiables
Grammar there was / there were p.191
Vocabulary Prepositions of place p.272
(instructions p.256)
Communicative What's different? p.239
(instructions p.210)
Teacher's Resource Centre
Video A haunted castle
For students
Workbook 8C
Online Practice 8C

OPTIONAL LEAD-IN (BOOKS CLOSED)

Play the *Long sentence* game to revise *there is* and furniture. You begin the game. Say *In my living room there's a sofa*. Then choose a student to continue. He / She must repeat your sentence, and add one more piece of furniture, e.g. *In my living room there's a sofa and two armchairs*.
Now point to another student, who must continue, repeating the sentence and adding to it, e.g. *In my living room there's a sofa, two armchairs, and a table*.
After all the Sts have added their words, see if the whole class can repeat the list from memory.

1 READING & LISTENING identifying paragraph topics

a Books open. Focus on the task, making sure Sts know the meaning of *ghost* (= the form of a dead person that a living person thinks he / she sees) and *haunted* (= if a place is haunted, people think there are ghosts there). Elicit answers. You could start the activity by telling Sts whether or not you believe in ghosts.

b Focus on the photos and tell Sts that this is a real hotel in London.
Now focus on the instructions, and give Sts time to read the article.

EXTRA CHALLENGE Put Sts in pairs and get them to discuss what each of the three paragraphs is about. Elicit answers.

Paragraph 1 is about the history of the hotel and famous people who stayed there.
Paragraph 2 is about the hotel's ghosts, and a journalist who saw them.
Paragraph 3 is about the experiences of the English cricket team when they stayed at the hotel.

Put Sts in pairs and get them to answer questions 1–5. Check answers.

EXTRA SUPPORT Before Sts read the article, check whether you need to pre-teach any vocabulary.

1 The Duke of Windsor, Napoleon III, Oscar Wilde, Arthur Conan Doyle
2 *GoldenEye*
3 The ghost of a Victorian doctor who murdered his wife
4 A ghost moves the bed.
5 He was in the hotel and couldn't sleep because the bathroom taps turned on and off.

c 🔊 8.19 Focus on the question and make sure Sts know the meaning of *guest*. Model and drill pronunciation.
Before you play the audio, you might want to tell Sts that the hotel stories that they are going to hear are based on real TripAdvisor reports.
Play the audio for Sts to listen and answer the question. Check the answer.

EXTRA SUPPORT Read through the script and decide if you need to pre-teach any new lexis before Sts listen.

No, but they both heard strange noises.

8.19

(script in Student's Book on *p.121*)

1 We stayed at The Langham for two nights. It's a wonderful place – a very elegant, very English hotel. The service, atmosphere, and room were excellent, and we really enjoyed our stay. But we had a very strange experience. On the first night we woke up at about five thirty. There was a strange noise coming from outside our door. It was like somebody was scratching the door with their fingers. To tell you the truth, we were a little bit frightened. Then we thought that probably it was other guests coming back late from a party, maybe they were drunk or something, and we went back to sleep. But the second night exactly the same thing happened. So we just thought, strange, maybe it's because it's an old hotel. But when we got home, we told the story to a friend, and he told us that The Langham is haunted. We looked on the internet, and we read that people say that room 333 has a ghost! And our room was 332, the next room! We sent an email to The Langham and told them about it and they sent us some really interesting information about the ghost stories. We'd really like to stay in this fantastic hotel again, but maybe not in room 333!

2 I stayed at The Langham in November last year with my husband. It's a beautiful hotel, with a wonderful location. It's between Hyde Park and Regent's Park. We were in a room on the second floor. We knew that people said there were ghosts, and we knew about room 333, but we weren't worried at all. We had a nice meal in the hotel restaurant and then we went to bed. But in the middle of the night – about three in the morning – we suddenly woke up and we could hear loud noises from the room above us. They were really loud noises – like people were moving the bed or moving a heavy chair. Anyway, after two or three minutes, the noises stopped and we went back to sleep. There weren't any more strange noises, and we slept for the rest of the night. The next morning, we went to Reception and said, 'We slept really badly last night – the people in the room above us made a terrible noise.' The man at reception asked for our room number and said, 'Let me check.' He looked on the computer and he said, 'The room above you is empty, madam.' So I said, 'Are you sure?' And he said, 'Yes, madam. The room above yours is room 333. There wasn't anybody in that room last night.' We checked out of the hotel the same morning. Never again!

d Focus on the task. Give Sts time to read 1–8, and make sure they understand all the vocabulary.

Play the audio again for Sts to listen and complete the task.

Check answers (M = The man, W = The woman).

1 W	2 M / W	3 M / W	4 M	5 W	6 M	7 W	8 W

e Focus on the task and give Sts time to complete the verb phrases.

 Before Sts complete the gaps, elicit the infinitive of the five verbs, e.g. *got – get*. Now tell Sts, in pairs, to read the article again and complete the gaps. When they find one of the verb phrases, they should discuss its meaning.

 Get Sts to complete the gaps without looking at the article. Then put Sts in pairs and get them to compare answers and discuss what each verb phrase means.

Check answers, getting Sts to explain each verb phrase.

1	got **up**	got out of bed
2	turned **on / off**	opened / connected
3	woke **up**	opened your eyes after sleeping
4	went **back**	returned, do sth again
5	checked **out**	paid your bill and left

Deal with any other new vocabulary. Model and drill the pronunciation of any tricky words.

 If there's time, you could get Sts to listen again with the script on *p.121*, so they can see exactly what they understood / didn't understand. Translate / Explain any new words or phrases.

f Do this as a whole-class activity. You could tell the class whether you would like to stay there.

2 GRAMMAR *there was / there were*

a 8.20 Focus on the four sentences and get Sts to complete them.

Play the audio for Sts to listen and check.

Check answers.

1	was
2	weren't
3	were
4	wasn't

8.20

1 There was a strange noise outside our door.
2 There weren't any more strange noises.
3 We knew that people said there were ghosts.
4 There wasn't anybody in that room last night.

b Tell Sts to go to **Grammar Bank 8C** on *p.138*.

Grammar notes

There is / are can be used in any tense simply by changing the form of *be*, thus the past is *there was / were*.

Although it works in exactly the same way as *there is / are*, Sts have a tendency to forget the plural form *there were*.

8.21 Focus on the example sentences and play the audio for Sts to listen and repeat. Then go through the rules.

Now focus on the exercises for **8C** on *p.139*. Sts do the exercises individually or in pairs.

Check answers, getting Sts to read the full sentences.

a
1 There were   2 There was   3 there were   4 Was there
5 there wasn't   6 there was   7 Was there   8 there was
9 there weren't   10 were there
b
1 there was a   2 there wasn't a   3 there were some
4 there weren't any   5 there weren't any   6 there was a
7 there wasn't a

Tell Sts to go back to the main lesson **8C**.

 If you think Sts need more practice, you may want to give them the **Grammar** photocopiable activity at this point.

3 VOCABULARY prepositions: place and movement

a Get Sts to complete the two sentences with prepositions. Check answers.

> **1** in **2** through

 Demonstrate the meaning of the prepositions using, e.g. a chair in the classroom.

b Tell Sts to go to **Vocabulary Bank** Prepositions on *p.162*.

Vocabulary notes

Highlight the difference between *in* (= inside an enclosed space, e.g. *in a drawer*) and *on* (= touching an external surface, e.g. *on the wall*), and between *opposite* (= face-to-face) and *in front of* demonstrating with objects / people in the classroom.

Focus on **1 Place** and get Sts to do **a** individually or in pairs.

◖◗ **8.22** Now do **b**. Play the audio for Sts to listen and check. Check answers.

◖◗ **8.22**

Prepositions, 1 Place

2 in **5** in front of **9** on **3** under **1** behind **7** between
8 opposite **6** next to **4** over

Then either use the audio to drill the pronunciation of the prepositions, or model and drill them yourself.

EXTRA IDEA Give more practice with the prepositions by asking questions about things / people in the classroom.

Now focus on the example in **Activation**. Sts cover the prepositions and test each other in pairs by pointing to pictures and asking *Where's the ghost?*.

Go through the ***above*** and ***below*** box with the class.

Focus on **2 Movement** and get Sts to do **a** individually.

Vocabulary notes

Highlight that with *into* and *out of* if we use them without a place, we just use *in* and *out*, e.g. *Come in. Come into the garden. Go out. Go out of the room.*

◖◗ **8.23** Now do **b**. Play the audio for Sts to listen and check. Check answers.

◖◗ **8.23**

2 Movement

11 from…to **10** into **14** out of **15** through
12 up **13** down

Then either use the audio to drill the pronunciation of the prepositions, or model and drill them yourself.

Now focus on the example in **Activation**. Sts cover the prepositions and test each other in pairs by pointing to pictures and asking *Where's the ghost going?*.

Tell Sts to go back to the main lesson **8C**.

EXTRA SUPPORT If you think Sts need more practice, you may want to give them the **Vocabulary** photocopiable activity at this point.

4 PRONUNCIATION silent letters

Pronunciation notes

Encourage and help Sts to cross out silent letters when they learn new words, like this: *listen*.

Emphasize that if Sts can recognize the phonetic transcriptions next to words in the dictionary, this will help them to identify silent letters.

a ◖◗ **8.24** Go through the **Silent letters** box, and elicit the pronunciation of *ghost*, so Sts can hear the *h* isn't pronounced. Point out the phonetics also make this clear.

Get Sts to say the words aloud to themselves to help them decide which they think is the silent letter in each word, and then cross it out. Meanwhile write the words on the board to help check answers.

Play the audio for Sts to listen and check.

Check answers by eliciting which letter is silent and crossing it out (the silent letters are in red below).

◖◗ **8.24**

coul**d** cu**p**board fri**e**nd **g**uest hal**f** **h**our is**l**and **k**now
lis**t**en tal**k** w**h**at **w**rite

Highlight that in words that begin with *kn-* (e.g. *knee*) or *wr-* (e.g. *wrong*), the *k* and the *w* are always silent.

EXTRA IDEA If Sts have dictionaries, you could get them to check their answers with the phonetics in their dictionary. This will help build their confidence in dictionary use.

b Get Sts to practise saying the words.

5 SPEAKING

Put Sts in pairs, **A** and **B**, and tell them to go to **Communication** Room 333, **A** on *p.106*, **B** on *p.111*.

Give Sts one minute to look at the photo. Then focus on the questions, and elicit that they start with *Was there…?* for singular nouns and *Were there…?* for plural nouns.

EXTRA SUPPORT You could get Sts to write the questions.

Get Sts to sit face-to-face if possible. **A** (book open) asks his / her questions to **B** (book closed), who has to answer.

Then they swap roles.

Get feedback. Who had the most correct answers, **A** or **B**?

Tell Sts to go back to the main lesson **8C**.

6 ▶ VIDEO LISTENING

a Tell Sts they are going to watch a documentary about Portchester Castle and its ghosts. Portchester Castle is on the south coast of England, near Portsmouth.

Focus on the question and play the video for Sts to watch.

Get Sts to compare with a partner, and then check the answer.

EXTRA SUPPORT Read through the script and decide if you need to pre-teach any new lexis before Sts watch.

Two of the four ghosts are frightening.

A haunted castle

Hi, I'm Ned. Welcome to Portchester Castle. Portchester Castle is over one thousand seven hundred years old. It's near Portsmouth, a city on the south coast of England. The castle is part of English Heritage. English Heritage is a charity, which manages over four hundred old buildings and monuments in England.

With so many old buildings, there are also lots of reports of ghosts. And ghosts are sometimes a problem for staff and visitors at English Heritage. In fact, some staff decided to leave their jobs because of the ghosts. I've come here to Portchester to find out more about reports of not one, but four ghosts! And many of the ghosts come from different times in Portchester's long history. Portchester Castle dates back to Roman Britain; the Romans built the original castle here in the year two hundred and ninety. The first ghost report also comes from Roman times. Visitors report that they see the ghost of a Roman soldier guarding the walls, but they say they don't feel frightened.

In the Middle Ages, Portchester became a favourite castle for the kings and queens of England. During this time, a small monastery was built. There's a church here now in place of the monastery. People say that they see a man dressed in black here and they think he is the ghost of a monk from the monastery. Surprisingly, people don't feel frightened when they see him. They say that he disappears when they look at him. Our first two ghosts are not frightening, but the next ghost really frightens people – the White Lady. Some people believe that this is the ghost of Charlotte White. She was a woman who visited the castle in the nineteenth century. Charlotte's baby fell into the water and poor Charlotte also died when she tried to save her child.

The most frightening ghost of all is a man on a black horse. Both castle visitors and staff say that they see him. One of the staff who saw the ghost said, 'It got bigger and bigger. It started to come towards me and I screamed and ran away'. People also say they hear the sound of horses; one visitor even heard the sound of horses on a video he filmed. One of the strange things about the man on the horse is that we don't know who he is or which part of Portchester's long history he is from.

I was quite sure I didn't believe in ghosts before I came here, but, after a day at Portchester, I'm not so sure.

EXTRA IDEA Ask Sts if they noticed anything strange on the video (there is interference before the presenter goes into the castle, and a hooded figure, perhaps the ghost of the monk, appears four times).

b Focus on the task. Go through 1–8 with Sts, making sure they understand all the lexis, e.g. *charity*, etc.

Now play the video again.

Get Sts to compare with a partner, and then check answers.

1 1,700 **2** English **3** ghosts **4** soldier **5** look
6 baby / child **7** away **8** horses

EXTRA SUPPORT If there's time, you could get Sts to watch again with subtitles / showing the script, so they can see exactly what they understood / didn't understand. Translate / Explain any new words or phrases.

c Finally, focus on the question and ask the whole class.

For instructions on how to use these pages, see *p.39*.

<table>
<tr><td>More materials</td></tr>
<tr><td>For teachers</td></tr>
<tr><td>Teacher's Resource Centre
Video Can you understand these people? 7&8
Quick Test 8
File 8 Test</td></tr>
<tr><td>For students</td></tr>
<tr><td>Online Practice Check your progress</td></tr>
</table>

GRAMMAR

1 b 2 a 3 b 4 a 5 c 6 a 7 c 8 c 9 b 10 a
11 b 12 b 13 a 14 b 15 c

VOCABULARY

a
1 actor 2 artist 3 painter 4 musician 5 scientist
b
1 have 2 get 3 go 4 get 5 have
c
1 out 2 by 3 to 4 in 5 back
d
1 an armchair 2 a carpet 3 a bed 4 a cooker 5 a sofa
e
1 behind 2 next to 3 up 4 down 5 on

PRONUNCIATION

c
1 h**a**ll /ɔː/ 2 h**ere** /ɪə/ 3 liv**ed** /d/ 4 look**ed** /t/
5 th**ere** /eə/
d
1 <u>sci</u>entist 2 a<u>go</u> 3 <u>yes</u>terday 4 be<u>tween</u> 5 <u>fire</u>place

CAN YOU understand this text?

b
1 T 2 F 3 F 4 T 5 T 6 F

▶ CAN YOU understand these people?

1 a 2 a 3 b 4 a 5 b

◉ 8.25

1 Rebecca
I = interviewer, R = Rebecca
I Where were you born?
R I was born in Italy.
I Do you have family there?
R Yes, all my family lives there.
I Where do you live now?
R I live in the UK.
I Where in the UK?
R I live in Newcastle.

2 James
I = interviewer, J = James
I Did you go out last weekend?
J Er, yes, I did.
I What did you do?
J Er, I went with some friends to a pub, um, in Banbury, a town near here, and we watched a band. It was really good.

3 Maura
I = interviewer, M = Maura
I What's your favourite room in your house?
M Probably my bedroom. I love sleeping.
I Can you describe it?
M Er, yes, it's got a bed, and two bedside tables, a wardrobe, and a chest of drawers.

4 Asya
I = interviewer, A = Asya
I What did you do yesterday evening?
A Last night I had dinner with my brother in Brooklyn.
I What time did you go to bed?
A I went to bed around 1.00 a.m.

5 David
I = interviewer, D = David
I What did you do on New Year's Eve last year?
D So, last, last New Year's Eve, my wife and I, we met some friends in downtown New York, in Manhattan. We went to a very nice steakhouse, and then went for some cocktails, and er, sang in the New Year in, er, in New York.
I Did you have a good time?
D We had a very, very good time.

G countable / uncountable nouns, *a / an*, *some / any*
V food and drink
P the letters *ea*

Lesson plan

Food and drink provide the context for looking at the grammar of countable and uncountable nouns and the related use of *a*, *an*, *some*, and *any*. The lesson begins with a quiz on food and drink words that have come up so far in Elementary, and Sts then go to the Vocabulary Bank to learn more words. Sts then read part of a blog where a man describes why he eats the same thing every day. The Reading leads into the grammar focus, and Sts go on to practise the new grammar. Sts then listen to four people describing their dinner the previous night. The pronunciation focus looks at the vowel combination *ea*, which can be pronounced in several different ways, and which occurs in many common food words, e.g. *bread*, *meat*, and *steak*. Finally, in Speaking Sts tell each other what they ate and drank yesterday, and discuss their eating habits to find out if they are similar or not.

More materials
For teachers
Photocopiables
Grammar countable / uncountable nouns; *a / an*, *some / any p.192*
Vocabulary Food *p.273* (instructions *p.256*)
Communicative Shopping list *p.241* (instructions *p.210*)
For students
Workbook 9A
Online Practice 9A

OPTIONAL LEAD-IN (BOOKS CLOSED) Play *Hangman* (see *p.24*) with the word RESTAURANT.

Then ask Sts *When did you last eat in a restaurant? Who were you with? Did you enjoy it?*

1 VOCABULARY food and drink

a Books open. Focus Sts' attention on the instructions and point out that the first answer (*pizza*) has been done for them. Go through the clues, eliciting / explaining any words Sts don't know.

Put Sts in pairs and give them two minutes to try to write down all words in the quiz.

Check answers by getting Sts to spell the words, and write them on the board. Model and drill the pronunciation.

1 pasta **2** milk, sugar **3** meat **4** mineral water **5** ice cream **6** potato **7** eggs **8** chocolate **9** sandwich **10** breakfast, lunch, dinner

b Tell Sts to go to **Vocabulary Bank Food and drink** on *p.163* and get them to do **a** individually or in pairs. There are more words than usual, but Sts will probably already know some of them.

🔊 **9.1** Now do **b**. Play the audio for Sts to listen and check.

Check answers.

🔊 **9.1**
Food and drink
Breakfast
9 bread
12 butter
8 cereal
1 cheese
4 coffee
11 eggs
2 jam
6 juice
7 milk
10 sugar
3 tea
5 toast

Lunch or dinner
18 fish, for example salmon, tuna
17 herbs
15 meat, for example chicken, sausages, steak, ham
14 oil
21 pasta
27 rice
26 salad
23 seafood
28 spices

Vegetables
30 carrots
16 chips
13 a lettuce
29 mushrooms
20 onions
24 peas
19 peppers
22 potatoes
25 tomatoes

Fruit
41 apples
39 bananas
35 oranges
32 a pineapple
36 strawberries

Desserts
42 cake
38 fruit salad
33 ice cream

Snacks
37 biscuits
43 chocolate
34 crisps
40 nuts
31 a sandwich
44 sweets

Then either use the audio to drill the pronunciation of the words, or model and drill them yourself. Give further practice of any words your Sts find difficult to pronounce.

Focus on **Activation**. Get Sts to cover the words and use the photos to test themselves or their partner.

Tell Sts to go back to the main lesson **9A**.

 If you think Sts need more practice, you may want to give them the **Vocabulary** photocopiable activity at this point.

c Focus on the questions and give Sts time to think about their answers. Elicit / Teach words for any food which is very common in your Sts' country, but is not in the **Vocabulary Bank**.

Put Sts in pairs or small groups to discuss the questions. You could demonstrate by telling Sts what your favourite breakfast is and if there is any food or drink you don't like.

Get some feedback from various pairs or groups.

2 GRAMMAR countable / uncountable nouns, *a / an*, *some / any*

a Focus on the instructions, making sure Sts know what *a blogger* is (= a person who has a website where they write regularly about topics that interest them).

Do the questions as a whole-class activity, and teach Sts any food words they don't know.

> smoked salmon, avocado, bread, cream cheese, lime

b Do this as a whole-class activity.

Tell Sts to read his blog and find the answer.

Check the answer.

> Because he doesn't want to spend a lot of time deciding what to eat.

c Tell Sts to read the blog again, and then, in pairs, to answer questions 1–6.

When Sts have finished, check answers to questions 1–3, and elicit opinions for questions 4–6.

> **1** They all wear / wore the same clothes every day.
> **2** He spends less time and money buying food, and never needs to worry if his diet is healthy or not.
> **3** No, because he changes his meals a bit.

d Give Sts time to complete the gaps in sentences 1–3. Check answers.

> **1** a **2** some, an **3** some, some

e Tell Sts to go to **Grammar Bank 9A** on *p.140*.

Grammar notes
Countable / uncountable nouns

The concept of countable and uncountable nouns shouldn't cause too many problems (unless they do not exist in the Sts' own language), but what may cause confusion is that some words are countable in English, but uncountable in other languages or vice versa.

You may need to give more examples of when a noun can be countable or uncountable. This occurs when we can think of e.g. *a chicken* (a whole chicken) and *chicken* (e.g. chicken pieces).

Other examples: *a beer* (= a can or glass of beer), *beer* (= the liquid in general); *a coffee* (= a cup of coffee), *coffee* (= the drink in general).

a / an, some / any

Sts have already learned the rules for *a / an*, *some*, and *any* plus singular and plural countable nouns in **8B**. Here they learn that *some* can also be used with singular uncountable nouns to mean 'a quantity of', 'not an exact amount', e.g. *some butter, some milk*.

Sts may find it strange using *some* and *any* with 'singular' words, e.g. *butter*, since they previously used *some* and *any* with plural nouns, and may have translated them in their heads as plural words.

Make sure you point out the exception of using *some* for requests and offers. Sts usually assimilate this rule instinctively through learning set phrases like *Would you like some coffee?*.

9.2 Focus on the example sentences and play the audio for Sts to listen and repeat. Then go through the rules with the class. You could point out that a good dictionary will tell Sts if a noun is countable or uncountable.

Focus on the **some in** [?] box and go through it with the class.

Now focus on the exercises for **9A** on *p.141*. Sts do the exercises individually or in pairs.

Check answers, getting Sts to read the full sentences in **b**.

> **a**
> **1** some milk **2** a sandwich **3** some chips **4** a lettuce
> **5** an egg **6** some carrots **7** some chocolate **8** a cake
> **b**
> **1** any **2** some **3** any **4** some **5** any **6** any **7** some
> **8** an **9** some **10** a

Tell Sts to go back to the main lesson **9A**.

 If you think Sts need more practice, you may want to give them the **Grammar** photocopiable activity at this point.

f 9.3 Focus on the instructions and make sure Sts understand what they have to do. Point out the example.

Play the audio for Sts to listen and write the shopping list. If necessary, play the audio again.

Check answers. If Sts just answer with the food word, elicit whether it should be *a* or *some*.

some coffee, *some milk*, some orange juice, some apple juice, a pineapple, some (four or five) oranges, some bananas, some onions, some (two or three big) potatoes, a bottle of wine, a lettuce

9.3

(script in Student's Book on *p.121*)

W = woman, M = man

W We need food for the weekend – can you do the shopping on your way home this evening?
M OK, I suppose so. What do we need?
W Let's see. We need some coffee, we don't have *any*.
M OK…coffee…
W And some milk. And some juice.
M Orange juice?
W Fine. And maybe apple juice, too.
M OK. What else?
W Get a pineapple if they have them.
M One pineapple…
W And some oranges – four or five oranges – and some bananas. And I want to make a vegetable curry, so get some onions, some potatoes, some tomatoes…
M Hold on, wait a minute…! Potatoes…
W Yes, two or three big ones. Oh, and forget the tomatoes – we've got some in the fridge. And a bottle of wine.
M White? Red?
W Don't mind. Oh, and a lettuce, I want to make a salad.
M A lettuce…Do we need any tomatoes?
W No, I said no tomatoes!
M Sorry, yes, you did. Is that everything?
W Yes, I think so. And don't forget anything!

3 LISTENING hypothesizing about photos to prepare for listening

a Focus on the photos and the instructions and explain what *a hashtag* is (= a word or phrase with the symbol # in front of it, included in some messages sent using the Twitter social networking service, so that you can search for all messages with the same subject). You might want to pre-teach *takeaway* (= food that you buy at a restaurant that sells hot food you can take and eat somewhere else) and *foodie* (= a person who is very interested in cooking and eating different kinds of food), and tell Sts that foodies often post photos on Instagram.

Put Sts in pairs and get them to match the photos to 1–4.

EXTRA SUPPORT Ask Sts what different foods they can see in the photos (A = turkey, Brussels sprouts, potatoes, carrots, pie, mashed potatoes; B = lettuce, onion, tomatoes, chicken, mushrooms; C = chicken, carrots, tomatoes, lettuce, and some pieces of fried bread; D = eggs in tomato sauce, onion, coriander).

b 9.4 Point out the **Glossary**. Now play the audio for Sts to listen and check.

Check answers, and get Sts to say what they can see in the photos.

EXTRA SUPPORT Read through the script and decide if you need to pre-teach any new lexis before Sts listen.

1 B **2** C **3** D **4** A

9.4

(script in Student's Book on *pp.121–122*)

1

This is for my foodie friends. In case you thought lettuce was only for salads, here I'm cooking it in some butter with an onion. Then I add some mushrooms, chicken, fresh tomatoes, and some other things – not sure yet. Lettuce is also great in soups, or you can grill it and serve it with blue cheese.

2

We didn't feel like cooking last night, and anyway we didn't have any food in the house, so we decided to order some takeaway salads from our wonderful local pizzeria. They were all very good, but my favourite was a chicken salad with carrots, tomatoes, peppers, lettuce, and some pieces of fried bread.

3

Dinner last night at a restaurant in Piccadilly, called NOPI. We had lots of different sharing plates. I loved everything, especially this dish called *shakshuka*, which is North African, and it's basically eggs in a tomato sauce, but the mixture of herbs and spices makes it just fantastic. And the bread we had to dip in the sauce was wonderful, too. Go there. Soon.

4

OK guys, this is it! Our Thanksgiving dinner – which we had at six thirty last night. All the usual things: turkey with cranberry sauce, roast potatoes, mashed potatoes, lots of vegetables, and more… and more… Mom said, 'Why not go to a restaurant this year – maybe have seafood?', but I said, 'No, I want it home-made and traditional' – so she did it. Thanks, Mom. I now need to spend a few hours on the sofa before I even think of going to bed. So how was yours?

You might want to point out that the fourth speaker is American, so he uses the word *Mom* instead of the British English *Mum*.

c Focus on the task. Tell Sts they are going to listen to the audio again, and this time they need to decide which speaker talks about what. Make sure Sts understand all the lexis, e.g. *ingredients*.

Play the audio for Sts to listen and complete the task.

Check answers.

Speaker 2 a good restaurant near their house
Speaker 1 ways of preparing something
Speaker 3 a dish with two main ingredients
Speaker 4 a meal for a special occasion

EXTRA SUPPORT If there's time, you could get Sts to listen again with the script on *pp.121–122*, so they can see exactly what they understood / didn't understand. Translate / Explain any new words or phrases.

d Focus on the questions and elicit / explain the difference between *a meal* (= breakfast, lunch, dinner) and *a dish* (= food prepared in a particular way, e.g. *a pizza*, *spaghetti carbonara*, etc.).

Put Sts in small groups or pairs to discuss the questions.

Get some feedback. You could tell Sts your answers, too.

4 PRONUNCIATION the letters *ea*

Pronunciation notes

The combination of vowels *e* + *a* has different possible pronunciations, several of which seem quite irregular to Sts, e.g. *great* /greɪt/. In this exercise, we focus on common examples of this spelling occurring in food words.

a Focus on the words in the list and elicit that they all have the vowels *ea*, but that the pronunciation is not the same.

Now focus on the sound pictures and elicit the three words and sounds (*tree* /iː/, *egg* /e/, *train* /eɪ/).

Get Sts, in pairs, to put the words in the correct columns. Encourage them to say the words aloud to help them.

b ◀)) **9.5** Play the audio once for Sts to listen and check. Check answers.

◀)) **9.5**

tree /iː/	eat, ice cream, meat, peas, tea
egg /e/	bread, breakfast, healthy
train /eɪ/	steak

EXTRA SUPPORT Play the audio again, pausing after each word (or group of words) for Sts to repeat.

Sts now practise saying the words.

Elicit that the most common pronunciation is /iː/, but they will need to learn unusual ones, e.g. *steak*, by heart.

EXTRA CHALLENGE On the board, write some more words with *ea* that Sts know, and that have one of these three pronunciations for Sts to put in the columns, e.g. *repeat*, *easy*, *headphones*, *read* (/e/ and /iː/), *great*, *mean*, *please*, *speak*. You may want to point out that the letters *ear* have a different pronunciation from *ea* + other consonants, and is either /ɪə/, e.g. *hear*, or /eə/, e.g. *wear*. Sts saw this in **8B**.

5 SPEAKING

a Tell Sts to make a food diary for yesterday, i.e. write down what they had to eat and drink. They can use the **Vocabulary Bank Food and drink** on *p.163* to help them. Monitor and help with any new words they need, but try not to overdo new vocabulary. Encourage Sts to use more general food words, e.g. *meat*, *fish*, *vegetables*, rather than specific words (e.g. *lamb*, *hake*, *aubergines*, etc.), which they probably won't know. Tell them to write *a* / *an* or *some* with each word, and to group them under meals.

Tell Sts to go back to the main lesson **9A**.

b You could demonstrate the activity by telling Sts what you had yesterday, where you had it, and who made it. In pairs, Sts tell each other their answers. Monitor and help with pronunciation, and correct mistakes with *a* / *an* or *some*.

Get some feedback. Did anyone have a very similar meal to their partner?

c Focus on the questions and make sure Sts understand all the lexis.

Put Sts in pairs to ask and answer the questions.

Monitor and help.

Get feedback from some pairs.

EXTRA IDEA Tell Sts they are now going to write their own blogs, so they need to write a short text like the ones they heard in the Listening about what they ate yesterday.

G quantifiers: *how much / how many, a lot of*, etc.
V food containers
P linking, /ʃ/ and /s/

Lesson plan

This lesson continues the theme of food and focuses on sugar and salt, which were both known at different times in history as 'white gold'. The lesson begins with a vocabulary focus on containers, e.g. *packet* and *tin*. The context for the grammar presentation is the amount of sugar and salt that there is in some common food items. Sts learn about quantifiers, e.g. *much* and *a lot of*, and asking about quantity, e.g. *How much sugar is there in dark chocolate?*. Pronunciation looks at two sounds, /ʃ/ and /s/. The reading text *Fascinating facts about sugar and salt* is based on several recent articles and studies. The lesson ends with Sts interviewing each other, using a questionnaire to find out how much salt and sugar they eat every day.

More materials
For teachers
Photocopiables
Grammar quantifiers: *how much / how many, a lot of,* etc. *p.193*
Communicative How much / many board game *p.242* (instructions *p.211*)
For students
Workbook 9B
Online Practice 9B

OPTIONAL LEAD-IN (BOOKS CLOSED)

Revise food and countability by playing the *Long sentence* game (see **Optional lead-in** for **8C** on *p.113*). You begin by saying *In my fridge there's* (e.g. *some milk*). Sts continue, remembering what the previous people have said, then adding an item of their own. Make sure they use *a*, *an*, or *some* before the food word.

1 VOCABULARY & PRONUNCIATION
food containers; linking

a ◖ **9.6** Books open. Focus on the photos and explain that they are all containers which are often used for food. Then tell Sts to match the words and photos.

Play the audio for Sts to listen and check.

Check answers.

◖ **9.6**

3 a bottle
5 a box
6 a can
2 a carton
7 a jar
1 a packet
4 a tin

Play the audio again, pausing for Sts to listen and repeat.

b ◖ **9.7** Tell Sts they are going to hear five conversations in shops and they must listen and write what people want to buy, using the words in **a**, e.g. *a jar of honey*.

Play the audio, pausing after each conversation to give Sts time to write.

Check answers. Highlight that the container words and *of* are always linked, and the pronunciation of *of* is /əv/.

1 a bottle of olive oil   **2** a packet of (basmati) rice
3 a tin of tomatoes   **4** a box of chocolates   **5** a carton of orange juice

◖ **9.7**
(script in Student's Book on *p.122*)
1
A Hi. I'd like a bottle of oil.
B Olive oil?
A Yes, please.
2
A Can I help you?
B Yes, I'm looking for a packet of rice.
A Ordinary rice, basmati, brown rice?
B Er, basmati, please.
3
A Excuse me. I need a tin of tomatoes, but I can't see them anywhere.
B They're over there, next to the eggs.
A Thanks.
4
A Hi. I want a box of chocolates – a nice one. It's for my girlfriend's birthday.
B How much do you want to spend?
A Oh, not very much. I mean, nothing very expensive…
5
A A carton of juice, please.
B Apple juice? Orange juice?
A Er, orange juice.
B That's one pound fifty, please.

EXTRA SUPPORT If there's time, you could get Sts to listen again with the script on *p.122*, so they can see exactly what they understood / didn't understand. Translate / Explain any new words or phrases.

c Sts now have to make their own phrases using a container from **a** and a word from the list. Point out the example. Tell Sts to think about how they buy these things in their country.

Get Sts to compare their ideas with a partner, and then check answers.

Possible answers
a box of biscuits
a carton of cereal / a packet of cereal / a box of cereal
a bottle of Coke / a can of Coke
a packet of crisps
a jar of jam
a bottle of milk / a carton of milk
a packet of salt / a box of salt
a packet of sugar
a tin of tuna

2 GRAMMAR quantifiers

a Focus on the photos of food items, and give Sts time to think about how much sugar and salt is in each item and number them *0* (no sugar / salt) to *3* (a lot of sugar / salt).

b Focus on the pictures of the spoons and make sure Sts understand the expressions for quantities from *none* to *a lot*. Highlight that *quite a lot* = a medium quantity, between a lot and a little.

Now focus on the speech bubbles and remind Sts that the question is *How much…?*, not *How many…?*, because *sugar* and *salt* are uncountable.

Put Sts in pairs and get them to ask each other how much sugar / salt is in each item.

Get some feedback from the class about what they think for each item, but <u>don't</u> correct their guesses at this stage.

c Tell Sts to go to **Communication Sugar and salt** on *p.106*. Go through the facts with the class, establishing whether there is a lot / quite a lot / a little sugar or salt, or none in each food item.

> **Sugar**
> a can of Coke: a lot   an apple: quite a lot   a small bar of dark chocolate: a little   an egg: none
> **Salt**
> a large packet of crisps: a lot   a slice of white bread: quite a lot
> a bottle of mineral water: a little   a bottle of olive oil: none

Get feedback from some Sts. Were their answers in **a** correct? Did they find any facts surprising?

Tell Sts to go back to the main lesson **9B**.

d Focus on the sentences. Sts should, from memory, try to complete the sentences with a food item or drink from **2a**. Highlight that you have to say *There isn't any salt* NOT ~~*There's none salt*~~.

Get Sts to compare with a partner, and then check answers.

> **1** olive oil   **2** dark chocolate   **3** white bread
> **4** (a can of) Coke

e Tell Sts to go to **Grammar Bank 9B** on *p.140*.

> **Grammar notes**
> ### *a lot of*
> In positive sentences native speakers normally use *a lot of* for big quantities. It is also possible to use *a lot of* in negatives and questions, although it is more common to use *much / many*.
> We use *a lot* (NOT ~~*a lot of*~~) in short answers or when we don't give the noun, e.g. *I eat a lot of chocolate*, but *I eat a lot*.
> In colloquial English, people often use *lots of* as an alternative to *a lot of*. It's useful for Sts to recognize both forms, but at this level, we only include *a lot of* in the **Grammar Bank** exercises.

> ### *much / many*
> *Much* and *many* are used mainly in negative sentences and questions. *Many* is also sometimes used in positive sentences in formal English, e.g. *Many people live in houses in the UK*. However, *much* is not normally used in positive sentences, e.g. NOT ~~*British people drink much tea*~~.
> Tell Sts to think of *much* as singular and *many* as plural to help them to remember which one to use.

🔊 **9.8** Focus on the example sentences and play the audio for Sts to listen and repeat. Then go through the rules with the class.

Focus on the **a lot and lots of** box and go through it with the class.

Now focus on the exercises for **9B** on *p.141*. Sts do the exercises individually or in pairs.

Check answers, getting Sts to read the full sentences. In **a** sentence 4, elicit / explain the difference between *some chocolate* (a bar, some pieces, etc.) and *chocolates* (individual sweets covered in chocolate).

> **a**
> **1** How much   **2** How many   **3** How much   **4** How many
> **5** How much   **6** How much   **7** How many   **8** How many
> **9** How much   **10** How many
> **b**
> **1** a lot of   **2** A little.   **3** much   **4** Quite a lot.   **5** a lot of
> **6** not much   **7** many   **8** None.   **9** a little   **10** much, any

Tell Sts to go back to the main lesson **9B**.

EXTRA SUPPORT   If you think Sts need more practice, you may want to give them the **Grammar** photocopiable activity at this point.

f Focus on the instructions. Elicit / Explain the meaning of the question *How about you?* and check Sts can remember the meaning of *fast food*.

Put Sts in pairs, **A** and **B**. Demonstrate the activity by saying how much you eat of one of the things in the list. Then turn to a student and ask *How about you?*.

A should start by saying how much fish he / she eats, give extra information, and ask **B**. They then swap roles.

Get some feedback from various pairs. Find out if pairs have a similar diet, or if they found out something surprising about their partner's eating habits.

3 PRONUNCIATION /ʃ/ and /s/

> ### Pronunciation notes
> **/ʃ/**
> *sh* and *-tion* are always pronounced /ʃ/, e.g. *shop*, *station*.
> *c* before *iou* and *ia* is usually /ʃ/, e.g. *delicious*, *special*.
> **/s/**
> *c* before *e* and *i* is pronounced /s/, e.g. *city*, *centre* (*c* before other vowels is usually /k/).
> *s* at the beginning of a word is always /s/. The only two exceptions are *sure* /ʃʊə/ and *sugar* /ʃʊgə/.
> *s* in the middle of a word or at the end is sometimes /s/ and sometimes /z/.
> See **Sound Bank** *p.167*.

a ◉ **9.9** Focus on the two sound pictures and play the audio for Sts just to listen. Make sure Sts can hear the difference between them.

◉ **9.9**
See sounds and words in Student's Book on *p.72*

Now play the audio again for Sts to listen and repeat.

 If these sounds are difficult for your Sts, it will help to show them the mouth position. You could model this yourself or use the Sound Bank videos on the *Teacher's Resource Centre.*

b ◉ **9.10** Sts should say each word aloud and then put it in the correct row in **a**.

Get Sts to compare with a partner, then play the audio for them to check.

Check answers, and elicit when *c* is pronounced /s/ (before *e* and *i* although *ci* can sometimes be /ʃ/).

◉ **9.10**

shower /ʃ/   sugar, fish, delicious, fresh, information, reception, shopping, special, sure

snake /s/   salt, sweets, centre, cereal, cinema, crisps, rice, salad, science

---

Now play the audio, pausing after each word for Sts to repeat.

c ◉ **9.11** Focus on the conversation. Play the audio once and get Sts to listen and read.

◉ **9.11**
See conversation in Student's Book on *p.72*

Then play the audio again, pausing after each sentence for Sts to listen and repeat.

Now get Sts to practise it in pairs. Monitor, helping and correcting.

Finally, you could get one pair to 'perform' for the rest of the class.

4 READING categorizing information

a Tell Sts they are going to read an article entitled *Fascinating facts about sugar and salt*. Elicit / Explain the meaning of *fascinating* (= very interesting). Model and drill pronunciation. Point out the **Glossary**.

In pairs, Sts read the article and complete the gaps with *sugar* or *salt*. Highlight the meaning of *too much* (= more than what is good for you) before gap 12.

 Before Sts read the article, check whether you need to pre-teach any vocabulary, but not the verbs in **c**.

b ◉ **9.12** Play the audio for Sts to listen and check.

Check answers. Don't ask Sts about the facts at this stage, as they will be discussing them later.

1 Salt	2 Sugar	3 sugar	4 sugar	5 salt	6 sugar	7 salt
8 salt	9 sugar	10 sugar	11 Salt	12 salt		

◉ **9.12**
Fascinating facts about sugar and salt
At different times in history, both sugar and salt were called 'white gold' because they were so expensive and difficult to get. But there are many more interesting facts about sugar and salt…

Salt is used to make glass, washing powder, and paper.

Sugar really helps the medicine go down! It's an important ingredient of many modern medicines.

Christopher Columbus introduced sugar to the New World in 1493, on his second voyage.

If you put sugar into a vase of flowers, the flowers last longer.

If you want to check if an egg is fresh, put it in a cup with water and salt. If the egg floats, it isn't very fresh.

In the UK, there's a club for people who collect the little packets of sugar you get when you order tea or coffee in a café or restaurant.

If your dog or cat has fleas, and they are now living in your carpets, put some salt on the carpets and leave it for twelve hours. This kills all the fleas.

Only six per cent of the salt used in the USA is used in food; another seventeen per cent is used for de-icing roads in the winter months.

Sure and *sugar* are the only two words in the English language that begin with 's-u' and are pronounced 'sh'.

Scientists use sugar to make different kinds of plastic, e.g. for food packaging.

Salt removes red wine stains (though probably not from your new white carpet).

If you eat too much salt (about one gram per kilogram of weight), you can die. This was a method of ritual suicide in ancient China.

c Tell Sts to read the article again and find the verbs. In pairs, they should to try to guess the meaning and pronunciation of the verbs.

Check answers, either explaining in English or translating into Sts' L1. Model and drill the pronunciation, and get Sts to underline the stressed syllable in each verb.

intro<u>duce</u> /ˌɪntrəˈdjuːs/ = to bring in something new

float /fləʊt/ = to stay on top of water

co<u>llect</u> /kəˈlekt/ = to bring together things that are the same in some way, to study or enjoy them

<u>order</u> /ˈɔːdə/ = to ask for food or drink in a restaurant, bar, etc.

de-<u>ice</u> /ˌdiː ˈaɪs/ = to take the ice away from something

re<u>move</u> /rɪˈmuːv/ = to take something away

Deal with any other new vocabulary. Model and drill the pronunciation of any tricky words.

d Do this as a whole-class activity.

5 SPEAKING

a Focus on the questionnaire about sugar and salt. Give Sts a few minutes to complete the gaps with *How much* or *How many*.

Check answers by going through the questions, making sure Sts understand all the lexis, e.g. *spoon* and *add*.

1 How many	2 How many	3 How much	4 How many
6 How much	7 How much	8 How many	

b You could demonstrate the activity by getting Sts to interview you first. Answer the questions, giving a bit of extra information where you can, as a model for Sts, e.g. *I don't have sugar in my coffee; I hate fizzy drinks.*

Sts interview each other in pairs. When they have finished, they should tell each other if they need to eat less sugar or salt. If you didn't teach it earlier, you may want to teach Sts the phrase *too much*.

Get some feedback from individual Sts about their partner.

G comparative adjectives: *bigger*, *more dangerous*, etc.
V high numbers
P /ə/, sentence stress

Lesson plan

The context of this lesson is general knowledge quizzes, through which comparative adjectives are presented and practised, and high numbers introduced. The lesson starts with a vocabulary focus on numbers greater than 100. In Listening, Sts decide if they think some statements are true or false, and then listen to a contestant answering the questions on a quiz show. The quiz questions lead into the grammar focus on comparative adjectives. This is followed by a pronunciation focus on stress in comparative sentences, and the sound /ə/ in *than* and in *-er* endings. In Speaking, Sts put the grammar and high numbers into practice and role-play taking part in a quiz show. The lesson finishes with a reading text about pub quizzes in the UK.

More materials
For teachers
Photocopiables
Grammar comparative adjectives *p.194*
Vocabulary Guess the number *p.274* (instructions *p.256*)
Communicative Guess the comparative *p.243* (instructions *p.211*)
For students
Workbook 9C
Online Practice 9C

OPTIONAL LEAD-IN (BOOKS CLOSED)
Revise numbers up to 100 by writing some sums on the board and eliciting answers from the class.

1 VOCABULARY high numbers

a Books open. Focus on the lesson title and elicit / explain the meaning.

Put Sts in pairs and give them a few minutes to answer the three radio quiz questions. If they don't know the answers, tell them to guess. Tell Sts at this point just to answer *a*, *b*, or *c* rather than trying to say the long numbers.

b ◗ **9.13** Tell Sts they are going to hear a contestant on the radio quiz show answering the three questions. Play the audio for Sts to listen and check their answers to **a**.

Check answers.

1 c **2** b **3** b

◗ **9.13**
(script in Student's Book on *p.122*)

P = presenter, C = contestant

P Question one. What is the population of the UK? Is it approximately **a** forty-seven million, **b** fifty-seven million, or **c** sixty-seven million?
C I think it's c, sixty-seven million.
P C is the right answer! Question two. How far is it from New York City in the east to Los Angeles in the west? Is it **a** about two thousand five hundred kilometres, **b** about four thousand kilometres, or **c** about five thousand kilometres?
C About four thousand kilometres.
P Are you sure?
C Yes. I'm sure.
P B is the right answer! Question three. How many politicians are there in the British Parliament? Is it **a** four hundred and fifty, **b** six hundred and fifty, or **c** seven hundred and fifty?
C I think it's c, seven hundred and fifty.
P Final answer?
C Final answer, seven hundred and fifty.
P I'm sorry, the right answer is **b**. There are six hundred and fifty politicians in the British Parliament.

Play the audio again and tell Sts this time to pay attention to how the numbers are said. Pause the audio after each answer and elicit the number from Sts, and write it on the board.

1 sixty-seven million   **2** (about) four thousand   **3** six hundred and fifty

Vocabulary notes

Highlight:
- there is no *s* on *million* or *thousand*.
- the use of *and* between hundreds and tens, e.g. *six hundred **and** fifty*.

EXTRA SUPPORT If there's time, you could get Sts to listen again with the script on *p.122*, so they can see exactly what they understood / didn't understand. Translate / Explain any new words or phrases.

c Tell Sts to go to **Vocabulary Bank** Days and numbers on *p.148* and get them to do **Part 4**.

Focus on **4 High numbers** and get Sts to do **a** individually or in pairs.

◗ **9.14** Now do **b**. Play the audio for Sts to listen and check.

Check answers.

three hundred and **fifty**
eight hundred **and** seventy-five
1,500
two thousand and **twelve**
five thousand four **hundred** and twenty
25,000
a hundred **thousand**
two million **three** hundred thousand

◆) 9.14

4 High numbers
a hundred and five
two hundred
three hundred and fifty
eight hundred and seventy-five
a thousand
one thousand five hundred
two thousand and twelve
five thousand four hundred and twenty
twenty-five thousand
a hundred thousand
a million
two million three hundred thousand

Now either use the audio to drill the pronunciation of the numbers, or model and drill them yourself. Give further practice of any numbers your Sts find difficult to pronounce.

Focus on **Activation**. Get Sts to cover the words on the right and say the numbers. They could test themselves or their partner.

Tell Sts to go back to the main lesson **9C**.

EXTRA SUPPORT Write the numbers and words below on the board, and tell Sts to correct the mistakes:

175	A HUNDRED SEVENTY-FIVE
2,150	TWO THOUSAND AND ONE HUNDRED AND FIFTY
3,009	THREE THOUSAND NINE
20,000	TWENTY THOUSANDS
3,000,000	THREE MILLIONS

EXTRA SUPPORT If you think Sts need more practice, you may want to give them the **Vocabulary** photocopiable activity at this point.

d ◆) 9.15 Tell Sts they are going to hear ten numbers and they must write down the number (using figures, not words). Focus on the example. Tell Sts that they are going to hear the audio twice.

! This is a difficult exercise. Pause the audio after each number, to give Sts time to think and write.

Get Sts to compare with a partner, and then check answers, getting Sts to write the figures on the board.

2	450
3	920
4	1,300
5	3,437
6	7,700
7	50,000
8	120,000
9	40,000,000
10	2,600,000

◆) 9.15
1 a hundred and ninety-nine
2 four hundred and fifty
3 nine hundred and twenty
4 one thousand three hundred
5 three thousand four hundred and thirty-seven
6 seven thousand seven hundred
7 fifty thousand
8 a hundred and twenty thousand
9 forty million
10 two million six hundred thousand

Finally, either use the audio to drill the pronunciation of the numbers, or model and drill them yourself.

EXTRA CHALLENGE Get Sts to write out the numbers in words as well, and then elicit both versions of the numbers onto the board.

e In pairs, Sts answer the four questions. If Sts don't know the answers and they have access to the internet in class, you could set a time limit for them to find the answers online.

Get some feedback from the class.

EXTRA CHALLENGE Sts write their own four questions with high numbers as answers. Put Sts in pairs and get them to ask each other their questions.

2 LISTENING

a ◆) 9.16 Focus on the task. Tell Sts that they are going to listen to another quiz show called *Quiz Night*, and give them a few minutes to read questions 1–4. Make sure all the questions are clear – check, for example, that Sts know *How long* (= How much time), *contestant*, *to win*, and *to lose*.

Play the audio twice.

Get Sts to compare with a partner, and then check answers.

EXTRA SUPPORT Read through the scripts and decide if you need to pre-teach any new lexis before Sts listen.

1 Ten seconds
2 a £100 **b** £200 **c** £400 **d** £12,800
3 All the money
4 Phone a friend

◆) 9.16
(script in Student's Book on *p.122*)

P = presenter, E = Eddie
P Good evening. Welcome to *Quiz Night*. Tonight's show comes from Manchester. And our first contestant is Eddie from Chorley. Hi, Eddie. Are you nervous?
E No, not really. I think I'm, er, well-prepared.
P Well, let's hope so. The rules are the same as always. I'm going to read you some sentences, and you have ten seconds to say if the sentence is true or false. If you get the first answer right, you win one hundred pounds. Then for each correct answer, you double your money, so if you get the second answer right, you win two hundred pounds, and for the third correct answer, you win four hundred pounds. For eight correct answers, you win twelve thousand eight hundred pounds. But if you get an answer wrong, you lose all the money. Remember, you can also phone a friend, so if you're not sure about one of the answers, you can phone your friend to help you. Is that OK, Eddie?
E Yeah, OK.

b Focus on the picture and elicit *whale* and *lion*. Write the new words on the board, and model and drill pronunciation.

Focus on sentences 1–8 in *Quiz Night*. Elicit / Teach that the sentences are comparing two things, e.g. the first one is comparing a whale and a lion, using the adjective *loud*. Highlight that the *-er* ending means *more*.

Get Sts to read the sentences in pairs and decide whether they are true or false. <u>Don't</u> check answers yet.

c 🔊 **9.17** Tell Sts they are now going to hear Eddie doing the quiz. They should listen and check their answers to **b**.

Play the audio and get Sts to check their answers in pairs. Check answers.

> 1 T   2 T   3 F   4 T   5 F   6 T   7 F   8 F

🔊 **9.17**
(script in Student's Book on *p.122*)

P = presenter, E = Eddie, S = Sandra

P OK, Eddie, first question for one hundred pounds. A whale can make a louder noise than a lion. True or false?

E A whale can make a louder noise than a lion. Er, true.

P Correct. Blue whales can make a sound of up to one hundred and eighty-eight decibels whereas a lion's roar is never more than one hundred and fourteen decibels. Ro-a-rrrr. Now, for two hundred pounds, the First World War was shorter than the Second World War. True or false?

E Er, I think it's true.

P Correct. It's true. The First World War lasted four years, from nineteen fourteen to nineteen eighteen, but the Second World War lasted six years, from nighteen thirty-nine to ninettn forty-five. Next, for four hundred pounds, the American film industry is bigger than the Indian film industry.

E I think it's false. You know, Bollywood and all that is huge. I think it's false.

P Correct. The Indian film industry is much bigger than the American one. It produces about one thousand films every year, which is double what Hollywood produces. In fact, America isn't even the second country that makes the most films, which is Nigeria. Next, for eight hundred pounds, in July, Edinburgh is hotter than Sydney. True or false?

E In July, Edinburgh is hotter than Sydney. Er, true.

P Correct. The average temperature in July in Edinburgh is fifteen degrees, and in Sydney it's thirteen degrees. Of course, Australia's in the southern hemisphere, so it's winter there. Next, for one thousand six hundred pounds, silver is heavier than gold. True or false?

E Er, true. No, er, false.

P Do you want to phone a friend?

E No, I think it's false. I remember from science lessons at school. Gold is heavier than silver.

P Correct. Gold weighs about nineteen grams per cubic centimetres, and silver weighs only ten point five grams. That means that gold is almost twice as heavy as silver. OK, for three thousand two hundred pounds, the mountain K2 is more difficult to climb than Mount Everest.

E Er, true.

P Correct. Thirty per cent of the people who try to climb K2 die, usually on the way down, whereas only five per cent of the people who try to climb Everest die. OK, Eddie, now for six thousand four hundred pounds, driving in Italy is more dangerous than driving in Belgium. True or false?

E Er, I think that's a trick question. We all think the Italians drive really fast, but maybe they're good drivers. I think it's false.

P Well done, Eddie! It may be hard to believe, but in fact, out of every one hundred thousand people, six people died because of car accidents in Italy, compared to seven in Belgium. And finally, the last question. Be very careful, Eddie. If you get it right, you win twelve thousand eight hundred pounds, but if you get it wrong, you get nothing. Are you ready?

E Yes, ready.

P OK, for twelve thousand eight hundred pounds, it's better to do exercise in the morning than in the afternoon.

E Er…er…

P Quickly, Eddie, your time is nearly up.

E I think it's false, but I'm not sure. I want to phone a friend.

P Right, Eddie. So, who do you want to call?

E Sandra.

P Is she your girlfriend?

E Yes, she is.

P OK then. Hello, is that Sandra?

S Yes, it is.

P I'm phoning from *Quiz Night*. Eddie needs some help. You have thirty seconds, Eddie. Here she is.

E Hi. Sandra?

S Yes.

E Listen. It's the last question. It's better to do exercise in the morning than in the afternoon. True or false? I think it's false.

S Er, I think it's true. I always see people running in the park in the morning…

E Google it. Quickly. On your phone.

S What do I put in?

E Just that sentence and see what comes up! 'It's better to do exercise in the morning than in the afternoon.' Come on!

S Yes, I'm writing it. Oh sorry, I just got a message.

E Hurry up, Sandra!

P Time's up, I'm afraid. OK, Eddie. So, true or false?

E Er. True.

P Final answer?

E Final answer. True.

P I'm sorry, Eddie, it's false. It's better to do exercise in the afternoon, between four and five. Eddie, you had six thousand four hundred pounds, but now you go home with…nothing.

E Why did I phone Sandra? Why didn't I phone my friend Dave?

Find out if any pairs got all the answers right. Now ask how much money Eddie wins.

> He doesn't win anything.

d Tell Sts to listen again and write down why the answers are true or false. They must also write the important numbers they hear in the answers.

Play the audio, pausing after each answer to give Sts time to write. Play the audio again if necessary.

Check answers.

> 1 T – Blue whales can make a sound of up to **188** decibels, whereas a lion's roar is never more than **114** decibels.
> 2 T – The First World War lasted **four** years, from **1914** to **1918**, but the Second World War lasted **six** years, from **1939** to **1945**.
> 3 F – …the Indian film industry produces about **1,000** films every year, which is double what Hollywood produces.
> 4 T – The average temperature in July in Edinburgh is **15** degrees, and in Sydney it's **13** degrees.
> 5 F – Gold weighs about **19** grams per cm³ and silver weighs only **10.5** grams.
> 6 T – **Thirty** per cent of the people who try to climb K2 die, usually on the way down, whereas only **five** per cent of the people who try to climb Everest die.
> 7 F – …out of every **100,000** people, **six** people died because of car accidents in Italy, compared to **seven** in Belgium.
> 8 F – It's better to do exercise in the afternoon, between **4.00** and **5.00**.

EXTRA SUPPORT If there's time, you could get Sts to listen again with the scripts on *p.122*, so they can see exactly what they understood / didn't understand. Translate / Explain any new words or phrases.

3 GRAMMAR comparative adjectives

a Focus on the instructions. Give Sts time to answer the questions in pairs.

Check answers.

> **1** *-er* **2** Because you double the final *g*. **3** Change *y* to *i* and add *-er*. **4** more **5** better **6** than

b Tell Sts to go to **Grammar Bank 9C** on *p.140*.

> **Grammar notes**
>
> There are clear rules governing the formation of comparative adjectives.
>
> In one-syllable adjectives, a final *-w* after a vowel doesn't count as a consonant, and is not doubled, e.g. *new*, *newer*.
>
> Depending on your Sts' L1, they may try to use *that* instead of *than* after comparative adjectives.

9.18 Focus on the example sentences and play the audio for Sts to listen and repeat. Then go through the rules with the class.

Now focus on the exercises for **9C** on *p.141*. Sts do the exercises individually or in pairs.

Check answers. Get Sts to spell the *-er* adjectives in **a** and write them on the board. In **b**, get them to read the full sentences.

> **a**
>
> **1** higher **2** dirtier **3** more important **4** later **5** lower **6** more bored **7** wetter **8** more modern **9** more comfortable **10** happier
>
> **b**
>
> **1** cheaper than **2** easier…than **3** more tired…than **4** busier than **5** better than **6** more interesting than **7** further…than **8** shorter than **9** worse than **10** more difficult than

Tell Sts to go back to the main lesson **9C**.

EXTRA SUPPORT If you think Sts need more practice, you may want to give them the **Grammar** photocopiable activity at this point.

4 PRONUNCIATION & SPEAKING /ə/, sentence stress

a **9.19** Focus on the sentence from the quiz. Play the audio once for Sts to hear how *-er* and *than* are pronounced, and then check answers. Tell Sts that the final *-er* is never stressed, e.g. *safer* NOT ~~safer~~.

> The final *-er* is always pronounced /ə/.
> *than* is pronounced /ðən/.

9.19
See sentence in Student's Book on *p.75*

b **9.20** Tell Sts they are going to hear six comparative sentences and they must write them down.

Play the audio, pausing after each sentence to give Sts time to write.

Check answers by eliciting the sentences onto the board.

9.20
1 Carrots are sweeter than tomatoes.
2 Air travel is safer than train travel.
3 London is wetter than Milan.
4 A horse is heavier than a car.
5 Oranges are healthier than strawberries.
6 Istanbul is further north than New York.

c Play the audio again, pausing after each sentence for Sts to repeat. Highlight that *is / are* and *than* are not stressed.

Play the audio again, pausing after each sentence, and elicit whether the sentence is true or not.

> **1** T **2** T **3** F **4** F **5** F **6** T

d Put Sts in pairs, **A** and **B**, and tell them to go to **Communication Quiz Night**, **A** on *p.107*, **B** on *p.112*.

Go through the instructions with them carefully. They are going to play a slightly simplified version of the game.

Then give Sts time to complete their sentences with comparative adjectives. Before they start, you could quickly check they have the correct comparative forms.

Student A	Student B
1 smaller	**1** older
2 colder	**2** smaller
3 older	**3** higher
4 shorter	**4** bigger
5 more expensive	**5** more popular
6 drier	**6** larger
7 further	**7** warmer
8 hotter	**8** busier

Write the amounts of money that they win on the board, e.g. 1 = 100 (pounds or a currency that your Sts are familiar with), 2 = 200, 3 = 400, etc. (up to 12,800), and check Sts can say the numbers correctly. Explain that if you get, for example question 4 wrong, you continue playing, but you lose the money you had and the prize starts again from 100 pounds.

Sit **A** and **B** face-to-face if possible. **A** reads his / her sentences to **B**. Monitor and help Sts to get the rhythm right when they read their quiz sentences.

B then reads **A** his / her sentences.

EXTRA SUPPORT You could do the above activity in groups of four instead of pairs. Divide the class into groups of four and have two **A**s and two **B**s in each group. They prepare their quiz sentences together, and take turns to read them to the other pair.

EXTRA CHALLENGE Encourage **A** to 'play the role' of the presenter. Give Sts a few minutes to look at the script and make a note of any useful language (e.g. *Good evening, I ask the questions*).

When both Sts have played the game, get feedback to see who won the most money.

Tell Sts to go back to the main lesson **9C**.

5 READING identifying section topics

a Tell Sts they are now going to read an article about pub quizzes in the UK. Make sure they understand the question and that they only read the first part. Before they start, you might want to elicit / explain the meaning of *general knowledge*.

When Sts have finished, elicit some responses to the question.

EXTRA SUPPORT Before Sts read the article, check whether you need to pre-teach any vocabulary, but <u>not</u> the words in **c**.

b Focus on the instructions and elicit the meaning of *tips*. Now focus on A–G and make sure Sts understand them.

Tell Sts to read the tips and complete the gaps with *A–G*. Point out that the first one (*D*) has been done for them. Check answers.

> **2** A   **3** C   **4** F   **5** G   **6** E   **7** B

c Tell Sts to read the article again and find the words. In pairs, they should try to guess the meaning and pronunciation.

Check answers, either explaining in English or translating into Sts' L1. Model and drill the pronunciation, and get Sts to underline the stressed syllable in each item.

> a team /tiːm/ = a group of people who play a game together against another group
>
> a <u>quiz</u>master /ˈkwɪzmɑːstə/ = a person who asks questions in a game, especially on TV
>
> an <u>ex</u>pert /ˈekspɜːt/ = a person who knows a lot about something
>
> to cheat /tʃiːt/ = to do something dishonest in order to gain an advantage, especially in a game, a competition, an exam, etc.
>
> to <u>mem</u>orize /ˈmeməraɪz/ = to learn something so that you can remember it exactly
>
> to be a bad <u>los</u>er /bi ə bæd ˈluːzə/ = to behave badly when you lose a game
>
> to win /wɪn/ = to be the best or first in a game

Deal with any other new vocabulary. Model and drill the pronunciation of any tricky words.

d Put Sts in pairs and get them to discuss the five questions. You could demonstrate the activity by answering a few questions yourself.

Get some feedback from various pairs.

Function ordering a meal
Vocabulary understanding a menu

Lesson plan

In this lesson Sts learn some common vocabulary related to menus and practise ordering a meal in a restaurant. In the storyline, Jenny and Rob are chatting in the office when Jenny gets a call from Eddie. Eddie sings 'Happy Birthday' to Jenny, which Rob overhears, and he takes the chance to invite Jenny out for dinner. But before she can reply, Daniel comes out of his office and invites Jenny to go out for a working dinner that evening.

More materials
For teachers
Teacher's Resource Centre
Video Practical English Episode 5
Quick Test 9
File 9 Test
For students
Workbook Practical English 5
Can you remember? 1–9
Online Practice Practical English 5
Check your progress

OPTIONAL LEAD-IN (BOOKS CLOSED)   Elicit from the class what happened in the previous episode. Ask some questions, e.g. *What did Rob and Jenny want to do on their free morning? Why couldn't they do this? What happened to Jenny when she tried to find the gallery? Why did Daniel call Jenny?*. Alternatively, you could play the last scene of Episode 4.

1 ▶ AN INVITATION TO DINNER

a ◗ **9.21** Books open. Focus on the photo and elicit what Sts think is happening. <u>Don't</u> tell them if they are right or not yet.

Focus on sentences 1–5 and give Sts time to read them.

Then play the video / audio once the whole way through for them to mark the sentences *T* (true) or *F* (false). Make it clear that they don't need to correct the false sentences yet. Play again if necessary.

Get Sts to compare with a partner, and then check answers.

1 T **2** T **3** F **4** T **5** F

◗ **9.21**
R = Rob, J = Jenny, E = Eddie, D = Daniel
J Thanks for showing me around London yesterday. I had a great time.
R Me too. So, what did you do last night?
J Nothing, really. I had a lot of work to do. Emails, phone calls… What did you do?
R I wrote my article about the artist that I interviewed yesterday morning.
J Can I see it?
R Sure, it's on my laptop. Hang on a second. There.
J Oh, sorry. Hi, Eddie.
E Happy Birthday to you! Happy Birthday to you!
J Thanks! But listen, I can't talk right now. I'm in the office.
E OK.
J Yeah, later.
E Have fun!
J OK. Sorry, but…it's my birthday today.
R Really? Happy Birthday! Maybe we could have dinner tonight?
D Jennifer.
J Oh, hi, Daniel.
D I'd like to take you out for dinner this evening.
J This evening?
D Yes, for a working dinner. We have a lot to talk about before you go back to New York. I know a very good restaurant.
J Yes, of course.
D Great. See you later.
J Yes, sure. Sorry, Rob.

b Play the video / audio again so Sts can watch or listen and correct the false sentences.

Get Sts to compare with a partner, and then check answers.

3 It's **Jenny's** birthday.   **5** Jenny says *yes* to **Daniel**.

EXTRA SUPPORT   If there's time and you are using the video, you could get Sts to watch again with subtitles / showing the script, so they can see exactly what they understood / didn't understand. Translate / Explain any new words or phrases.

c ◗ **9.22** Focus on the **Responding to what somebody says** box and go through it with the class. Elicit / Explain that *congratulations* and *well done* are similar, but *congratulations* is used for something important, like getting engaged, getting a new job, passing an important exam, etc., whereas *well done* is used for smaller things, like getting an exercise right.

Now play the video / audio for Sts to watch or listen and repeat **B**'s phrases. Encourage them to copy the rhythm and intonation.

◗ **9.22**
See script in Student's Book on *p.76*

d ◗ **9.23** Tell Sts they are going to hear some phrases and they must respond using a phrase from the **Responding to what somebody says** box. Now focus on the example.

Play the video / audio, pausing for Sts to respond.

1
A I got two goals this afternoon.
B Well done!
2
A I passed my exams. I'm a doctor!
B Congratulations!
3
A I'm thirty today.
B Happy Birthday!
4
A I didn't pass my driving test.
B Oh dear! Never mind.
5
A I have my English exam tomorrow.
B Good luck!

Now repeat the activity, eliciting responses from individual Sts.

2 ▶ VOCABULARY understanding a menu

a Focus on the menu and get Sts to complete the three gaps. Check answers, and model and drill the pronunciation of the words. Focus especially on the stress in *desserts* /dɪ'zɜːts/ (you could point out that if they stress it on the first syllable, it will sound like *deserts*).

1 Starters   **2** Main courses   **3** Desserts

b 🔊 **9.24** Tell Sts to look at the highlighted words on the menu and, in pairs, to try and guess their meaning.

Check answers, either explaining in English, translating into Sts' L1, or getting Sts to check in their dictionaries.
courses /'kɔːsɪz/ = separate parts of a meal
soup /suːp/ = liquid food that you make by cooking things like vegetables or meat in water
grilled /grɪld/ = cooked on metal bars under or over heat
home-made /ˌhəʊm 'meɪd/ = made in your house, not bought in a shop or made in a factory
sauce /sɔːs/ = a thick liquid that you eat on or with other food
fresh /freʃ/ = made or picked not long ago

🔊 **9.24**
See highlighted words in Student's Book on *p.76*

Now play the video / audio for Sts to watch or listen and repeat the words.

c Get Sts to cover the menu or close their books. Write on the board STARTERS, MAIN COURSES, DESSERTS. In pairs, see if Sts can remember the two starters, three main courses and desserts.

Get feedback, asking the class to say what was on the menu.

EXTRA SUPPORT You could simply elicit the dishes from the whole class.

3 ▶ ORDERING A MEAL

a 🔊 **9.25** Focus on the photo and ask *Where are Jenny and Daniel?* (At the restaurant), *What are they doing?* (Looking at the menu and ordering).

Focus on the instructions and tell Sts to look at the menu on *p.76* as they listen. They should tick the dishes they hear.

Play the video / audio once the whole way through.

Get Sts to compare with a partner, and play the video / audio again if necessary.

Check answers. Ask *What's Jenny having for a starter?*, etc.

Jenny: soup; mushroom ravioli
Daniel: mozzarella salad; chicken

🔊 **9.25** 🔊 **9.26**
W = waiter, D = Daniel, J = Jenny
W Good evening. Do you have a reservation?
D Yes, a table for two. (*repeat*) My name's Daniel O'Connor. (*repeat*)
W Come this way, please.
***
W Are you ready to order?
J Yes. The soup and the mushroom ravioli, please. (*repeat*)
D I'd like the mozzarella salad and then the chicken, please. (*repeat*)
W What would you like to drink?
J Just water for me. (*repeat*)
D A bottle of mineral water, please. (*repeat*)
W Still or sparkling?
D Is sparkling OK? (*repeat*)
J Yes, sparkling. (*repeat*)
W Thank you, sir.
D Thank you. (*repeat*)

b Now focus on the conversation in the chart. Elicit that the **You hear** phrases are said by the waiter, and **You say** is what the customer says, here Daniel and Jenny. These phrases will be useful for Sts if they go to a restaurant.

Give Sts a minute to read through the conversation and think what the missing words might be. Then play the video / audio again, and get Sts to complete the gaps. Play again if necessary.

Get Sts to compare with a partner, and then check answers.

1 reservation   **2** way   **3** order   **4** like   **5** Still

Go through the conversation line by line with Sts, helping them with any words or expressions they don't understand.

Also make sure Sts understand the two kinds of mineral water, *still* (= no gas) and *sparkling* (= with gas).

c 🔊 **9.26** Now focus on the **You say** phrases. Tell Sts they're going to hear the conversation again. They should repeat the **You say** phrases when they hear the beep. Highlight the different ways of ordering, e.g. *The soup and the mushroom ravioli, please* or *I'd like (I would like) the mozzarella salad and then the chicken, please*, or *(Just) water for me*.

Play the video / audio, pausing if necessary for Sts to repeat the phrases. Encourage them to copy the rhythm and intonation, but <u>not</u> to try to copy Jenny's American accent. When Jenny pronounces *water* as /'wɔːdər/, Sts should use the British English pronunciation of *water* /'wɔːtə/.

🔊 **9.26**
Same as script 9.25 with repeat pauses

d Put Sts in groups of three **A**, **B**, and **C**. **A** is the waiter, and **B** and **C** are Daniel and Jenny. Get them to read the conversation aloud and then swap roles.

e Sts now role-play the conversation. **A** (book open) is the waiter. **B** and **C** (books closed) are customers. Tell the waiter to give **B** and **C** one of their books, open on *p.76*, to use as a menu.

If there's time, get Sts to swap roles at least once. Monitor and help.

When Sts have finished, get feedback to find out what Sts ordered.

 Print a menu for Sts to use in the role-play.

4 ▶ THE END OF THE MEAL

a 🔊 **9.27** Give Sts time to read the six questions.

Play the video / audio once the whole way through. Play it again if necessary.

Get Sts to compare with a partner, and then check answers. When you check the answer to 3, write what Daniel says (YOU'VE GOT BEAUTIFUL EYES) on the board. Point out to Sts that *you've got* is a contraction of *you have got*, which is a colloquial form of *you have*. You may also want to get Sts to speculate what the good news is when you check the answer to 5.

> 1 She goes out for dinner with friends or sees a film.
> 2 Coffee
> 3 He says 'You've got beautiful eyes.'
> 4 She thanks him and says they are from her mother.
> 5 Good news
> 6 She wants to go back to the hotel.

🔊 **9.27**

D = Daniel, J = Jenny, W = waiter, B = Barbara

D So, Jenny, I hear it's your birthday today.
J Yes, that's right.
D Well, Happy Birthday! How do you normally celebrate?
J Oh, nothing special. Maybe I go out for dinner with friends or see a movie.
D Well, we could go out somewhere, after dinner.
W Would you like a dessert?
J Not for me, thanks.
D OK, no.
W Coffee?
J A decaf espresso.
D The same for me, please.
W Two decaffeinated espressos. Certainly, sir.
D You know, Jenny, you've got beautiful eyes.
J I get them from my mother. Anyway, what are your plans for the July edition of the magazine?
D The, er, July edition? I, um…
J I have to take this. Sorry.
D No problem.
J Hi, Barbara.
B Jenny, just a quick call. We really like your idea about Rob Walker. He's a great writer.
J So can I ask him?
B Yes. Go ahead.
J That's great.
B Good luck. I hope he says yes.
J Me too.
D Good news?
J Yeah. That was Barbara, my boss from the New York office. She just gave me a little birthday present.
D So, would you like to go somewhere else?
J I'm sorry, Daniel. I'm a little tired.
D Yes. Of course. Waiter, could I have the bill, please?

 If there's time and you are using the video, you could get Sts to watch again with subtitles / showing the script, so they can see exactly what they understood / didn't understand. Translate / Explain any new words or phrases.

b Focus on the **Social English** phrases and go through them with the class.

In pairs, get Sts to decide who says them.

c 🔊 **9.28** Play the video / audio for Sts to watch or listen to the eight phrases and check.

Check answers. If you know your Sts' L1, you could get them to translate the phrases.

> **1** J **2** D **3** J **4** J **5** D **6** B **7** D **8** D

🔊 **9.28**

See Social English phrases in Student's Book on *p.77*

Now play the video / audio again, pausing after each phrase, for Sts to watch or listen and repeat.

d Focus on the instructions and make sure Sts understand what they have to do.

Get Sts to compare with a partner, and then check answers.

> **A** 7 **B** 2,3 **C** 8 **D** 1 **E** 4 **F** 5 **G** 6

Now put Sts in pairs and get them to practise the conversations.

Finally, focus on the **CAN YOU…?** questions and ask Sts if they feel confident they can now do these things. If they feel that they need more practice, tell them to go to *Online Practice* to watch the episode again and practise the language.

G superlative adjectives: *the biggest, the best,* etc.
V places and buildings
P consonant groups

Lesson plan

A reading text about the most dangerous place in the world to cross the road and other geographical superlatives provides the context to present and practise superlative adjectives and the lexis of places and buildings. The lesson starts with Vocabulary, where Sts learn the words for buildings and landmarks in a town or city. In Grammar, Sts make the logical progression from comparatives to superlatives, and look at some 'extreme' places in the world, e.g. *the biggest station, the oldest bridge,* etc. Pronunciation focuses on consonant groups, which occur in superlatives, e.g. *the most expensive,* and then Sts do a role-play about their town, using superlatives. Then an article from the British press gives Sts information about the most dangerous place in the world to cross the road. Writing focuses more directly on the Sts' own environment, and they write about their own town / city.

More materials
For teachers
Photocopiables
Grammar superlative adjectives *p.195*
Vocabulary Places and buildings puzzle *p.275* (instructions *p.256*)
Communicative What do you know about the UK? *p.244* (instructions *p.211*)
For students
Workbook 10A
Online Practice 10A

OPTIONAL LEAD-IN (BOOKS CLOSED)

Write on the board RUSSIA and CHINA. Ask Sts if they are big or small countries, and elicit that they are big. Then ask which is bigger, and elicit that Russia is bigger. (For reference, Russia is about 17 million km², and China is about 9.6 million km²).

Now rub CHINA off the board. Ask Sts if they know any country which is bigger than Russia (there isn't one). Elicit / Teach *Russia is the biggest country in the world.* Write the sentence on the board.

1 VOCABULARY places and buildings

a Books open. Tell Sts to look at sentences 1–6, which are all about famous tourist sights in the UK and the USA. In each one a word is missing. Sts should complete each gap with a word from the list.

Get Sts to compare with a partner.

b ◗)) **10.1** Play the audio for Sts to listen and check their answers to **a** or you could elicit the answers first, and then play the audio.

Check answers. Point out the silent *t* in *castle.*

1 Bridge	**2** Street	**3** Castle	**4** Park	**5** Gallery	**6** Square

---

◗)) **10.1**
1 The Brooklyn Bridge connects Manhattan and Brooklyn.
2 Downing Street is where the British Prime Minister lives.
3 Windsor Castle is the Royal Family's weekend home, and the largest inhabited castle in the world.
4 Central Park is a green space in the middle of New York.
5 The National Gallery is London's most famous art museum.
6 Times Square is the centre of New York's theatre district.

Finally, ask Sts if any of them have seen any of these places.

c Tell Sts to go to **Vocabulary Bank Places and buildings** on *p.164* and get them to do **a** individually or in pairs.

Vocabulary notes

You may want to highlight the difference between *a road* (= connects different towns or cities) and *a street* (= in a town or city).

◗)) **10.2** Now do **b**. Play the audio for Sts to listen and check.

Check answers.

◗)) **10.2**
Places and buildings
3 a chemist's
9 a church
4 a department store
6 a hospital
5 a market
2 a park
11 a police station
8 a post office
10 a shopping centre
7 a supermarket
1 a town hall
15 an art gallery
16 a castle
14 a museum
12 a theatre
13 a zoo
20 a bridge
19 a river
18 a road
21 a square
17 a street
23 a bus station
24 a car park
22 a railway station

Then either use the audio to drill the pronunciation of the words, or model and drill them yourself. Remind Sts that in compound nouns (e.g. *post office, art gallery*), the main stress is on the first word. Don't forget to remind Sts of the silent *t* in *castle,* and that *ch* is pronounced /k/ in *chemist's.* Give further practice of any other words your Sts find difficult to pronounce.

Focus on the **Other places of worship** box and go through it with the class.

Now focus on **c**. Get Sts to cover the words and use the photos to test themselves or their partner.

Finally, focus on **Activation** and model and drill the question. Put Sts in pairs to ask and answer the question. Tell Sts to go back to the main lesson **10A**.

 If you think Sts need more practice, you may want to give them the **Vocabulary** photocopiable activity at this point.

2 GRAMMAR superlative adjectives

a Tell Sts to look at photos 1–6 and ask if they know or can guess which countries they are in. Don't tell them if they are right.

b Focus on the instructions. In pairs, Sts complete sentences 1–6 using phrases from the list. Establish that the phrases are all superlative adjectives.

c 🔊 **10.3** Before you play the audio, tell Sts they are going to hear a little more information about each place. Play the audio for Sts to listen and check their answers to **a** and **b**.

Check answers. If you have a map of the world in class, you could show Sts where each country is.

> **a**
> 1 the UK   2 the USA   3 Italy   4 Egypt   5 Vietnam
> 6 Germany
> **b**
> 1 The busiest
> 2 The biggest
> 3 The oldest
> 4 The longest
> 5 The most dangerous
> 6 The tallest

🔊 **10.3**
1 The busiest shopping street in Europe is Oxford Street. Five hundred thousand shoppers a day visit the street in the centre of London, capital of the UK.
2 The biggest railway station in the world is Grand Central Terminal in New York. It has forty-four platforms, and covers nearly two hundred thousand square metres.
3 The oldest bridge in Europe is the *Ponte Fabricio*. It's in Rome, Italy, and it was built more than two thousand years ago.
4 The longest river in the world is the Nile. It's six thousand eight hundred and fifty-three kilometres long, and goes through eleven different African countries.
5 The most dangerous place in the world to cross the road is Ho Chi Minh City, in Vietnam. There are five million scooters in this city, as well as cars, trucks, and buses.
6 The tallest cathedral in the world is *Ulm Münster*, in Germany. It is one hundred and sixty-one metres tall.

 Get Sts to listen again and write down any extra information they hear about each place.

d Focus on the chart and the three column headings. Get Sts to complete the chart with the adjectives from **b**.

Check answers. Model and drill pronunciation.

> tall   longer   the biggest   busy   the most dangerous

e Do this as a whole-class activity.

> For one-syllable adjectives, we add *-est* (and not *-er*) to the end of the adjective. For longer adjectives with two or more syllables, we put *the most* instead of *more* before the adjective.

f Tell Sts to go to **Grammar Bank 10A** on *p.142*.

Grammar notes

Make sure Sts are clear about the difference between comparatives (to compare two things or people, etc.) and superlatives (to say which is, e.g. the smallest / largest in a group of three or more). In your Sts' L1, they may just use the comparative form + *the*. (Typical error: ~~the better place in the world…~~)

Formation of superlatives is very easy once Sts know comparatives. *-er* changes to *-est* with most short adjectives, and *more* changes to *the most* before long adjectives.

Spelling rules

These are exactly the same as for comparatives, e.g. *hotter / the hottest; prettier / the prettiest.*

Highlight that we use **in** the world, *in the class*, etc. after superlatives, NOT ~~of~~.

🔊 **10.4** Focus on the example sentences and play the audio for Sts to listen and repeat. Then go through the rules with the class.

Now focus on the exercises for **10A** on *p.143*. Sts do the exercises individually or in pairs.

Check answers. Get Sts to spell the *-est* adjectives in **a** where there's a spelling change and write them on the board. In **b**, get them to read the full sentences, helping them with the rhythm.

> **a 1** the hottest   **2** the cheapest   **3** the worst   **4** the easiest
> **5** the wettest   **6** the tallest / longest   **7** the furthest   **8** the dirtiest
> **b 1** the biggest   **2** the best   **3** the smallest   **4** the most comfortable   **5** the noisiest   **6** the most stressed   **7** the youngest   **8** The most beautiful

Tell Sts to go back to the main lesson **10A**.

 If you think Sts need more practice, you may want to give them the **Grammar** photocopiable activity at this point.

g 🔊 **10.5** Tell Sts they are going to hear six questions with superlatives and they must write them down.

Play the audio, pausing after each question to give Sts time to write. Play again if necessary.

Check answers, eliciting the questions onto the board.

🔊 **10.5**
1 What's the noisiest city in the world?
2 What's the foggiest city in Europe?
3 Which US city has the biggest population?
4 What's the highest capital city in the world?
5 Which city has the busiest airport in the world?
6 Which city has the worst traffic in the world?

h Focus on the possible answers and make sure Sts know where they all are.

Put Sts in small groups and get them to ask the questions from **g** and choose an answer from **h**.

Elicit answers from the class.

> 1 Tokyo   2 Milan   3 New York   4 La Paz   5 Atlanta
> 6 Brussels

3 PRONUNCIATION & SPEAKING

consonant groups

a 🔊 **10.6** Focus on the **Consonant groups** box and go through it with the class.

Tell Sts to look at the speech bubble and play the audio once for them just to listen.

🔊 **10.6**
See word and phrases in Student's Book on *p.79*

Now play the audio again and get Sts to listen and repeat.

b 🔊 **10.7** Now tell Sts they are going to do the same with the adjectives in 1–4. Tell them the word in brackets is the noun they must use with the adjective. If Sts are confused, write BEAUTIFUL (SQUARE) on the board and show them the speech bubble in **a**.

Then play the audio for Sts to listen and repeat.

🔊 **10.7**
1 old – the oldest – the oldest building – What's the oldest building?
2 interesting – the most interesting – the most interesting museum – What's the most interesting museum?
3 good – the best – the best shopping street – What's the best shopping street?
4 nice – the nicest – the nicest place – What's the nicest place?

You may want to repeat it, pausing after each word / phrase, and get individual Sts to say the phrase and question.

EXTRA CHALLENGE   Get Sts to say the word, phrases, and question first. Then play the audio for them to listen and check.

c Put Sts in pairs, **A** and **B**, and tell them to go to **Communication I'm a tourist. Help!**, **A** on *p.107*, **B** on *p.112*.

Go through the instructions with Sts carefully. Highlight that the tourist only speaks English, so the local person must explain everything in English. Highlight, too (if your Sts are from the same town), that the tourist should pretend not to know anything and to ask for as much information as possible, and the local person should try to answer all his / her questions in as much detail as possible.

Now focus on questions 1–6 and the examples, and explain that Sts have to complete the questions with the superlative of the adjective in brackets. You might want to elicit / explain the meaning of *typical* and *popular*.

EXTRA SUPPORT   Get Sts to write in the superlatives, and check them before they start.

Student A	Student B
1 the most beautiful	1 the oldest
2 the easiest	2 the nicest
3 the most interesting	3 the best
4 the best	4 the most typical
5 the nicest	5 the most popular
6 the most famous	6 the most beautiful

If you are not from the same city / country as your Sts, get them to interview you first with their first two questions to find out about your town / city.

! Don't be afraid to say *I don't know, but I think it's…* This will provide a good model for Sts.

Get Sts to role-play the conversation. First, Sts **A** are the tourist. Monitor and help, especially with superlatives.

Then tell Sts to swap roles, so now Sts **B** are the tourist.

Get some feedback. Where Sts are from the same town / city, see if they agree.

Tell Sts to go back to the main lesson **10A**.

4 READING   identifying paragraph endings

a Focus on the photo and the title of the article, and ask Sts where it is (Ho Chi Minh City). Elicit / Explain the meaning of the title.

Tell Sts to read the article and decide which suggestion in the article is the most useful.

When Sts have finished, elicit responses.

EXTRA SUPPORT   Before Sts read the article the first time, check whether you need to pre-teach any vocabulary.

b Now set a time limit for Sts to read the article again and complete the gaps with *A–E*.

Get Sts to compare with a partner, and then check answers.

Keep walking D
Cross with a local person E
Cross in a group B
Find a policeman A
Take a taxi C

c Tell Sts to cover the article, and elicit / explain the meaning of *vehicles* (= a thing that takes people from one place to another). Model and drill pronunciation.

In pairs or as a whole-class activity, Sts try to remember all seven words.

If Sts worked in pairs, check answers. You could draw a mind map on the board with *vehicles* in the middle. Elicit / Explain that a *scooter* is a light motorbike with a small engine.

cars, lorries, bikes, buses, motorbikes, scooters, taxi

Deal with any other new vocabulary. Model and drill the pronunciation of any tricky words.

d Focus on the six questions and make sure Sts understand all the lexis.

Put Sts in small groups and get them to discuss the questions.

Get some feedback from various groups. You could also tell Sts if you have had problems crossing a road.

5 WRITING

Focus on the instructions and read the example about Kielce. Tell Sts to write an advert for their town / city, and to include some superlatives. If your Sts are all from the same town / city, you could give them the option to write about another place they know well. You could set this as homework and ask Sts to add some photos to their advert.

Put the adverts around the class for Sts to read.

Ask Sts if they found out anything new / interesting about the places.

G *be going to* (plans), future time expressions
V city holidays: *stay in a hotel*, etc.
P sentence stress

Lesson plan

The context of this lesson is travel and city breaks. The lesson starts with Grammar, where *be going to* for future plans is presented and practised by listening to and reading about two people who are planning to travel to five continents in one day. Pronunciation focuses on sentence stress in *going to* sentences. In Listening, Sts listen to an expert from a website called Responsible Travel giving advice about how to plan a holiday. In Vocabulary and Speaking, Sts look at some common holiday phrases and then plan their own dream trip. Finally, in Writing they write a formal email, booking some accommodation for a holiday.

More materials
For teachers
Photocopiables
Grammar be going to (plans) *p.196*
Communicative Future plans *p.245* (instructions *p.212*)
For students
Workbook 10B
Online Practice 10B

OPTIONAL LEAD-IN (BOOKS CLOSED)

Revise continents. Play *Hangman* (see *p.24* for instructions) with the word EUROPE.

Then ask Sts what it is (a continent).

Finally, elicit the other five continents and write them on the board.

1 GRAMMAR *be going to* (plans)

a Books open. Focus on the instructions and do this as a whole-class activity. Point out the example.

> Punta Cana is in the Dominican Republic, North America.
> Casablanca is in Morocco, Africa.
> Paris is in France, Europe.
> Istanbul is in Turkey, Europe / Asia.

b ◉ **10.8** Focus on the task and make sure Sts understand what Gunnar and Adrian are planning to do. You could tell Sts that in order to break the record, Gunnar and Adrian have to leave the airport in each place, even for just a short time. Make sure Sts cover the interview and look at the map.

Before playing the audio, you might want to tell Sts that Gunnar is from Norway and has a slight accent. Play the audio for Sts to listen and draw the route. Play the audio again if necessary.

Check answers. Ask Sts which continent they are not planning to visit (Australia).

> Istanbul > Casablanca > Paris > Punta Cana > Caracas

◉ **10.8**

I = interviewer, G = Gunnar, A = Adrian

I Gunnar, Adrian, tell us your plan. How can you visit five continents in one day?

G We're going to start in Istanbul. Part of Istanbul is in Asia, which is our first continent. At ten past one in the morning we're going to fly to Casablanca, which is in Morocco, in North Africa. Continent number two.

I Are you going to get another flight immediately?

A No, first we're going to visit the famous mosque – it's the largest mosque in Morocco. Then our next flight is to Paris, at seven thirty-five in the morning.

I So Europe is your third continent. How long are you going to be in Paris?

G Five minutes, maybe? We're just going to go out of the airport – that's one of the rules of our challenge – and then go back in. We only have one hour fifty-five minutes before our next flight, to Punta Cana, in the Dominican Republic.

I So North America is your fourth continent?

G Yes, that's right. And from there, the final flight is to Caracas in Venezuela, South America – our last continent. We're going to arrive at five past ten. And then we're going to celebrate!

---

c Tell Sts to uncover the interview and look at the verbs in the list.

Give Sts time to quickly read the interview before playing the audio.

EXTRA CHALLENGE Get Sts to complete the gaps before they listen to the audio.

Play the audio for Sts to listen and complete the gaps.

Get Sts to compare with a partner, and then check answers.

> **1** start **2** fly **3** get **4** visit **5** be **6** go out **7** arrive **8** celebrate

d Either put Sts in pairs and get them to answer the questions, or do this as a whole-class activity.

If Sts worked in pairs, check answers.

> **1** infinitive **2** the future

e Tell Sts to go to **Grammar Bank 10B** on *p.142*.

Grammar notes

going to + infinitive is the most common way to express future plans and the main future form taught in this level. It is often used with time expressions like *tonight*, *next week*, and *next summer*. Sts don't usually find the concept of *going to* a problem, but the form needs plenty of practice. A typical error is the omission of the auxiliary *be*, e.g. ~~I going to have dinner~~, or using the present simple of *go*, e.g. ~~I go to have dinner~~.

In song lyrics, *going to* is sometimes spelled *gonna* because of the way it is pronounced (see **Pronunciation notes** in **2**). Discourage Sts from using this in written English.

Some Sts may know the future form *will* and may ask about this. Explain that both *going to* and *will* are used to talk about the future. In the *English File* series, *be going to* is presented first to talk about plans and predictions. *Going to* for predictions is practised in the next lesson. Sts will learn the grammar of *will* in *English File* Pre-intermediate, but will see some examples in **Practical English**.

◗) 10.9 Focus on the example sentences and play the audio for Sts to listen and repeat. Then go through the rules with the class.

Now focus on the exercises for **10B** on *p.143*. Sts do the exercises individually or in pairs.

Check answers, getting Sts to read the full sentences.

a
1 're going to book **2** 'm going to stay **3** 's going to study
4 are going to get **5** 's going to work **6** isn't going to go
7 aren't going to visit
b
1 'm going to call **2** are…going to have **3** isn't going to come **4** are…going to get **5** aren't going to buy
6 Are…going to watch

Tell Sts to go back to the main lesson **10B**.

EXTRA SUPPORT If you think Sts need more practice, you may want to give them the **Grammar** photocopiable activity at this point.

f ◗) 10.10 Remind Sts of Gunnar and Adrian's plan. Focus on the question.

Play the audio for Sts to listen and find out if Gunnar and Adrian succeeded.

Check the answer.

Yes, they did.

◗) 10.10
(script in Student's Book on *p.122*)

I = interviewer, G = Gunnar

I Gunnar, can you give us a quick summary of your journey?
G OK, so we left Istanbul twenty minutes late, at one thirty in the morning – not a good start. But we arrived in Casablanca more or less on time. We visited the mosque at four thirty in the morning. We couldn't go inside though – we just saw it from the outside! Then we went back to the airport and flew to Paris. When we arrived, we rushed outside and took some photos, and then went back in to a different terminal. It was really stressful, the most stressful part of the trip – but we just got to the gate in time for our flight to Punta Cana. When we got there, we went to a beach that was just twenty kilometres from the airport, and we relaxed there for a bit, and then went back to the airport and got our flight to Caracas. And we arrived here at ten at night, and we officially entered the country at ten fifteen. So – five continents in one day! We did it!

EXTRA IDEA Before playing the audio, you could ask Sts what they think success or failure depended on, e.g. the airlines, the weather, etc.

g Focus on the question and the three options, eliciting / explaining any lexis Sts don't know, especially the word *trip*.

Do this as a whole-class activity, by getting a show of hands for each option. Elicit some reasons. You could also tell the class what you think.

2 PRONUNCIATION & SPEAKING
sentence stress

Pronunciation notes

When native speakers speak quickly, they tend to pronounce *going to* as *gonna* /ˈɡənə/. It is a good idea to point out this pronunciation to Sts as they will hear it if they have contact with native speakers or listen to songs, and they will see it written down in song lyrics. This pronunciation is widespread in British and American English, particularly in conversation, although it might not be appropriate in some formal situations.

At this level, we recommend that it is better to teach the more 'correct' pronunciation, i.e. pronouncing both *going* and *to* (using the weak form of *to*). Sts can use the more colloquial form later when their speed of speech increases.

a ◗) 10.11 Tell Sts they are going to listen to the two conversations. Before playing the audio, focus on the first question and ask Sts which words are stressed (*What*, *do*, and *summer*).

Play the audio once for Sts just to listen.

◗) 10.11
See conversations in Student's Book on *p.81*

Play the audio again, pausing after each line for Sts to listen and repeat. Encourage Sts to get the right rhythm.

EXTRA IDEA Get Sts to read the conversations aloud in pairs.

b Put Sts in pairs, **A** and **B**, and tell them to go to
Communication What are you going to do?, **A** on
p.107, **B** on *p.112*.

Tell Sts they need to complete their questions with *going to*. Point out the example.

Sit **A** and **B** face-to-face if possible. **A** asks his / her
questions to **B**. Monitor and help Sts to get the rhythm
right when they read their questions.

B then asks **A** his / her questions.

When both Sts have answered the questions, get
feedback from the class.

Tell Sts to go back to the main lesson **10B**.

3 LISTENING using prior knowledge to predict stages

a Focus on the task and make sure Sts understand *plan*.

Give Sts time to read the four questions and make sure
they understand *previous*.

Now get Sts to number the questions.

Put Sts in pairs and get them to compare answers.

Get some feedback.

b 🔊 **10.12** Focus on the task and make sure Sts understand
who Justin Francis is.

Play the audio for Sts to listen and complete the task.

Check answers. Find out, with a show of hands, if anyone
had the same order as Justin. <u>Don't</u> ask Sts if they agree
with Justin, as they will be doing this later in the lesson.

EXTRA SUPPORT Read through the script and decide if you
need to pre-teach any new lexis before Sts listen.

> **1** What am I going to do?
> **2** Who am I going to go with?
> **3** What previous holidays did I really enjoy?
> **4** Where am I going to go?

🔊 **10.12**

(script in Student's Book on *pp.122–123*)

If you're thinking of having a holiday or travelling somewhere nice,
the planning can be complicated. The internet is full of reviews of
hotels, restaurants, and attractions. There are so many different ways
of travelling, and thousands of places to go. Where do you start?
Why not follow these three simple steps to find the right holiday
for you?

Step one. Think about what you want to do on your holiday. The first
thing people usually try to decide is *where* they want to go, but it's
probably better to start by thinking about *what* you want to do.
Do you want to relax? Then think about *how* you relax. For
example, do you like reading or doing yoga, or do you like doing
something more active? Do you want to go somewhere completely
different? Do you want to visit an exciting new city, or see some
countryside and animals that are different from where you live?
Seeing something completely new is a great way to forget about
your normal life. Do you want to have an adventure? Perhaps you're
dreaming about climbing Everest or living with an African tribe. You
could use your holiday to make one of those dreams come true.
Do you want to learn something new? Not everybody wants to sit
in a classroom learning Spanish, or be in a kitchen learning to cook
when they're on holiday, but some people love it. And nowadays
you can do courses in many countries and experience a different
culture at the same time.

So now step two. Think about the people you're going to go with.
Are they family or friends? Do they have children? What do they
want to do? People have different needs and interests, and if you're
all going to enjoy the holiday, you need to make sure you all want

the same things. But if what you really want to do is to meet new
people, perhaps it would be better to travel alone.

And finally, step three. Think about good holidays you had in the
past. Why were they good? Perhaps it was the people you were with.
Perhaps it was something you learned, or an experience you had.
What can you repeat from those holidays?

Of course, there are always other things you need to consider, like
how much money you can spend, and how much time you can be
away. But first follow these three steps, and then you're ready to start
thinking about *where* you want to go!

EXTRA IDEA Ask Sts what else Justin said is important to
think about.

> How much money you can spend and how much time you can
> be away

c Now tell Sts they are going to hear the audio again and
they must answer questions 1–5.

Go through the questions before Sts listen, making sure
they understand all the lexis, e.g. *skill*, *to make sure*, etc.

Now play the audio again, pausing after Justin has
answered each question.

Get Sts to compare with a partner, and then check
answers.

> **1** • Reading, doing yoga
>   • Visit an exciting new city, or see some countryside and
>   animals that are different from where you live
>   • Climb Everest or live with an African tribe
>   • Learn Spanish or learn to cook
> **2** Make sure everyone wants the same things.
> **3** To travel alone
> **4** The people you were with, something you learned, or an
>   experience you had
> **5** Where you want to go

Deal with any new vocabulary. Model and drill the
pronunciation of any tricky words.

EXTRA SUPPORT If there's time, you could get Sts to listen
again with the script on *pp.122–123*, so they can see exactly
what they understood / didn't understand. Translate /
Explain any new words or phrases.

d Either put Sts in pairs and get them to answer the
questions, or do this as a whole-class activity.

If Sts worked in pairs, get feedback.

4 VOCABULARY & SPEAKING city holidays

a Tell Sts to look at the nine phrases related to holidays and
to complete each one with a verb from the list.

Check answers. You might want to point out that
accommodation is uncountable.

> **1** book **2** go **3** rent **4** stay **5** eat **6** visit **7** buy
> **8** have **9** meet

Now get Sts to cover phrases 1–9 (but not the verbs in the
list) and see if they can remember the holiday phrases.

b Focus on the task and put Sts in pairs.

Monitor and help while Sts try to find things they both like
doing on holiday.

Get some feedback from various pairs.

c Focus on the task and the five questions. Tell Sts that they are going to plan a dream trip in their pairs. Their plan must be a visit to three cities in the same continent, and the holiday can be a maximum of ten days.

Before Sts start, go through the **Making suggestions** box with the class, and encourage them to use these phrases when planning their trip with their partner. You could write them on the board to serve as an extra reminder.

Give Sts about five minutes to make their plans for each of the five questions. Monitor and help, encouraging them to use *Why don't we…?*, etc. for making suggestions. Monitor and help.

d Now tell Sts to change partners and to tell their new partner the agreed plan from **c**. Focus on the example in the speech bubble before they start.

e Finally, ask Sts if they are still happy with their original plan, or if they prefer their new partner's plan. Get some Sts to tell the class their plans.

EXTRA IDEA Get one pair to come out to the front of the class. Act as a TV presenter and interview them, using the questions from **c**, e.g. *What cities are you going to visit?*.

5 WRITING a formal email

Remind Sts of / Elicit the difference between informal and formal writing: *informal* = e.g. to a friend, and *formal* = e.g. to a person we don't know, or to a company or institution. We need to use a different style of writing depending on whether it is an informal or formal situation. Before going to the **Writing** section, quickly elicit what Sts can remember about writing an informal email, e.g. how you begin (*Hi / Dear…*) and end (*Best wishes / Write soon*, etc.).

Now tell Sts to go to **Writing A formal email** on *p.117*.

a Focus on the advertisement and the email. Make sure Sts know what a *Bed and Breakfast* is. Tell Sts to complete the gaps in Pascale's email with the words in the list. Check answers.

> **1** Dear **2** double **3** from **4** are **5** about **6** would
> **7** hope **8** confirm **9** Regards

Ask Sts some comprehension questions to make sure they understand the email, e.g. *Who are Mr and Mrs Buckingham?* (the owners of the Bed and Breakfast), *Why is Pascale writing to Mr and Mrs Buckingham?* (to confirm her reservation, ask about parking, and arrange to have dinner there), *How many nights does Pascale want to stay?* (three nights), etc.

b Focus on the task and give Sts time to think of their answers.

c Focus on the **Formal emails** box and go through it with the class. Elicit / Remind Sts of the difference between *Mrs* and *Ms* (some married women use *Mrs*. Most women use *Ms* as this gives no indication of marital status). Highlight that we don't usually use contractions in formal writing.

Now tell Sts to write their email to the Bed and Breakfast. They must include answers to the questions in **b**, i.e. who they are travelling with, which rooms they want, how many nights they want to stay, etc.

As this writing task is fairly short, you may like to get Sts to do it in class.

EXTRA IDEA If your Sts also need to write formal letters, not just emails, tell them that they can use exactly the same language to begin and end as in an email, but they should put:

◾ their address in the top right-hand corner

◾ the name and address of the person / company they're writing to on the left-hand side, slightly lower down

◾ the date under the name and address

◾ *Yours faithfully* (if the letter is addressed *Dear Sir / Madam*) or *Yours sincerely* (if it is addressed to a name, e.g. *Dear Mrs Richards*)

You could also teach as a set phrase *I look forward to hearing from you*.

G *be going to* (predictions)
V verb phrases: *become famous*, etc.
P word stress

Lesson plan

This lesson looks at another use of the future *be going to* to express predictions (what we think or are sure is going to happen in the future). The context is a short story about a fortune teller, which has also been dramatized on video. The lesson starts with Sts discussing fortune telling and looking at related verb phrases. In Pronunciation, Sts look at stress in two-syllable words. Then Sts read and listen to a short story about a fortune teller, which has a 'twist' at the end. As they read / listen to the story, Sts have to make a series of predictions about the outcome. After reading and listening to the first four parts of the story, Sts then have the possibility of watching them on video, and then finally discovering what happens in the end. However, if you are unable to use video in class, you can simply use the audio for the end of the story, and tell Sts to watch the video at home. After the story, Sts look at the grammar of using *going to* for predictions, and the lesson ends with Sts telling each other's fortunes. If you would like to give Sts the actual cards to use for this stage, go to *p.248* to photocopy them and cut them up.

More materials
For teachers
Photocopiables
Grammar *be going to* (predictions) *p.197*
Communicative Predictions *p.246* (instructions *p.212*)
Teacher's Resource Centre
Video It's written in the cards
For students
Workbook 10C
Online Practice 10C

OPTIONAL LEAD-IN (BOOKS CLOSED)

Revise *going to* for plans. Write the following prompts on the board:

TONIGHT   TOMORROW NIGHT   NEXT WEEKEND   NEXT SUMMER

Get Sts to ask you *What are you going to do…?* with the prompts.

Sts ask each other in pairs.

1 VOCABULARY verb phrases

a Books open. Focus on the cards and ask Sts what they think they are for. Elicit / Tell them they are for fortune telling, i.e. predicting somebody's future.

Now focus on the questions and elicit answers from the class. Tell Sts if you believe in fortune telling, and if you have had any experience of it. Find out if any of the Sts have, too.

b Sts match the cards and verb phrases. Point out that the first one (*be lucky*) has been done for them.

Check answers, and model and drill pronunciation.

B	have a surprise
C	fall in love
D	get married
E	become famous
F	travel
G	meet somebody new
H	move house
I	get a new job
J	get a lot of money

Get Sts to test each other's memory by covering the phrases and pointing at the cards.

2 PRONUNCIATION word stress

a Focus on the **Word stress in two-syllable words** box and go through it with the class.

Now focus on the words in the list and tell Sts that all these words are in a story they are going to hear. They must look at the words and decide which four are stressed on the second syllable. Remind Sts that exercises like this are easier if they say the words aloud.

Get Sts to compare answers with a partner.

b 🔊 **10.13** Play the audio for Sts to listen and check.

Check answers.

be<u>lieve</u>   i<u>dea</u>   sur<u>prise</u>   to<u>day</u>

🔊 **10.13**
See words in the list in Student's Book on *p.82*

Put Sts in pairs and get them to practise saying the words.

EXTRA SUPPORT Play the audio again, pausing after each word for Sts to listen and repeat. Then put them in pairs and get them to practise saying the words.

3 READING & LISTENING following the events of a story

a Focus on the title of the story and help Sts to explain / translate it. Elicit some ideas about the story.

b 🔊 **10.14** Focus on questions 1–3. Now play the audio and get Sts to read and listen to **Part 1** of the story.

Get Sts to answer the questions in pairs and then check answers. Elicit / Teach the meaning of any words you think Sts may not have understood, e.g. *a voice*.

EXTRA SUPPORT Read through the scripts and decide if you need to pre-teach any new lexis before Sts listen.

! Although the story is in the past, it is more natural to ask and answer questions about it in the present.

1 Madame Yolanda, the fortune teller
2 A man because Madame Yolanda isn't there.
3 Because the room was dark.

🔊 10.14
See *It's written in the cards* Part 1 in Student's Book on *p.83*

c 🔊 10.15 Sts now listen to **Part 2**. Tell Sts you are going
to play the audio twice. Sts, in pairs, complete the gaps in
1–4. Play again if necessary.

Check answers. Elicit / Teach the meaning of any words
you think Sts may not have understood, e.g. *face down*,
turn over.

1 boyfriend   2 five   3 (very) lucky   4 stay

🔊 10.15
(script in Student's Book on *p.123*)
J = Jane, Ji = Jim, N = narrator
Part 2
J   Well, I have a problem with my boyfriend. We argue all the time.
     I'm not sure that he loves me. I want to know if we're going to stay
     together.
Ji Please choose five cards, but don't look at them.
N   *The fortune teller put the cards on the table, face down. Jane took*
     five cards. The fortune teller turned over the first card.
Ji Ah, this is a good card. This means you're going to be very lucky.
J   But am I going to stay with my boyfriend?
N   *Jane asked.*
Ji Maybe.
N   *…said the fortune teller.*
Ji We need to look at the other cards first.

d 🔊 10.16 Focus on questions 1–5. Then play the audio
and tell Sts to read and listen to **Part 3**.

Give Sts time to answer the questions in pairs.

Check answers and elicit some ideas for question 5.

1 A house. She is going to move to another country.
2 Her boyfriend can't move.
3 A heart. She's going to fall in love.
4 Jim is an actor from New York. She met him at a party.

🔊 10.16
See *It's written in the cards* Part 3 in Student's Book on *p.83*

e 🔊 10.17 Focus on sentences 1–4. Then play the audio
and tell Sts to listen to **Part 4**.

Give Sts time to complete the sentences in pairs.

Check answers. Elicit / Teach the meaning of any words
you think Sts may not have understood, e.g. *ring*, *note*.

1 leave, another country   2 get married   3 happy, very happy
4 50

🔊 10.17
(script in Student's Book on *p.123*)
Part 4
N   *The fortune teller turned over a card with two rings.*
Ji Now I can see everything clearly. You're going to leave your
     boyfriend and go away with the other man, with Jim…to another
     country. And very soon you're going to get married.
J   Married? To Jim! But am I going to be happy with him?
Ji You're going to be very happy together. I'm sure of it.

N   *Jane looked at her watch.*
J   Oh no, look at the time. I'm going to be late for work.
N   *She stood up, left a fifty-pound note on the table, and ran out of the*
     room.

4 ▶ VIDEO LISTENING

a 🔊 10.18 Tell Sts they are going to watch or listen to
Parts 1–4 again. Get them to close their books and try to
follow the story. Play the video / audio once the whole
way through.

Ask Sts what they think is going to happen.

🔊 10.18
See scripts 10.14–10.17

 You could get Sts to listen again to the four
parts of the audio with the scripts in the main lesson and on
p.123, so they can see exactly what they understood / didn't
understand. If you are using the video, you could get Sts to
watch again with subtitles / showing the script.

b 🔊 10.19 Focus on the three questions. Then play the
video / audio and tell Sts to watch or listen to **Part 5**.

Give Sts time to answer the questions in pairs.

Check answers and elicit some ideas for question 3.

1 Jim, the actor that Jane met at the party
2 Because she helped him.
3 A plane
    Accept any reasonable predictions: her plane is going to
    crash. If he travels with her, he is going to die, too.

🔊 10.19
N = narrator, Y = Yolanda, J = Jim
Part 5
N   *The fortune teller stood up. He turned on the light. At that moment, a*
     woman came in.
Y   So, what happened?
N   *…she asked.*
J   It was perfect! She believed everything.
N   *…said Jim.*
J   I told you I'm a very good actor. She was sure I was a fortune
     teller!
N   *He gave the woman one hundred pounds.*
J   That's Jane's fifty pounds and another fifty pounds from me.
     Thanks very much, Madame Yolanda. Bye.
N   *Madame Yolanda took the money. The fifth card was still on the*
     table, face down. She turned it over. It was the plane. She looked at it
     for a minute and then she shouted.
Y   Wait, young man! Don't travel with that girl – her plane is going to…
N   *But the room was empty.*

 If there's time and you are using the video,
you could get Sts to watch again with subtitles / showing
the script, so they can see exactly what they understood /
didn't understand. Translate / Explain any new words or
phrases.

5 GRAMMAR *be going to* (predictions)

a Focus on the two sentences and make sure Sts
understand *a prediction* (= something you think is going
to happen). Do this as a whole-class activity.

1 is a prediction and 2 is a plan.

b Tell Sts to go to **Grammar Bank 10C** on *p.142*.

Grammar notes

Sts learned the use of *going to* to express future plans in
the previous lesson. Here, the same structure is used to
make predictions (what we think or are sure will happen).
Will can also be used to make predictions. This is taught in
Pre-intermediate.

10.20 Focus on the example sentences and play the
audio for Sts to listen and repeat. Then go through the
rules with the class.

Focus on the exercises for **10C** on *p.143*. Sts do the
exercises individually or in pairs.

Check answers, getting Sts to read the full sentences.

a **1** They're going to have dinner.
   2 It's going to be a nice day.
   3 She's going to get the bus.
   4 He's going to make an omelette.
   5 She's going to send an email.

b **1** 're going to have
   2 isn't going to pass
   3 are going to buy
   4 'm not going to finish
   5 're going to win
   6 're going to be
   7 'm not going to like
   8 's going to forget
   9 's going to sleep
  10 're going to have

Tell Sts to go back to the main lesson **10C**.

EXTRA SUPPORT If you think Sts need more practice, you
may want to give them the **Grammar** photocopiable
activity at this point.

c Tell Sts to write one prediction for each category – the
weather, sport, their town / country, and the student
himself / herself. All four sentences should start with
I think. Point out the example.

d In pairs, Sts now read their predictions to each other
and say whether or not they agree with their partner's
predictions.

Get some feedback.

6 SPEAKING

Go through the instructions with Sts and focus on the
example in the speech bubbles. Then put Sts in pairs,
A and **B**, and get them to sit face-to-face if possible.

Sts individually number the cards *1–10*. Stress that it
should be in random order. Number your cards, too.

Demonstrate the activity. Get a student to tell you a
number, and 'tell his / her fortune', depending on the card
he / she has chosen.

Student **A** is the fortune teller first. **B** chooses five
numbers between one and ten, and tells **A**, who writes
them down. **A** predicts **B**'s future according to the 'cards'
he / she has chosen. Then Sts swap roles.

! If you have odd numbers, have a group of three, where
A tells **B**'s fortune, **B** tells **C**'s, and **C** tells **A**'s.

Get feedback by asking a few Sts what's going to happen
to them.

EXTRA IDEA You could photocopy the **Communicative**
photocopiable activity and cut out the cards. Give each pair
a pack of cards. Sts don't need to think of any numbers, they
simply choose five cards from the pack.

9&10 Revise and Check

For instructions on how to use these pages, see *p.39*.

GRAMMAR

1 a 2 b 3 a 4 c 5 a 6 b 7 c 8 b 9 b 10 a
11 b 12 a 13 c 14 c 15 c

VOCABULARY

a
1 dessert (the others are meals)
2 strawberries (the others are vegetables)
3 sugar (the others are drinks)
4 tomatoes (the others are, or are made from, potatoes)
5 chicken (the others are desserts)
b
1 beer 2 tomatoes 3 honey 4 rice 5 fruit juice
c
1 a hundred and twenty 2 million 3 department store
4 square 5 station
d
1 stay 2 go 3 become 4 get 5 fall 6 book 7 meet
8 visit 9 have 10 move

PRONUNCIATION

c
1 bread /e/ 2 chemist /k/ 3 oil /ɔɪ/ 4 town /aʊ/
5 wrote /r/
d
1 chocolate 2 dessert 3 supermarket 4 interesting
5 dangerous

CAN YOU understand this text?

a
1 C 2 B 3 A
b
1 A 2 B 3 A 4 C 5 C 6 A 7 B 8 C

▶ CAN YOU understand these people?

1 a 2 c 3 b 4 b 5 c

◀)) 10.21

1 Graziella
I = interviewer, G = Graziella
I Do you think you have a healthy diet?
G Um, for the most part, I would say I have a healthy diet. Er, lots of fruits and vegetables, and a little bit of chocolate, here and there.
I How much sugar and salt do you eat?
G Um, I don't have that much salt in my diet, but with all of the fruit that I have, I would say I have quite a bit of sugar, natural sugars.

2 Kara
I = interviewer, K = Kara
I Do you like cooking?
K I love to cook.
I Do you think you're a good cook?
K I do think I'm a good cook.
I What's your speciality?
K Um, my husband is Cuban, so I learned to cook Cuban food for him, so that's my specialty.

3 Maura
I = interviewer, M = Maura
I What's the most beautiful city you've ever been to? Why?
M Er, that's a difficult question, but I think I'd have to say Edinburgh. Um, it's very beautiful, it's got the sea, it's got an extinct volcano in the centre, and every street has, er, a different view.

4 Kevin
I = interviewer, K = Kevin
I Where are you going to go for your next holiday?
K Er, we've booked that for January and we're going to Thailand for two weeks.
I Where are you going to stay?
K We're staying three nights in Bangkok, three nights in an island called Ko Samui and five nights in an island called Ko Tao.
I How are you going to get there?
K We are flying from Edinburgh to, er, Dubai, Dubai to Bangkok, and then it's another flight from Bangkok to Ko Samui, and then a ferry from Ko Samui to Ko Tao.

5 Mica
I = interviewer, M = Mica
I What's the biggest difference between the US and the UK?
M Um, so the biggest difference between the US and the UK in New York City, er, food's very different here compared to the UK. Um, lots of burgers and pizza, and fast food and things like that.

G adverbs (manner and modifiers)
V common adverbs: *slowly*, *fast*, etc.
P connected speech

Lesson plan

People's first impressions of a new country provide the context for learning common adverbs of manner and modifiers. This lesson starts with Sts reading some posts on a forum written by people about what surprised them when they first arrived in the USA. This leads into the grammar focus on the formation and position of adverbs. In Listening, a British teacher talks about living in Costa Rica, which leads to Pronunciation, where the focus is on understanding connected speech. Sts then discuss habits and behaviour in their own country / city. Finally, Sts write three short posts about habits in their country which might surprise a visitor.

More materials
For teachers
Photocopiables
Grammar adverbs (manner and modifiers) *p.198*
Communicative Read slowly *p.247* (instructions *p.212*)
For students
Workbook 11A
Online Practice 11A

OPTIONAL LEAD-IN (BOOKS CLOSED)

Tell Sts to imagine that they have to go and live for a year in a foreign city. Then tell them, in pairs, to decide which city they would like to go to, and why.

Get feedback about the cities Sts chose and their reasons.

1 READING

a Books open. Do this as a whole-class activity. You could tell the class about your own experience.

b Focus on the title of the forum and the question below it. Make sure Sts understand the topic.

Give Sts a few minutes to read the posts and decide which topic isn't mentioned.

Check the answer.

EXTRA SUPPORT Before Sts read the posts the first time, check whether you need to pre-teach any vocabulary , but not the words and phrases in **e**.

exercise

c Get Sts to read the posts again and match sentences 1–9 to the people who said them. The sentences are paraphrases and not the exact wording in the posts.

Get Sts to compare with a partner, and then check answers.

1 J 2 L 3 N 4 R 5 L 6 N 7 T 8 N 9 T

d Tell Sts to read sentences 1–9 again and, with a partner, discuss whether each one is true in their country. You could do the first one with the whole class to start them off. If your Sts come from the same country, you could do this as a whole-class activity.

e Focus on the words in the list. Elicit the pronunciation from the phonetics, and drill.

Then Sts work alone or in pairs.

Check answers, either explaining in English, translating into Sts' L1, or getting Sts to check in their dictionaries.

salary – the money that you get from your job insurance – something that you buy to protect yourself if you have an accident, need an operation, etc. tip – extra money that you give to a taxi driver, a waiter, etc. earn money – get money from your job pay bills – pay for electricity, gas, phone, etc.

Deal with any other new vocabulary. Model and drill the pronunciation of any tricky words.

2 GRAMMAR adverbs

a Tell Sts to look at the highlighted phrases in sentences 1–9 in **1c** and choose option *a* or *b* in questions 1–3.

Check answers.

1 a 2 b 3 b, a

EXTRA SUPPORT Get Sts to work in pairs.

b Tell Sts to go to **Grammar Bank 11A** on *p.144*.

Grammar notes
Adverbs of manner
Sts usually find formation of these adverbs fairly straightforward.
The most common word order with these kinds of adverbs is to put the adverb <u>after</u> a verb or verb phrase, e.g. *He drives very quickly, I speak English very well* (typical error: ~~I speak very well English~~).
Sts may try to use *hardly* instead of *hard*, e.g. ~~I work hardly~~. Explain that *hard* is irregular and doesn't add *-ly*.
Hardly is a word which means *almost not*, e.g. *I hardly slept last night, I hardly ever go to the theatre*. Sts learned *hardly ever* in **4C**.
Modifiers
The position of these is quite straightforward. You may want to point out that you can't use *very* with strong adjectives, e.g. *great, fantastic, awful*, etc.

Focus on the example sentences and play both audio ◀)) **11.1** and ◀)) **11.2** for Sts to listen and repeat. Then go through the rules with the class.

Focus on the **Words ending in -ly** box and go through it with the class.

Now focus on the exercises for **11A** on *p.145*. Sts do the exercises individually or in pairs.

Check answers, getting Sts to read the full sentences. Help with rhythm, and tell them that adverbs are always stressed.

Tell Sts to go back to the main lesson **11A**.

 If you think Sts need more practice, you may want to give them the **Grammar** photocopiable activity at this point.

c **11.3** Tell Sts they're going to hear six sound effects, and for each one, they must write a sentence using the present continuous and an adverb to describe what's happening.

Play the audio and pause after number 1, so Sts can see how the example sentence describes what they heard.

Now play the other five sound effects, pausing after each one to give Sts time to write.

Elicit ideas from Sts.

11.3
(sound effects for the following)
1 *two people whispering*
2 *car screeching round corners, plus male voice*
3 *stepping on feet, two voices*
4 *two people eating together, slurping spaghetti*
5 *lovely female opera voice*
6 *very loud piano playing*

3 LISTENING & PRONUNCIATION
connected speech

a **11.4** Focus on the photo of Jack and the caption, and ask Sts if they know where Costa Rica is (Central America), and what they can see in the big photo (a man selling fruit and vegetables). Make sure Sts understand the task. You could tell Sts that Jack Horton is from the UK.

Tell Sts that the first time they listen, they don't need to understand everything. They just need to decide how Jack feels about living in Costa Rica.

Play the audio for Sts to listen and answer the question.

Check the answer.

 Read through the script and decide if you need to pre-teach any new lexis before Sts listen.

He's positive.

11.4
(script in Student's Book on *p.123*)
The first thing that I really noticed when I arrived here was how incredibly friendly the people are. The 'ticos' – that's what they're called – are much friendlier than people in Europe. They always say *buenos días* to you even if they don't know you. And if something's good, like a beautiful day or a good meal, they say *pura vida*, which I love. It literally means 'pure life', but I think it really means 'things are great', or something like that. One thing that can be difficult though, their sense of time is completely different from ours – they call it 'tico time'. If they have an appointment at, let's say, seven in the evening, they probably leave home at seven o'clock, so they're always late. Luckily, my school works on what they call 'British time', so classes start punctually!
Another thing that surprised me was the weather. I thought Costa Rica was hot and sunny all the time. That's true in the dry season, and the temperature's about twenty-five degrees all year round, but in the rainy season, especially in September and October, it rains really heavily for maybe two hours a day. Really amazing rain, nothing like in England.
Everyone told me that the scenery was beautiful in Costa Rica, but it was even more beautiful than I expected. Incredible animals, birds, trees – and volcanoes. Some of them are active and smoke quietly, and then suddenly there's a big bang and they start erupting. I was quite frightened the first time it happened.
What else? Er, I thought that life here was going to be very cheap, but in fact, food is very expensive, especially imported food. The only thing that's cheap is fruit, vegetables, and coffee – wonderful, wonderful coffee. And the fruit and vegetables are very different from what we have in Europe. One day I went to a market and I didn't recognize any of the fruit.
I like San José. I don't feel that it's dangerous, but it probably is. A colleague of mine was in a taxi the other day, and the taxi driver took out a gun and asked him for all his money! And the roads are terrible, especially in the rain! But in general, I love it here.

b **11.5** Tell Sts they are now going to hear eight phrases taken from the listening and they must write each one down. Each phrase has three or four words in it. Point out the example.

Play the audio, pausing after each phrase to give Sts time to write. Play again if necessary.

Check answers.

11.5
1 how incredibly friendly
2 things are great
3 their sense of time
4 seven in the evening
5 hot and sunny
6 all year round
7 two hours a day
8 took out a gun

Now play the audio again, pausing after each one for Sts to listen and repeat.

c Tell Sts they are going to listen to Jack again, and this time they need to complete the gaps in 1–11. Give Sts time to read 1–11.

Play audio 🔊 **11.4** again for Sts to complete the task.

Get Sts to compare with a partner, and then check answers.

1 friendlier   **2** are great   **3** late   **4** 25 degrees   **5** rains, heavily   **6** more beautiful   **7** quite frightened   **8** fruit, vegetables, coffee   **9** coffee   **10** dangerous   **11** terrible

 If there's time, you could get Sts to listen again with the script on *p.123*, so they can see exactly what they understood / didn't understand. Translate / Explain any new words or phrases.

d Do this as a whole-class activity and give your opinion.

4 VOCABULARY & SPEAKING
common adverbs

Focus on the task. Then look at the questions and make sure Sts understand all the verb phrases, e.g. *treat tourists*, *behave*, etc.

Put Sts in small groups. Focus on the example, or demonstrate first if you are from a different country / city, by telling Sts, e.g. *In Britain, I think most people drive very carefully. I drive…*

Give Sts time in their groups to discuss all the points. Remind them to first say what they think about the people in their country and then about themselves.

Get some feedback from various groups.

5 WRITING

Tell Sts to look back at all the topics in the posts in **1** and to choose three they want to write about, e.g. *transport*, *food*, *money*. They need to write one post about their own country for each topic.

When Sts have finished, ask them to compare their posts. If your Sts are all from the same country, ask them if they wrote about the same things, and if they agree. If they're from different countries, ask if anything surprises them, and if they'd like to visit the other country.

G verb + *to* + infinitive
V verbs that take the infinitive: *want to*, *need to*, etc.
P weak *to*, sentence stress

Lesson plan

This lesson is based on a blog written by a German girl who is passionate about travel and new experiences. In the first half of the lesson, Sts read and talk about people's dreams or 'bucket lists'. In Grammar, they focus on the structure verb + *to* + infinitive, which is common when talking about dreams, e.g. *I want to climb a mountain*, and they learn some common verbs that are followed by the infinitive. In the second half of the lesson, Sts work on the weak pronunciation of *to* in verb phrases and sentence stress, and talk about their dreams and plans for the future. The Writing task, which links back to the reading, gets Sts to write their own bucket lists and then compare them.

More materials
For teachers
Photocopiables
Grammar verbs + *to* + infinitive *p.199*
Communicative Dreams and plans *p.248*
(instructions *p.212*)
For students
Workbook 11B
Online Practice 11B

OPTIONAL LEAD-IN (BOOKS CLOSED)
Tell Sts to imagine that they have won, for example €1,000 in the lottery. Ask who would buy something with it (what?), and who would spend it on an experience, e.g. a trip (where to?).

1 READING & SPEAKING scanning for information

a Books open. Read the definition and elicit answers from the class. Don't ask Sts if they have a bucket list as they will be doing this later in the lesson. The term *bucket list* comes from the expression *to kick the bucket*, meaning to die. You might want to point out that the definition here says 'before you die', but the term *bucket list* also often means any list of special things that you want to do – in this lesson, Stef makes a new bucket list for each year.

b Focus on the task and make sure Sts can remember what *a blog* is. Give Sts time to read the *About me* section and answer the questions. Point out that the first one has been done for them.

Get Sts to compare with a partner, and then check answers. Don't ask Sts any questions about Stef's lifestyle at this stage as they will be doing this later in the lesson.

EXTRA SUPPORT Before Sts read the blog check whether you need to pre-teach any vocabulary, but not the phrases in **d**.

2 She went to Australia in 2011. She worked in a pub. Then she travelled all over Australia and New Zealand.
3 She got a job there as a project assistant.
4 She went there on holiday when she worked for the IT company.
5 Having experiences is more important than working to pay for a flat and buying things she doesn't need.
6 Three months ago, she left her job and decided to work in different jobs.

c Focus on the task and the *My dreams* section of the blog. Check Sts know all the lexis in the list, e.g. *a balloon*, *a field*, *to dive*, etc.

Now give Sts time to go through the list and tick the five things they would most like to do. You could demonstrate the activity by telling Sts five you would like to do, and explaining why.

Put Sts in pairs and get them to compare their lists. Tell them to say why they have chosen each item.

Get some feedback from individual Sts.

d Now tell Sts to cover the text and look at the phrases in 1–8. Can they remember the verbs?

Check answers.

1 make **2** go **3** ride **4** learn **5** go **6** make **7** cook **8** get

Deal with any other new vocabulary. Model and drill the pronunciation of any tricky words.

e Do this as a whole-class activity.

You could also tell Sts what you think. You could find out with a show of hands if any Sts would like to live like Stef.

2 GRAMMAR verb + *to* + infinitive

a Tell Sts to match the sentence beginnings on the left to the endings on the right, and then answer the question.

Check answers.

I decided to go to Australia.
I needed to save some money.
Learn to play the guitar.

The missing word is *to*.

b Tell Sts to go to **Grammar Bank 11B** on *p.144*.

Grammar notes

There are two forms of the infinitive in English, e.g. *live* and *to live*.

Live is often known as the 'base form' and *to live* as the 'infinitive with *to*' or 'the full infinitive'. The negative is formed by adding *not*, e.g. *to be or not to be*.

The base form (*live*) is used, for example, in questions and negatives with *do / does* and *did*, e.g. *Where do you live?*, *I don't live here*.

The full infinitive (*to live*) is used very widely in English. One of its main uses is after a lot of common verbs, like *want*, *need*, *decide*, *hope*, etc., e.g. *I want to live in the city centre*.

Some verbs – a smaller group – are followed by the gerund (*-ing*), e.g. *like*, *love*, *hate* (*I like cooking*), which Sts learned in **6B**.

However, some native speakers, particularly Americans, use the infinitive after *like*, e.g. *I like to cook*.

11.6 Focus on the example sentences and play the audio for Sts to listen and repeat. Highlight the pronunciation of *would* /wʊd/, reminding Sts that the *l* is silent. Then go through the rules with the class.

Focus on the **would like and like** box and go through it with the class.

Now focus on the exercises for **11B** on *p.145*. Sts do the exercises individually or in pairs.

Check answers, getting Sts to read the full sentences.

a
1 to drive **2** to buy **3** to be **4** to call **5** to stay **6** to see **7** to get married **8** to have **9** to go **10** to leave
b
1 to have **2** to speak **3** to travel **4** relaxing **5** to play **6** to get **7** going **8** reading **9** to wear **10** cooking

Tell Sts to go back to the main lesson **11B**.

 If you think Sts need more practice, you may want to give them the **Grammar** photocopiable activity at this point.

3 PRONUNCIATION weak *to*, sentence stress

a **11.7** Tell Sts they are going to hear six sentences with verb + *to* + infinitive in them, and they must write them down.

Play the audio, pausing after each sentence for Sts to listen and write down the sentence.

Get Sts to compare with a partner, and then check answers, by eliciting the sentences onto the board.

11.7
1 I'm planning to buy a new car.
2 He decided to walk home.
3 I hope to hear from you soon.
4 Do you want to stop now?
5 I need to go to the shops.
6 They'd like to have dinner with us.

Now play the audio again, pausing after each sentence for Sts to listen and repeat.

Ask the class how *to* is pronounced. If necessary, play the audio again.

It is pronounced /tə/.

b **11.8** Remind Sts that all the stressed words are in bigger font. Play the audio once the whole way through for Sts just to listen.

11.8
See conversation in Student's Book on *p.89*

Play the audio again, pausing after each line for Sts to listen and repeat. Encourage them to copy the rhythm by saying the stressed words more strongly.

Put Sts in pairs and get them to practise the conversation.

Get a few pairs to read the conversation to the class.

 Ask Sts to memorize the conversation, then close their books and practise saying it.

c Put Sts in pairs and focus on the task. First, they need to look at the five things their partner ticked in Stef's bucket list in **1c**, and then they should ask their partner five more questions, using *Would you like to…?* followed by an item in the list. Before they start, focus on the speech bubbles and tell Sts to ask and answer like this, and if possible, as in **3b**, they should give a reason. You might want to point out that Sts need to change *my* in certain items to *your*, e.g. *Would you like to go on holiday with your best friend?*

Get some feedback from various pairs on their partner's dreams.

4 VOCABULARY verbs that take the infinitive

a Focus on the task and get Sts to do it in pairs.

 Elicit the past tense of each verb from the class and write it on the board. Then ask the class to divide the list into regular and irregular verbs.

Check answers.

Forget is irregular (*forgot*).
Learn can be regular or irregular (*learned / learnt*).

b Tell Sts to complete 1–10 with the verbs in **a**. Point out that the first one (*wanted*) has been done for them.

Get Sts to compare with a partner, and then check answers.

2 remembered **3** decided **4** forgot **5** tried **6** learned / learnt **7** hoped **8** promised **9** planned **10** needed

5 SPEAKING

Give Sts a few minutes to look at the ten phrases and think about their answers.

Now focus on the instructions and example.

Put Sts in pairs. Monitor and help, especially correcting any errors with infinitives.

Get some feedback. Find out if any Sts had the same answers, or if any answers were surprising.

6 WRITING

a Tell Sts to write a bucket list like Stef's, with five things they want to do this year.

b Put Sts in pairs and get them to compare lists. They should see if any of the items are the same or if their partner wrote something they also want to include in their list.

Get some feedback from various pairs.

11C How smart is your phone?

G definite article: *the* or no *the*
V phones and the internet
P *the*

Lesson plan

The topic of this lesson is phones and the internet. The lesson starts with the introduction of some useful phone and internet related language. Sts then listen to three people saying what they use their phones for, and Sts do the same. Reading focuses on life before the internet – something that you and your Sts may not have experienced. This is followed by the grammar focus, which looks at the uses of the definite article, with a special focus on the non-use of articles when generalizing, e.g. talking about things or people in general. The lesson finishes with a Speaking activity that revises the different uses of articles.

More materials
For teachers
Photocopiables
Grammar definite article: *the* or no *the* p.200
Communicative Speak for 30 seconds p.249
(instructions p.213)
For students
Workbook 11C
Online Practice 11C

OPTIONAL LEAD-IN (BOOKS CLOSED)

Write on the board DIGITAL NATIVE and DIGITAL IMMIGRANT and ask Sts what they think the terms mean.

Elicit / Explain that a *digital native* is somebody who was born after the internet was already an important part of life, and a *digital immigrant* is somebody who was born before then and has had to learn how to use it.

Ask Sts if they know any digital immigrants.

1 VOCABULARY phones and the internet

a Books open. Focus Sts' attention on the phone screen. Give them time to look at all the apps and functions, and count how many they have on their phone.

Elicit some answers.

b Get Sts to match the icons in **a** to the activities.

Check answers.

1 Facebook (or Twitter) **2** App Store **3** Skype **4** Messages **5** YouTube (or Facebook) **6** WhatsApp **7** Twitter **8** Mail **9** Camera **10** Google Maps **11** Kindle **12** MyFitnessPal **13** Spotify (or YouTube)

Now ask the class which ones can be used without internet connection.

Calendar, Camera, Kindle, Photos, Messages, Phone

c �))) **11.9** Tell Sts they are going to hear 1–13 in **b**, and they must listen and repeat.

Play the audio, pausing for Sts to listen and repeat.

�))) 11.9
See activities 1–13 in **b** in Student's Book on *p.90*

Play the audio again if necessary.

d �))) **11.10** Tell Sts to match the words related to the internet to the pictures.

Play the audio for Sts to listen and check.

Check answers, making sure Sts understand what each item is. Model and drill pronunciation.

1 wi-fi **2** attachment **3** log in **4** search **5** broadband

◍))) 11.10
2 attachment **5** broadband **3** log in **4** search **1** wi-fi

EXTRA SUPPORT Play the audio again, and get Sts to listen and repeat.

2 LISTENING & SPEAKING using visual clues to support understanding

a ◍))) **11.11** Focus on the instructions and tell Sts they are going to hear three different conversations. They must listen for the first activity the three people do with their phones.

Play the audio once the whole way through.

Check answers.

EXTRA SUPPORT Read through the scripts and decide if you need to pre-teach any new lexis before Sts listen.

Speaker A	the internet
Speaker B	receiving phone calls from other people
Speaker C	email

I = interviewer

A

I What make of phone do you have?

A I have an iPhone.

I How old is it?

A Er, about two years old.

I How often do you change phones?

A Not very often, I would say. I like to, er, I'm not particularly worried about having the latest phone. I just want one that works well. Er, I usually keep my phone about four years – if I don't lose it, that is.

I What do you use your phone for the most?

A Probably the internet. And messaging. Things like WhatsApp, Facebook messenger.

I So you don't use it much to actually talk to people?

A No, I don't.

I What other apps do you use a lot?

A I use the weather one quite a lot. And I have a couple of games I like playing. And Skype. I use Skype from time to time to talk to my brother because he lives in Spain.

I Do you have any unusual apps that you sometimes use?

A I have one to track the food that I eat, but I don't use it every day. And I have a photo-editing app.

B

I What kind of phone do you have?

B An Android smartphone. A Samsung, er, Galaxy, I think.

I Is it new?

B About six months old.

I How often do you change phones?

B About every two to three years.

I What do you use it for the most?

B Receiving phone calls from other people, or looking up things on the internet.

I What apps do you have that you use a lot?

B An online banking app. I use that a lot. Email, of course. And the Kindle app, the e-reader.

I Do you like reading on your phone?

B No, I much prefer reading real books, paper books, but as I always have my phone with me, there are lots of times, like on the bus or if I'm waiting for somebody, I can read a book on my phone.

I Do you have any unusual apps that you sometimes use?

B Er, I have an app so I can order a taxi from my local taxi company.

C

I What kind of phone do you have?

C An iPhone.

I How often do you change your phone?

C When my contract lets me upgrade it, which is, I don't know, every two or three years.

I What do you use your phone for the most?

C Er, email, text messages, internet, and phone, I mean, talking. In that order.

I What apps do you use a lot?

C Apart from mail and Google, you mean?

I Yes.

C Er, Twitter, er, BBC news, and various transport apps for booking trains or seeing what time they are.

I Do you have any unusual apps that you sometimes use?

C I have a 'night sky' app. If it's a starry night, I sometimes use that. You point your phone at the sky and it tells you the names of the stars and planets and things.

b Tell Sts they are going to hear the three speakers again, and this time they must listen and label 1–9 according to which speaker says it.

Give Sts time to read 1–9.

Play the audio, pausing after each speaker to give Sts time to complete the task.

Check answers.

1 speaker A	**2** speaker C	**3** speaker B	**4** speaker B
5 speaker A	**6** speaker C	**7** speaker B	**8** speaker C
9 speaker A			

EXTRA SUPPORT If there's time, you could get Sts to listen again with the script on *p.123*, so they can see exactly what they understood / didn't understand. Translate / Explain any new words or phrases.

c Put Sts in pairs and get them to ask and answer questions 1–5.

Get some feedback from various pairs. You could also tell Sts how you use your phone.

3 READING

a Do this as a whole-class activity. <u>Don't</u> tell Sts if they are right or not at this stage.

b Focus on the article. You might want to model and drill the pronunciation of *encyclopaedia* /ɪnˌsaɪkləˈpiːdiə/. Tell Sts to read the article to check their answers to **a** and to find out what people used the things for.

Check answers. If you used any of these things yourself, tell the class about your experiences.

EXTRA SUPPORT Before Sts read the article, check whether you need to pre-teach any vocabulary.

1 Encyclopaedias: people used them to look up information.

2 Teletext: people used it like a basic internet on their TV.

3 Fax machines: people used them to send printed messages over the phone.

4 Walkmans: people used them to listen to music.

5 The Yellow Pages: people used them to look up the names and contact details of local businesses.

6 An A–Z: people used them to find streets in their city.

Deal with any new vocabulary. Model and drill the pronunciation of any tricky words.

c Focus on the task and example.

Put Sts in pairs and get them to tell their partner if they do any of the activities (the chances are they rarely do any of them – the objective here is to get them to explain how they do these things, e.g. book tickets, find information, etc., nowadays).

Get some feedback from various pairs.

4 GRAMMAR definite article

a You could do this as a whole-class activity, discussing each sentence in turn, or Sts could do it in pairs or small groups.

If Sts worked in pairs or small groups, get some feedback.

b Tell Sts to look at the three sentences in **a** and complete rules 1–4 in **b**.

Check answers.

1 Use *the*   **2** Don't use *the*   **3** Don't use *the*   **4** Use *the*

c Tell Sts to go to **Grammar Bank 11C** on *p.144*.

Grammar notes

This lesson focuses on the use and non-use of the definite article. It also revises the uses of the indefinite article that Sts have seen so far in Elementary.

The **Grammar Bank** information covers several uses / non-uses of the article, but is not exhaustive, as some of the more complex rules, e.g. the use of articles with geographical words, will be dealt with at a higher level. The difficulties your Sts have with articles will depend, to a large extent, on how articles are used or not used in their L1.

11.12 Focus on the example sentences and play the audio for Sts to listen and repeat. Then go through the rules with the class.

Focus on the **a / an or the?** box and go through it with the class.

Now focus on the exercises for **11C** on *p.145*. Sts do the exercises individually or in pairs.

Check answers, getting Sts to read the full sentences.

a
1 at university   **2** by train   **3** at the weekend   **4** at home
5 novels   **6** the best   **7** the moon   **8** the man   **9** the door
10 breakfast
b
1 –   **2** –   **3** The   **4** –   **5** –   **6** The   **7** the   **8** the   **9** –
10 the

Tell Sts to go back to the main lesson **11C**.

 If you think Sts need more practice, you may want to give them the **Grammar** photocopiable activity at this point.

5 PRONUNCIATION & SPEAKING *the*

a **11.13** Focus on the task and play the audio for Sts just to listen. If necessary, play it again.

Check the answer.

1 /ðiː/   **2** /ðə/

11.13
See phrases in Student's Book on *p.91*

Now ask what difference there is between the words after *the* in each group. Elicit that in group 1 the words after *the* (= /ðiː/) begin with a vowel, and in group 2 the words after *the* (= /ðə/) begin with a consonant.

b Put Sts in pairs and get them to practise saying the phrases.

 Play the audio again, pausing after each phrase for Sts to listen and repeat. Then get Sts to practise saying the phrases.

c The aim of this exercise is to get Sts talking about topics, often generalizing, which will encourage them to use the definite article correctly.

Go through the instructions with Sts. Focus on the speech bubbles and highlight that because the person is speaking in general, they say *women* and *men*, and not *the women* and *the men*.

Give Sts time to read the circles. Then put Sts in pairs, **A** and **B**.

A chooses a circle and talks about the three things.
B listens, reacts, and asks extra questions. Monitor and help Sts, making sure that they use articles correctly.

B then chooses a circle and talks about three things, and **A** asks for more information. Monitor and help as before.

When **B** has finished, **A** should choose another circle, and they should continue, alternating until they've talked about all the circles.

Get feedback to see if any of the information was surprising / funny / interesting, etc.

Function getting to the airport
Vocabulary public transport

Lesson plan

In this final Practical English lesson, Sts learn some vocabulary related to transport, and functional language for using public transport. It's Jenny's final morning in London, and Rob goes to the hotel to say goodbye. Jenny says that she has shown some of his articles to Barbara, her boss in New York, and that they would like him to go to New York for a month and write a column for *New York 24seven*, and a daily blog. Rob is excited at the idea, but asks for time to think about it. Jenny takes a taxi and then a train to get to Heathrow Airport, but when she arrives, she discovers that she has left her phone in the hotel. At that moment, Rob arrives with the phone and tells her that he wants to accept Barbara's offer and go to New York. He finally discovers who Eddie is.

The story is continued in New York in *English File* Pre-intermediate.

More materials
For teachers
Teacher's Resource Centre
Video Practical English Episode 6
Quick Test 11
File 11 Test
For students
Workbook Practical English 6
Can you remember? 1–11
Online Practice Practical English 6
Check your progress

OPTIONAL LEAD-IN (BOOKS CLOSED)

Elicit what happened in the last episode by asking some questions, e.g. *Where did Daniel take Jenny? What did Daniel say to Jenny after the meal? Was she happy about this? Who called her during the meal? Was it good news or bad news?*

Alternatively, you could play the last scene of Episode 5.

1 ▶ JENNY'S LAST MORNING

a 🔊 **11.14** Books open. Focus on the photo and elicit what Sts think is happening.

Focus on sentences 1–5 and go through them with Sts.

Then play the video / audio once the whole way through, for them to mark the sentences *T* (true) or *F* (false). Make it clear that they don't need to correct the false sentences yet. Play again if necessary.

Get Sts to compare with a partner, and then check answers.

1 T 2 F 3 F 4 F 5 T

🔊 **11.14**
R = Rob, J = Jenny
J Rob!
R Jenny, hi. Sorry I'm a bit late.
J No problem.
R Really?
J Really!
R I got your message.
J Would you like a coffee or something?
R No, I'm fine, thanks. So what did you want to talk about? You think London is the best city in the world and you don't want to go home.
J Not exactly. We'd like *you* to come to New York.
R Me? To New York?
J I talked to Barbara about you. You know, Barbara, my boss? She loves your articles, too. So…would you like to come over to New York and work for us? Just for a month. And write a column for *New York 24seven*. And maybe a daily blog?
R Wow, sounds great! What could I call it? *An Englishman in New York*?
J Why not? Are you interested?
R Yes, very. It's amazing! But I need to think about it.
J Of course.
R When do I need to decide?
J Before the end of the week.
R OK, great. Thank you.
J And now, I really have to go.

b Play the video / audio again, so Sts can watch or listen and correct the false sentences.

Get Sts to compare with a partner, and then check answers.

2 He **doesn't** want a coffee.
3 Jenny has **good** news.
4 He thinks *An Englishman* in New York is a good name.

Ask Sts what they think Rob is going to do, but <u>don't</u> tell them yet.

EXTRA SUPPORT If there's time and you are using the video, you could get Sts to watch again with subtitles / showing the script, so they can see exactly what they understood / didn't understand. Translate / Explain any new words or phrases.

2 ▶ VOCABULARY public transport

a Focus on the task and get Sts to match the words and pictures.

Get Sts to compare with a partner.

b 🔊 **11.15** Play the video / audio for Sts to watch or listen and check.

Check answers.

1 train **2** plane **3** bus **4** tram **5** coach **6** taxi

🔊 **11.15**
3 bus **2** plane **6** taxi **1** train **5** coach **4** tram

Now play the video / audio again, pausing after each word for Sts to watch or listen and repeat.

Finally, tell Sts to cover the words and look at the pictures to test themselves.

c Focus on the task and get Sts to complete the four headings with a word from **a**.

Get Sts to compare with a partner, and then check answers.

1 taxi **2** plane **3** train **4** bus

Go through the four texts, dealing with new vocabulary, and model and drill pronunciation.

d Write the four types of transport on the board. Get Sts to close their books. Then elicit two facts for each type, e.g. ask *Where can you get a taxi?* (at a taxi rank) *What's another word for* a taxi? (a cab), etc.

3 ▶ GETTING TO THE AIRPORT

a 🔊 **11.16** Focus on the photos and elicit what Sts think is happening and who the people are (*a ticket clerk and a taxi driver*). Model and drill the pronunciation of *clerk* /klɑːk/.

Focus on the instructions and the question. Alternatively, you could get Sts to close their books and write the question on the board.

Play the video / audio once the whole way through.

Get Sts to compare with a partner, and play the video / audio again if necessary.

Check the answer.

She gets a taxi and a train.

🔊 **11.16** 🔊 **11.17**
J = Jenny, R = receptionist, T = taxi driver, TC = ticket clerk
J Could you call me a taxi, please? (*repeat*)
R Yes, of course. Where to?
J To Paddington Station. (*repeat*)
R And when would you like it for?
J Now, please. (*repeat*)
J How much is it? (*repeat*)
T That's thirteen sixty, please.
J Make it fifteen pounds. (*repeat*) And could I have a receipt? (*repeat*)
T Thank you very much, madam.
J Could I have a ticket to Heathrow Airport, please? (*repeat*)
TC Single or return?
J Single, please. (*repeat*)
TC Standard or first class?
J Standard, please. (*repeat*)
T That's eighteen pounds.
J Can I pay by credit card? (*repeat*)
TC Yes, of course.

b Now focus on the conversations in the chart. Ask Sts *Who says the **You hear** sentences in each conversation?* and elicit that first it is the receptionist, then the taxi driver, and then the man at the ticket office.

Then ask *Who says the **You say** sentences?* and elicit that it is Jenny. Tell Sts that if they want someone to call them a taxi, or want to use public transport, they will need the **You say** phrases.

Give Sts a minute to read through the conversations and think what the missing words might be. Then play the video / audio again, and get Sts to complete the gaps. Play again if necessary.

Get Sts to compare with a partner, and then check answers.

1 Where **2** for **3** 13.60 **4** madam **5** return **6** first **7** course

Go through the conversations line by line with Sts, helping them with any words or expressions they don't understand. Highlight that *a single ticket* = one way only, *a return ticket* = to a place and then back again, *standard* = a normal ticket, and *first class* = you pay more and travel in a more comfortable part of the train. Highlight also the useful phrase *Could I have a receipt?* and elicit that a *receipt* /rɪˈsiːt/ is a piece of paper showing what you paid for something. Point out that the *p* is not pronounced in *receipt*.

c 🔊 **11.17** Now focus on the **You say** phrases. Tell Sts they're going to hear the conversations again. They should repeat the **You say** phrases when they hear the beep.

Play the video / audio, pausing if necessary for Sts to repeat the phrases. Encourage them to copy the rhythm and intonation.

🔊 **11.17**
Same as script 11.16 with repeat pauses

d Put Sts in pairs, **A** and **B**. Tell Sts **A** to read the part of the receptionist, the taxi driver, and the ticket clerk, and Sts **B** to read Jenny.

In pairs, Sts read the conversations aloud.

Then Sts swap roles.

e Sts now role-play the conversation. In the same pairs, get them to read the information for their roles. Tell Sts that Gatwick is the other main London airport.

 You could write VICTORIA STATION and GATWICK AIRPORT on the board to help Sts **B** remember where they want to go.

Make sure Sts swap roles when they have finished.

You could get some pairs to perform in front of the class.

4 ▶ SAYING GOODBYE

a ◀) **11.18** Focus on the photo and ask Sts what's happening.

Focus on the sentence beginnings and give Sts time to read them.

Play the video / audio once the whole way through.

Get Sts to compare with a partner, and then play again if necessary.

Check answers.

1 she can't find her phone.
2 he wants to give Jenny her phone.
3 come and work in New York.
4 he lives in California.
5 Jenny's younger brother.
6 she needs to get her plane.

◀) **11.18**
J = Jenny, R = Rob, A = announcement
J Where is it? Where's my phone?!
R Are you looking for this?
J Rob! I can't believe it! My phone! You're a hero, thank you so much.
R No problem. It gave me a chance to see you again. And I had more time to think about your offer.
J And?
R I'd love to accept. I really want to come and work in New York.
J That's great, Rob! I'm so happy.
R Me, too. Oh, you had a call from Eddie. I didn't answer it. Is he going to meet you at the airport?
J Eddie? No. He's at college in California.
R In California? Does he teach there?
J Teach? No, he's a student.
R A student?
J Well, he's only nineteen. Eddie's my brother.
A Next departure, flight 232 to New York, is now ready for boarding.
J I need to go.
R Well, have a good journey.
J Thanks, Rob. Bye.
R Bye. And see you in New York!

 If there's time and you are using the video, you could get Sts to watch again with subtitles / showing the script, so they can see exactly what they understood / didn't understand. Translate / Explain any new words or phrases.

b Focus on the **Social English** phrases and go through them with the class.

In pairs, get Sts to decide who says them.

c ◀) **11.19** Play the video / audio for Sts to watch or listen to the five phrases and check.

Check answers. If you know your Sts' L1, you could get them to translate the phrases.

1 J **2** J **3** J **4** R **5** R

◀) **11.19**
See Social English phrases in Student's Book on *p.93*

Now play the video / audio again, pausing after each phrase for Sts to watch or listen and repeat.

d Focus on the instructions and make sure Sts understand what they have to do.

Get Sts to compare with a partner, and then check answers.

A 5 **B** 2 **C** 3 **D** 1 **E** 4

Now put Sts in pairs and get them to practise the conversations.

Finally, focus on the **CAN YOU…?** questions and ask Sts if they feel confident they can now do these things. If they feel that they need more practice, tell them to go to *Online Practice* to watch the episode again and practise the language.

I've seen it ten times!

G present perfect
V irregular past participles
P sentence stress

Lesson plan

The topic of films and TV series that are based on books provides the context to introduce the present perfect. The lesson begins with the grammar presentation through a conversation about films, TV series, and books. The pronunciation focus is on sentence stress, and Vocabulary looks at common irregular past participles. The main context of the final Listening and Speaking activity is a survey asking about film, TV, and book experiences, and Sts learn how to ask present perfect questions with *ever*.

NB In **12B** Sts learn other regular and irregular past participles, and contrast the present perfect with the past simple.

More materials
For teachers
Photocopiables
Grammar present perfect *p.201*
Communicative Have you done it? *p.250*
(instructions *p.213*)
For students
Workbook 12A
Online Practice 12A

Write the following cinema questionnaire on the board:
HOW OFTEN DO YOU GO TO THE CINEMA?
HOW OFTEN DO YOU WATCH A FILM ON TV OR ONLINE?
WHAT KIND OF FILMS DO YOU LIKE?
WHAT'S THE LAST FILM YOU SAW? DID YOU LIKE IT? WHY (NOT)?
DO YOU HAVE A FAVOURITE ACTOR OR DIRECTOR?

Get Sts to ask you first, then they ask and answer in pairs.
Get some feedback from various pairs.

1 GRAMMAR present perfect

a Books open. Focus on the images from two films and a TV series, and get Sts to match them to the books.

Check answers. Ask Sts if they have read any of the books or seen any of the films.

1 B   2 A   3 C

b 🔊 **12.1** Tell Sts they are going to listen to three conversations about the items in **a**, and they must complete the gaps with the phrases in the list. Point out that the first one has been done for them.

Play the audio, pausing after each conversation to give Sts time to complete the gaps with the phrases.

Check answers.

1 Yes, I have, I've read the book
2 No, I haven't
3 I haven't seen it

🔊 **12.1**
1 **Stella** The first *Jurassic Park* is on TV tonight. Have you seen it?
  Paul Yes, I have. And I've read the book. The film's better than the book, I think.
  Stella Let's watch it then. I know it's an old film, but I haven't seen it.
2 **Matt** Have you read the Game of Thrones books?
  Tom No, I haven't. They're really long! Life's too short for seven-hundred-page books!
  Matt Have you watched the TV series?
  Tom Yes, I've watched the first three seasons, and I've downloaded the fourth.
3 **Ann** Have you seen the film *It*? The recent one.
  Mike Is it the film of the Stephen King book?
  Ann Yes.
  Mike I've heard of it, but I haven't seen it. I've read the book – it's fantastic.

EXTRA CHALLENGE Get Sts to complete the gaps before they listen to the audio. They then listen and check their answers.

c Tell Sts to read the conversations whilst they listen again. Play the audio the whole way through.

Now focus on the chart and ask Sts, in pairs, to complete it, using the conversations to help them, and to answer questions 1–5. Point out that the first one (*I've read*) has been done for them.

Check answers.

—	**I haven't read** the book.
?	**Have you read** the book?
✓	**Yes, I have.**
✗	**No, I haven't**.

1 I have read   2 has, hasn't   3 see, read, hear
4 watch, download   5 No, we don't.

EXTRA CHALLENGE Get Sts to complete the chart before they listen to the audio again. They then listen and check their answers.

d Tell Sts to go to **Grammar Bank 12A** on *p.146*.

Grammar notes
Present perfect

The present perfect is presented here in two of the most basic uses, i.e. for recent past actions and past experience when the time is not referred to. These uses may be difficult for Sts if they don't have an equivalent in their language.

The form of the present perfect may also be problematic as it is the first time Sts have seen *have* used as an auxiliary verb with all its contractions (*I've…*, *he's…*, etc.).

Regular and irregular past participles

Past participles of regular verbs should not cause any problems for Sts since they are the same as the past simple. Sts simply have to remember the pronunciation rules for *-ed* endings.

Many irregular past participles also have the same form as the past simple. However, ones which are different (e.g. *speak–spoke–spoken*) may cause problems as Sts may confuse the two forms. For this reason, it is worth giving special attention to these verbs.

12.2 Focus on the example sentences and play the audio for Sts to listen and repeat. Then go through the rules with the class.

Now focus on the exercises for **12A** on *p.147*. Sts do the exercises individually or in pairs.

Check answers, getting Sts to read the full sentences. In **a**, write the contracted forms on the board. In **b** and **c**, tell Sts to use contractions in ➕ and ➖ after *I*, *he*, etc.

a 1 She hasn't read the book.
   2 You haven't finished your ice cream!
   3 We've heard the news.
   4 He's arrived at the airport.
   5 They haven't asked for the bill.
   6 We haven't seen him before.
   7 It's stopped raining.
b 1 I've changed my email address.
   2 My boyfriend hasn't worked abroad.
   3 Have you decided what to do?
   4 They haven't passed the exam.
   5 Has he accepted the invitation?
   6 She's studied three languages.
   7 The train hasn't arrived.
   8 Have the children tidied their room?
   9 My girlfriend hasn't phoned me.
  10 My father's helped me a lot.
c 1 They've seen 2 He's passed 3 She hasn't finished
   4 He's painted 5 She's asked

Tell Sts to go back to the main lesson **12A**.

 If you think Sts need more practice, you may want to give them the **Grammar** photocopiable activity at this point.

e Tell Sts to complete sentences 1–10 with the past participle of a verb from the list. Point out that the first one (*opened*) has been done for them.

Get Sts to compare with a partner, and then check answers. When checking answers, get Sts to read the full sentences, e.g. *I've never opened a bank account.*

2 booked 3 acted 4 played 5 killed 6 worked
7 believed 8 asked 9 travelled 10 downloaded

f In pairs, Sts say which sentences are true for them.

Get some feedback from various pairs. Encourage Sts to say why, but don't correct misuse of tenses at this point.

Finally, go through each sentence and find out, with a show of hands, how many Sts have done each one.

2 PRONUNCIATION sentence stress

a **12.3** Focus on the conversation. Play the audio once for Sts just to listen.

12.3
See conversation in Student's Book on *p.95*

Now play the audio again, pausing after each line for Sts to listen and repeat. Remind Sts that the larger words are the ones which they should stress more strongly.

Get Sts to practise the conversation in pairs, swapping roles.

b Tell Sts to think of three more films or TV series from books. Monitor and help Sts write their three titles. The titles can be in any language, depending which country the films or series are from – but in a monolingual class, for British or American films and series, tell Sts the original title in English if you can.

 Some Sts might have trouble thinking of films and TV series, so put Sts in pairs to brainstorm some names, and then write them on the board.

Sts ask and answer with a partner. Monitor, helping Sts get the right rhythm in their questions.

Get feedback from the class.

 If Sts have seen a film and read the book, ask which one they preferred and why.

3 VOCABULARY irregular past participles

a Tell Sts to focus on the last column of the chart. Explain that these are irregular past participles and that Sts need to write the infinitive and the past simple in the relevant columns. Remind Sts that past participles of irregular verbs are sometimes the same as the past simple, but sometimes different.

Get Sts to compare their answers with a partner.

b **12.4** Play the audio for Sts to listen and check.

Check answers. Elicit that the verbs where the past participles are different from the past simple are *fall*, *give*, and *see*.

2 fall, fell 3 give, gave 4 hear, heard 5 leave, left 6 read, read 7 see, saw 8 tell, told

12.4

1	buy	bought	bought
2	fall	fell	fallen
3	give	gave	given
4	hear	heard	heard
5	leave	left	left
6	read	read	read
7	see	saw	seen
8	tell	told	told

Now ask Sts what the difference is between the infinitive of the verb *read* and the past simple and past participle.

read infinitive = /riːd/
read past simple and past participle = /red/

Play the audio again, pausing after each past participle for Sts to listen and repeat the three forms. Help with pronunciation where necessary.

c 🔊 **12.5** Focus on the instructions and the example, and tell Sts they are going to hear the infinitive and they must say the past simple and the past participle. Tell Sts that the verbs are from **a**, but they will hear them in a different order. Play the audio for Sts to see what they have to do. Get Sts to either cover **a** or to close their books. If Sts close their books, write PAST SIMPLE and PAST PARTICIPLE on the board.

Play the audio, pausing after each infinitive, and elicit the past simple and past participle from the whole class.

🔊 **12.5**
buy (*pause*) bought, bought
see (*pause*) saw, seen
give (*pause*) gave, given
fall (*pause*) fell, fallen
leave (*pause*) left, left
read (*pause*) read, read
tell (*pause*) told, told
hear (*pause*) heard, heard

Now repeat the activity, eliciting responses from individual Sts.

d Tell Sts to look at 1–8 and to complete the **Verb** column in each one with a past participle from **a**.

Get Sts to compare with a partner, and then check answers.

1 read   **2** fallen   **3** told   **4** heard   **5** seen   **6** bought
7 left   **8** given

e Tell Sts to cover the **Verb** column, and to say the sentences, completing them from memory.

4 LISTENING & SPEAKING recognizing topic questions

a Focus on the *Films, books, and TV* questionnaire and go through 1–12, making sure Sts understand the vocabulary, e.g. *soundtrack, subtitles*, etc.

Give Sts a few minutes to put the verbs in brackets into the past participle, and then check answers. Model and drill pronunciation.

1 fallen   **2** bought   **3** left   **4** seen   **5** cried   **6** seen
7 told   **8** read   **9** stopped   **10** listened   **11** given
12 watched

Don't get Sts to ask and answer the questions at this stage as they will be doing it later in the lesson.

b 🔊 **12.6** Now tell Sts they are going to listen to six people (A–F), each answering one of the 12 questions in **a**. Elicit / Teach that *ever* in the question *Have you ever…?* means (at some time) in your life.

Play the audio, pausing after each speaker to give Sts time to work out which question each speaker is answering.

Get Sts to compare with a partner, and then check answers.

 Read through the script and decide if you need to pre-teach any new lexis before Sts listen.

Speaker A 10   **Speaker B** 4   **Speaker C** 1   **Speaker D** 12
Speaker E 8   **Speaker F** 2

🔊 **12.6**
(script in Student's Book on *p.123*)
A Yes, I have. I drive a lot in my job, several hours a day, and I like listening to books – it's much better than listening to the radio. I probably listen to a couple of books every week.
B Yes, I've seen *Blade Runner* at least ten times. It's a really great film, I never get tired of it, I always notice something new.
C No, never. I've definitely fallen asleep watching TV, but never in the cinema.
D Yes, I have. I got a box set of *Downton Abbey* for Christmas last year, and the next day I watched four episodes one after another.
E No, I haven't. It usually takes me a long time to finish a book, so I never read them again.
F Yes, I bought the soundtrack of *Catching Fire*, you know, *The Hunger Games*, after I saw the film. It's got some amazing music: Coldplay, Imagine Dragons, Christina Aguilera.

---

c Now tell Sts that they should listen again and write down each speaker's answer. Play the audio, pausing after each speaker to give Sts time to write.

Check answers.

See script 12.6

 If there's time, you could get Sts to listen again with the script on *p.123*, so they can see exactly what they understood / didn't understand. Translate / Explain any new words or phrases.

d Focus on the instructions and the follow-up question. Get Sts to ask you question 1. If you answer *Yes, I have*, get them to ask *What film was it?* If you answer *No, I haven't*, get them to continue with the other questions until you answer *Yes, I have*.

Give Sts time to choose six questions in **a** that they want to ask their classmates.

Set a time limit, e.g. five minutes. Tell Sts to stand up and start. Take part in the activity yourself. Tell Sts that for each question they must try to find a different person who answers *Yes, I have*. Remind them to write down people's answers.

Stop the activity after five minutes (or when you think Sts have had enough time, or when someone has found people for all the questions). Get Sts to sit down again.

 If it is difficult for Sts to mingle in your classroom, you could get Sts to interview each other in pairs with the 12 questions.

e Get Sts to look at their answers and choose two that they think are the most interesting.

Get Sts to tell the class their two most interesting answers.

12B He's been everywhere!

G present perfect or past simple?
V learning irregular verbs
P irregular past participles

Lesson plan

The main context of the lesson is a conversation between a group of friends about where to go for dinner. One of the friends has tried all the restaurants his friends suggest. Their conversation contrasts the present perfect and the past simple in a natural context: *Have you been to…? When did you go? Why did you go there?*. The lesson starts with a Listening activity in which Sts are exposed to both the present perfect (for past experiences) and the past simple. This leads into the grammar focus. In Vocabulary and Pronunciation, Sts get more practice in forming and pronouncing irregular past participles. The lesson finishes with a Speaking activity in which Sts ask opening questions in the present perfect with *recently* and *ever*, and then simple follow-up questions using the past simple.

More materials		
For teachers		
Photocopiables		
Grammar present perfect or past simple? *p.202*		
Communicative Have you ever…? *p.251*		
(instructions *p.213*)		
For students		
Workbook 12B		
Online Practice 12B		

OPTIONAL LEAD-IN (BOOKS CLOSED)

Write the names of the following dishes on the board:

DIM SUM   GREEN CHICKEN CURRY   FAJITAS   MOUSSAKA
SASHIMI   TAPAS   RISOTTO   TANDOORI CHICKEN

Then ask Sts *In what kind of restaurants would you find them? Have you tried them? Do you like them?*

1 LISTENING identifying key information

a Books open. Focus on the task. Put Sts in pairs to ask and answer the questions.

Tell Sts the answer to 1 and elicit some feedback for 2 and 3.

1 Indian, Chinese, Italian

b 12.7 Focus on the task and play the audio for Sts to listen and answer the question.

Check the answer.

EXTRA SUPPORT Read through the script and decide if you need to pre-teach any new lexis before Sts listen.

No, they don't agree which restaurant to go to.

12.7
(script in Student's Book on *p.123*)

A = Alison, B = Brett, C = Clare, J = Joe

A Let's go out for dinner next Saturday. We can celebrate that it's nearly the end of term.
B Good idea. Where?
A Let's try somewhere new, somewhere that we haven't been to before.
B Yeah, good idea.
C How about that Indian restaurant near the station, Curry Up?
J Curry Up? I've been there. It wasn't very good.
C OK. Joe says it's not great. What about Chinese then? Somebody told me The Great Wall is very good.
A Yes, I haven't been there, but people say it's great.
J The Great Wall? I've been there. I went there last week. It is good, but I don't really want to go again.
B Well, there's a new Thai place, Thai-Chi. It opened really recently.
J Thai-Chi? I've been there, too. I went on Wednesday.
A Well, I don't know. Have you been to Mexican Wave?
J Mexican Wave? Yes, I have.
A When did you go there?
J Last month. I went for dinner with people from work.
A The Acropolis? That Greek place?
B I'm sure Joe's been there!
J No, I haven't. I haven't been to The Acropolis. But it closed a few months ago.
B Oh, this is ridiculous!
A OK, Joe, here's the answer. You cook dinner for us!

---

c Tell Sts they are going to listen to the conversation again, and this time they need to complete the chart about Joe. Focus on the restaurant names and elicit what kind of food each one serves.

Play the audio again.

Get Sts to compare with a partner, and then check answers. You could elicit anything else Sts can remember about the restaurants, e.g. *the Indian restaurant (Curry Up) wasn't very good, people say the Chinese restaurant (The Great Wall) is very good*, etc.

	Has he been there?	When?
Curry Up (Indian)	✓	?
The Great Wall (Chinese)	✓	last week
Thai-Chi (Thai)	✓	on Wednesday
Mexican Wave (Mexican)	✓	last month
The Acropolis (Greek)	✗	

EXTRA SUPPORT If there's time, you could get Sts to listen again with the script on *p.123*, so they can see exactly what they understood / didn't understand. Translate / Explain any new words or phrases.

d Do this as a whole-class activity, making sure Sts understand *annoying*.

2 GRAMMAR present perfect or past simple?

a Focus on the extract from the conversation and give Sts time, in pairs, to read it and answer questions 1–3. Check answers.

> **1** present perfect **2** past simple **3** When did you go there?

b Tell Sts to go to **Grammar Bank 12B** on *p.146*.

Grammar notes
Present perfect or past simple?
This is intended as a gentle introduction to the contrast between the present perfect and the past simple.

Many conversations typically begin with an opening question in the present perfect, e.g. *Have you been to the new French restaurant? Yes, I have*, and continue in the past tense, e.g. *What did you think of it? I loved it*.

This grammar point will be dealt with in more detail in *English File* Pre-intermediate.

been or *gone*?
This can be a tricky grammar point for Sts to assimilate. Instead of *Have you been to Mexico?*, Sts often say (incorrectly) *Have you gone to Mexico?* or *Have you been in Mexico?*.

Focus on the example sentences and play both audio ◉ **12.8** and ◉ **12.9** for Sts to listen and repeat. Then go through the rules with the class.

Now focus on the exercises for **12B** on *p.147*. Sts do the exercises individually or in pairs.

Check answers, getting Sts to read the full sentences.

> **a**
> **1** haven't finished **2** gave **3** bought **4** Have you ever danced **5** went
> **b**
> **1** gone **2** been **3** gone **4** been **5** been
> **c**
> **1** Have…visited **2** went **3** did…go **4** paid **5** Were
> **6** were **7** did…stay **8** had **9** Has…invited **10** stopped

EXTRA IDEA Get Sts to read the conversation in **c** to practise their pronunciation.

Tell Sts to go back to the main lesson **12B**.

EXTRA SUPPORT If you think Sts need more practice, you may want to give them the **Grammar** photocopiable activity at this point.

c You could demonstrate this yourself first. Write on the board the names of a restaurant you've been to recently, a film you've seen recently, and a place you've visited recently. Then ask Sts *Have you been to / seen / visited* x? If they say *Yes*, ask more questions with the past simple. Then get Sts to write down their two restaurants, films, and places.

d Put Sts in pairs to ask and answer their questions.

3 VOCABULARY learning irregular verbs

a ◉ **12.10** Focus on the task and point out that these five irregular verbs have the same form for the past simple and the past participle.

Get Sts to write the infinitives of the verbs.

Play the audio for Sts to listen and check.

Check answers. You could tell Sts that of the 50 most common irregular verbs in English, 27 have the same form for the past simple and the past participle.

> **1** get **2** have **3** lose **4** meet **5** win

◉ **12.10**

1	get	got
2	have	had
3	lose	lost
4	meet	met
5	win	won

Play the audio again, pausing after each past participle for Sts to listen and repeat the two forms. Help with pronunciation where necessary.

b ◉ **12.11** Tell Sts that they are now going to look at some verbs where the past simple form and the past participle are not the same. Give them time to write both the infinitive and the past simple.

Play the audio for Sts to listen and check.

Check answers.

> **1** be, was / were **2** do, did **3** eat, ate **4** speak, spoke
> **5** sing, sang

◉ **12.11**

1	be	was / were	been
2	do	did	done
3	eat	ate	eaten
4	speak	spoke	spoken
5	sing	sang	sung

Play the audio again, pausing after each past participle for Sts to listen and repeat the three forms. Help with pronunciation where necessary.

c Tell Sts to go to **Irregular verbs** on *p.165*, and get them to underline the verbs that have the same form for the past simple and the past participle.

Check answers by eliciting the infinitive of the verbs.

> bring, build, buy
> catch, cost
> feel, find
> get
> have, hear
> leave, lose
> make, meet
> pay, put
> read
> say, send, sit, sleep, spend, stand
> teach, tell, think
> understand
> win

Then tell Sts to highlight the verbs where the past participle is different from the past simple and try to learn them.

Tell Sts to go back to the main lesson **12B**.

4 PRONUNCIATION irregular past participles

a Focus on the seven sound pictures and elicit the word and sound (*clock* /ɒ/, *fish* /ɪ/, *tree* /iː/, *up* /ʌ/, *phone* /əʊ/, *horse* /ɔː/, and *egg* /e/).

Now focus on the verbs in the list. Elicit that the first one (*bought*) has the /ɔː/ sound, so Sts should write it in the *horse* column.

Put Sts in pairs, and get them to put the past participles into the correct columns. Remind them that this kind of exercise is easier if they say the words aloud to themselves.

b 🔊 **12.12** Play the audio for Sts to listen and check. Check answers.

🔊 **12.12**

clock /ɒ/	got, lost
fish /ɪ/	given
tree /iː/	eaten, seen
up /ʌ/	done, sung, won
phone /əʊ/	spoken
horse /ɔː/	bought, fallen
egg /e/	left, met, read

Now play the audio again, pausing after each group for Sts to listen and repeat. Give extra practice as necessary.

Put Sts in pairs and get them to practise saying the past participles.

5 SPEAKING

a Focus on the questionnaire and highlight the two groups of questions, one group about *Recently* (= in the last few days / weeks) and the other about *In your life*. Model and drill the pronunciation of *recently*.

Point out to Sts that the first column has the heading *Present perfect* and the second *Past simple*. Elicit which words are missing from the questions (column 1: *Have you*, and column 2: *did you*). Then elicit what form is needed for the verb in bold (the past participle). Finally, elicit all the questions for 1 (*Have you been to the cinema recently? What did you see? Did you like it?*).

Give Sts time to read all the questions.

b Demonstrate the activity by getting Sts to ask you some of the questions from each section. Then put Sts in pairs, **A** and **B**, and get them to take turns to interview each other. You could get Sts **A** to ask Sts **B** questions 1–5 under *Recently* and Sts **B** to ask Sts **A** 1–5 under *In your life*. Then they swap roles.

Monitor and help.

Finally, get feedback from a few Sts. Ask *Who has been to the cinema recently?*, and then get the details.

G revision: question formation

Lesson plan

In this final lesson, Sts revise Grammar, Vocabulary, and Pronunciation from the whole course, with a special focus on question formation. The lesson is based on an interview Sir Ian McKellen kindly gave to the *English File* authors. Sts first read the interview with Ian McKellen and do some comprehension exercises. Then, in Grammar and Speaking, they revise question formation before interviewing each other. Finally, Sts watch or listen to a programme about Judi Dench, an actress who has worked in famous productions with Ian McKellen.

More materials
For teachers
Photocopiables
Grammar revision: question formation *p.203*
Communicative Revision questions *p.252*
(instructions *p.213*)
Teacher's Resource Centre
Video Judi Dench – a life in acting
For students
Workbook 12C
Online Practice 12C

1 READING understanding topics

a Books open. Tell Sts to look at the characters in the photos and ask them if they know Sir Ian McKellen. They might recognize him from films such as *The Lord of the Rings*, *X-Men*, *Mr Holmes*, *The Da Vinci Code*, or *The Golden Compass*.

Find out if any Sts have seen any of the films.

b Tell Sts that the interview was given exclusively for *English File* and that Sir Ian McKellen answered questions based on lessons in Elementary.

Get Sts to read the interview and match a heading to each section. Point out that the first one (*Your tastes*) has been done for them.

Get Sts to compare with a partner, and then check answers.

EXTRA SUPPORT Before Sts read the interview the first time, check whether you need to pre-teach any vocabulary.

B Your lifestyle   **C** Your home   **D** Your abilities   **E** Your places
F Your work experiences

c Put Sts in pairs and tell them to decide in which sections of the interview they think they will find 1–10.

Check which section of the interview the sentences might be in. Also elicit some feedback on which sentences are true and which are false. <u>Don't</u> tell Sts at this stage if they are right or not.

1 F   **2** C   **3** B   **4** E   **5** B   **6** F   **7** C   **8** C   **9** B   **10** D

d Tell Sts to read the interview again and to mark sentences 1–10 *T* (true) or *F* (false). Remind them to say why the *F* ones are false.

Get Sts to compare with a partner, and then check answers.

1 T
2 F (He lives in London.)
3 F (Sometimes he doesn't get up until 10 a.m.)
4 T
5 T
6 F (He read *The Lord of the Rings* when he was preparing to play Gandalf.)
7 T
8 F (He loves dogs.)
9 T
10 F (He'd like to learn to sing, play the piano, and speak foreign languages.)

Deal with any other new vocabulary. Model and drill the pronunciation of any tricky words.

e Put Sts in pairs and get them to discuss what three things they found the most interesting from the interview.

Get some feedback from the class.

2 GRAMMAR & SPEAKING revision: question formation

a Put Sts in pairs and get them to complete all the questions in groups 1–6. Point out that the first one (*do*) has been done for them.

b 🔊 **12.13** Play the audio for Sts to listen and check. Check answers after each group.

1 do, did   **2** 's, Are, Did   **3** can, Can, are   **4** 's, did, are
5 's, are, do   **6** have, 's, Have

1   Your lifestyle
What do you usually do in the morning?
How do you relax?
What did you do last weekend?
2   Your home
What's your favourite room in your home?
Are you tidy or untidy?
Did you do a lot of housework last week?
3   Your abilities
What languages can you speak?
Can you sing or play a musical instrument?
Why are you learning English?
4   Your places
What's your favourite place to spend the weekend?
Where did you go for your last holiday?
Where are you going to go for your next holiday?
5   Your tastes
What's your favourite time of year?
What book are you reading at the moment?
What kind of TV programmes do you like watching?
6   Your experiences
What films have you seen recently?
What's the most beautiful place you've ever been to?
Have you ever been to Britain or the USA?

c Focus on the task and the example.

Put Sts in pairs, **A** and **B**. **A** starts by interviewing **B** with group 1. Encourage Sts to ask for more information and react to their partner's answers.

EXTRA SUPPORT Write some phrases on the board to help Sts react and show interest, e.g. *Really? How interesting! Me too! What about you?*.

When Sts **A** have finished asking the questions in group 1, Sts **B** ask the questions in group 2. Make sure they keep swapping roles.

When they have finished, elicit some interesting answers from the class for each group of questions.

EXTRA CHALLENGE Get Sts to write the interview they just had with their partner. They should follow the style used in the interview with Sir Ian McKellen.

EXTRA IDEA Tell Sts that they are going to role-play being a journalist and a famous person. Tell them to think of a famous person who is still alive. When they are ready, put them in pairs, **A** and **B**. Tell Sts **A** they are journalists and Sts **B** they are the famous person. Tell Sts **B** to use their imagination and invent answers. When Sts **A** have finished their interview, they swap roles.

3 ▶ VIDEO LISTENING understanding biographical information

a Tell Sts they are going to watch a documentary about Judi Dench, one of Britain's best known and most successful actresses.

Focus on the film titles and check that Sts understand / recognize them. Then play the video for Sts to watch and complete the task.

Get Sts to compare with a partner, and then check answers.

EXTRA SUPPORT Read through the script and decide if you need to pre-teach any new lexis before Sts watch or listen. You may want to tell Sts that *The Old Vic* and *The Royal Court* are famous theatres in London.

The six films mentioned are *Macbeth*, *A Room with a View*, *Henry V*, *GoldenEye*, *Mrs Brown*, and *Shakespeare in Love*.

Judi Dench – a life in acting

Judi Dench is one of a golden generation of British actors who have had long and successful careers, including Maggie Smith, Vanessa Redgrave, Ian McKellen, Michael Caine, and Anthony Hopkins. She has acted in the theatre, on television, and in films in a career of nearly sixty years.

Judith Olivia Dench was born on the ninth of December nineteen thirty-four in York in the north of England. Dench's father was a doctor, but she had connections from a very early age to the Theatre Royal in York – her father was the theatre's doctor and her mother made costumes for the theatre. As a teenager, Judi Dench acted in the York Mystery Plays. These religious plays have been performed in York every four years since the fourteenth century.

In the late nineteen fifties and nineteen sixties, she acted with Britain's most important theatre companies, the Old Vic, the Royal Court, and the Royal Shakespeare Company.

In the nineteen seventies and nineteen eighties, Dench continued to work in the theatre and on British television. In nineteen seventy-eight, she acted in Shakespeare's *Macbeth* with the actor Ian McKellen, both in the theatre and on film. Many people think it was one of the best ever performances of the play. She also appeared in British films like *A Room with a View* in nineteen eighty-five and *Henry V* in nineteen eighty-nine.

In the nineteen nineties, her career changed with two films. The first of these was the James Bond film, *GoldenEye*, where Dench played Bond's boss, M, normally a part for a man. Dench was a great success in the part. She was hard, and at the same time funny. She played the part in eight films, with both Pierce Brosnan and Daniel Craig as James Bond. The second film that changed her career was *Mrs Brown* in nineteen ninety-seven. Dench played Queen Victoria. This small, British film was a great success and she was nominated for an Oscar for Best Actress.

In nineteen ninety-eight, she played Queen Elizabeth I in the comedy, *Shakespeare in Love*. The film was another big hit. It won the nineteen ninety-nine Oscar for Best Film, and Judi Dench won the Oscar for Best Supporting Actress. She's only in the film for eight minutes, but, as ever, she's absolutely brilliant.

Finally, ask Sts if they've seen any of the films, and if they liked them.

b Focus on the task and give Sts time to read the events in Judi Dench's life. Point out that the first one has been done for them.

Play the video for Sts to watch again and number the events in the order in which they happened.

Get Sts to compare with a partner, and then check answers.

2 She acted in the York Mystery Plays.
3 She worked with the Royal Shakespeare Company.
4 She was in a production of *Macbeth* with Ian McKellen.
5 She appeared in *A Room with a View*.
6 She appeared in her first James Bond film.
7 She played Queen Victoria in the film *Mrs Brown*.
8 She played Queen Elizabeth I.
9 She won an Oscar.

EXTRA SUPPORT If there's time, you could get Sts to watch again with subtitles / showing the script, so they can see exactly what they understood / didn't understand. Translate / Explain any new words or phrases.

c Do this as a whole-class activity.

For instructions on how to use these pages, see *p.39*.

More materials
For teachers
Teacher's Resource Centre
Video Can you understand these people? 11&12
Quick Test 12
File 12 Test
Progress Test Files 7–12
End-of-course Test
For students
Online Practice Check your progress

GRAMMAR

1 b 2 a 3 b 4 b 5 a 6 c 7 b 8 a 9 c 10 a
11 c 12 a 13 a 14 c 15 c

VOCABULARY

a
1 slowly 2 dangerous 3 badly 4 quiet 5 cold
6 strongly
b
1 learn 2 need 3 promise 4 want
c
1 online 2 download 3 website 4 attachment 5 wi-fi
d
1 in 2 up 3 for 4 with
e
1 seen 2 gone 3 known 4 given 5 fallen 6 taken

PRONUNCIATION

b
1 b**ough**t /ɔː/ 5 sp**o**ken /əʊ/ 2 w**a**nt /ɒ/ 4 wi-f**i** /aɪ/
3 w**o**men /ɪ/
c
1 poli<u>te</u>ly 2 <u>dan</u>gerously 3 de<u>cide</u> 4 a<u>ttach</u>ment
5 <u>web</u>site

CAN YOU understand this text?

a
C is the most positive. B is the most negative.
b
1 C 2 B 3 E 4 A 5 D 6 C 7 A 8 E

▶ CAN YOU understand these people?

1 a 2 c 3 a 4 b 5 a

◀)) 12.14

1 Anna
I = interviewer, A = Anna
I What are you doing in the UK?
A In the UK, er, I just came for a visit. I'm here the second time in my life, and it was always a dream of mine to come to London. Er, yes.
I Was there anything that surprised you about the UK when you arrived?
A I think that the people are very open, and that, um, just everybody is so nice, and I also saw some monuments and some places I wanted to see, so I was also very impressed about the architecture, etc.

2 Madeleine
I = interviewer, M = Madeleine
I How do people in your country drive?
M I think it depends where you are. Where I live in Oregon, everything is very safe, much slower, but in New York City everything is very fast, very dangerous.
I Are you a typical driver for where you live?
M I would say so, I d-, I'm a very cautious driver.

3 Chris
I = interviewer, C = Chris
I Do you have any ambitions for this year?
C Um, yes, I'd like to visit my daughter in Australia, and also plan towards my retirement.
I Do you think you're going to do them?
C Certainly the planning, whether or not I achieve the visit is something else.

4 Talitha
I = interviewer, T = Talitha
I Have you ever seen a film more than three times?
T Yes, I really like *Lord of the Rings*, so I've definitely seen that more than three times.
I What do you like about it?
T I love the scenery, um, and I love the imagination.

5 Martin
I = interviewer, M = Martin
I What phone do you have?
M I have an iPhone.
I How old is it?
M I believe, I believe my iPhone is now two years old.
I How often do you change phones?
M I change phones maybe every three years.
I What do you use it for the most?
M I mostly use my phone for social media.

Photocopiable activities

Overview

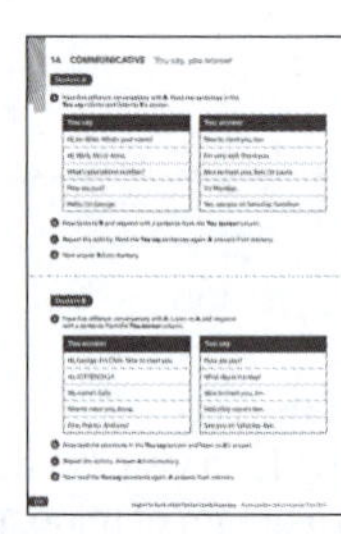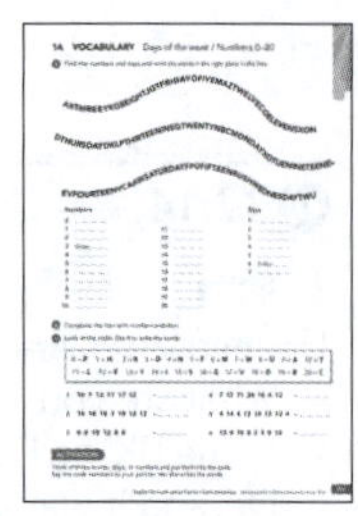

- There is a **Grammar activity** for each main (A, B, and C) lesson of the Student's Book.
- There is a **Communicative activity** for each main (A, B, and C) lesson of the Student's Book.
- There is a **Vocabulary activity** for each section of the Vocabulary Bank in the Student's Book.

All the photocopiable material is also available on the **Teacher's Resource Centre** (TRC). It is also available on the **Classroom Presentation Tool** (CPT), allowing you to display the worksheets on an interactive whiteboard or projector. This will make it easier to set up and demonstrate the activities, and show answers.

Using extra activities in mixed ability classes

Some teachers have classes with a very wide range of levels, and where some Sts finish Student's Book activities much more quickly than others. You could give these fast finishers a photocopiable activity (Grammar, Vocabulary, or Communicative) while you help the slower Sts. Alternatively, some teachers might want to give faster Sts extra oral practice with a communicative activity while slower Sts consolidate their knowledge with an extra grammar activity.

Tips for using Grammar activities

- The grammar activities are designed to give Sts extra practice in the main grammar points from each lesson. How you use these activities depends on the needs of your Sts and the time available. They can be used in the lesson if you think all of your class would benefit from the extra practice or you could set them as homework for some or all of your Sts.
- Before using the worksheets in class, check for any vocabulary that may be either new or difficult for your Sts.
- All of the activities start with a writing stage. If you use the activities in class, get Sts to work individually or in pairs. Allow Sts to compare before checking answers.
- If Sts are having trouble with any of the activities, make sure they refer to the relevant Grammar Bank in the Student's Book.
- All of the activities have an **Activation** section. Some of them have a task that gets Sts to cover the sentences and test their memory. If you are using the activities in class, Sts can work in pairs and test their partner. If you set them for homework, encourage Sts to use this stage to test themselves. Alternatively, you could set the main activity for homework and then get Sts to do the **Activation** at the start of the next class.

- Make sure that Sts keep their worksheets and that they review any difficult areas regularly. Encourage them to go back to activities and cover and test themselves.

Tips for using Communicative activities

- Before using the worksheets in class, check for any vocabulary that may be either new or difficult for your Sts.
- We have suggested the ideal number of copies for each activity. However, you can often manage with fewer, e.g. one worksheet per pair instead of one per student.
- When Sts are working in pairs, if possible get them to sit face-to-face. This will encourage them to really talk to each other and also means they can't see each other's worksheet.
- If your class doesn't divide into pairs or groups, take part yourself, get two Sts to share one role, or get one student to monitor, help, and correct.
- If some Sts finish early, they can swap roles and do the activity again, or you could get them to write some of the sentences from the activity.

Tips for using Vocabulary activities

- These worksheets are intended to recycle and consolidate Sts' understanding of the vocabulary in the Student's Book Vocabulary Banks. As such, we suggest not using them directly after doing these exercises. Instead, get Sts to do them in a subsequent lesson.
- If Sts are having trouble with any of the activities, make sure they refer to the relevant Vocabulary Bank page.
- You could ask Sts to check their answers by referring to the relevant Student's Book Vocabulary Bank.
- All the activities are suitable for use in class. However, you may wish to set some of the tasks for homework.
- Most of the Vocabulary worksheets have an **Activation** task and this can be treated in a similar way to the Grammar ones.
- Make sure that Sts keep their and that they review any difficult areas regularly. Encourage them to go back to activities and cover and test themselves.

Customisable worksheets

There are customisable versions of some of the Grammar, Communicative, and Vocabulary activities on the **Teacher's Resource Centre**. These allow you to adapt the material to make it more applicable and/or relevant to your Sts. For instance, you could:

- change some of the names to the names of Sts in your class.
- change place names to ones that are more relevant and/or familiar to your Sts.
- change items of grammar or vocabulary to focus on the needs and interests of your Sts and/or adapt the level of challenge.
- reduce the number of items if you are short of time.

Grammar activity answers

1A verb *be* [+], subject pronouns

a 2 She's   3 You're   4 They're   5 It's   6 I'm   7 We're
8 They're   9 We're   10 You're   11 It's   12 He's
b 2 She is   3 You are   4 They are   5 It is   6 I am   7 We are
8 They are   9 We are   10 You are   11 It is   12 He is

1B verb *be* [−] and [?]

1 2 is   3 Are   4 am   5 's   6 'm   7 's   8 are   9 'm
10 'm   11 Are   12 'm not   13 'm   14 's   15 's   16 Is
17 isn't   18 's   19 are   20 Are   21 aren't   22 're
2 2 's   3 Are   4 'm not   5 are   6 'm   7 Is   8 is   9 Are
10 'm not   11 'm   12 are   13 Is   14 's   15 Is   16 isn't
17 Is   18 isn't   19 Are   20 aren't   21 're

1C possessive adjectives: *my, your,* etc.

2 his   3 our   4 their   5 your   6 our   7 Their   8 your
9 my   10 her   11 our   12 my

2A singular and plural nouns

a 2 a; magazines
3 a; children
4 an; airports
5 a; universities
6 a; dictionaries
7 an; addresses
8 a; men
9 a; laptops
10 a; cities
b 3 What are they? They're headphones.
4 What is it? It's a (mobile) phone.
5 What are they? They're keys.
6 What are they? They're newspapers.
7 What are they? They're chairs.
8 What is it? It's a pizza.
9 What are they? They're tissues.
10 What is it? It's an umbrella.
11 What is it? It's a wallet.
12 What are they? They're sandwiches.

2B adjectives

2 It's a cheap hotel.   3 They're expensive watches.
4 It's a fast train.   5 It's an easy exercise.   6 She's a beautiful
actress.   7 They're long snakes.   8 They're old women.
9 It's a small car.   10 They're new boots.   11 It's a dangerous
road.   12 They're tall men.

2C imperatives, *let's*

a 3 Don't take   4 listen   5 Don't stop   6 Turn off
7 Have   8 Be   9 Sign   10 Slow down
b 2 Let's go   3 Let's have   4 Let's cross   5 Let's ask
6 Let's check

3A present simple [+] and [−]

2 She plays the guitar.
3 She doesn't eat meat.
4 She doesn't play tennis.
5 She goes to the gym.
6 She drinks coffee.
7 She studies French.
8 She listens to music.
9 She doesn't live in Oxford.
10 She has a cat.
11 She wears glasses.
12 She doesn't smoke.

3B present simple [+], [−] and [?]

a 2 live   3 do…do   4 do…work   5 Do…like
6 love   7 Do…work   8 don't work
b 2 teaches   3 Does   4 doesn't   5 works   6 like
7 doesn't like   8 rains   9 Do   10 doesn't   11 Do   12 Do

3C word order in questions

2 Are you a vegetarian?
3 Where are your parents from?
4 What phone do you have?
5 How many languages do you speak?
6 Do you need a new phone?
7 How do you spell your surname?
8 When do you listen to the radio?
9 Where do you do your homework?
10 Who is your favourite singer?
11 What do you do at the weekend?
12 What TV programmes do you watch?

4A possessive *'s, Whose…?*

3 It's Pete's CD.   4 It's Rachel's book.   5 It's Pete's
ticket.   6 They're Rachel's scissors.   7 They're Pete's music
books.   8 It's Keira's white coat.   9 They're Rachel's board
pens.   10 It's Toby's shirt.   11 It's Pete's piano.   12 It's
Keira's car.   13 They're Toby's tennis balls.   14 It's Rachel's
dictionary.   15 They're Toby's trainers.   16 It's Keira's bag.

4B prepositions of time and place (*in, on, at, to*)

a 2 at   3 on   4 on   5 in   6 at   7 in   8 on   9 in
10 at   11 on   12 on   13 at   14 in   15 at
b 1 in   2 to   3 in   4 at   5 to   6 in / at   7 at   8 to
9 in / at   10 at

4C adverbs and expressions of frequency

2 He always sleeps for eight hours.
3 They sometimes go to the cinema on Friday.
4 She meets her friends once a week.
5 He is always tired in the morning.
6 She never eats meat.
7 He often does his homework on the bus.
8 He is sometimes late for class.
9 They do yoga twice a week.
10 He hardly ever goes to the hairdresser.
11 He often goes to the doctor.
12 She studies English every day.

5A *can / can't*

2 can't take   3 Can…sit   4 can't find   5 can cook   6 can't
hear   7 Can…open   8 can't park   9 can't speak   10 Can…
help   11 can't swim   12 can dance

5B present continuous: *be* + verb + *-ing*

1 2 's washing   3 's listening   4 is…doing   5 are…
doing   6 'm getting
2 7 Are…watching   8 's happening   9 're
winning   10 aren't playing   11 aren't…watching   12 'm
working   13 is watching
3 14 are…doing   15 're counting   16 aren't
counting   17 're playing   18 's…doing   19 's looking
4 20 's…doing   21 Is…working   22 're
travelling   23 are…doing   24 'm not working   25 'm
looking for

5C present simple or present continuous?

1 do…think **2** takes **3** are having **4** are…going **5** go
6 are…doing **7** 'm waiting **8** 's having **9** 'm listening
10 Do…wear **11** don't like **12** 's raining **13** rains
14 are…crying **15** 'm watching **16** 's…stopping **17** stops
18 do…see **19** meet **20** Do…finish **21** 'm working
22 are…looking **23** put **24** do…do **25** swim
26 's…trying **27** watches

6A object pronouns: *me, you, him*, etc.

2 us **3** it **4** me **5** you **6** them **7** me **8** her **9** him
10 them **11** us **12** it **13** her **14** me **15** it **16** you
17 him **18** them **19** her **20** us

6B *like* (+ verb + *-ing*)

2 I don't mind doing
3 I love swimming
4 I hate going
5 I don't like sitting
6 I love having
7 I don't like waiting
8 I don't mind living
9 I like listening
10 I love cooking
11 I hate looking for
12 I don't like watching
13 I hate getting up
14 I like shopping

6C *be or do?*

2 'm **3** Is **4** isn't **5** 's **6** do **7** 're **8** do **9** are
10 's **11** don't **12** Is **13** Are **14** am **15** 's **16** 's
17 Do **18** don't **19** are **20** Do **21** is **22** don't **23** 's

7A past simple of *be: was / were*

2 wasn't (He was American.)
3 was
4 weren't (They were from Scandinavia.)
5 was
6 wasn't (He was a writer.)
7 were
8 was
9 weren't (They were philosophers.)
10 was
11 wasn't (He was German.)
12 were
13 wasn't (Her first album was *19*.)
14 weren't (They were from Peru.)
15 was
16 were
17 weren't (They were Italian.)
18 was
19 were
20 wasn't (He was a German physicist.)

7B past simple: regular verbs

1 **2** didn't study **3** studied **4** lived **5** did…live
    6 rented **7** Did…talk **8** wanted **9** learned
2 **10** Did…like **11** loved **12** didn't want **13** Did…
    travel **14** didn't travel **15** Did…stay **16** stayed
3 **17** Did…watch **18** didn't **19** worked **20** didn't finish
    21 started **22** missed **23** didn't arrive
4 **24** called **25** didn't answer **26** texted **27** didn't…text
    28 didn't talk **29** chatted **30** didn't chat **31** wanted
    32 danced

7C past simple: irregular verbs

a **2** was **3** were **4** bought **5** got **6** had **7** got **8** wore
    9 was **10** got **11** was **12** went **13** found **14** drank
    15 put on **16** went **17** were **18** said **19** couldn't
    20 wasn't **21** felt **22** got **23** spent **24** didn't have
b **2** did they wear **3** did they get **4** was
    5 did they do / drink **6** did they do
    7 did some people say **8** Did they get
    9 did they spend **10** Did they have

8A past simple: regular and irregular verbs

2 didn't come **3** did you see **4** Did you do **5** was
6 woke up **7** had **8** drove **9** didn't have **10** went
11 came **12** did **13** made **14** did you come
15 arrived **16** sat **17** read **18** checked **19** had
20 watched **21** went to sleep **22** Did you speak
23 did she say **24** didn't talk **25** said **26** called
27 heard **28** took **29** closed **30** didn't say **31** left

8B *there is / there are, some / any* + plural nouns

a **3** Is there a double bed in the bedroom? Yes, there is.
    4 Is there a piano in the living room? No, there isn't.
    5 Is there a plant in the study? No, there isn't.
    6 Is there a dishwasher in the kitchen? Yes, there is.
    7 Are there any cupboards in the bathroom? Yes, there are.
    8 Are there any chairs in the bedroom? No, there aren't.
b **2** There are some plants in the living room.
    3 There's a mirror in the hall.
    4 There aren't any books in the living room.
    5 There's a computer in the study.
    6 There isn't a clock in the kitchen.
    7 There's a fireplace in the living room.
    8 There are some shelves in the study.

8C *there was / there were*

1 **2** there wasn't **3** There was **4** Were there **5** there
    weren't **6** there was **7** there were
2 **8** there was **9** Was there **10** there were **11** Were
    there **12** There were
3 **13** There was **14** there were **15** Were there **16** there
    were **17** there was
4 **18** There were **19** Were there **20** there
    were **21** there weren't

9A countable / uncountable nouns; *a / an, some / any*

a **2** Is there any butter? No, there isn't.
    3 Are there any carrots? No, there aren't.
    4 Is there any cheese? Yes, there is.
    5 Is there any fish? No, there isn't.
    6 Is there a / any chicken? Yes, there is.
    7 Are there any eggs? Yes, there are.
    8 Is there any orange juice? No, there isn't.
b **2** There's some tomato juice.
    3 There's a / some pineapple.
    4 There aren't any strawberries.
    5 There aren't any peppers.
    6 There's some milk.
    7 There are some mushrooms.
    8 There isn't any ice cream.

9B quantifiers; *how much / how many, a lot of,* etc.

2 many / He eats a lot of burgers.
3 many / He doesn't eat many chips.
4 much / She doesn't eat any meat.
5 many / She eats a lot of vegetables.
6 much / She doesn't drink much Diet Coke.
7 much / She drinks a lot of milk.
8 much / She doesn't eat much bread.
9 many / She doesn't eat any apples.
10 much / He doesn't eat any rice.
11 much / He eats a lot of pasta.
12 many / He doesn't drink many cups of espresso.

9C comparative adjectives

2 Skype is older than Facebook.
3 A Cartier watch is more expensive than a Swatch watch.
4 New York is hotter than London (in the summer).
5 An orange is healthier than an apple.
6 Rome is drier than Buenos Aires.
7 A man is slower than a horse.
8 Russia is bigger than Canada.
9 Shanghai is more crowded than Istanbul.
10 Travelling by car is more dangerous than travelling by plane.
11 The Burj Khalifa tower is taller than the Empire State Building.
12 Stockholm is sunnier than Paris.

10A superlative adjectives

a 2 What's the wettest town in the world?
3 What's the smallest country in the world?
4 What's the highest city in the world?
5 What's the longest beach in the world?
6 What's the driest desert in the world?
7 What's the busiest train station in the world?
8 What's the most populated city in the world?
9 What's the most popular tourist destination in the world?
10 What's the most expensive city in the world?

b 2 Cherrapunji in India
3 Vatican City
4 La Rinconada in Peru
5 Praia do Cassino in Brazil
6 the Atacama Desert in Chile
7 Shinjuku Station in Tokyo
8 Shanghai in China
9 France
10 Zurich in Switzerland

10B *be going to* (plans)

1 2 'm going to watch
2 3 aren't going to study   4 're going to live
3 5 'm not going to go out   6 'm going to go to bed
4 7 Is…going to be   8 's going to bring
5 9 are…going to do   10 're going to stay   11 Are…going to take   12 're going to visit
6 13 's going to buy   14 's…going to do   15 's going to give

10C *be going to* (predictions)

2 He's going to listen
3 He's going to win
4 They aren't going to eat
5 She's going to make
6 It's not going to snow
7 She's not going to buy
8 He's going to play
9 She's going to get married.
10 He's going to take
11 They're going to visit
12 She's going to paint

11A adverbs (manner and modifiers)

a badly   dangerously   well   noisily   carefully   easily   hard   quietly   patiently   fast   loudly   slowly

b 2 slowly   3 carefully   4 easily   5 well   6 quietly   7 fast   8 hard   9 patiently   10 dangerously   11 badly   12 loudly

11B verb + *to* + infinitive

a 2 to be   3 to play   4 to drive   5 to buy   6 to have   7 to get   8 to do

b 1 Would   2 Do   3 Does   4 Would   5 Would

11C definite article: *the* or no *the*

1 3 –   4 –
2 5 –   6 the
3 7 –   8 –   9 –
4 10 –   11 the   12 –
5 13 the   14 –
6 15 the   16 the   17 The
7 18 –   19 The   20 the
8 21 the   22 the
9 23 the   24 –   25 –
10 26 –   27 the   28 –

12A present perfect

1 Have…seen   2 've broken   3 haven't worn   4 've bought   5 has travelled   6 Have…met   7 've eaten   8 hasn't finished   9 Has…arrived   10 's taken

12B present perfect or past simple?

1 2 did…leave
2 3 Have…been   4 went   5 was
3 6 Has…arrived   7 phoned
4 8 saw   9 didn't like   10 Have…seen   11 saw   12 loved
5 13 Have…seen   14 haven't   15 stayed   16 didn't see
6 17 Have…been   18 have   19 did…go   20 was   21 Did…have   22 was
7 23 've been   24 've…visited   25 've seen   26 went   27 had   28 did…enjoy   29 met   30 was
8 31 Have…spoken   32 haven't   33 got   34 did…say   35 got

12C revision: question formation

2 How did you get
3 What was
4 Are you having
5 Would you…to try
6 Where did you go
7 Why is…leaving
8 Can you play
9 Why didn't you have
10 Have you done
11 Are you going to go out
12 Whose…is
13 How often do…have
14 Why did…go
15 When was…born
16 Have you…eaten
17 Are you going to fly
18 What time does…finish
19 How many…do you sleep
20 What's…going to do

1A GRAMMAR verb *be* ⊞, subject pronouns

a Complete the sentences with a pronoun (*I*, *You*, etc.) and 'm, 're, or 's.

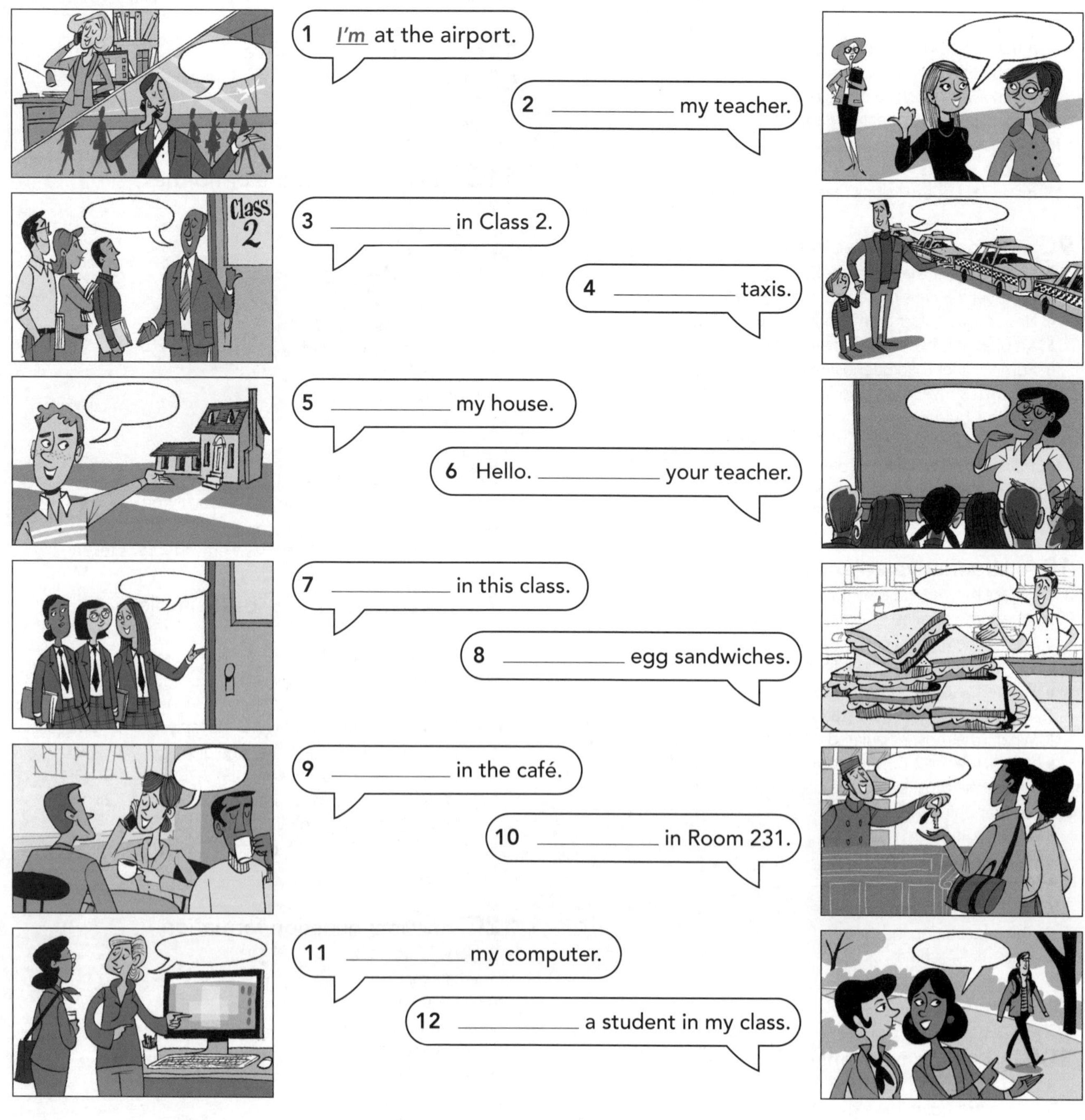

b Rewrite sentences 1–12 with the full forms (**NOT** contractions).

1 *I am* at the airport.
2 __________ my teacher.
3 __________ in Class 2.
4 __________ taxis.
5 __________ my house.
6 __________ your teacher.

7 __________ in this class.
8 __________ egg sandwiches.
9 __________ in the café.
10 __________ in Room 231.
11 __________ my computer.
12 __________ a student in my class.

ACTIVATION

Test your memory. Cover the sentences in **a** and look at the pictures.
Say the sentences. Use contractions.

English File fourth edition Teacher's Guide Elementary   Photocopiable © Oxford University Press 2019

1B GRAMMAR verb *be* ⊟ and ?

Complete the conversations with a form of the verb *be*. Use contractions where possible.

1

Juan Hi.

Petra [1]*Is* this Class 2?

Juan Yes, it [2]__________. [3]__________ you in this class, too?

Petra Yes, I [4]__________. What [5]__________ your name?

Juan I [6]__________ Juan.

Petra My name [7]__________ Petra.

Juan Where [8]__________ you from, Petra?

Petra I [9]__________ from the Czech Republic. And you?

Juan I [10]__________ from Madrid.

Petra [11]__________ you Spanish?

Juan No, I [12]__________. I [13]__________ Mexican, but I live in Spain.

Petra Who [14]__________ our teacher?

Juan Her name [15]__________ Diane.

Petra [16]__________ she English?

Juan No, she [17]__________. She [18]__________ American.

Petra Where [19]__________ the other students? [20]__________ they in class?

Juan No, they [21]__________. They [22]__________ in the café!

2

Chris Hi, I [1]*'m* Chris.

Oliver Hello. My name [2]__________ Oliver. It's my first day here.

Chris [3]__________ you German, Oliver?

Oliver No, I [4]__________. I'm Swiss.

Chris Oh, which city [5]__________ you from?

Oliver I [6]__________ from Lucerne, in the centre of Switzerland.

Chris [7]__________ it nice in Lucerne?

Oliver Yes, it [8]__________. It's beautiful. [9]__________ you English?

Chris No, I [10]__________. I [11]__________ Irish.

Oliver Where [12]__________ you from in Ireland?

Chris Dublin, the capital.

Oliver Really. [13]__________ Dublin nice?

Chris Yes, it [14]__________ great!

Oliver [15]__________ this my computer?

Chris No, it [16]__________. This is your computer here.

Oliver Thanks. [17]__________ the boss here?

Chris No, he [18]__________. He's in a meeting.

Oliver [19]__________ the other people in the office English?

Chris No, they [20]__________. They [21]__________ from all over the world. Have a good first day at work!

ACTIVATION

Practise the conversations with a partner.

1C GRAMMAR possessive adjectives: *my, your,* etc.

● Look at the pictures. Complete the sentences with *my, your, his, her, our,* or *their.*

ACTIVATION

Test your memory. Cover the sentences and look at the pictures. Say the sentences.

2A GRAMMAR singular and plural nouns

a Complete the **SINGULAR** column with *a* or *an*. Then complete the **PLURAL** column.

SINGULAR	PLURAL
1 *a* ___ credit card	*credit cards*
2 ___ magazine	
3 ___ child	
4 ___ airport	
5 ___ university	

SINGULAR	PLURAL
6 ___ dictionary	
7 ___ address	
8 ___ man	
9 ___ laptop	
10 ___ city	

b Look at the pictures. Write a question with *it* or *they* and complete the answers.

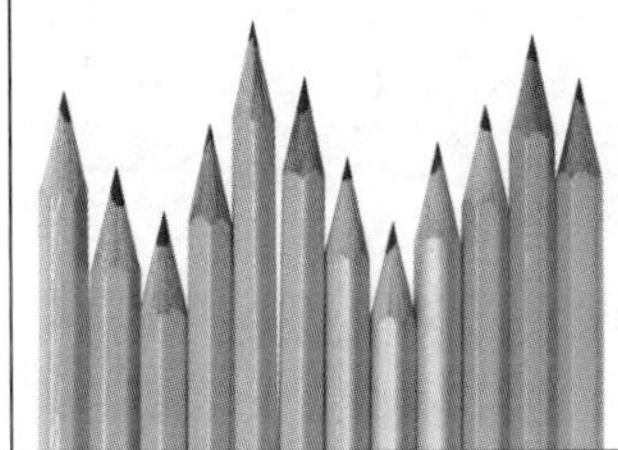

1 *What are they?*
  They're pencils.

2 *What is it?*
  It's a lamp.

3 ___________________?

4 ___________________?

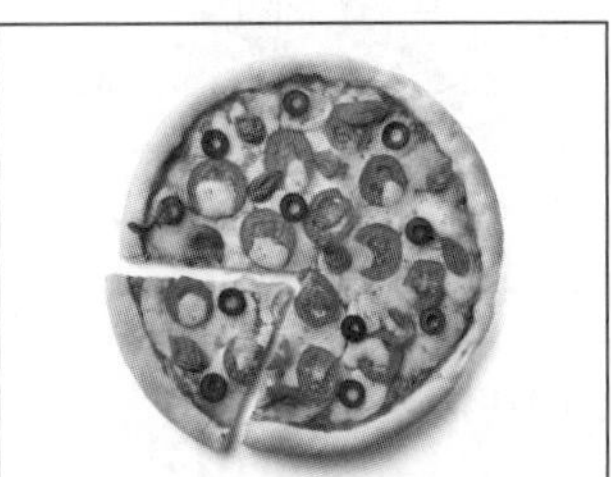
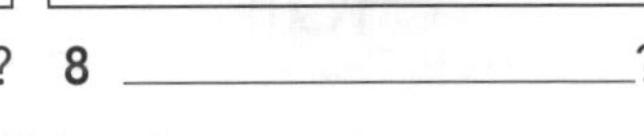

5 ___________________?

6 ___________________?

7 ___________________?

8 ___________________?

9 ___________________?

10 ___________________?

11 ___________________?

12 ___________________?

ACTIVATION

Test your memory. Cover the sentences and look at the pictures. Take turns to ask and answer.

What is it?) (*It's a…*   *What are they?*) (*They're…*

2B GRAMMAR adjectives

Write sentences for pictures 1–12. Use an adjective from the list.

small tall beautiful rich new
easy expensive OLD LONG
cheap FAST DANGEROUS

1 *He's a rich man.*   7 _______________________
2 _______________________   8 _______________________
3 _______________________   9 _______________________
4 _______________________   10 _______________________
5 _______________________   11 _______________________
6 _______________________   12 _______________________

ACTIVATION

Test your memory. Cover the sentences and adjectives. Look at the pictures and say the sentences.

English File fourth edition Teacher's Guide Elementary   Photocopiable © Oxford University Press 2019

2C GRAMMAR imperatives, *let's*

a Complete the conversations with a ⊞ or ⊟ imperative using a verb from the list.

~~be~~ be ~~close~~ have listen sign slow down stop take turn off

1 A I'm cold. *Close* the window, please.
   B OK.

2 A What time is the exam?
   B Tomorrow at 9.00. *Don't be* late!

3 A _______________ photos!
   B Why not?
   A Look at that sign – 'No photographs in the museum'.

4 A Sh! Be quiet and _______________ to the teacher.
   B Sorry.

5 A _______________ here!
   B Why not?
   A It's a bus stop.

6 A _______________ the TV and finish your homework!
   B OK, Dad.

7 A _______________ a good weekend.
   B You too. See you on Monday.

8 A _______________ careful! The coffee is very hot.
   B OK. Thank you.

9 A _______________ your name here, please.
   B Sure. Can I have a pen?

10 A _______________! The speed limit is 60 kph on this road!
   B I know, but we're very late!

b Complete the conversations with *Let's…* and a verb from the list.

ask check cross go have ~~stop~~

1 A I'm tired.
   B OK. *Let's stop* and sit down.

2 A I'm really thirsty.
   B Me too. _______________ to a café and have a drink.

3 A I'm hungry.
   B Me too! _______________ a sandwich.

4 A _______________ the road here.
   B No! It's really dangerous.

5 A Where's the bus station?
   B I don't know. _______________ that man.

6 A What's the capital of Turkey?
   B I think it's Ankara, but I'm not sure. _______________ on the internet.

Practise the conversations with a partner.

3A GRAMMAR present simple ⊞ and ⊟

a Look at the picture of Carla's room. Write positive ⊞ and negative ⊟ sentences about Carla.

1 like Coldplay *She likes Coldplay.*
2 play the guitar ____________________
3 eat meat ____________________
4 play tennis ____________________
5 go to the gym ____________________
6 drink coffee ____________________

7 study French ____________________
8 listen to music ____________________
9 live in Oxford ____________________
10 have a cat ____________________
11 wear glasses ____________________
12 smoke ____________________

b **Test your memory.** Cover the sentences in **a**. Look at the picture and say ⊞ and ⊟ sentences.

ACTIVATION

Work with a partner. Look at the picture and say true sentences about yourself.
Remember your partner's answers.

I don't play the guitar. I eat meat.

Now tell a different partner about your first partner's answers.

Paula doesn't play the guitar. She eats meat.

English File fourth edition Teacher's Guide Elementary Photocopiable © Oxford University Press 2019

3B GRAMMAR present simple ⊞, ⊟, and ?

a Complete the conversation in the present simple. Use ⊞, ⊟, and ? forms. Use the verbs from the list and auxiliaries *do* and *don't* where necessary.

do   like   live   love   ~~speak~~   work (x3)

A Where are you from?

B Poland.

A You ¹*speak* English very well.

B Thanks. I ²__________ here.

A What ³__________ you __________?

B I'm a nurse.

A Really? Where ⁴__________ you __________?

B At St Thomas's Hospital, in London.

A ⁵__________ you __________ your job?

B Yes, I ⁶__________ it! But I work very long hours.

A ⁷__________ you __________ at night?

B Sometimes. It depends on the week. But luckily, I ⁸__________ at weekends.

b Choose the right word to complete the rest of the conversation.

A Are you married?

B Yes, I'm married to an Englishman.

A What ¹*does* he do? (do / does)

B He's a teacher. He ²__________ science. (teach / teaches)

A ³__________ he work at the local school? (Do / Does)

B No, he ⁴__________. (don't / doesn't) He ⁵__________ in London. (work / works)

A Does he ⁶__________ his job? (like / likes)

B No, he ⁷__________ it very much. It's a difficult school. (doesn't like / doesn't likes)

A Are you happy in England?

B I like the country, but not the weather. It ⁸__________ all the time. (rain / rains)

A ⁹__________ you want to go back to Poland one day? (Do / Does)

B Of course, but it isn't easy. My husband ¹⁰__________ speak Polish. (don't / doesn't)

A ¹¹__________ you have children? (Do / Does)

B Yes, two boys.

A ¹²__________ they speak Polish? (Do / Does)

B Yes, perfectly.

ACTIVATION

Practise the conversation with a partner.

3C GRAMMAR word order in questions

a Put the words in order to make questions.

		YOUR PARTNER
1	favourite What your film is? *What is your favourite film?*	
2	you vegetarian a Are?	
3	your are parents from Where?	
4	phone have you do What?	
5	many speak do languages you How?	
6	new you Do need phone a?	
7	surname spell you do your How?	
8	to do the listen radio When you?	
9	Where homework you your do do?	
10	singer Who your favourite is?	
11	the you do do What at weekend?	
12	TV programmes watch you do What?	

b Work with a partner. Ask and answer the questions. Use contractions with *be* where possible, e.g. *What's*. Note the answers.

ACTIVATION

Cover the questions and look at the answers. Say the questions.

4A GRAMMAR possessive 's, Whose…?

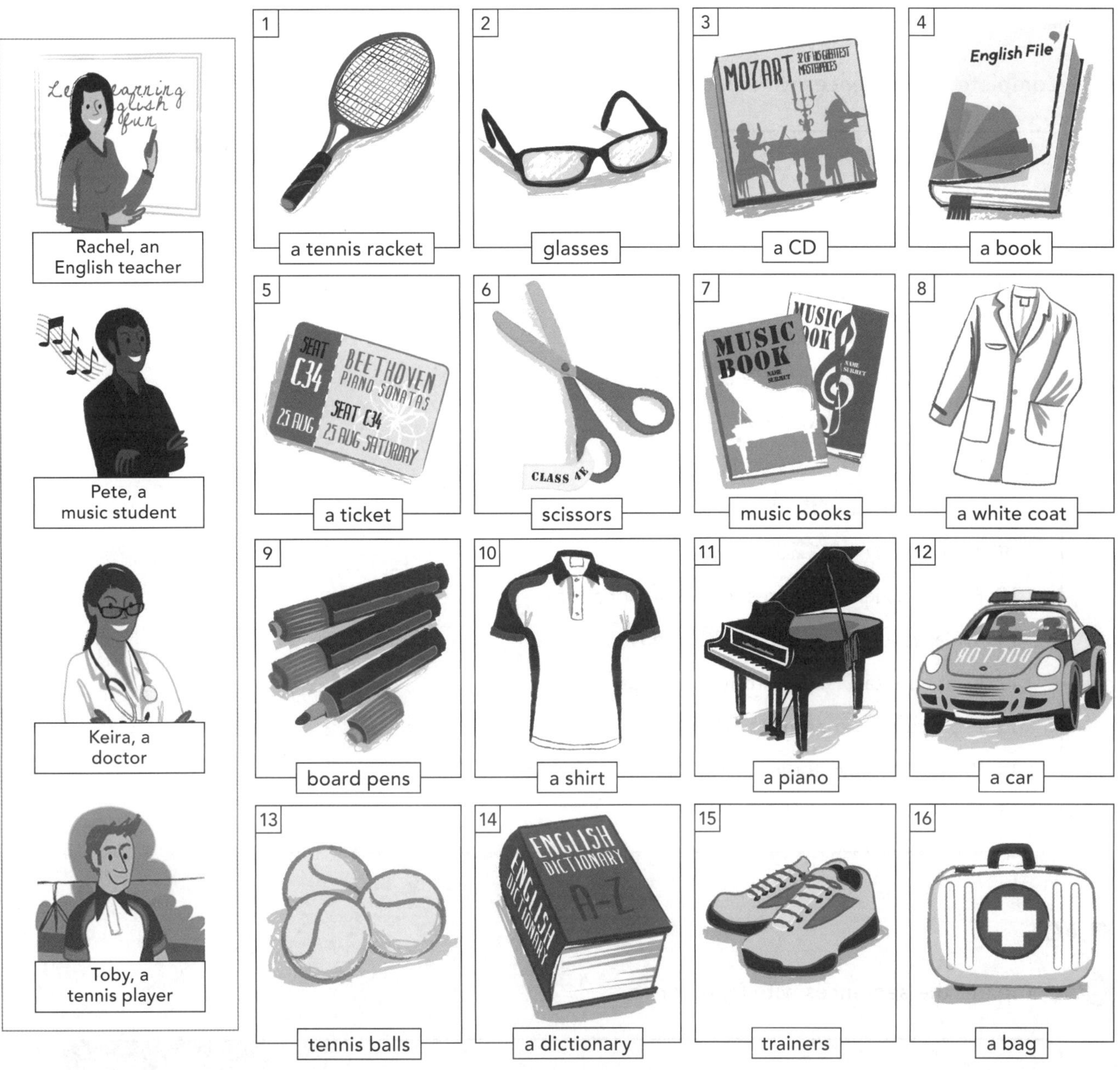

Look at objects 1–16. Whose are they? Write 14 more sentences.

1 *It's Toby's tennis racket.*
2 *They're Keira's glasses.*
3 _______________
4 _______________
5 _______________
6 _______________
7 _______________
8 _______________
9 _______________
10 _______________
11 _______________
12 _______________
13 _______________
14 _______________
15 _______________
16 _______________

ACTIVATION

Cover the sentences. Test a partner or say the sentences.

Whose is the book?

It's Rachel's. Whose are the glasses?

They're Keira's.

4B GRAMMAR prepositions of time and place (*in, on, at, to*)

TIME

a Complete the sentences with *in*, *on*, or *at*.

	PREPOSITION
1 I usually wake up ▰▰ 7.00 every day.	*at*
2 I never work ▰▰ the weekend.	________
3 I see my family ▰▰ Sundays.	________
4 The party is ▰▰ 21st December.	________
5 We hardly ever watch TV ▰▰ the evening.	________
6 I usually go to bed ▰▰ 11.00 p.m.	________
7 I go skiing ▰▰ the winter.	________
8 I always go out ▰▰ Friday night.	________
9 My birthday is ▰▰ January.	________
10 People usually give presents ▰▰ Christmas.	________
11 We always go shopping ▰▰ Friday.	________
12 I get up late ▰▰ Saturday mornings.	________
13 I sometimes go home ▰▰ lunchtime.	________
14 We usually have three classes ▰▰ the afternoon.	________
15 Nurses often work ▰▰ night.	________

PLACE

b Complete the sentences with *in*, *at*, or *to*.

	PREPOSITION
1 I live ▰▰ a small flat in the city centre.	________
2 She usually goes ▰▰ the gym after work.	________
3 Do you have a TV ▰▰ your bedroom?	________
4 I always have lunch ▰▰ home.	________
5 We often go ▰▰ the cinema on Friday evenings.	________
6 Let's play football ▰▰ the park.	________
7 The children aren't ▰▰ school today. It's a holiday.	________
8 I usually go ▰▰ work by train.	________
9 On Saturdays, we sometimes have dinner ▰▰ a restaurant.	________
10 My wife isn't here at the moment. She's ▰▰ work.	________

ACTIVATION

Test your memory. Cover the **PREPOSITION** columns. Say the sentences.

English File fourth edition Teacher's Guide Elementary　Photocopiable © Oxford University Press 2019

4C GRAMMAR adverbs and expressions of frequency

Look at the pictures and put the words in order to make sentences.

1 *She goes to the gym every day.*

2 _______________________________

3 _______________________________

4 _______________________________

5 _______________________________

6 _______________________________

7 _______________________________

8 _______________________________

9 _______________________________

10 _______________________________

11 _______________________________

12 _______________________________

ACTIVATION

Look at the pictures and make true sentences about you.

I go to the gym once or twice a week.

Look at the pictures. Complete the sentences with *can / can't* and a verb from the list.

cook   dance   hear   help   find   open   park   ~~play~~   sit   speak   swim   take

1 He _can't play_ the guitar.

2 You ___________________ photos in here!

3 ___________________ I ___________________ there, please?

4 He ___________________ his glasses.

5 Jamie ___________________ very well.

6 The boy ___________________ the old man.

7 ___________________ I ___________________ the window?

8 Stop! You ___________________ there.

9 They ___________________ French.

10 ___________________ you ___________________ me, please?

11 She ___________________ ___________________.

12 They ___________________ very well.

ACTIVATION

Test your memory. Cover the sentences and look at the pictures. Say the sentences.

5B GRAMMAR present continuous: *be* + verb + *-ing*

● Complete the sentences with the verb in brackets in the present continuous. Use contractions where possible.

1
A What's that noise?
B It's our neighbour.
A Not again! What [1]*'s he doing* (do) now?
B He [2]_____________ (wash) his car and he [3]_____________ (listen) to the radio.
A What? At 7.30 on a Sunday morning! Why [4]_____________ he _____________ (do) it now?
B I don't know.
A What [5]_____________ you _____________ (do)?
B I [6]_____________ (get) up. I can't sleep with this noise!

2
A [7]_____________ you _____________ the match (watch)?
B Of course we are.
A What [8]_____________ (happen)?
B We [9]_____________ (win) 1–0, but we [10]_____________ (not play) very well. Why [11]_____________ you _____________ (not watch) the match?
A I [12]_____________ (work) and my boss [13]_____________ (watch) me.

3
A What can you see?
B There are three men downstairs.
A What [14]_____________ they _____________ (do)?
B They [15]_____________ (count) money, I think. No, sorry. They [16]_____________ (not count) money. They [17]_____________ (play) cards.
A Can you see Jim?
B Yes, he's upstairs.
A What [18]_____________ he _____________ (do)?
B He [19]_____________ (look) at me!

4
A How's your sister?
B She's fine.
A What [20]_____________ she _____________ (do) now? [21]_____________ she _____________ (work)?
B No, she's in Thailand at the moment, with two friends. They [22]_____________ (travel) round the world.
A What [23]_____________ you _____________ (do) now?
B I [24]_____________ (not work) at the moment. I [25]_____________ (look for) a job.

Practise the conversations with a partner.

5C GRAMMAR present simple or present continuous?

Put the verbs in the present simple or present continuous. Use contractions where possible.

1   A   What _are_ you _doing_? (do)
    B   I_'m checking_ my emails. (check)

2   A   What [1]__________ you __________ of your new phone? (think)
    B   It's great! It [2]__________ really good photos. (take)

3   A   What's that music?
    B   My neighbours [3]__________ a party. (have)

4   A   Where [4]__________ you __________? (go)
    B   To my parents' house for lunch. We usually [5]__________ there for lunch on Sundays. (go)

5   A   Hi, Nora! What [6]__________ you __________ here? (do)
    B   I [7]__________ for a friend. (wait)

6   A   Where's Simon?
    B   In the bathroom. He [8]__________ a shower. (have)

7   A   What's the answer to number five?
    B   Sh! I [9]__________ to the teacher. (listen)

8   A   [10]__________ you __________ a uniform for work? (wear)
    B   Yes. I [11]__________ it. It's horrible. (not like)

9   A   Look! It [12]__________. (rain)
    B   Again? It [13]__________ a lot here. (rain)

10 A   Why [14]__________ you __________? (cry)
    B   Because I [15]__________ a very sad film. (watch)

11 A   Why [16]__________ the train __________? (stop)
    B   Because this is the slow train. It [17]__________ at every station. (stop)

12 A   When [18]__________ you usually __________ your friends? (see)
    B   On Friday night. We always [19]__________ after work. (meet)

13 A   What time [20]__________ you usually __________ work? (finish)
    B   About 6.00, but I [21]__________ late this evening. (work)

14 A   What [22]__________ you __________ for? (look)
    B   My car keys! I always [23]__________ them in my bag, but they aren't there now. (put)

15 A   How often [24]__________ you __________ exercise? (do)
    B   I [25]__________ in the sea every morning. (swim)

16 A   Be quiet! Your mum [26]__________ to watch a film on TV. (try)
    B   Sorry! She hardly ever [27]__________ TV in the afternoon. (watch)

| | 27 |

21–27   Excellent. You understand the difference between the present continuous and the present simple.

15–20   Quite good, but check the rules in the Grammar Bank (Student's Book p.132) and look at the exercise again.

0–14   This is difficult for you. Read the rules in the Grammar Bank (Student's Book p.132). Then ask your teacher for another photocopy and do the exercise again at home.

ACTIVATION

Work with a partner. Talk about two things you do every day, and two things you're doing at the moment.

6A GRAMMAR object pronouns: *me, you, him,* etc.

Complete the sentences with *me, you, him, her, it, us,* or *them.* Write in the **PRONOUN** column.

		PRONOUN
1	It's a great song. I love ▮▮▮!	*it*
2	We can't speak Italian very well. Can you help ▮▮▮?	
3	The phone's ringing! Can you answer ▮▮▮?	
4	I often call Ellie, but she hardly ever calls ▮▮▮.	
5	Can you go to the boss's office? She wants to see ▮▮▮.	
6	Where are my keys? I can't find ▮▮▮!	
7	Hello again! Do you remember ▮▮▮? My name's Matt.	
8	Lorna really likes Nick, but I don't think he likes ▮▮▮.	
9	Is Kate's boyfriend nice? I don't know ▮▮▮.	
10	**A** What do you think of these shoes? **B** I don't like ▮▮▮. They're a horrible colour.	
11	We don't know this city. Can you tell ▮▮▮ some places to visit?	
12	This hotel's very noisy. I don't like ▮▮▮.	
13	My sister works in Germany. I don't see ▮▮▮ very often.	
14	I'm free tonight. Do you want to come to the cinema with ▮▮▮?	
15	This exercise is very difficult. I can't do ▮▮▮.	
16	Your sister phoned. She needs to speak to ▮▮▮.	
17	My husband gets home late, but I always have dinner with ▮▮▮.	
18	George and Natalia are really nice. I like ▮▮▮.	
19	**A** Excuse me, Julia Parker is here. **B** Thanks. Please ask ▮▮▮ to wait in reception.	
20	We're going to the cinema tonight. Do you want to come with ▮▮▮?	

Test your memory. Cover the **PRONOUN** column. Say the sentences again with the pronouns.

Complete the sentences with *I love / like / don't mind / don't like / hate* and the *-ing* form of a verb from the list.

cook   do   ~~eat~~   get up   go   have   listen   live   look for   shop   sit   swim   wait   watch

😄	1	*I love eating* in restaurants.
😐	2	________________________ housework.
😄	3	________________________ in the sea in summer.
😣	4	________________________ to the dentist.
🙁	5	________________________ at the front of the class.
😄	6	________________________ a big party on my birthday.
🙁	7	________________________ for the bus.
😐	8	________________________ in a flat.
🙂	9	________________________ to loud music in the car.
😄	10	________________________ dinner for my family.
😣	11	________________________ somewhere to park.
🙁	12	________________________ films in English.
😣	13	________________________ early in winter.
🙂	14	________________________ online.

😄 = I love   🙂 = I like   😐 = I don't mind   🙁 = I don't like   😣 = I hate

ACTIVATION

Work with a partner. Tell your partner if the sentences are true about you.

I don't like eating in restaurants.

6C GRAMMAR *be* or *do?*

Complete the conversations with a form of the verb *be* or *do*. Use contractions where possible.

Interviewer Excuse me. ¹*Do* you have time to answer a few questions?

Daniel Yes, sure. I ²__________ just waiting for some friends.

Interviewer Great, thanks. ³__________ this your first time at the Glastonbury Festival?

Daniel No, it ⁴__________. I come every year. It ⁵__________ quite expensive, but I love it!

Interviewer And which bands ⁶__________ you really want to see this year?

Daniel Coldplay and Muse. They ⁷__________ my favourite bands

Interviewer Why ⁸__________ you like their music?

Daniel I think their songs ⁹__________ great.

Interviewer And what about the weather? It ¹⁰__________ awful!

Daniel Oh, I ¹¹__________ mind the rain. It always rains at Glastonbury!

Interviewer Good evening. ¹²__________ it OK if I ask you some questions?

Charlotte Yes, fine.

Interviewer ¹³__________ you enjoying the concert this evening?

Charlotte Yes, I ¹⁴__________. I think it ¹⁵__________ really good. The orchestra ¹⁶__________ playing very well.

Interviewer ¹⁷__________ you have a favourite orchestra?

Charlotte Mmm, no, I ¹⁸__________. I think all the orchestras that play at the Proms ¹⁹__________ very good.

Interviewer ²⁰__________ you often come to the Proms?

Charlotte Yes, this ²¹__________ my fifth concert this season. And when I ²²__________ come, I listen to the concerts on the radio.

Interviewer Oh, I think the concert ²³__________ starting again. Thank you for talking to me.

Charlotte No problem.

ACTIVATION

Practise the conversations with a partner.

7A GRAMMAR past simple of *be*: *was / were*

● Complete with *was / were* or *wasn't / weren't* to make true sentences.

1 Mother Teresa <u>*wasn't*</u> born in India.

2 Kurt Vonnegut ___________ an English writer.

3 Tchaikovsky ___________ the composer of *Swan Lake*.

4 The Vikings ___________ from Germany.

5 Gustave Eiffel ___________ a famous French engineer.

6 Roald Dahl ___________ a famous British musician.

7 The Beatles ___________ from Liverpool.

8 Jennifer Lawrence ___________ in the *Hunger Games* films.

9 Socrates and Plato ___________ Greek artists.

10 Pablo Picasso ___________ Spanish.

11 Beethoven ___________ a Swiss composer.

12 Neil Armstrong and Buzz Aldrin ___________ the first men to walk on the moon.

13 Adele's first album ___________ *25*.

14 The Incas ___________ from Mexico.

15 Marco Polo ___________ born in Venice.

16 The Olympic Games ___________ in Brazil in 2016.

17 Michelangelo and Leonardo da Vinci ___________ famous German painters.

18 Barack Obama ___________ the 44th President of the USA.

19 Monet and Gauguin ___________ French painters.

20 Albert Einstein ___________ a German politician.

ACTIVATION

Work with a partner. Make questions and test your partner's memory. Correct the information if you can.

Was Mother Teresa born in India?) (*No, she wasn't. She was born in Albania.*

 GRAMMAR   past simple: regular verbs

● Complete the conversations in the past tense. Use the verbs in brackets.

1

Annie	[1]*Did you study* French at university? (study)
Beth	No, I [2]___________ French; I [3]___________ Italian. I [4]___________ in Rome for six months in my third year. (not study, study, live)
Annie	Where [5]___________ you ___________ in Rome? (live)
Beth	Near the Forum. I [6]___________ a house with some Italian students. (rent)
Annie	[7]___________ you ___________ in Italian all the time? (talk)
Beth	Not always, because they [8]___________ to practise their English. But I [9]___________ to cook great pasta! (want, learn)

2

Alan	[10]___________ you ___________ Brazil? (like)
Ben	We [11]___________ it! We [12]___________ to come home. (love, not want)
Alan	[13]___________ you ___________ around the country? (travel)
Ben	We [14]___________ much, because we were only there for two weeks. (not travel)
Alan	[15]___________ you ___________ in hotels? (stay)
Ben	No, we [16]___________ with Brazilian friends. (stay)

3

Dave	[17]___________ you ___________ the match? Arsenal and Real Madrid? (watch)
Carl	No, I [18]___________.
Dave	Why not?
Carl	I [19]___________ late last night. I [20]___________ until 7.00. (work, not finish)
Dave	But the match [21]___________ at 7.45. (start)
Carl	Yeah, but I [22]___________ my train. I [23]___________ home until 9.30. (miss, not arrive)
Dave	What a pity! It was a great game.

4

Sam	I [24]___________ you three times last night, but you [25]___________. (call, not answer)
Lucy	Sorry. I was at the cinema with my sister.
Sam	And I [26]___________ you, too. Why [27]___________ you ___________ me back? (text, not text)
Lucy	Because I was angry.
Sam	Angry? Why?
Lucy	Because you [28]___________ to me at the party last week. You [29]___________ to Eva for about an hour. (not talk, chat)
Sam	I [30]___________ to Eva for an hour! She had a problem, and she just [31]___________ to tell me about it. (not chat, want)
Lucy	A problem? Is that why you [32]___________ with her for 20 minutes? (dance)

ACTIVATION

Practise the conversations with a partner.

a Complete the blog with the past simple form of the verbs in brackets.

A MEMORABLE NEW YEAR'S EVE

This happened to me a couple of years ago. Some university friends and I wanted to celebrate New Year's Eve at the famous street party in Edinburgh. We [1]_**knew**_ (know) it [2]________ (be) difficult to get tickets for the party, but we [3]________ (be) really lucky and [4]________ (buy) some online six months before. On 31st December, we [5]________ (get) a fast train from London.

We arrived in Edinburgh at 6.00 p.m. and walked from the station to our hotel. We relaxed, [6]________ (have) dinner, and then [7]________ (get) ready to go out. We [8]________ (wear) warm clothes, because it [9]________ (be) really cold. We [10]________ (get) to the city centre at about 9.30 p.m. It [11]________ (be) wet and quite windy. We [12]________ (go) into the first warm bar we [13]________ (find) and [14]________ (drink) some whisky. At about 10.30 p.m., we [15]________ (put on) our warm coats again and [16]________ (go) back outside. The streets [17]________ (be) nearly empty! Some people [18]________ (say) 'The street party is cancelled because of the terrible weather.' We [19]________ (not can) believe it! The weather [20]________ (not be) good, but it [21]________ (feel) like a normal winter night in Scotland.

In the end, we [22]________ (get) a taxi back to our hotel and [23]________ (spend) midnight in our rooms! We [24]________ (not have) a very happy New Year's Eve!

b Complete these questions about the blog.

1	Where _did they buy_ tickets for the party?	They bought tickets for the party online.
2	Why ________________ warm clothes?	Because it was really cold.
3	What time ________________ to the city centre?	They got there at about 9.30 p.m.
4	What ________________ the weather like?	It was wet and quite windy.
5	What ________________ in the bar?	They drank some whisky.
6	What ________________ at 10.30 p.m.?	They put on their coats and went outside.
7	What ________________ to them?	They said 'The street party is cancelled.'
8	________________ a bus back to their hotel?	No, they didn't. They got a taxi.
9	Where ________________ midnight?	They spent midnight in their rooms.
10	________________ a good time?	No, they didn't.

ACTIVATION

Work with a partner. Cover the answers. Take turns to answer the questions.
Then cover the questions and take turns to make the questions from the answers.

 GRAMMAR past simple: regular and irregular verbs

Complete the conversation with the past tense of the verb in brackets.

• A NEW LIFE •

Inspector	OK, Mr Thomas. Please just relax and tell me the problem.
Mr Thomas	It's my wife. She [1] _went_ (go) out yesterday evening. And she [2]______________ (not come) back.
Inspector	When [3]______________ (you / see) your wife for the last time?
Mr Thomas	Yesterday evening, at about nine thirty.
Inspector	Tell me what happened yesterday. [4]______________ (you / do) anything unusual?
Mr Thomas	No, it [5]______________ (be) just a normal day. We [6]______________ (wake up) at seven. I [7]______________ (have) breakfast. Then I [8]______________ (drive) to work. My wife [9]______________ (not have) breakfast. In the morning, I think she [10]______________ (go) shopping. She [11]______________ (come) home at lunchtime. I don't know what she [12]______________ (do) in the afternoon. She probably [13]______________ (make) dinner.
Inspector	When [14]______________ (you / come) home?
Mr Thomas	I [15]______________ (arrive) home at about seven thirty. I [16]______________ (sit) down and [17]______________ (read) the newspaper, and [18]______________ (check) my emails. We [19]______________ (have) dinner at about eight. After dinner, I [20]______________ (watch) TV. I [21]______________ (go to sleep) in my chair.
Inspector	[22]______________ (you / speak) to your wife at all? What [23]______________ (she / say) to you?
Mr Thomas	We [24]______________ (not talk) during dinner. After dinner, she [25]______________ (say), 'This isn't a life. I need to go out.' She [26]______________ (call) a taxi. I [27]______________ (hear) the taxi about 15 minutes later. She [28]______________ (take) her bag and her coat and [29]______________ (close) the door. She [30]______________ (not say) goodbye.
Inspector	I see, Sir. I think I know why she [31]______________ (leave).

ACTIVATION

Read the conversation again. Then cover it. Can you remember five things that Mr and Mrs Thomas did yesterday?

a Write the questions and short answers.

1 shower / bathroom?   *Is there a shower in the bathroom?*   *Yes, there is.*
2 pictures / hall?   *Are there any pictures in the hall?*   *No, there aren't.*
3 double bed / bedroom?
4 piano / living room?
5 plant / study?
6 dishwasher / kitchen?
7 cupboards / bathroom?
8 chairs / bedroom?

b Write ➕ or ➖ sentences.

1 table / kitchen   *There's a table in the kitchen.*
2 plants / living room
3 mirror / hall
4 books / living room
5 computer / study
6 clock / kitchen
7 fireplace / living room
8 shelves / study

ACTIVATION

Test your memory. Work with a partner. Look at the picture again for 30 seconds.
Then **A** (picture face up) ask **B** (picture face down) five questions about the house. Change roles.

Is there a plant in the study?   *Are there any chairs in the hall?*

    English File fourth edition Teacher's Guide Elementary   Photocopiable © Oxford University Press 2019

● Complete the sentences with the correct form ($\boxed{+}$, $\boxed{-}$, or $\boxed{?}$) of *there was / were*.

1

A [1]*Was there* a supermarket in this town when you were a child?

B No, [2]___________. [3]___________ a baker's and a small shop.

A [4]___________ any Italian restaurants? I love pizza!

B No, [5]___________, but [6]___________ a café. And [7]___________ two pubs!

2

A We stayed in a great hotel in Spain. It was on the beach and [8]___________ a really big swimming pool, too.

B Cool! [9]___________ a gym?

A Yes, and [10]___________ two tennis courts.

B [11]___________ any restaurants in the hotel?

A [12]___________ three! And the food was delicious!

3

A [13]___________ a very old castle in the town, near where I lived when I was a child. People said [14]___________ secret rooms in it.

B Really? [15]___________ any ghosts in the castle, too?

A Yes, [16]___________. My aunt saw one once. She said that suddenly [17]___________ a strange light, and then she saw a face looking in through the window – but she was on the second floor!

4

A Did you get anything nice in the sale?

B Yes, I did. [18]___________ some lovely sweaters. I got two.

A Great! [19]___________ any jeans?

B Yes, [20]___________, but [21]___________ any in my size.

Work with a partner. Say three things that were in the street or area where you live, but which are not there now.

9A GRAMMAR countable / uncountable nouns; *a / an, some / any*

a Look at what's in the fridge. Write the questions and short answers with *Is there / Are there + a, an,* or *any.*

1 sushi? *Is there any sushi?* *Yes, there is.*

2 butter?

3 carrots?

4 cheese?

5 fish?

6 chicken?

7 eggs?

8 orange juice?

b Write ⊞ or ⊟ sentences with *a / an, some,* or *any.*

1 onions *There aren't any onions.*

2 tomato juice

3 pineapple

4 strawberries

5 peppers

6 milk

7 mushrooms

8 ice cream

ACTIVATION

Test your memory. Work with a partner. **A** (picture face up) asks **B** (picture face down) five questions about what's in the fridge. Then change roles.

9B GRAMMAR quantifiers; *how much / how many, a lot of,* etc.

● (Circle) *much* or *many*. Then answer the question with a complete sentence.
Use *a lot of, not…much, not…many,* or *not…any.*

Fast Food Phil

1 How **much** / **many** orange juice does he drink?
He doesn't drink any orange juice.

2 How **much** / **many** burgers does he eat?
____

3 How **much** / **many** chips does he eat?
____

Valerie the Vegetarian

4 How **much** / **many** meat does she eat?
____

5 How **much** / **many** vegetables does she eat?
____

6 How **much** / **many** Diet Coke does she drink?
____

Baby Belinda

7 How **much** / **many** milk does she drink?
____

8 How **much** / **many** bread does she eat?
____

9 How **much** / **many** apples does she eat?
____

Fabio the Italian Food Fan

10 How **much** / **many** rice does he eat?
____

11 How **much** / **many** pasta does he eat?
____

12 How **much** / **many** cups of espresso does he drink?
____

ACTIVATION

Work with a partner. Ask and answer questions 1–12 about yourself.

How much orange juice do you drink?) (*I don't drink much orange juice.*

9C GRAMMAR comparative adjectives

● Use the information to make comparative sentences.

1 Length

the Akashi Kaikyō Bridge
(Japan): 1,991m

the Golden Gate Bridge
(USA): 1,280m

`short`

2 Inventions

Facebook: 2004

Skype: 2003

`old`

3 Price

a Cartier watch: £4,500

a Swatch watch: £38

`expensive`

4 Average summer temperature

London: 24°C

New York: 28.5°C

`hot`

5 Vitamin C

an orange: approx. 70mg per orange

an apple: approx. 9mg per apple

`healthy`

6 Annual rainfall

Buenos Aires: 983mm

Rome: 584mm

`dry`

7 Speed

a man: 44.88kph

a horse: 76.44kph

`slow`

8 Size

Russia: 17,075,200 km^2

Canada: 9,984,670 km^2

`big`

9 People per km^2

Shanghai: 4,000

Istanbul: 2,500

`crowded`

10 Deaths per year worldwide

travelling by car: approx. 1,250,000

travelling by plane: approx. 600

`dangerous`

11 Height

the Burj Khalifa tower
(Dubai): 828 m

the Empire State Building
(New York): 381 m

`tall`

12 Weather

Paris (France) average hours
sunlight per day: 4.9

Stockholm (Sweden) average hours
sunlight per day: 5.4

`sunny`

1 *The Golden Gate Bridge is shorter than the Akashi Kaikyō Bridge.*

2 ___________________________

3 ___________________________

4 ___________________________

5 ___________________________

6 ___________________________

7 ___________________________

8 ___________________________

9 ___________________________

10 ___________________________

11 ___________________________

12 ___________________________

ACTIVATION

Test your memory. Cover the sentences and look at the information. Compare the things.

10A GRAMMAR superlative adjectives

a Write the questions.

1 big / country / world
   What's the biggest country in the world?

2 wet / town / world
   _______________________?

3 small / country / world
   _______________________?

4 high / city / world
   _______________________?

5 long / beach / world
   _______________________?

6 dry / desert / world
   _______________________?

7 busy / train station / world
   _______________________?

8 populated / city / world
   _______________________?

9 popular / tourist destination / world
   _______________________?

10 expensive / city / world
   _______________________?

b Match questions 1–10 to the answers below.

Vatican City	☐	Cherrapunji in India	☐
Shinjuku Station in Tokyo	☐	Zurich in Switzerland	☐
Praia do Cassino in Brazil	☐	the Atacama Desert in Chile	☐
Shanghai in China	☐	La Rinconada in Peru	☐
Russia	1	France	☐

ACTIVATION

Test your memory. Work with a partner. Cover the questions and look at the answers.
Take turns to make sentences about each place.

Vatican City is the smallest country in the world.

● Complete the conversations with *be going to*. Use the verb in brackets. Use contractions where possible.

1

A [1]*Are* you *going to watch* the match tonight? (watch)

B Yes, but I [2]_______________ it at a friend's house – nobody in my family likes football. (watch)

2

A Juan and Pablo [3]_______________ here next year. (not study)

B Why not?

A Because they [4]_______________ in Washington. (live)

3

A I [5]_______________ this evening. (not go out)

B Why not?

A I need to get up early tomorrow morning. I [6]_______________ at 10.00. (go to bed)

4

A [7]_______________ Emma _______________ at the party? (be)

B Yes, and she says that she [8]_______________ her new boyfriend. (bring)

5

A What [9]_______________ you _______________ next weekend? (do)

B We [10]_______________ with our friends in London. (stay)

A [11]_______________ you _______________ the children? (take)

B Yes. We [12]_______________ the Science Museum and then go sightseeing. (visit)

6

A Where's your sister?

B She's out shopping. She [13]_______________ a new laptop. (buy)

A What [14]_______________ she _______________ with the old one? (do)

B She [15]_______________ it to me! (give)

ACTIVATION

Practise the conversations with a partner.

10C GRAMMAR *be going to* (predictions)

Write a prediction with *going to* for each picture. Use a verb from the list.

not buy   not eat   get married   ~~learn~~   listen   make   paint   play   not snow   take   visit   win

1 *He's going to learn* Italian.

2 _______________________ to music.

3 _______________________ the match.

4 _______________________ their lunch.

5 _______________________ a salad.

6 _______________________ next week.

7 _______________________ any shoes.

8 _______________________ the guitar.

9 _______________________ next month.

10 _______________________ his dog for a walk.

11 _______________________ the museum.

12 _______________________ the bathroom.

ACTIVATION

Test your memory. Cover the sentences and look at the pictures. Say the predictions.

11A GRAMMAR adverbs (manner and modifiers)

a Make adverbs from the adjectives.

bad ___________	noisy ___________	hard ___________	fast ___________
dangerous ___________	careful ___________	quiet ___________	loud ___________
good ___________	easy ___________	patient ___________	slow ___________

b Write sentences for pictures 1–12. Use an adverb from **a**.

1 She's eating very _noisily_.

2 He's driving really ___________.

3 He's writing ___________.

4 She passed the exam very ___________.

5 They're dancing very ___________.

6 She's opening the door ___________.

7 She's running very ___________.

8 He's working ___________.

9 She's waiting ___________.

10 He's driving ___________.

11 She's singing really ___________.

12 They're talking ___________.

ACTIVATION

Test your memory. Cover the sentences and look at the pictures. Say the sentences.

She's eating very noisily.

11B GRAMMAR verb + *to* + infinitive

a Look at the pictures. Complete the sentences with *to* + a verb in the infinitive. Use a verb from the list.

be   buy   do   drive   get   ~~go~~   have   play

1 We're planning *to go* on holiday to Mexico next summer.

2 We need ___________ at the airport by 7.00 a.m.!

3 Would you like ___________ basketball on Saturday?

4 She's learning ___________.

5 Steve wants ___________ a new computer.

6 They decided ___________ a swim.

7 I'm hoping ___________ a job in a London restaurant.

8 I promise ___________ my homework when the programme finishes.

b Complete the conversations with *Would* or *Do / Does*.

1 A ___________ your flatmates like to come to dinner?

B Why don't you ask them? I'm sure they'd like to.

2 A ___________ you like classical music?

B No, I prefer rock music.

3 A ___________ your husband like cooking?

B Yes, he loves it.

4 A ___________ you like another coffee?

B No, thanks. Just a glass of water, please.

5 A ___________ you like to come to the cinema with us tonight?

B Sorry, I can't. I'm going out to a restaurant with Mark tonight.

ACTIVATION

Test your memory. Cover the sentences in **a** and look at the pictures. Say the sentences.

● Complete with *the* or –.

1 **A** Which country has [1]*the* best food in [2]*the* world?

    B Italy, definitely! I love Italian food! I often have [3]__________ pasta for [4]__________ dinner.

2 **A** What time do you usually go to [5]__________ bed?

    B Usually at around 10.00 p.m., but later at [6]__________ weekend.

3 **A** Do you think [7]__________ men are more interested in football than [8]__________ women?

    B No! I'm a woman and I really like [9]__________ football.

4 **A** How often do you travel by [10]__________ train?

    B Every weekday. It's [11]__________ easiest way to get to [12]__________ work.

5 **A** In your family, who has [13]__________ most interesting job?

    B I think [14]__________ my brother's job is really interesting. He's an architect.

6 **A** Do [15]__________ men in this class talk more than [16]__________ women?

    B No! [17]__________ men are really quiet.

7 **A** Do you like [18]__________ animals?

    B Yes, I love them! I have a cat and a dog. [19]__________ dog is frightened of [20]__________ cat!

8 **A** How often do you go shopping in [21]__________ city centre?

    B Hardly ever! I prefer shopping on [22]__________ internet.

9 **A** What are you going to do when [23]__________ lesson finishes today?

    B I'm going to have [24]__________ lunch with [25]__________ my mother-in-law.

10 **A** Do you think [26]__________ children behave worse now than in [27]__________ past?

    B Yes, I do. I think [28]__________ teachers have a really difficult job!

ACTIVATION

Work with a partner. Ask each other the questions and answer with your own ideas.

English File fourth edition Teacher's Guide Elementary   Photocopiable © Oxford University Press 2019

12A GRAMMAR present perfect

● Write sentences in the present perfect. Use contractions where possible.

1 ____________ you ____________ this film? (see)

2 Oh no! I ____________ my glasses. (break)

3 It was a mistake. I ____________ it. (not wear)

4 They ____________ a new car. (buy)

5 Alex ____________ all over the world (travel)

6 ____________ you ____________ Jake, my boyfriend? (meet)

7 They ____________ all the biscuits! (eat)

8 Don't turn it off! The film ____________. (not finish)

9 ____________ the boss ____________? (arrive)

10 He ____________ my bag! (take)

ACTIVATION

Test your memory. Cover the sentences and look at the pictures. Say the sentences.

12B GRAMMAR present perfect or past simple?

● Write the verbs in the present perfect or past simple. Use contractions where possible.

---

1 **A** Where's Suzie?

   B She [1] *'s gone* home. (go)

   A When [2] _______________ she _______________? (leave)

   B About half an hour ago.

---

2 **A** [3] _______________ you _______________ to the new Italian restaurant in Queen Street? (be)

   B Yes, we have. We [4] _______________ last week. The food [5] _______________ great. (go, be)

---

3 **A** [6] _______________ Mr Hamilton _______________? (arrive)

   B No, he [7] _______________ a few minutes ago. He's going to be late. (phone)

---

4 **A** I [8] _______________ the new Star Wars film at the cinema last night. I [9] _______________ it. [10] _______________ you _______________ it? (see, not like, see)

   B Yes, I have. I [11] _______________ it last week and I [12] _______________ it. (see, love)

---

5 **A** [13] _______________ you ever _______________ a ghost? (see)

   B No, I [14] _______________. I [15] _______________ in a haunted hotel a few months ago, but I [16] _______________ anything. (stay, not see)

---

6 **A** [17] _______________ you _______________ to Paris? (be)

   B Yes, I [18] _______________.

   A When [19] _______________ you _______________ there? (go)

   B When I [20] _______________ at school, for an end-of-year trip. (be)

   A [21] _______________ you _______________ a good time? (have)

   B Yes. It [22] _______________ great. (be)

---

7 **A** Where do you want to go on holiday this summer?

   B Well, we [23] _______________ to North America a few times, but we [24] _______________ never _______________ South America. How about Peru? (be, visit)

   A Oh, good idea. I [25] _______________ a lot of photos of Machu Picchu, and it looks fantastic! (see)

   B Yes, it does! My friend Ruby [26] _______________ there last month, and she [27] _______________ a great time. (go, have)

   A What [28] _______________ she _______________ most about her trip? (enjoy)

   B She [29] _______________ lots of really friendly people, and the food [30] _______________ delicious. (meet, be)

---

8 **A** [31] _______________ you _______________ to Jake recently? (speak)

   B No, I [32] _______________. What about you?

   A Well, I [33] _______________ a surprising phone call from him yesterday. (get)

   B Really? What [34] _______________ he _______________? (say)

   A He [35] _______________ a new job last week and is planning to move to Australia. (get)

   B Wow!

Practise the conversations with a partner.

12C **GRAMMAR** revision: question formation

● Write questions for the answers.

1 _What does_ **your brother** _do_**? (do)** — He's a doctor.

2 _____________________ **to class today? (get)** — I came by bus.

3 _____________________ **the weather like in New York last weekend? (be)** — Awful! It was foggy and really cold.

4 _____________________ **a good time? (have)** — Yes, I am. This place is great.

5 _____________________ **like** _____________________ **windsurfing? (try)** — No, I wouldn't. I can't swim!

6 _____________________ **on holiday last year? (go)** — We went to Tenerife.

7 _____________________ **he** _____________________ **now? (leave)** — Because he needs to get up early tomorrow.

8 _____________________ **a musical instrument? (play)** — Yes, I can. I can play the guitar.

9 _____________________ **breakfast this morning? (not have)** — Because I wasn't hungry.

10 _____________________ **the homework? (do)** — No, I haven't. I'm going to do it this evening.

11 _____________________ **on Friday night? (go out)** — Yes, we are. We have tickets for a concert.

12 _____________________ **coat** _____________________ **this? (be)** — It's mine. Thanks.

13 _____________________ **you** _____________________ **English classes? (have)** — Twice a week. On Tuesdays and Thursdays.

14 _____________________ **Maria** _____________________ **home early? (go)** — Because she didn't feel well.

15 _____________________ **Shakespeare** _____________________**? (be born)** — In 1564.

16 _____________________ **ever** _____________________ **Mexican food? (eat)** — Yes, I have. It's delicious!

17 _____________________ **to Scotland? (fly)** — No, we're going to go by train.

18 _____________________ **your wife** _____________________ **work? (finish)** — She finishes at 7.00 p.m.

19 _____________________ **hours** _____________________ **a night? (sleep)** — Usually seven or eight.

20 _____________________ **your brother** _____________________ **after university? (do)** — He's going to work in television.

ACTIVATION

Test your memory. Cover the questions and look at the answers. Say the questions.

Communicative activity instructions

1A You say, you answer

A pairwork matching activity

Sts play matching games to practise greeting phrases, numbers, and days of the week. Copy one worksheet per pair and cut into **A** and **B**.

- Write HELLO, I'M SALLY. on the board. Then write NICE TO MEET YOU, BEN. and HI, SALLY, I'M BEN. Ask students which answer they think is correct, HI, SALLY, I'M BEN.
- Put Sts in pairs, **A** and **B**. Give out the worksheets and focus on **a**. Give Sts time to read their sentences.
- Explain that Sts **A** start by reading the sentences in the **You say** column and Sts **B** choose their answers from the **You answer** column.
- Monitor and help if necessary.

STUDENT A	STUDENT B
Hi, I'm Mike. What's your name?	My name's Sally.
Hi, Mark, this is Anna.	Nice to meet you, Anna.
What's your phone number?	It's 07478203124.
How are you?	Fine, thanks. And you?
Hello, I'm George.	Hi, George. I'm Chris. Nice to meet you.
STUDENT B	**STUDENT A**
How are you?	I'm very well, thank you.
What day is it today?	It's Monday.
Nice to meet you, Jim.	Nice to meet you, too.
Hello! My name's Ben.	Nice to meet you, Ben. I'm Laura.
See you on Saturday. Bye.	Yes, see you on Saturday. Goodbye.

- Finally, get Sts to repeat the activity, covering the **You answer** column.

1B Nationalities bingo

A bingo game activity

Sts play bingo to practise nationalities and the names of countries. Copy one worksheet and cut up one bingo card per student. The list of nationalities is for the teacher.

- Give each student a bingo card. With classes of more than 12, give more than one student the same card or give one card per pair.
- Explain that Sts are going to play a bingo game. Tell Sts that you will say a nationality. If they have that country on their card, they should cross it out. The first student / pair to cross out all the countries should shout *Bingo!*
- Say the nationalities at random, ticking them off as you go.
- When a student / pair shouts *Bingo!* ask them to say the countries on their card. Check that they are the ones you have already ticked. If not, continue the game. The first student / pair to cross off all the countries on their card correctly is the winner.

EXTRA IDEA Put Sts in groups of three or four to play a second game. Tell the groups to choose one person to be the caller. Give each caller the list of nationalities and each student a new bingo card. Tell the callers to say the nationalities at random. Remind them to keep a note of the nationalities as they say them.

1C Personal information

A mingle activity

Sts ask and answer questions to complete business cards with personal information. Copy and cut up one worksheet per eight Sts.

- If necessary, revise the alphabet and numbers before starting.
- Put Sts in groups of eight (or fewer, e.g. if you have 20 Sts, have two groups of eight and one of four). Use one set of cards per group.
- Give each student one strip. Focus on the first card and tell them that they are that person. Check that they know how to say the @ sign (*at*) and the . (*dot*). Tell them not to worry if they can't pronounce the names perfectly.
- Now focus on the blank cards, and elicit and drill the questions they need to ask to get that information (see **Language**). If necessary, write them on the board.
- Tell Sts they are at a conference. They must complete the blank business cards with information about two other people from their group. Demonstrate with a student first.
- Sts mingle and complete their forms.
- When Sts have finished, get them to check the information they have written down.

2A Mystery objects

A pairwork guessing game

Sts talk about close-up photos of everyday objects. Copy one worksheet per pair.

- Copy the questions and answers in **Language** onto the board. Model and drill pronunciation.
- Put Sts in pairs and give out the worksheets. They take turns to ask and answer questions pointing at the photos.
- If a pair has answered all the questions they can, but still don't know what some of the objects are, they can ask other pairs.
- At the end of the activity, go through all the photos and ask Sts what they are.

1 scissors **2** a watch **3** a laptop **4** pens
5 headphones **6** coins **7** an identity card **8** a charger
9 photos **10** magazines **11** an umbrella **12** glasses
13 a credit card **14** a lamp **15** a wallet **16** keys

2B Can you name…?

Sts fill in a column with vocabulary

Sts read some adjective + noun phrases and write the names of well-known people and objects. Copy one worksheet per pair.

- Put Sts in pairs and give out the worksheets. Tell them that they are going to play a game. Each pair has to fill in the blank column with names. You could start by eliciting expensive makes of watches, e.g. *Rolex*. Tell Sts that if they are the only pair with their answer, they get 3 points; if another pair has the same answer, they only get 1 point.
- Set a time limit, e.g. five minutes, or up to ten minutes, depending on the level of your class. Alternatively, stop the game when the first pair fills in the whole column.
- When time is up get feedback. Remind Sts of the point system. Continue until Sts have shared all their answers. Sts add up their points to find the winner.

EXTRA IDEA Say some of the Sts' answers to the class, e.g. *skiing* (a dangerous sport), *Bill Gates* (a rich person) and elicit the adjective + noun phrases.

2C Dominoes

A dominoes game

Sts match different sentences. Copy and cut up one worksheet per group of three or four Sts.

- Tell Sts they are going to play dominoes. Let them help you explain if they know the rules. Use an example from the worksheet if necessary.

| This is a library. | This room's hot. | Turn on the air conditioning! | I'm thirsty. |

- Put Sts in groups of three or four. Give each group a set of cards.
- In groups of three, each student takes four dominoes; in groups of four, each student takes three. There should be some left.
- Sts look at their cards. Clarify any vocabulary problems before they start.
- One student in each group places a card on the table. The person on his / her left places the card that matches the sentence correctly at one end of his / her card. If he / she doesn't have a card that matches, he / she misses a turn and takes a card from the middle.
- Monitor that the game is being played correctly.
- The game continues until all the cards are on the table. The winner is the first student to use all his / her cards.

3A I work… He works…

Sts use cards to make true sentences about themselves and their classmates

Sts make true statements about themselves and in the third person singular. Copy and cut up one worksheet per group of three or four Sts.

- Write the verb *work* on the board. Elicit phrases that go with *work*, e.g. *in an office, late*. Make sentences using *I*, e.g. *I work in an office. I work late.*, etc., asking Sts if these are true for you. If they aren't true, change them to *I don't work late.*, etc.
- Put Sts in groups of three or four. Give each group a set of cards.
- Sts take turns to pick up a card and make a sentence that is true for them with *I / I don't*, until there are no cards left.
- Tell Sts to stay in their groups and that they are going to play again, but a bit differently. They have to shuffle the cards and repeat, but this time trying to remember what other students said, e.g. *David doesn't work in an office.*, *Maria drinks coffee.*
- Monitor to make sure Sts are using the third person correctly.
- The game ends when Sts have used all the cards.
- Get feedback from various groups.

EXTRA IDEA Sts shuffle the cards again and try to make only positive sentences using the verbs and a collocate which makes the sentence true for them, e.g. *I drink Diet Coke. I read magazines.*, etc.

3B Present simple questionnaire

A pairwork questionnaire

Sts make questions in the first and third person singular and note down their partners' answers. Copy one worksheet per pair and cut into **A** and **B**.

> **LANGUAGE**
> Present Simple all forms
> *Do you live near a supermarket? No, I don't.*
> *Does Paula live near a supermarket? Yes, she does.*

- Put Sts in pairs, **A** and **B**, and give out the worksheets. Give Sts time to look at their questions and check any vocabulary problems.
- Tell Sts to ask each other the questions and to mark a tick (✔) or a cross (✗) in the first column, **Do you…?**
- Monitor and help if necessary.
- When Sts have finished, they do **b** and Sts change partners. Put two Sts **A** and two Sts **B** together in new pairs. Sts tell their partner the name of the person they interviewed first. Sts write the name in the gap at the top of the second column.
- Sts ask each other questions about their partner's first partner. Sts put a tick (✔) or a cross (✗).
- Monitor the correct use of *Does* in the questions.

EXTRA IDEA Write WHAT? / WHERE? / WHO? / WHEN? / WHY? on the board and get students to ask for extra information using the question words.

Do you live near a supermarket?

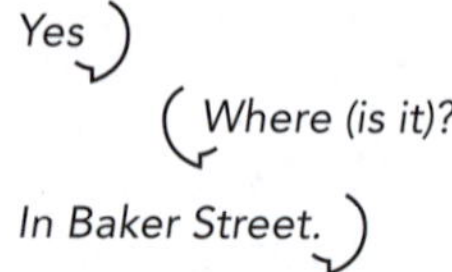

3C Famous people

A pairwork information exchange activity

Sts ask for information to complete sentences. Copy one worksheet per pair and cut into **A** and **B**.

> **LANGUAGE**
> Word order in questions, question words, present simple ⊞, ⊟
> *What instrument does Samuel L Jackson play? He plays the trumpet.*
> *What restaurants does Jennifer Lawrence like? She likes fast food restaurants.*

- Put Sts in pairs, **A** and **B**, and give out the worksheets. Focus on the photos of the famous people, and the incomplete questions. Explain that Sts **A** and Sts **B** have different information, so they will need to ask each other questions to complete the information.
- Give Sts time to write their questions. Monitor and help.
- When Sts are ready, get Sts **A** to ask Sts **B** their first question, and to complete the answer. Sts **B** then ask their first question.
- Sts continue until they have completed the information.
- Finally, get Sts to compare their sentences, and check all questions and answers.

4A Everyday objects

A *Happy Families* game

Sts practise everyday objects and possessive 's. Copy and cut up one set of cards per group of three or four Sts.

> **LANGUAGE**
> Everyday objects, possessive 's
> *Do you have Kate's dictionary?*
> *Yes, here you are. / No, sorry.*

- Tell Sts they are going to play a game called *Happy Families*. Sts may have a similar game in their language you can refer to.
- There are five sets of cards. Write the names of the five people on the board and under one of the names, the four objects they possess. Point to an object word and ask *What's this?* Elicit *It's Robin's book. They're Robin's headphones.* Model and drill pronunciation.
- Put Sts in groups of four. Give each group a set of cards. One student shuffles and deals the cards face down so that each student has five cards.
- Tell Sts to look at their cards. Point out the name at the top of each card and explain that the three small pictures at the bottom are the other objects they need to collect for that person.
- Sts collect a set of cards by asking the other Sts in the group. Tell Sts they can ask anyone in their group, but must address one person when asking the question.
- When a student is given the card he / she wants, he / she must give one of his / her cards to the other student. Sts must always have only five cards in their hands.
- Now drill the questions and answers in **Language**.
- Demonstrate with one group first.
- Sts play the game. One student starts and then it's the turn of the student on his / her left. The game finishes when a student has collected a complete set of four cards for one of the people. The cards are re-dealt and the game starts again.
- Monitor to make sure Sts are playing correctly.
- The game could be played in groups of five. In this case each student has four cards.

4B Prepositions questionnaire

A pairwork question and answer activity

Sts complete the questions and then ask a partner. Copy one worksheet per pair and cut into **A** and **B**.

- Put Sts in pairs, **A** and **B** and give out the worksheets.
- Give Sts time to complete the questions in **a** with a preposition. Then check answers.

> **A 1** at **2** at, on **3** in **4** to, on **5** at **6** at **7** in **8** in **9** on
> **10** in, at **11** in
> **B 1** to, on **2** in **3** on **4** to, at **5** on **6** at **7** at **8** in, in
> **9** in **10** to, on **11** at
> **C 1** at **2** on **3** on **4** to, in **5** in **6** on **7** in **8** on **9** to, at
> **10** to, at **11** at, in

- Tell Sts that the questions are different on worksheets **A** and **B**. Now tell them to do **b** and ask each other their questions. Encourage Sts to ask their partner for more information. Remind them to 'return' the questions with: *What about you? And you?*

4C *How often?* board game

A group board game

Sts talk about how often they do activities using adverbs and expressions of frequency. Copy one worksheet for each group of three or four students. You will also need one counter per student and a dice per group.

- Tell Sts they are going to play a board game.
- Write on the board GET UP AFTER 10 O'CLOCK and HAVE A BIG BREAKFAST. Ask Sts to make a sentence with the phrase and include an adverb or expression of frequency, e.g. *every day*.
- Put Sts in small groups of three or four. Give each group a worksheet, a dice and a counter or coin for each student. Tell Sts to put their counters on the square marked **START**.
- Sts roll the dice and move clockwise to the corresponding square. They make a true sentence using the phrase and one of the adverbs or expressions of frequency.
- Set a time limit. Students continue until one of them gets back to **START** square or time is up. Monitor and help.

EXTRA IDEA Ask Sts if they can remember any of their group's sentences, e.g. *Chris buys clothes once a month*.

5A What can you do?

A group card game

Sts turn over cards and try to do the tasks or answer the questions. Copy and cut up one worksheet per group of three or four Sts.

- Put Sts in groups of three or four. Give each group a set of cards face down or in an envelope.
- Demonstrate the activity by asking a student to turn over a card and read the question. You then do the task or answer the question.
- Tell Sts to continue playing. One student turns over a card and the next student has to do the task or answer the question. The others in the group decide if it's correct.
- If a card is correctly used, Sts put it aside. If not, the next student tries to answer the question or do the task on the card.
- Sts play until they run out of cards or time is up.

5B Guess what I'm doing!

A miming activity

Sts take a card, mime the action and the others guess what he / she is doing. Copy and cut up one worksheet per group of three or four Sts.

- Demonstrate the activity. Write on the board YOU ARE… Tell Sts you are going to mime a sentence and they need to guess *exactly* what is on the card. Pick up a card and mime what's on it, making sure you elicit the correct sentence from Sts.
- Put Sts in groups of three or four and give each group a set of cards face down.
- One student picks up a card and mimes the action. The others in the group have to guess the sentence on the card.
- Monitor to make sure the mimers don't speak.
- Set a time limit. Sts play until they run out of cards or until time is up.

EXTRA IDEA Students can write their own present continuous sentences and mime them in front of the class if they want to (or give them to someone else to mime). Make sure Sts who mime in front of the class are outgoing and comfortable with it.

EXTRA IDEA Cut up one sheet, and put Sts in groups. Give one card to a student in each group to mime. When someone has said the correct sentence, they bring you the card and exchange it for another one.

5C It's Friday evening

A pairwork information gap activity

Sts ask questions to find out what people are doing or what they usually do. Copy one worksheet per pair and cut into **A** and **B**.

- Write on the board:
  PETER USUALLY _________________ ON FRIDAY EVENINGS.
  PETER _________________ THIS EVENING.

- Elicit the questions to complete the missing information (*What does Peter usually do on Friday evenings? What is Peter doing this evening?*). Complete the sentences with *goes to the cinema* and *is doing homework*. Now rub PETER out and write SAM AND CHRIS. Elicit the changes in the questions and in the sentences (*What do / are Sam and Chris…?*)

- Put Sts in pairs, **A** and **B**, and give out the worksheets. Focus on the examples. Give Sts time to look at the chart and think what questions they have to ask.

- Sts ask and answer questions to complete their charts. Monitor to make sure Sts are asking their questions correctly.

- When they have finished, tell Sts to compare their charts.

6A The pronoun game

A group matching pairs game

Sts match nouns and pronouns in a game of pelmanism. Copy and cut up one worksheet per group of three or four Sts. Divide the cards into sentences and pronouns.

- Tell Sts they are going to play a game where they have to match the pronouns to the nouns in sentences.

- Put Sts in groups of three or four and give each group a set of the shuffled sentence cards and a set of the shuffled pronouns cards face down on the desk.

- Sts take it in turns to turn over one sentence card and one pronoun card. If the cards match, the student should say the sentence aloud, replacing the noun or nouns with the pronoun. If the sentence is correct, the student keeps the cards and has another turn. If the cards don't match, the student turns the cards over again and puts them at the bottom of each pile.

- Sts play till there are no more cards. The student with the most pairs of cards is the winner.

NON-CUT ALTERNATIVE Copy one worksheet per pair. Get Sts to decide which pronoun they should use to replace the underlined words. Check answers.

6B Likes and dislikes

A group activity

Sts use cards to ask each other questions about their likes / dislikes. Copy and cut up one worksheet per group of three or four Sts.

- Demonstrate with an example on the board: / LIKE DO SPORT OR EXERCISE. Elicit the full question (*Do you like doing sport or exercise?*) and point out that they need to put the underlined verb (*do*) in the -*ing* form. Ask several Sts the question and elicit *Yes, I do / No, I don't*. Now write WHAT ABOUT YOU? on the board and get a student to ask you. Answer the question. Give more information e.g. *No, I don't. I hate doing sport* or *Yes, I do. I like going to the gym.*

- Put Sts in groups of three or four and give each group a set of cards. Set a time limit. One student picks up a card and thinks about the question he / she needs to ask, using the prompt. The student asks the question and everyone in the group answers. Highlight that if a student answers *No, I don't*, he / she should say how he / she feels about the activity with another verb. The last student to answer should then return the question with *What about you?* Sts continue picking up cards and asking the question to the group.

- Sts continue playing until they run out of cards or until time is up.

EXTRA CHALLENGE Encourage Sts to give a reason and/or an example when they answer ther questions.

6C Tell me about you

A pairwork revision activity

Sts complete the questions and then ask a partner. Copy one worksheet per pair and cut into **A** and **B**.

- Write a couple of examples on the board and elicit what is needed to complete each question:
  WHAT _________________ YOUR FAVOURITE COLOUR?
  HOW OFTEN _________________ YOU GO TO THE CINEMA?
  _________________ YOU SPANISH?
  _________________ YOU LIKE ENGLISH CLASS?

- Put Sts in pairs, **A** and **B**, and give out the worksheets.

- Give them time to complete their questions. Check answers.

A 1 is **2** do **3** Do **4** are **5** is **6** is **7** are **8** do **9** do **10** do
B 1 do **2** do **3** is **4** do **5** are **6** do **7** is **8** Do **9** Do **10** Are

- Now tell Sts to ask each other the questions. Point out that the questions are different for **A** and **B**. Remind Sts that when they ask questions beginning *What is…?* they should contract and say *What's…?*

- Get feedback from various pairs.

7A Where were you?

A pairwork activity

Sts ask each other where they were at various times in the past. Copy one worksheet per pair and cut into **A** and **B**.

LANGUAGE

Past simple verb *be: was / were*

- Draw a clock on the board and quickly revise the time.
- Demonstrate the activity. On the board, draw a clock showing the time 8:15 and write underneath YESTERDAY MORNING. Write WHERE…YOU AT…? and elicit the full question (*Where were you at 8.15 yesterday morning?*).
- Elicit answers from different Sts. You may need to revise prepositions of place *in / at / on* (**Grammar Bank 4B**) and write them on the board.
- Put Sts in pairs, **A** and **B**, and give out the worksheets.
- Tell Sts to ask each other where they were at those times. Point out that they need to use *last night* and *yesterday* too, not just the times.
- Give students a minute to look at the times. Monitor and help.
- Sts **A** then ask their first question and Sts **B** answer. Then Sts **B** ask their first question and Sts **A** answer. Monitor and help.
- When Sts have finished, get feedback to find out where various Sts were at different times.

7B Are we in Australia?

A pairwork story-telling activity

Sts put a story in order and then re-tell it. Copy one worksheet per pair and cut into cards.

LANGUAGE

Past simple regular verbs: *booked, arrived, asked*

- Ask Sts to give you names of cities in Australia. Elicit any information Sts may know about Sydney.
- Write the first sentence of the story on the board. LAST APRIL TWO BRITISH TEENAGERS, RAOUL AND EMMA, WANTED TO GO TO AUSTRALIA FOR THEIR SUMMER HOLIDAY. Tell them that this is the beginning of a story, and that they are going to put the story in order.
- Put Sts in pairs and give them a set of cards. Tell them to find the first sentence and then try to put the rest of the cards in order.
- Check answers. Get Sts to underline the regular verbs and drill the pronunciation of the past tense verbs.
- Tell Sts to turn the cards over, keeping them in the right order, and try to remember the story, turning the cards to check. Monitor and help.

EXTRA CHALLENGE See if any pair can tell a version of the story in their own words from memory.

EXTRA IDEA Keep back the last sentence and give Sts only eight cards. When they have put the story in order, get Sts to guess what the last sentence is. Elicit any ideas and then give out the last card for them to check.
You can also let them create different endings for the story with their guesses, Sts share their ideas and then you give them the last card. Sts decide which is the best ending.

7C Born on 31st December

A pairwork activity

Sts ask for information to complete a text about a famous person. This is a two-page activity. Copy one worksheet (**A** and **B**) per pair.

LANGUAGE

Past simple regular and irregular verbs

- Write ANTHONY HOPKINS and ELIZABETH ARDEN on the board and ask Sts if they know anything about them. Then tell Sts that the two people have something in common, and elicit ideas. Then tell them that they were both born on 31st December.
- Explain that Sts are going to ask and answer questions to complete a text about these two people. On the board write ANTHONY HOPKINS WAS BORN ON __________. and elicit the question (*When was Anthony Hopkins born?*). Tell them that they will have gaps in one of their texts and need to make questions in the same way.
- Put Sts in pairs, **A** and **B**, and give out the worksheets. Focus on **a** and go through the *Glossary* with the class.
- Tell Sts **A** to complete their questions about Anthony Hopkins, and Sts **B** to read the text about him. Monitor and help with the questions and any vocabulary problems.
- When they are ready, Sts **A** ask their questions, and Sts **B** answer. Sts **A** complete the text with the information.
- They then swap roles for the next text.
- When Sts have finished, they can compare their worksheets to check their answers.
- Finally, focus on **d**. Sts cover their worksheets and try to remember five facts about Anthony Hopkins and Elizabeth Arden.

8A Past simple question time

A pairwork activity

Sts practise making questions using prompts. Copy and cut up one worksheet per group of three Sts.

LANGUAGE

Past simple regular and irregular verbs
What time did you get up? I got up at 7.
Did you make your bed? Yes, I did.

- Tell Sts that they are going to revise the past simple by asking and answering questions.
- Demonstrate the activity. Take a card, write the first prompt on the board and elicit the question from Sts. Now ask a student the question. Then write another prompt and repeat the process. Remind Sts of how the rhythm of the question changes depending on whether it has a question word or not.
- Put Sts in groups of three and give each group a set of cards. Set a time limit. Sts then take a card, and ask one of the other Sts all the questions on the card. They repeat until there are no cards left or time is up.
- Monitor and help.

8B A place to rent

A pairwork information gap activity

Sts role-play a phone call for information about a place to rent. This is a two-page activity. Copy one worksheet (**A** and **B**) per pair.

> **LANGUAGE**
>
> *there is / there are* $\boxed{+}$, $\boxed{?}$
>
> *Is there a garage? Yes, there is.*
> *How many bedrooms are there? There are two bedrooms.*

- Pre-teach *estate agent*. Put Sts in pairs, **A** and **B**, and give out the worksheets. Explain that they are going to role-play a phone conversation to rent a place to live.
- Focus on **a** and get Sts to read the instructions. Tell Sts **A** that they are estate agents and have a flat that they want to rent out. They must read the instructions and information about the flat. Tell Sts **B** that they are looking for a flat to rent. They must read the instructions and prepare their questions. Highlight that all the questions are with *there is / there are* except the first two and the last two, which are with *is*. Encourage Sts **B** not to write the missing words, but to remember them.
- Monitor and help.
- Tell Sts **B** to focus on the speech bubble and start the conversation. Remind Sts that the conversation is on the phone.
- At the end of the role-play, find out how many Sts **B** decided to rent the flat.
- Focus on **b** and get Sts to swap roles and do the second role-play.

8C What's different?

A spot the differences pairwork activity

Sts describe the same room in the present and in the past, using furniture vocabulary and *there is / there are* and *there was / there were*. This is a two page activity. Copy one worksheet (**A** and **B**) per pair.

> **LANGUAGE**
>
> *there is / there are* + *there was / there were* $\boxed{+}$, $\boxed{-}$
> Prepositions of place
> Furniture

- Revise the furniture vocabulary for the activity.
- Put Sts in pairs, **A** and **B**, and give out the worksheets. Focus on Room 1 and explain that Sts have pictures of the same room, but Sts **A** have it as it is now and Sts **B** as it was in the 1960s. Ask them to look at their pictures for one minute.

- Write THERE IS / THERE ARE and THERE WAS / THERE WERE on the board. Elicit which they should use for the present and which for the past.
- Get Sts **A** to describe Room 1 to Sts **B**, using *there is / there are*. Tell Sts **B** to circle the differences on their picture. Point out that there are at least nine differences. Monitor and help.
- Now Sts **B** describe Room 1, using *there was / there were* and the Sts **A** circle the differences.
- Sts repeat the activity with Room 2, but this time Sts **B** start and use *there is / there are*. Sts **A** then describe their bedroom in the 1960s using *there was / there were*. Point out that there are at least nine differences. Monitor and help.
- Tell Sts to compare pictures and then elicit some sentences for each picture from the class. Finally, ask Sts which version of each room they prefer.

> **Room 1 differences:**
> 1 In the 1960s there were three armchairs. Now there is a sofa.
> 2 In the 1960s there was one table (in front of the armchairs). Now there are two tables (one in front of the sofa and one next to it).
> 3 In the 1960s there was a painting above the fireplace. Now there are three above the sofa.
> 4 In the 1960s there was a carpet. Now there is a wooden floor.
> 5 In the 1960s there was a bookcase. Now there isn't a bookcase.
> 6 In the 1960s there were two lamps on the floor. Now there is one lamp on the table.
> 7 In the 1960s there wasn't a plant (in front of the window). Now there's a plant.
> 8 In the 1960s there wasn't a clock (on the wall). Now there is a clock.
> 9 In the 1960s there was a TV next to the fireplace. Now there is a TV on the wall.

> **Room 2 differences:**
> 1 In the 1960s there was a rug. Now there isn't a rug.
> 2 In the 1960s there wasn't a TV. Now there is a TV.
> 3 In the 1960s there were two posters on the wall (above the desk). Now there is one poster.
> 4 In the 1960s there were two chairs. Now there's one chair.
> 5 In the 1960s there wasn't a computer (on the desk). Now there is a computer.
> 6 In the 1960s there was a radio. Now there isn't a radio.
> 7 In the 1960s there was a shelf with some books. Now there isn't a shelf.
> 8 In the 1960s there was a plant next to the desk. Now there isn't.
> 9 In the 1960s there was a mirror (next to the bed). Now there isn't a mirror.

9A Shopping list

A pairwork checking activity

Sts check items on a shopping list to see what is needed. Copy one worksheet per pair and cut into **A** and **B**.

> **LANGUAGE**
>
> *Do we need any…? Yes, we need some… / No, we don't need any…*

- Demonstrate the activity by writing a shopping list for classroom material on the board, e.g. PENS, PAPER, DICTIONARIES, READERS, DVDS etc. Then ask Sts *Do we need any pens?* Try to elicit *Yes, we need some pens* or *No, we don't need any pens* and write the two answers on the board. Continue with the other things on the list, ticking or crossing them according to what Sts think is needed.
- Put Sts in pairs, **A** and **B**, and give out the worksheets. Focus on **a**. Tell Sts **A** that they are in the supermarket and have made a list, but are not sure what they really need. They phone **B**, who is at home and will look in the fridge to see what they have and what they need.
- Tell Sts **A** to start the conversation with *Hi. I'm in the supermarket. Do we need any…* to ask **B** about the things on the list; **B** looks at his/her picture and answers. **A** then puts a tick (✔) for things they need and a cross (✗) for things they don't need. Monitor and help.
- When they have finished, Sts swap roles and do **b**.

9B *How much / many* board game

A board game activity

Sts play a game and complete questions with *much / many* and answer them. Copy one worksheet for each group of three or four students. You will also need one counter per student and a dice per group.

> **LANGUAGE**
>
> *How much fruit do you eat a day? Quite a lot.*
> *How many emails did you send yesterday? Not many.*

- Write on the board:

  How _______________ COFFEE DO YOU DRINK A DAY?

  How _______________ VEGETABLES DO YOU EAT A DAY?

  and elicit the missing words, reminding Sts that *coffee* is singular uncountable, and that *vegetables* are plural countable.
- Get Sts to ask you the questions and answer with a quantifier, e.g. *a lot / quite a lot / not many / not much / a little / a few / none* and then give a bit more detail, e.g. a reason or an example. Then ask some different Sts the questions and encourage them to answer in the same way.
- Put Sts in groups of three or four. Give each group a worksheet, a dice, and some counters. Focus on the quantifiers in the middle of the board and make sure Sts know what they all mean and how to use them.
- Sts roll the dice and move clockwise to the corresponding square. They have to complete the question they land on with *much / many* and then answer, using one of the quantifiers, giving a reason or an example where possible. Monitor to make sure Sts play the game correctly.
- Either set a time limit or stop the game when one group has a winner, i.e. a student who has gone the whole way round the board.

9C Guess the comparative

A pairwork activity

Sts read sentences and guess what the missing comparative adjective is. Copy one worksheet per pair and cut into **A** and **B**.

> **LANGUAGE**
>
> Comparatives: *colder, bigger, healthier*
> *Scotland is colder than England.*

- Demonstrate the activity. Write on a piece of paper *Scotland is colder than England*. Do not show this to Sts. Then write on the board SCOTLAND IS _______________ THAN ENGLAND.
- Elicit possible comparative adjectives, getting Sts to say the whole sentence. If what they say is *not* what you have on the piece of paper, e.g. *Scotland is smaller than England*, *Scotland is more beautiful than England*, etc. say *Try again*, until someone comes up with the sentence you have. Point out that their sentences are also correct, but that the objective is for them to guess the comparative that you had.
- Put Sts into pairs, **A** and **B**, and give out the copies. Tell Sts to work individually at first and complete the gaps. Remind them that the missing words are all comparative adjectives. Monitor, making sure Sts are writing correct and logical adjectives.
- Now get Sts to sit face to face if possible. **B** reads out his / her sentence 1 to **A**. If it's the same as what **A** has, he / she says *That's right*. If not **A** says *Try again*, and he / she continues guessing comparatives until he / she gets it right.
- Now **A** reads his / her completed sentence 2. Sts continue until they have said all the sentences.

10A What do you know about the UK?

A quiz about Britain

Sts revise superlatives. Copy one worksheet per student.

> **LANGUAGE**
>
> Superlatives: *busiest, most popular*, etc.
> *What's the busiest London airport?*
> *What's the most popular kind of restaurant?*

- If necessary, quickly revise the formation of superlatives with examples on the board, e.g.:
  THE (TALL) PERSON IN THE CLASS IS…
  THE (POPULAR) SPORT IN THE COUNTRY IS…
- Give out the worksheets. First, in **a** get Sts to complete the questions individually with superlative adjectives. Check answers.
- Check answers.

> **a** **1** busiest **2** most popular **3** biggest **4** longest **5** sunniest **6** the wettest **7** largest **8** most popular **9** oldest **10** most common **11** highest **12** biggest

- Now for **b**, put Sts in pairs and set a time limit for them to choose the correct answers. Monitor and help.

- Check answers. Find out who got the most answers right.

> **b** 1 a 2 c 3 b 4 b 5 b 6 a 7 b 8 a 9 a 10 c 11 a 12 c

- In the same pairs, Sts write five questions about their country or countries. Monitor and help. Sts then ask another pair/group their questions.
- In **d**, Sts ask another pair their questions.

10B Future plans
A pairwork activity

Sts use prompts to ask each other questions about their future plans using *going to*. Copy one worksheet per pair and cut into **A** and **B**.

> **LANGUAGE**
>
> Plans: *be going to* + verb

- Write on the board:

  / WATCH THE NEWS THIS EVENING?

  / GO TO A PARTY TONIGHT?

  / GO CAMPING NEXT SUMMER?

- Get Sts to ask you the questions and answer, giving reasons if possible. Then ask Sts the questions and some follow-ups (*Why? Why not? Where?*, etc.) and elicit the three questions with *going to*.
- Tell Sts they are going to ask their partner questions and they must also ask follow-up questions. Tell them the questions their partner has are different, so they can also ask *And you?*
- Put Sts in pairs, **A** and **B**. Give out the worksheets and tell Sts to ask each other questions using *Are you going to…?*
- Monitor and help. You can then ask Sts to tell you their partner's future plans, *He is going to have lunch with his family tomorrow*, etc.
- Get feedback, asking Sts to tell you their partner's future plans, e.g. *Pedro is going to have lunch with his family tomorrow*, etc.

EXTRA IDEA Tell Sts to cover the questions and tell them to ask you any questions they can remember.

10C Predictions
A pairwork role-play

Sts use cards to predict each other's future. Copy and cut up one worksheet per pair.

> **LANGUAGE**
>
> Predictions: *be going to* + verb

- These are the same cards that are used in the Student's Book lesson. Take a card, show it to the class and ask *What does this card mean?* Elicit *It means you're going to…* Repeat with the other cards.
- Tell Sts they are going to role-play a fortune teller and client activity. Put Sts in pairs, **A** and **B**. Sts **A** are the fortune tellers and Sts **B** are the clients.

- Give Sts **A** a set of cards and tell them to shuffle them and to lay them on the desk face down. Sts **B** now choose five cards, but <u>don't</u> turn them over.
- Now tell Sts **A** they are going to turn the cards over one by one and use them to predict Sts **B**s' future. Sts **B** should ask for more information.
- When Sts have finished, they swap roles and Sts **B** become the fortune tellers. Finally, get some feedback from the class and find out what Sts thought about their predicted future.
- Finally, get some feedback from the class and find out what Sts thought about their predicted future.

11A Read slowly
An adverb group activity

Sts get a sentence and an adverb and have to read their sentence in the way their adverb indicates. Copy and cut up one worksheet if you have up to 12 students, if not, one worksheet per eight students.

> **LANGUAGE**
>
> Adverbs: *fast, slowly, quietly*

- Write I AM VERY ANGRY RIGHT NOW! on the board. Read it in a happy voice. Ask Sts *How am I reading it?* and try to elicit *happily*. Demonstrate a couple more, e.g. *quietly, tiredly*. Make sure you point out you want the adverb and not the adjective and remind Sts of the -*ly* ending.
- Explain that they are going to read aloud some sentences for other Sts to guess the adverb. If you have a class of up to 12, do it as a class activity. For larger classes, divide the class into groups. Give each student a cut-out sentence, and an adverb.
- Sts now read the sentence in the way the adverb indicates and others guess the adverb.

EXTRA IDEA Repeat the activity giving Sts different sentences and adverbs.

11B Dreams and plans
A pairwork activity

Sts choose six questions from a list to ask their partner. Copy a worksheet per student.

> **LANGUAGE**
>
> Verbs + *to* + infinitive: *want to, need to, would like to, hope to, plan to, learn to, forget to*

- Put Sts in pairs and give out the worksheets. Give them time to read the questions and make sure there are no problems with vocabulary.
- Now tell Sts to choose six questions to ask their partner. Tell them to circle the questions.
- Sts ask each other their chosen questions. Encourage them to 'return' the questions with *What about you?* or *And you?* if their questions are different. Monitor and help.
- Get feedback to find out about different Sts dreams and plans.

11C Speak for 30 seconds

A board game activity

Sts practise speaking about different topics for 30 seconds. Copy one worksheet for each group of three or four Sts. You will also need one counter per student and a dice per group.

- Tell Sts they are going to play a board game.
- Put Sts in groups of three or four. Give each group a worksheet, a dice and some counters.
- Explain the rules of the game. Sts roll the dice and move their counters. When a student lands on a square, he / she must talk about the topic for 30 seconds. Then each of the other students can ask an extra question.
- Someone in the group times the 30 seconds.
- The game finishes when someone reaches **FINISH**, but they must roll the exact number. If they don't, they move any excess backwards.

12A Have you done it?

A pairwork information gap activity

Sts practise asking and answering present perfect questions. Copy one worksheet per student.

- Demonstrate the activity. Write two sentences in the present perfect on the board for yourself, one true, one not true, e.g. I'VE READ ALL THE GAME OF THRONES BOOKS. Ask Sts if they think it's true or not and why. Elicit some answers, e.g. *I think it's true because you love the TV series.* Then tell them if your sentences are true or not.
- Give each student a worksheet and quickly go through the questions, making sure Sts understand all the lexis. Tell them to complete the sentences using the verbs in brackets, so that half of the sentences are true and half of them not true.
- For **b**, explain that they are going to guess which of their partner's sentences are true and which are not.
- Put Sts in pairs, **A** and **B**. Tell Sts **A** to read their first sentence. Sts **B** then say whether they think it is true or not and why. Sts **A** then write *T* or *F* after the sentence depending on what their partner guessed. They continue until Sts **A** have read all their sentences. Then Sts **A** tell Sts **B** if they guessed correctly or not and why.
- Sts then swap roles.
- Get feedback and find out which pairs knew each other best. Ask Sts if they found out anything that surprised them.

EXTRA IDEA Let Sts try to guess how you would complete the sentences to make them true for you.

12B Have you ever…?

A class mingle speaking activity

Sts practise the present perfect and the past simple with question prompts. Copy and cut up one worksheet for a class of 14 Sts or two if more.

- Put Sts in groups of six or eight (even numbers where possible). A small class of up to 14 Sts can work as a whole. Ask each student to write *Yes, I have.* or *No, I haven't.* in big letters on two pieces of paper. Give every student in the class a question card and tell them to complete the first question with the past participle of the verb in brackets.
- Demonstrate first with a different question, e.g. *Have you ever been to the UK?* Sts should lift up either their *Yes, I have.* piece of paper or *No, I haven't.* one. Then ask a few past simple questions (e.g. *When did you go there? Did you like it?*) to those who answered *Yes, I have.*
- Now in their groups one student asks the group his / her first question (*Have you ever…?*). The rest of the group should lift either their *Yes, I have.* or *No, I haven't.* piece of paper.
- The student who asked the question then chooses a student who answered *Yes, I have.* to ask the follow-up questions to. Then another student continues with his / her question.
- When they have asked their questions, you could give out more cards if there are any left.

12C Revision questions

A revision activity

Sts revise and practise key structures from Files 1–12. This could be used as a last revision before the final exam. Copy and cut up one set of cards per pair.

- Tell Sts the object of this activity is to ask and answer as many questions as they can to revise the English they know. Demonstrate by taking a card and asking one student some of the questions. Then take another card and quickly copy some of it onto the board. Get Sts to use the prompts to ask you complete questions. Remind Sts that the symbol / means a word (or words) is missing.
- Put Sts in pairs. Give each pair a set of cards. Set a time limit, e.g. ten minutes. Sts take turns to take a card and ask their partner the questions. Encourage them to ask further questions. Monitor, help and correct.

1A COMMUNICATIVE You say, you answer

Student A

a Have five different conversations with **B**. Read the sentences in the **You say** column and listen to **B**'s answer.

You say	You answer
Hi, I'm Mike. What's your name?	Nice to meet you, too.
Hi, Mark, this is Anna.	I'm very well, thank you.
What's your phone number?	Nice to meet you, Ben. I'm Laura.
How are you?	It's Monday.
Hello, I'm George.	Yes, see you on Saturday. Goodbye.

b Now listen to **B** and respond with a sentence from the **You answer** column.

c Repeat the activity. Read the **You say** sentences again. **B** answers from memory.

d Now answer **B** from memory.

- -

Student B

a Have five different conversations with **A**. Listen to **A** and respond with a sentence from the **You answer** column.

You answer	You say
Hi, George. I'm Chris. Nice to meet you.	How are you?
It's 07478203124.	What day is it today?
My name's Sally.	Nice to meet you, Jim.
Nice to meet you, Anna.	Hello! My name's Ben.
Fine, thanks. And you?	See you on Saturday. Bye.

b Now read the sentences in the **You say** column and listen to **A**'s answer.

c Repeat the activity. Answer **A** from memory.

d Now read the **You say** sentences again. **A** answers from memory.

1B COMMUNICATIVE Nationalities bingo

- ☐ English
- ☐ Irish
- ☐ Mexican
- ☐ Hungarian
- ☐ Japanese
- ☐ Turkish
- ☐ Polish
- ☐ American
- ☐ Italian
- ☐ Czech
- ☐ German
- ☐ Scottish
- ☐ Brazilian
- ☐ Russian
- ☐ French
- ☐ Argentinian
- ☐ Spanish
- ☐ Egyptian
- ☐ Chinese
- ☐ Swiss

1 BINGO

the USA	Argentina	the Czech Republic
Japan	Poland	Turkey

7 BINGO

the USA	France	Brazil
Russia	Hungary	Mexico

2 BINGO

England	Germany	Brazil
Russia	France	China

8 BINGO

Brazil	Mexico	Germany
Japan	Egypt	Italy

3 BINGO

Ireland	Spain	Japan
Egypt	Italy	China

9 BINGO

Turkey	the USA	France
Scotland	Spain	Hungary

4 BINGO

Mexico	England	Hungary
Switzerland	Japan	Germany

10 BINGO

Ireland	Italy	Argentina
Japan	Poland	the Czech Republic

5 BINGO

Scotland	Turkey	Egypt
Russia	the Czech Republic	Switzerland

11 BINGO

Turkey	Switzerland	Brazil
England	Germany	Egypt

6 BINGO

Poland	Scotland	Argentina
China	Ireland	Spain

12 BINGO

China	Argentina	Mexico
Hungary	Scotland	the USA

1C COMMUNICATIVE Personal information

Name Joanna	**Name**	**Name**
Surname DUKE	**Surname**	**Surname**
Email joanna.duke@comet.com	**Email**	**Email**
Mobile 07700 960654	**Mobile**	**Mobile**
Name Claire	**Name**	**Name**
Surname HARVEY	**Surname**	**Surname**
Email c.harvey@basol.com	**Email**	**Email**
Mobile 07702 904678	**Mobile**	**Mobile**
Name Donna	**Name**	**Name**
Surname WILLIAMS	**Surname**	**Surname**
Email donna.williams@mail.com	**Email**	**Email**
Mobile 07708 990487	**Mobile**	**Mobile**
Name Celine	**Name**	**Name**
Surname CARSON	**Surname**	**Surname**
Email carson@compu.com	**Email**	**Email**
Mobile 07723 905124	**Mobile**	**Mobile**
Name Thomas	**Name**	**Name**
Surname RICHARDS	**Surname**	**Surname**
Email t.richards@freemail.com	**Email**	**Email**
Mobile 07711 990498	**Mobile**	**Mobile**
Name Ryan	**Name**	**Name**
Surname MANNERS	**Surname**	**Surname**
Email r.manners@freemail.com	**Email**	**Email**
Mobile 07700 943864	**Mobile**	**Mobile**
Name Dexter	**Name**	**Name**
Surname PITT	**Surname**	**Surname**
Email dexter.pitt@over.com	**Email**	**Email**
Mobile 07703 981290	**Mobile**	**Mobile**
Name Anthony	**Name**	**Name**
Surname EASTWOOD	**Surname**	**Surname**
Email a.eastwood@younder.com	**Email**	**Email**
Mobile 07706 977892	**Mobile**	**Mobile**

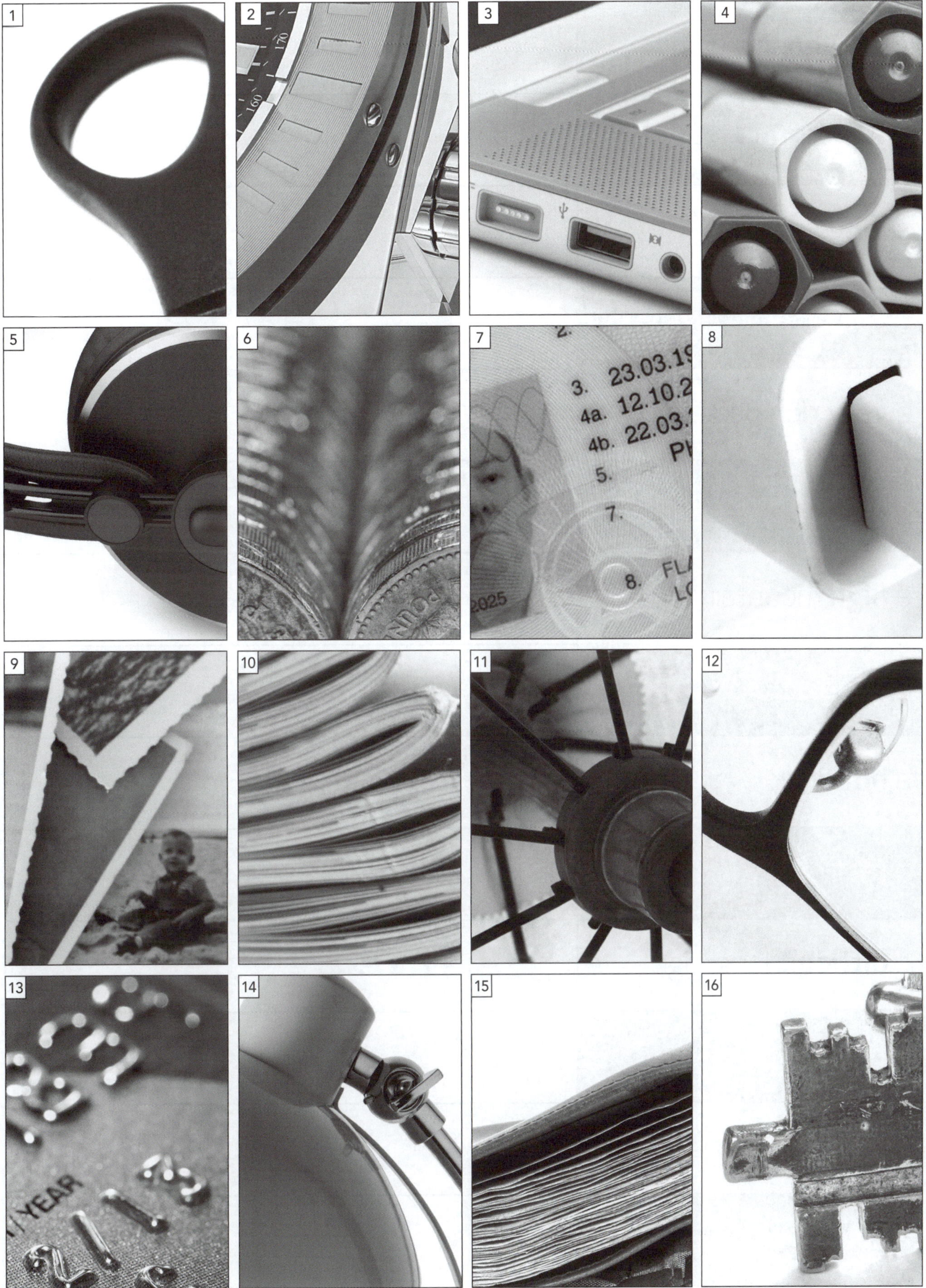

 COMMUNICATIVE   Can you name…?

an **expensive** watch	
a **dangerous** sport	
a **long** name	
an **old** song	
a **very rich** person	
a **strong** person	
a **high** mountain	
a **good** actor	
a **hot** drink	
a **fast** car	
a **difficult** language	
a **terrible** film	
a **very young** musician	
a **cold** country	
a **very beautiful** actress	

This is a library.	This room's hot.	**Turn on the air conditioning!**	I'm thirsty.
Have some water.	I'm tired.	**Sit down.**	I'm hungry.
Let's go to a café.	My camera's expensive.	**Please be careful with it!**	This road is dangerous.
Slow down!	I'm cold!	**Close the window.**	What's the matter?
I'm worried.	Let's stop for lunch.	**Good idea!**	Don't go in there!
The door is closed.	I'm stressed.	**Relax!**	I'm sad.
Cheer up!	Don't turn right!	**Turn left!**	This is a good hotel.
Let's go there!	The light is red.	**Don't cross!**	We're in class.
Please turn off your mobile.	I'm bored.	**Read a book.**	Be quiet, please.

work in an office	read a newspaper
drink coffee	listen to rock music
eat Japanese food	live in a big city
go to the gym	watch the news
do housework in the morning	need a new tablet
speak Spanish	play a musical instrument
study Chinese	have a pet
go to the cinema at the weekend	watch an American TV series
have a big family	live in a small flat
play basketball	want a sandwich
drive a car	cook Mexican food
like cats	speak three languages
wear a watch	work in the evening
take photos with my phone	do yoga

3B COMMUNICATIVE Present simple questionnaire

Student A

a Ask your partner the questions. Tick (✓) or cross (✗) the boxes in the **DO YOU…?** column.

Do you live near a supermarket? *Yes, I do. / No, I don't.*

	DO YOU…?	DOES ________…?
1 …live near a supermarket		
2 …watch TV in the morning		
3 …travel to other countries a lot		
4 …have a favourite food		
5 …read in bed		
6 …like computer games		
7 …speak French		
8 …play a team sport		

b Change partners and work with another **A**. Ask about your partner's first partner and tick (✓) or cross (✗) the boxes in the **DOES…?** column.

Does Paula live near a supermarket? *Yes, she does.*

- -

Student B

a Ask your partner the questions. Tick (✓) or cross (✗) the boxes in the **DO YOU…?** column.

Do you go to the cinema a lot? *Yes, I do. / No, I don't.*

	DO YOU…?	DOES ________…?
1 …go to the cinema a lot		
2 …cook Italian food		
3 …listen to music on your phone		
4 …drink a lot of water		
5 …wear headphones in the street		
6 …study in the evening		
7 …play the guitar		
8 …work or study at night		

b Change partners and work with another **B**. Ask about your partner's first partner and tick (✓) or cross (✗) the boxes in the **DOES…?** column.

Does Pablo go to the cinema a lot? *No, he doesn't.*

3C COMMUNICATIVE Famous people

Student A

Samuel
L Jackson

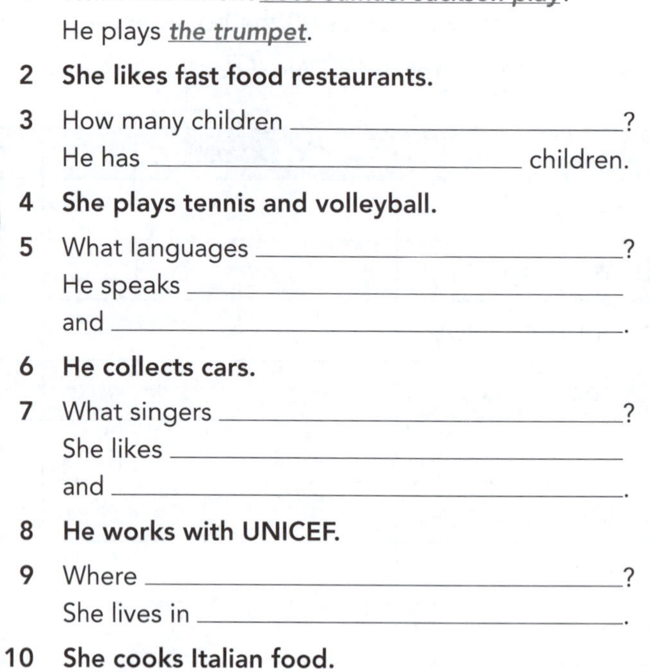

Jennifer
Lawrence

Hugh
Jackman

Rihanna

Brad Pitt

Cristiano
Ronaldo

1 What instrument *does Samuel Jackson play*?
He plays *the trumpet*.

2 **She likes fast food restaurants.**

3 How many children _________________?
He has _________________ children.

4 **She plays tennis and volleyball.**

5 What languages _________________?
He speaks _________________
and _________________.

6 **He collects cars.**

7 What singers _________________?
She likes _________________
and _________________.

8 **He works with UNICEF.**

9 Where _________________?
She lives in _________________.

10 **She cooks Italian food.**

11 What TV programme _________________?
He watches _________________.

12 **She has two dogs.**

Adele

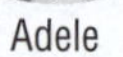

Tom
Hiddleston

Taylor
Swift

Scarlett
Johansson

Benedict
Cumberbatch

Charlize
Theron

- - -

Student B

Samuel
L Jackson

Jennifer
Lawrence

Hugh
Jackman

Rihanna

Brad Pitt

Cristiano
Ronaldo

1 **He plays the trumpet.**

2 What restaurants *does Jennifer Lawrence like*?
She likes *fast food* restaurants.

3 **He has two children.**

4 What sports _________________?
She plays _________________
and _________________.

5 **He speaks English and Japanese.**

6 What _________________?
He collects _________________.

7 **She likes Lauryn Hill and Alicia Keys.**

8 What organization _________________ with?
He works with _________________.

9 **She lives in New York.**

10 What food _________________?
She cooks _________________ food.

11 **He watches *The X Factor*.**

12 How many dogs _________________?
She has _________________ dogs.

Adele

Tom
Hiddleston

Taylor
Swift

Scarlett
Johansson

Benedict
Cumberbatch

Charlize
Theron

English File fourth edition Teacher's Guide Elementary   Photocopiable © Oxford University Press 2019

4A COMMUNICATIVE Everyday objects

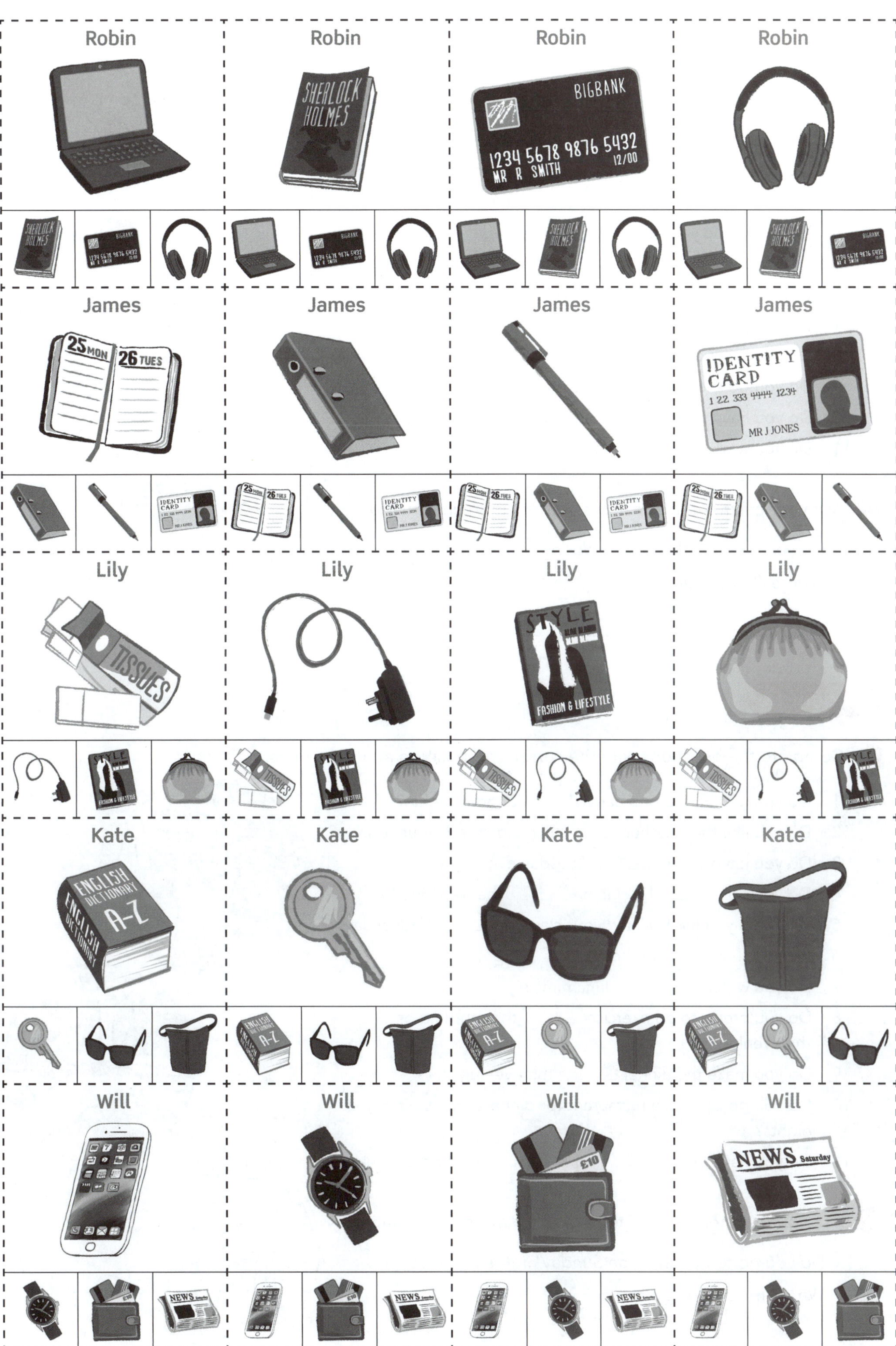

4B COMMUNICATIVE Prepositions questionnaire

Student A

a Complete the questions with the correct preposition *at*, *in*, *on*, or *to*.

1 Do you have lunch _______ home during the week?

2 Do you get up _______ 7.00 _______ Saturday mornings?

3 Where do you go on holiday _______ the summer?

4 What time do you go _______ bed _______ Fridays?

5 What do you usually do _______ Christmas?

6 How do you relax _______ the weekend?

7 Do you do your English homework _______ the evening?

8 Do you drink coffee _______ the morning?

9 Do you go shopping _______ Saturday mornings?

10 Do you have a shower _______ the morning or _______ night?

11 Do you work _______ an office?

b Ask your partner the questions. Ask for more information.

Do you have lunch at home during the week? *No, I don't.*
Where do you have lunch?

Student B

a Complete the questions with the correct preposition *at*, *in*, *on*, or *to*.

1 Do you go _______ bed early _______ Sunday nights?

2 Do you like the weather _______ the summer in your country?

3 Do you have classes _______ Tuesday evenings?

4 Do you go _______ the cinema _______ the weekend?

5 When do you finish work / your classes _______ Wednesdays?

6 Do you sleep for eight hours _______ night?

7 Do you watch TV _______ lunchtime?

8 Do you prefer to do exercise _______ the morning or _______ the evening?

9 Do you make the dinner _______ the evening?

10 Do you go _______ a restaurant for dinner _______ Friday nights?

11 Do you have lunch _______ work / school during the week?

b Ask your partner the questions. Ask for more information.

Do you go to bed early on Sunday nights? *Yes, I do.*
What time do you go to bed?

English File fourth edition Teacher's Guide Elementary   Photocopiable © Oxford University Press 2019

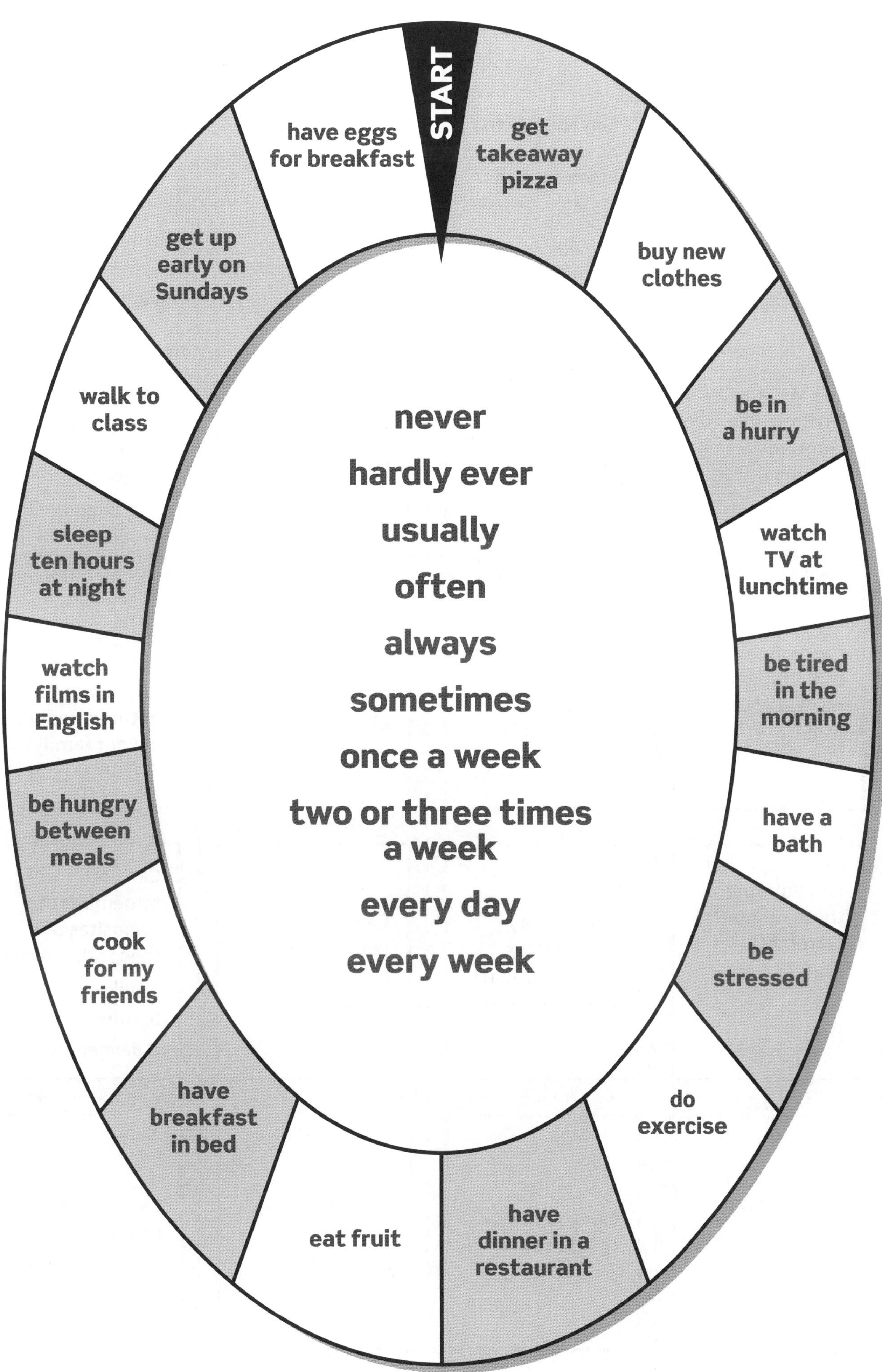
START
have eggs
for breakfast
get
takeaway
pizza
get up
early on
Sundays
buy new
clothes
walk to
class
be in
a hurry
sleep
ten hours
at night
watch
TV at
lunchtime
watch
films in
English
be tired
in the
morning
be hungry
between
meals
have a
bath
cook
for my
friends
be
stressed
have
breakfast
in bed
do
exercise
eat fruit
have
dinner in a
restaurant
never
hardly ever
usually
often
always
sometimes
once a week
two or three times
a week
every day
every week

Can you say three things you can do online?

Can you say the days of the week in ten seconds?

Can you sleep...
a) in a bus or a plane?
b) with the light on?

Can you play...
a) chess?
b) the violin?
c) volleyball?

Can you say 'Hello' in five languages?

Can you say three things you can do with your mobile?

Can you say three things you can't do in a library?

Can you sing...
a) a song in your language?
b) a song in English?

Can you say three things you have in your wallet?

Can you swim 2 km?

Can you drive...
a) a car?
b) a motorbike?

Can you remember the phone numbers of three people in your family?

Can you spell these numbers correctly?
a) 8
b) 15
c) 30

Can you say three places where you can't use your mobile?

Can you spell your name and address in English?

Can you remember the opposites of these adjectives?
a) full
b) strong
c) dangerous

Can you draw a map of your country?

Can you make spaghetti?

Can you run...
a) 1 km?
b) 10 km?

Can you count down from 20 to 1 in ten seconds?

You are waking up.	**You are having a shower.**
You are writing an email.	**You are doing your homework.**
You are drawing a picture.	**You are cooking.**
You are playing the piano.	**You are talking to your boyfriend / girlfriend on your phone.**
You are watching a horror film.	**You are waiting for somebody.**
You are drinking a hot coffee.	**You are dancing ballet.**
You are reading a funny book.	**You are taking a photo of your teacher.**
You are crying.	**You are looking for your keys.**

5C COMMUNICATIVE It's Friday evening

It's Friday evening. Look at the information and complete the table by asking **B** questions. Use the correct form of the verbs to answer **B**'s questions.

What's Mark doing this evening?

He's going to a football match.
What does he usually do on Friday evenings?

He plays football.

		What do / does _______ usually do on Friday evenings?	What is / are _______ doing this evening?
	MARK	play football	
	COLIN AND BETH		having a party at home
	PAULA	cook dinner for her friend	
	PHIL		watching a Star Wars film with a friend
	BRUCE AND ELLA	play computer games together	
	LUCY AND HANNAH		driving Lucy's sister to the airport

It's Friday evening. Look at the information and complete the table by asking **A** questions. Use the correct form of the verbs to answer **A**'s questions.

What does Mark usually do on Friday evenings?

He plays football.
What's he doing this evening?

He's going to a football match.

		What do / does _______ usually do on Friday evenings?	What is / are _______ doing this evening?
	MARK		going to a football match
	COLIN AND BETH	go out with friends	
	PAULA		meeting her friends at a restaurant
	PHIL	have dinner with his girlfriend	
	BRUCE AND ELLA		travelling to Spain
	LUCY AND HANNAH	sing in a choir	

I like <u>Anna</u>.	Wait for <u>Harry and me</u>!	Please call <u>Jack and Anna</u> this evening.	I agree with <u>Mrs Chapman</u>.
<u>Jack</u> is very angry.	<u>Sally and Jim</u> are getting married today.	<u>Mark and I</u> are cooking the dinner.	I can see <u>Matthew</u>.
Do you like <u>computer games</u>?	Are you sitting on <u>my purse</u>?	I can't come to <u>the meeting</u>.	<u>Silvia</u> can't come to the party.
<u>The dogs</u> are barking.	<u>The weather</u> is very cold.	My parents usually have lunch with <u>Simon and me</u> on Saturdays.	Can I speak to <u>Martin</u>?
This present is for <u>Anna and Richard</u>.	They are talking about <u>the children</u>.	**THEM**	**THEM**
WE	**THEY**	**HE**	**SHE**
HIM	**HIM**	**HER**	**HER**
IT	**IT**	**US**	**US**
THEY	**IT**	**THEM**	**THEM**

/ enjoy <u>meet</u> new people	/ like <u>do</u> the housework
/ enjoy <u>shop</u> online	/ hate <u>cook</u>
/ enjoy <u>travel</u>	/ hate <u>wait</u> for people
/ enjoy <u>do</u> homework	/ hate <u>watch</u> football
/ like <u>go</u> to museums	/ like <u>play</u> computer games
/ like <u>get</u> up early	/ hate <u>go</u> to the dentist
/ enjoy <u>go</u> to the beach	/ hate <u>be</u> late

English File fourth edition Teacher's Guide Elementary

6C COMMUNICATIVE Tell me about you

Student A

Complete the questions with *is / are* or *do*. Then ask your partner.

1 What _____________ your favourite season?

2 How _____________ you spell your surname?

3 _____________ you like dogs?

4 What TV series _____________ you watching at the moment?

5 When _____________ your birthday?

6 What _____________ your email address?

7 How often _____________ you in a hurry?

8 What kind of food _____________ you like?

9 What sports _____________ you like watching?

10 Where _____________ you usually have lunch?

Student B

Complete the questions with *is / are* or *do*. Then ask your partner.

1 When _____________ you usually see your friends?

2 Where _____________ you go when class finishes?

3 What _____________ your favourite kind of music?

4 How many cousins _____________ you have?

5 What do you think people in your family _____________ doing at the moment?

6 How _____________ you usually come to class?

7 What day _____________ it tomorrow?

8 _____________ you enjoy singing in the car?

9 _____________ you like going to the gym?

10 _____________ you learning another language, apart from English?

7A COMMUNICATIVE Where were you?

Look at the clocks. Ask **B** questions with
Where were you…? Answer **B**'s questions.

*Where were you at half past nine yesterday
morning?*

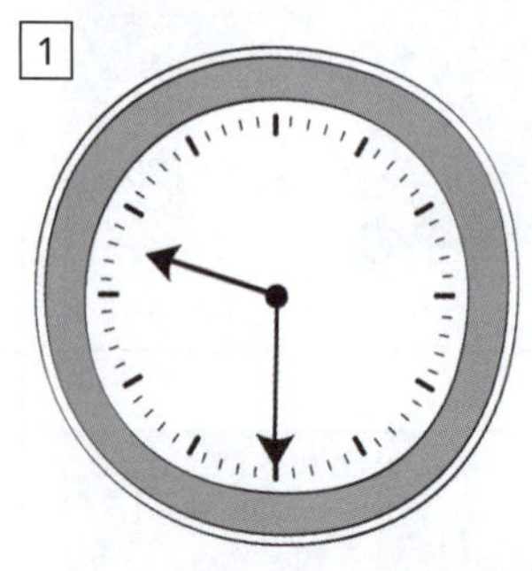

1

YESTERDAY MORNING

2

LAST NIGHT

3

YESTERDAY AFTERNOON

4

YESTERDAY EVENING

5

THIS MORNING

6

LAST SUNDAY MORNING

7

LAST SATURDAY
EVENING

8

YESTERDAY AFTERNOON

Look at the clocks. Ask **A** questions with
Where were you…? Answer **A**'s questions.

*Where were you at five o'clock yesterday
afternoon?*

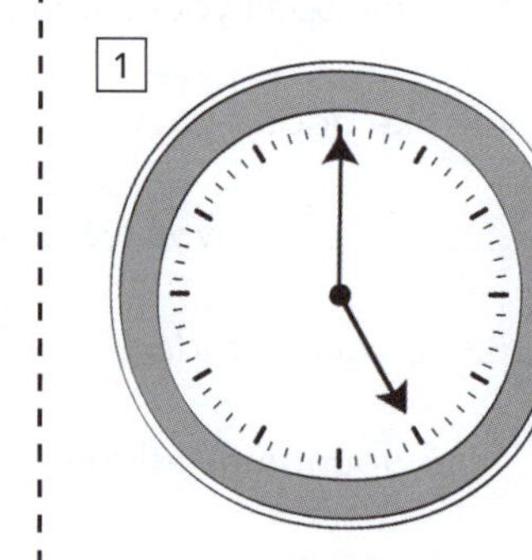
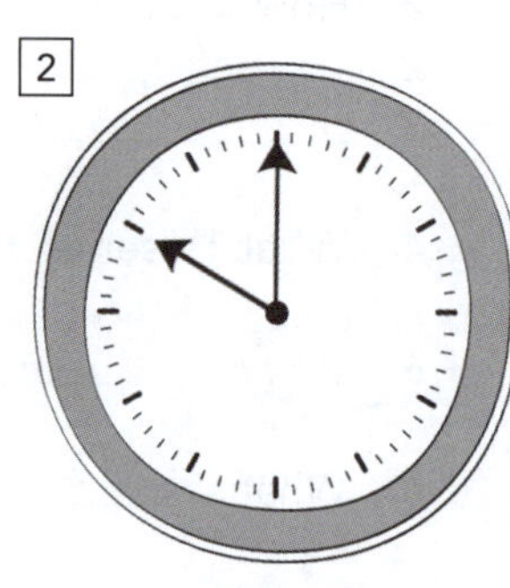

1

YESTERDAY AFTERNOON

2

LAST NIGHT

3

YESTERDAY MORNING

4

YESTERDAY EVENING

5

THIS MORNING

6

YESTERDAY AFTERNOON

7

LAST SUNDAY
AFTERNOON

8

LAST SATURDAY
EVENING

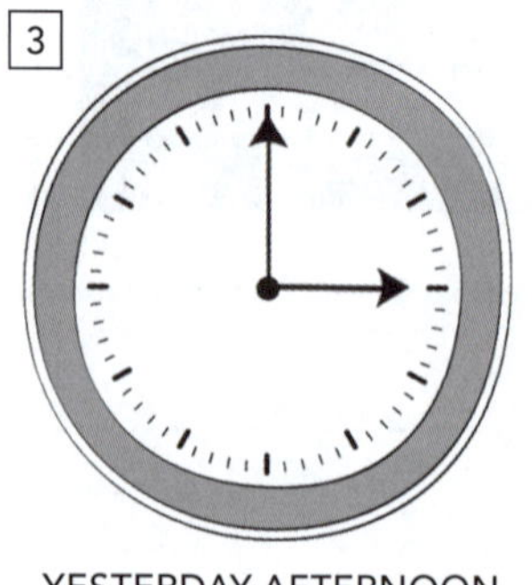
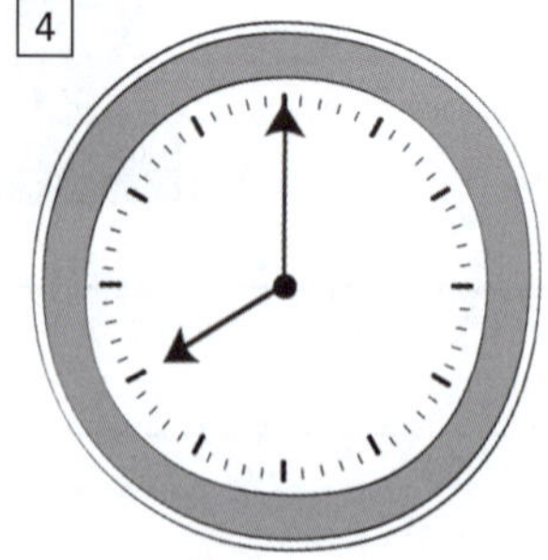
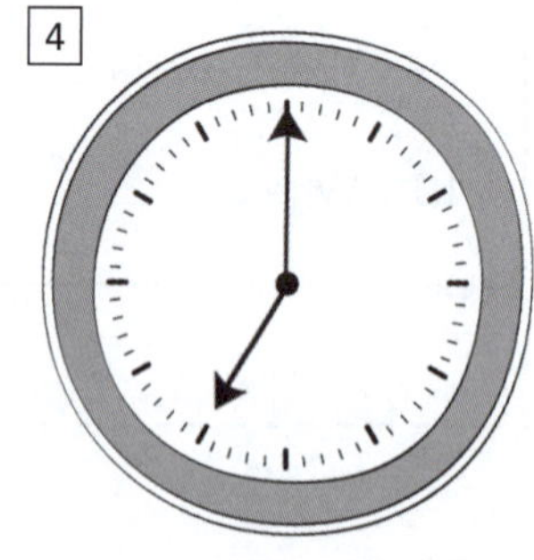
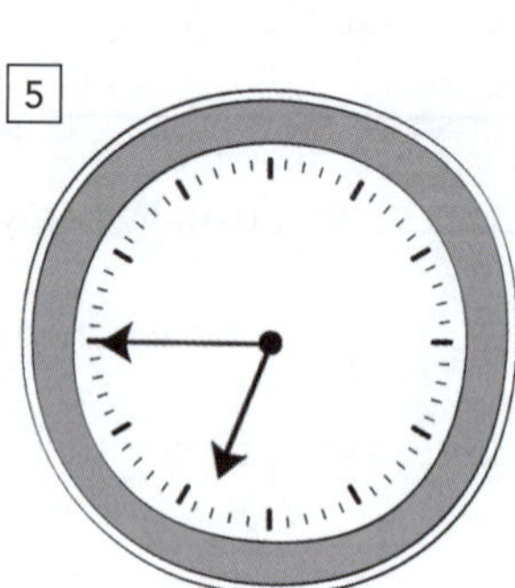
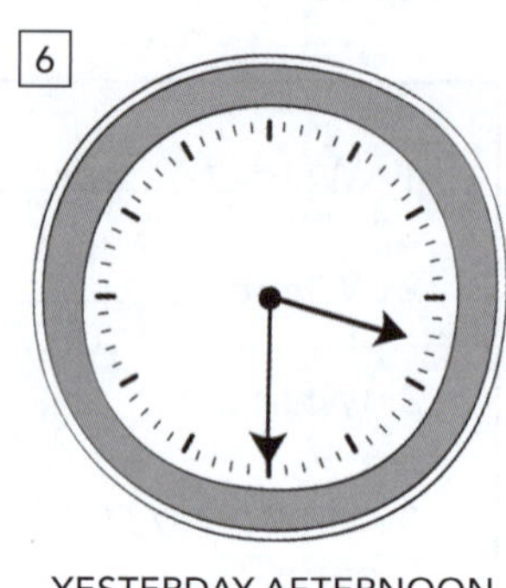
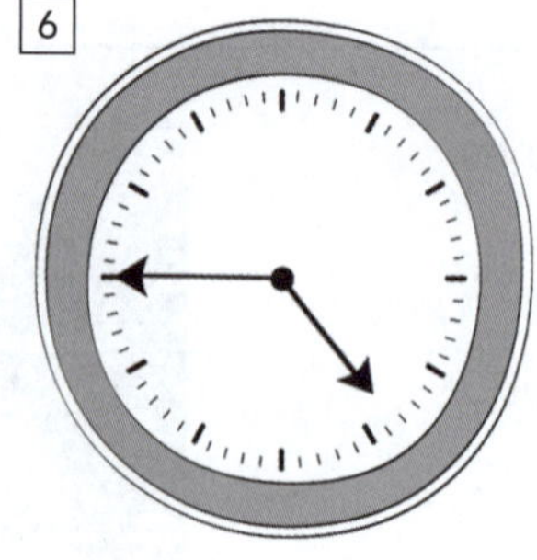

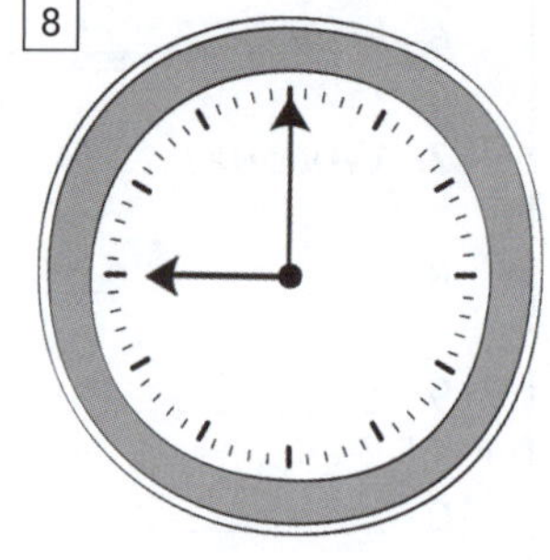

Last April two British teenagers, Raoul and Emma, wanted to go to Australia for their summer holiday.

But it was a 24-hour journey by plane and tickets were very expensive.

So, Raoul and Emma looked for cheap tickets on the internet. They booked two tickets to Sydney.

On 4th August they arrived at Heathrow airport. They checked in and waited for the plane to leave.

Six hours later they landed at a big airport and changed planes. The new plane was very small and Emma was worried.

After only an hour the plane landed. They looked out of the window. It was a very small airport!

They showed their tickets to a woman in the information desk. Raoul asked, 'When is our next flight?'

The woman was surprised. 'The next flight? This is the end of your journey. You're in Sydney.'

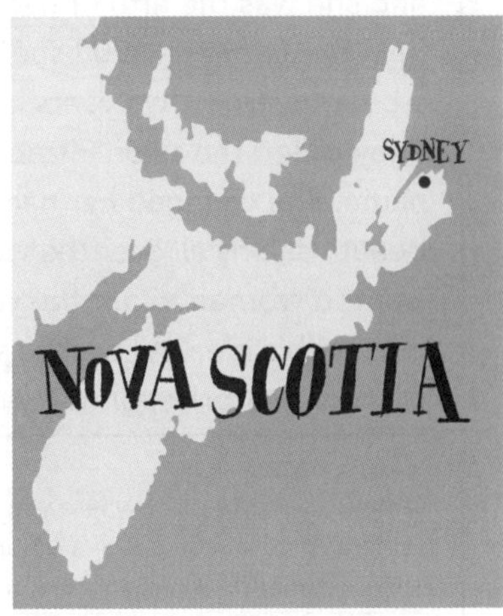

But Raoul and Emma weren't in Sydney, Australia. They were in Sydney, Nova Scotia, a small town in south-east Canada!

7C COMMUNICATIVE Born on 31st December

a Look at the text about Anthony Hopkins. Complete the questions about him.

b Ask **B** for the information and complete the text.

ANTHONY HOPKINS

Anthony Hopkins was born on 31st December 1937 in [1]_______________.
He went to the Royal Welsh College of Music and Drama when he was only
15 years old. Then he went to London to continue his studies and he met
[2]_______________, a very famous actor. He thought Anthony's acting was really
good and he gave him a job in his theatre. After that Hopkins acted in many plays
and critics loved him. He got his first film role in [3]_______________ in 1968, and
after that acted in more films and in the theatre, but he wasn't a big star. In
[4]_______________, he decided to go back to London and to forget about the
cinema. But in 1991 he won an Oscar for [5]_______________, and became very
famous. He went to live in America, and got three more Oscar nominations, but
he didn't win. In [6]_______________ he got a star on the Hollywood Walk of Fame.
Today he lives in [7]_______________, California. He is now Sir Anthony Hopkins.

Glossary
critic a journalist who writes about films, concerts, etc.
role an actor's part in a play, film/movie, etc.

1 Where *was* Anthony Hopkins born?
2 Who _______________ he _______________ in London?
3 _______________ _______________ did he get his first role in?
4 _______________ _______________ he decide to go back to London?
5 What film _______________ _______________ _______________ an Oscar for in 1991?
6 _______________ _______________ he get a star on the Hollywood Walk of Fame?
7 Where _______________ he _______________ today?

c Read about Elizabeth Arden. Then answer **B**'s questions.

ELIZABETH ARDEN

Elizabeth Arden's real name was Florence Nightingale Graham. She was born on
31st December 1884 in Ontario, Canada. Her family didn't have a lot of money
and she was the fifth of five children. She studied to be a nurse and worked to
help her family. In 1908 she moved to New York and got a job as an assistant in
a beauty salon. Two years later she opened her first beauty salon with a friend.
They called the salon Elizabeth Arden. The salon closed, but she liked the
name. She changed her name to Elizabeth Arden and used it for her beauty products. She opened
beauty salons all over the world and became very famous. Elizabeth was also a suffragette – she
wanted women to get the vote. In a protest march in 1912, all the women wore red lipstick, which was
Elizabeth's idea. All her life she never told people how old she was. When she died in 1966, her age,
81, was a surprise for many people.

Glossary
beauty salon a place where you can have beauty treatments, e.g. a manicure, a facial, etc.
suffragette a member of a group of women who worked for women to get the vote in the early 20th century
protest march an organized walk by many people in order to express their opinions

d Cover the information. With your partner, try to remember five facts
about Anthony Hopkins and Elizabeth Arden.

Student B

a   Read about Anthony Hopkins. Then answer **A**'s questions.

ANTHONY HOPKINS

Anthony Hopkins was born on 31st December 1937 in Port Talbot, Wales. He went to the Royal Welsh College of Music and Drama when he was only 15 years old. Then he went to London to continue his studies and he met Laurence Olivier, a very famous actor. He thought Anthony's acting was really good and he gave him a job in his theatre. After that Hopkins acted in many plays and critics loved him. He got his first film role in *The Lion in Winter* in 1968, and after that acted in more films and in the theatre, but he wasn't a big star. In 1990, he decided to go back to London and to forget about the cinema. But in 1991 he won an Oscar for *The Silence of the Lambs*, and became very famous. He went to live in America, and got three more Oscar nominations, but he didn't win. In 2003 he got a star on the Hollywood Walk of Fame. Today he lives in Malibu, California. He is now Sir Anthony Hopkins.

Glossary
critic a journalist who writes about films, concerts etc.
role an actor's part in a play, film/movie, etc.

b   Look at the text about Elizabeth Arden. Complete the questions about her.

c   Ask **A** for the information and complete the text.

ELIZABETH ARDEN

Elizabeth Arden's real name was ¹___________________. She was born on 31st December 1884 in Ontario, Canada. Her family didn't have a lot of money and she was the fifth of ²___________________ children. She studied to be a nurse and worked to help her family. In 1908 she moved to New York and got a job as an ³___________________ in a beauty salon. Two years later she opened her first beauty salon* with a friend. They called the salon ⁴___________________. The salon closed, but she liked the name. She changed her name to Elizabeth Arden and used it for her beauty products. She opened beauty salons all over the world and became very famous. Elizabeth was also a suffragette – she wanted women to get ⁵___________________. In a protest march in 1912, all the women wore ⁶___________________, which was Elizabeth's idea. All her life she never told people how old she was. When she died in 1966, her age, ⁷___________________, was a surprise for many people.

Glossary
beauty salon a place where you can have beauty treatments, e.g. a manicure, a facial, etc.
suffragette a member of a group of women who worked for women to get the vote in the early 20th century
protest march an organized walk by many people in order to express their opinions

1   What *was* Elizabeth Arden's real name?
2   ___________ _____________ children ___________ her parents have?
3   ___________ _____________ did she get in 1908?
4   What ___________ she and her friend ___________ their first salon?
5   What ___________ _____________ _____________ women to get?
6   ___________ _____________ all the women ___________ in a protest march in 1912?
7   How ___________ _____________ she when she died?

d   Cover the information. With your partner, try to remember five facts about Anthony Hopkins and Elizabeth Arden.

This morning

What time / get up? / make your bed?
What / have for breakfast?
When / leave home?
/ check your email?
How / go to work or school?

Yesterday

Who / have lunch with?
What time / finish work / school?
What / do in the evening?
Where / at 7.30?
/ watch TV? What / watch?
/ go to bed before or after midnight?

When you were 12 years old

Where / live?
Where / go to school?
What bands or singers / like?
/ have a mobile phone?
Who / your best friend?
What / like doing in your free time?

Last Saturday

/ get up early?
What / do in the morning?
Who / see in the evening?
Where / go in the afternoon?
/ go shopping? What / buy?
Where / be at 10.00?

Your last birthday

What presents / get?
/ go to work or school?
Who / celebrate it with?
/ have a party?
What / do in the evening?
/ have a good time?

Your last holiday

Where / go?
Who / go with?
Where / stay?
How long / stay?
What interesting things / do?
/ have any problems?

8B COMMUNICATIVE   A place to rent

a You are an estate agent. This is the advert you have put on your website.
B phones to ask for information. Answer his / her questions.

- First floor flat in quiet residential area.
- Two large double bedrooms and two bathrooms with shower.
- Big, light living room with modern TV and dining table and chairs.
- Modern kitchen with washing machine, dishwasher, and fridge freezer.
- Gas central heating.
- wi-fi internet connection.
- Private garage.
- 5 minutes from shops and public transport.
- Rent £900 a month.

b You are looking for a house to rent. You see this advert on a website.
Phone the estate agent, B, at Star Homes and ask for information about the house.

Hello. I'm phoning about a house.

The reference is 392117.

Can you tell me about it, please?

Student B

a You are looking for a flat to rent. You see this advert on a website.
Phone the estate agent, **A**, at Dream Flats and ask for information about the flat.

Hello. I'm phoning about a flat.

The reference is 268559.

Can you tell me about it, please?

What I want to know

Where / the flat?

What floor / on?

How many bedrooms and bathrooms / ?

/ big living room?

What / in the kitchen?

/ central heating?

/ wi-fi?

/ a garage?

How far / from shops and public transport?

How much / the rent?

b You are an estate agent. This is the advert you have put on your website.
A phones to ask for information. Answer his / her questions.

- Country house.
- 10 miles from Oxford.
- Big, light living room with fireplace / dining room.
- Eight double bedrooms, six bathrooms, study.
- New, modern kitchen with washing machine, dishwasher, and fridge freezer.
- Gas central heating.
- Big garden with swimming pool.
- Double garage.
- Rent £5,200 a month.

8C COMMUNICATIVE   What's different?

a Look at Room 1 for one minute. Then describe it to your partner. Say what there is and where.

> *It's a modern living room. There's a sofa. In front of the sofa there's a coffee table.*

b **B** has a picture of the same room in the 1960s. He/she is going to tell you how it was different. Circle the things in the picture.

Room 1   A modern living room

Room 2   A bedroom in the 1960s

c Now listen to **B** describe Room 2 as it is today. Circle things that were different in the 1960s.

d Tell **B** how the room was different in the 1960s.

> *There wasn't a computer on the desk. There was a poster of the Beatles above it.*

e Compare the pictures with **B**. Which rooms do you like best?

8C COMMUNICATIVE What's different?

a Look at Room 1 for one minute. It's a living room in the 1960s. Listen to **A** describe the same room today. Circle things that are different.

b Tell **A** how the room was different in the 1960s.

There wasn't a sofa, there were three armchairs. There wasn't a lamp on the table…

Room 1   A living room in the 1960s

Room 2   A modern bedroom

c Now describe Room 2 to **A**.

It's a modern bedroom. There's a computer on the desk.

d **A** has a picture of the same room in the 1960s. He/she is going to tell you how it was different. Circle the things in the picture.

e Compare the pictures with **A**. Which rooms do you like best?

9A COMMUNICATIVE Shopping list

Student A

a Look at the list. Ask **B** *Do we need any…?* for every item on the list.

Listen to **B**'s answers and put a tick (✓) for *yes* and a cross (✗) for *no* next to each item.

b Now listen to **B**'s questions and look at the picture.

Answer with *No, we don't need any…* or *Yes, we need some…*

Student B

a Listen to **A**'s questions and look at the picture.

Answer with *No, we don't need any…* or *Yes, we need some…*

b Now look at the list. Ask **A** *Do we need any…?* for every item on the list.

Listen to **A**'s answers and put a tick (✓) for *yes* and a cross (✗) for *no* next to each item.

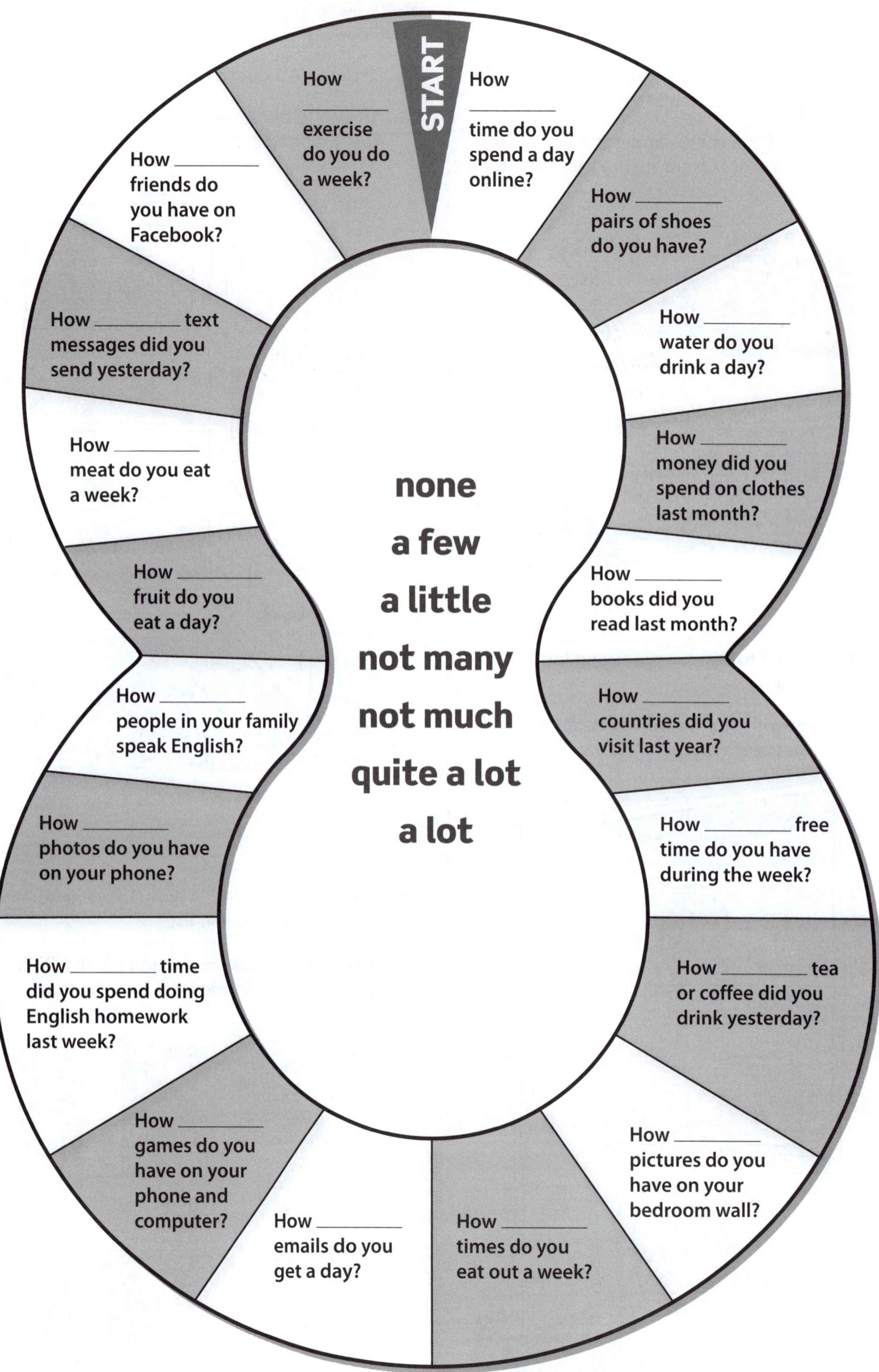
START
How _______ exercise do you do a week?
How _______ time do you spend a day online?
How _______ friends do you have on Facebook?
How _______ pairs of shoes do you have?
How _______ text messages did you send yesterday?
How _______ water do you drink a day?
How _______ meat do you eat a week?
How _______ money did you spend on clothes last month?
How _______ fruit do you eat a day?
How _______ books did you read last month?
How _______ people in your family speak English?
How _______ countries did you visit last year?
How _______ photos do you have on your phone?
How _______ free time do you have during the week?
How _______ time did you spend doing English homework last week?
How _______ tea or coffee did you drink yesterday?
How _______ games do you have on your phone and computer?
How _______ pictures do you have on your bedroom wall?
How _______ emails do you get a day?
How _______ times do you eat out a week?
none
a few
a little
not many
not much
quite a lot
a lot

9C COMMUNICATIVE Guess the comparative

Student A

1   Russia is **colder** than Spain.

2   **The Americans are** _________ **than the British**.

3   Swimming is **better** exercise than walking.

4   **Oranges are** _________ **than lemons**.

5   A Rolls Royce is **more expensive** than a BMW.

6   **Driving is** _________ **than flying**.

7   Chinese is **more difficult** to learn than English.

8   **Basketball players are** _________ **than footballers**.

9   Dark chocolate is **healthier** than white chocolate.

10   **Canada is** _________ **than Brazil**.

11   The weather in Britain is **worse** than the weather in Italy.

12   **Tom Cruise is** _________ **than George Clooney**.

- -

Student B

1   **Russia is** _________ **than Spain**.

2   The Americans are **friendlier** than the British.

3   **Swimming is** _________ **exercise than walking**.

4   Oranges are **sweeter** than lemons.

5   **A Rolls Royce is** _________ **than a BMW**.

6   Driving is **more dangerous** than flying.

7   **Chinese is** _________ **to learn than English**.

8   Basketball players are **taller** than footballers.

9   **Dark chocolate is** _________ **than white chocolate**.

10   Canada is **bigger** than Brazil.

11   **The weather in Britain is** _________ **than the weather in Italy**.

12   Tom Cruise is **shorter** than George Clooney.

10A COMMUNICATIVE   What do you know about the UK?

a Write the superlative form of the adjective.

1 What's the ____________ London airport? (busy)
  a Heathrow   **b** Gatwick   **c** Stansted

2 What's the ____________ kind of restaurant? (popular)
  a British   **b** Chinese   **c** Indian

3 Which is the ____________ city after London? (big)
  a Edinburgh   **b** Birmingham   **c** Manchester

4 Which is the ____________ river? (long)
  a The Thames   **b** The Severn   **c** The Avon

5 Which part of Britain is the ____________ (sunny)
  a the south-west   **b** the south-east   **c** the north-east

6 Which is the ____________ city? (wet)
  a Cardiff   **b** Belfast   **c** Manchester

7 What's the ____________ football stadium? (large)
  a Old Trafford   **b** Wembley   **c** Emirates Stadium

8 What's the ____________ outdoor activity? (popular)
  a fishing   **b** walking   **c** gardening

9 Which is the ____________ university? (old)
  a Oxford   **b** Cambridge   **c** London

10 What's the ____________ surname? (common)
  a Johnson   **b** Miller   **c** Smith

11 Where's the ____________ mountain? (high)
  a Scotland   **b** Northern Ireland   **c** Wales

12 What's the ____________ native animal? (big)
  a horse   **b** bull   **c** deer

b Work with a partner. Answer the questions.

c With your partner, write five questions about your country or countries.

d Find another pair and ask them your questions.

English File fourth edition Teacher's Guide Elementary   Photocopiable © Oxford University Press 2019

10B COMMUNICATIVE Future plans

Ask **B** questions about his / her plans using *going to*. Ask for more information.

Are you going to go abroad next summer?

Yes, I am.

Where are you going to go?

I'm going to go to China.

1 / go abroad next summer?

2 / go shopping this week?

3 / have lunch with your family tomorrow?

4 / go to bed early tonight?

5 / watch TV this evening?

6 / buy anyone a present this month?

7 / go out next Saturday night?

8 / study English at the weekend?

9 / celebrate a friend's birthday next week?

10 / do your homework this evening?

Ask **A** questions about his / her plans using *going to*. Ask for more information.

Are you going to make dinner tonight?

Yes, I am.

What are you going to make?

I'm going to make pasta I think.

1 / make dinner tonight?

2 / come to the next class?

3 / stay in bed late next Sunday?

4 / do any sport or exercise tomorrow?

5 / meet your friends next Friday?

6 / get up before 8 o'clock tomorrow?

7 / use your computer this evening?

8 / spend time with your family this weekend?

9 / work or study late this week?

10 / go for a walk later today?

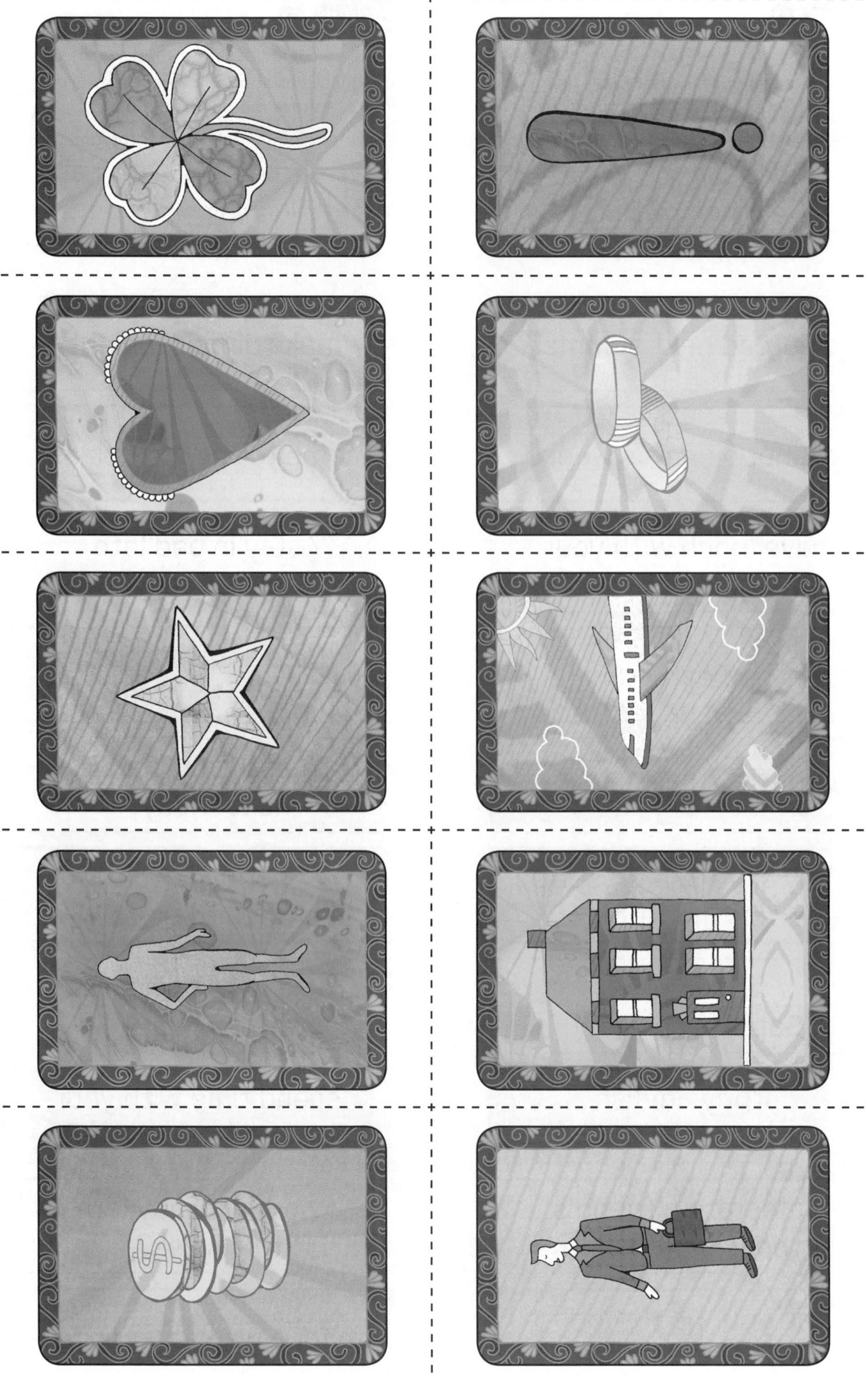

English File fourth edition Teacher's Guide Elementary   Photocopiable © Oxford University Press 2019

LOUDLY	**ANGRILY**	**SLOWLY**	**FAST**
NERVOUSLY	**QUIETLY**	**SADLY**	**HAPPILY**
TIREDLY	**POLITELY**	**SERIOUSLY**	**RUDELY**
Do you have a pen?	I lost my keys.	Can I come in?	Go away.
I know the answer.	Can you give me that book?	I don't like this exercise.	I need to help him.
I want to go to bed.	We bought some theatre tickets.	Don't go in there.	Turn off the TV.

a Choose six questions to ask your partner.

1 When did you learn to ride a bike?

2 What dish would you like to learn to cook?

3 What are two things you need to do this week?

4 What are you planning to do after class?

5 What's the next thing that you want to buy?

6 What things do you often forget to do?

7 Where would you like to go on your next holiday?

8 What did you want to be when you were little?

9 Which famous person would you like to have dinner with?

10 Who are you planning to go on holiday with?

11 Why do you want to learn to speak English?

12 What country would you like to live in?

13 What film do you really want to see?

14 What job do you hope to have in the future?

15 What hobby or activity would you like to try?

b Ask and answer the questions with your partner. Ask for more information.

START
FINISH
fast-food restaurants
selfies
my family
the sun
TV series
my house
SPEAK FOR
30 SECONDS
chocolate
the beach
modern clothes
reality TV shows
pop music
children
mobile phones
music festivals
neighbours
in my free time
the internet
cooking
ghosts

a Complete the sentences in the present perfect, ⊞ or ⊟, using the verb in brackets. Make six sentences true and six sentences not true for you.

Have you done it?

1 _________________________ the Game of Thrones books. (read)

2 _________________________ Beethoven's Fifth Symphony. (hear)

3 _________________________ in a fast food restaurant. (work)

4 _________________________ a Batman film. (see)

5 _________________________ new jeans recently. (buy)

6 _________________________ a multi-player game online. (play)

7 _________________________ in a five-star hotel. (stay)

8 _________________________ on TV. (be)

9 _________________________ by boat. (travel)

10 _________________________ asleep in class. (fall)

11 _________________________ caviar. (eat)

12 _________________________ to a famous person. (speak)

b Read your sentences to your partner. Can he / she guess which are true?

I haven't read the Game of Thrones books.

I think it's true because I don't think you like reading.

No, it's not true – I've read all the books and I've watched the series.

Have you ever _______________ (read) a book with more than 500 pages?

- What book was it?
- Did you like it?
- Did you recommend it to anyone?

Have you ever _______________ (eat) Thai food?

- Where did you eat it?
- What dishes did you eat?
- Did you like them?

Have you ever _______________ (forget) your PIN or password?

- When was it?
- Was it an important password?
- Did you remember it?
- What happened?

Have you ever _______________ (lose) your keys?

- When did you lose them?
- What happened?
- Did anybody help you?

Have you ever _______________ (be) late for something important?

- What was it?
- How late were you?
- Why was it important?

Have you ever _______________ (sleep) more than 12 hours?

- When was it?
- Why did you sleep so much?
- Did anybody wake you up?

Have you ever _______________ (buy) anything on eBay?

- What was it?
- How much did it cost?
- Did you have any problems with it?

Have you ever _______________ (have) a surprise birthday party?

- When was it?
- Where was the birthday party?
- Did you have a good time?

Have you ever _______________ (speak) in public?

- When was it?
- How did it go?
- Did you enjoy it?

Have you ever _______________ (send) an email or a text message to the wrong person?

- Who did you send it to?
- Who did you mean to send it to?
- Was it funny or was it a problem?

Have you ever _______________ (play) in a band?

- When did you do it?
- Did you like it?
- What kind of music did you play?

Have you ever _______________ (do) yoga or pilates?

- Where did you do it?
- When did you do it?
- Did you go alone or with a friend?

Have you ever _______________ (make) a cake?

- What kind of cake was it?
- Why did you make it?
- Was it good?

Have you ever _______________ (see) a famous singer or group in concert?

- Who did you see?
- Where was it?
- Did you go alone or with a friend?
- Did you have a good time?

Personal information

What / name?
How / spell your surname?
Where / you from?
What / your phone number?
What / do?
/ have a big family?
Why / need English?

Your flat/house

/ live in a house or a flat?
Where / it?
Can…tell me about it?
What / your favourite room?
Can…describe it?

Preferences

Which do you prefer? Why?
Coke / Pepsi?
summer / winter?
Facebook / Twitter?
watching sport / doing sport?
swimming in the sea / in a pool?

Can you…?

/ draw or paint well?
/ have a conversation in English?
/ play the guitar?
/ play chess?
/ drive?
/ wear jeans to work / school?

Time and dates

What / the time now?
What time / the class finish?
When / birthday?
What time / get up on Sundays?
When / your next class?
What / favourite day of the week? Why?
What / the date yesterday?

The past (*be*)

Where / you born?
Where / your mother born?
Where / you at 8.00 yesterday evening?
Who / you with?
What / your favourite food when you were little?
/ at home yesterday at 7.30 in the morning?

Future (*going to*)

Where / go after class?
/ watch TV this evening?
When / do your homework?
/ go to bed early today? What time?
Where / go this Saturday?

How often…?

/ go to the gym?
/ have dinner with friends?
/ eat meat?
/ go to bed after 11 o'clock?
/ watch TV in the evenings?
/ go to the doctor?

Now

What TV series / watching?
What book / read at the moment?
/ it rain now?
What / your teacher wearing?
How / feeling right now?

Have you ever…?

(be) to the UK?
(see) a ghost?
(break) your arm or leg?
(fall) in love?
(live) in a different place?
(be) to a pop festival?

Free time

How much free time / have?
What kind of books / like?
What / do when you want to relax?
What / like doing at weekends?
How often / go to the cinema?
What / your favourite kind of music?

Everyday activities

Where / usually have breakfast?
What time / usually leave home?
What / usually do in the morning?
What time / usually have lunch?
What time / usually get home?
What / usually do at weekends?

The past simple

What / do last night?
What / have for dinner?
What time / go to bed?
How many hours / sleep last night?
Who / dinner with yesterday?
How / come to class today?

Describe a friend

What / his or her name?
Where / live?
How often / see him or her?
What / do?
Where / you meet for the first time?
What / have in common?

Vocabulary activity instructions

1A Days of the week / Numbers 0–20

A pairwork spelling activity

LANGUAGE

Days of the week, numbers 0–20

• Give each student a worksheet and tell them to look at the letter snakes. Tell them to find the numbers and days and write them in the correct place in the lists.

> **a** eight, five, twelve, eleven, Thursday, thirteen, twenty, Monday, nineteen, fourteen, Saturday, fifteen, Wednesday

• For **b**, get Sts to complete the two lists with the missing numbers and days.

• Check answers.

• In **c**, get Sts to look at the code and write the words.

> **c** **1** twelve **2** goodbye **3** museum **4** welcome
> **5** nineteen **6** Saturday

• In **Activation**, each student thinks of three words, days, or numbers and puts them into the code. Put Sts in pairs and tell them to dictate the code numbers to a partner, and he / she works out what the words are.

• Put Sts in pairs and tell them to dictate the code numbers to a partner, and he / she works out what the words are.

1B The world

Filling in information

LANGUAGE

Countries and nationalities

• Give each student a worksheet. Focus on **a**, and tell Sts to complete the name of the country and write the nationality, using the photos to help them.

• Check answers.

> **a** **2** France, French **3** Germany, German **4** China, Chinese
> **5** Argentina, Argentinian **6** Turkey, Turkish
> **7** Poland, Polish **8** Mexico, Mexican

• For **b**, tell Sts to identify the countries and nationalities from the photos and complete the sentences.

• Check answers.

> **b** **1** Japan **2** Brazilian **3** Australia **4** African
> **5** Irish **6** Russia **7** Swiss **8** Czech Republic

• In **Activation**, Sts look at the photos in **a** and **b** and say the countries and nationalities.

1C Classroom language

Completing sentences

LANGUAGE

Common classroom expressions: *What page is it?*, etc.

• Give each student a worksheet. Tell Sts to look at the pictures and complete the conversations.

• Check answers.

> | **1** | **Student** | How do you say 'kot' in English? |
> |---|---|---|
> | | **Teacher** | It's 'cat'. |
> | | **Student** | How do you spell it? |
> | | **Teacher** | C-A-T. |
> | **2** | **Teacher** | Open your books, please. |
> | | **Student** | What page is it? |
> | | **Teacher** | Eighty-four. |
> | **3** | **Student** | Sorry I'm late! |
> | | **Teacher** | OK. Sit down. |
> | **4** | **Teacher** | Answer the questions. |
> | | **Student** | Can you help me, please? |
> | | **Teacher** | Yes, what' the problem? |
> | **5** | **Teacher** | Do exercise A. |
> | | **Teacher** | Can you match the words and definitions? |
> | | **Student** | I don't understand. |

• For **Activation**, put Sts in pairs and get them to practise the conversations.

2A Things

An anagram activity

LANGUAGE

Things: *key*, *sunglasses*, *coin*, etc.

• Explain to Sts that they are going to solve anagrams of common objects and match them to photos. If necessary, write a few anagram examples on the board, e.g. SITSUE – TISSUE.

• Give each student a worksheet. Tell Sts to first solve the anagram, and then write it with *a* / *an* if the noun is singular. Finally, they should match the word to a photo and write the number in the box.

• Check answers.

> **b** a coin 1 **c** a purse 11 **d** a watch 5 **e** a wallet 12
> **f** a file 10 **g** scissors 9 **h** a magazine 6
> **i** a laptop 4 **j** sunglasses 8 **k** a key 2 **l** a diary 3
> **m** a ticket 13 **n** a stamp 14 **o** an umbrella 15

• For **Activation**, put Sts in pairs and get them to cover the words and look at the photos to test each other.

2B Opposites crossword

A crossword activity

LANGUAGE

Common adjectives: *fast*, *slow*, etc.

• Tell Sts that they are going to solve a crossword. Explain / Elicit the meaning of *across* and *down*.

• You can either give each student a worksheet, or put Sts in pairs and give each pair a worksheet. Sts complete the crossword, using the opposites of the adjectives given.

- Check answers.

> **a** **DOWN** 2 difficult 4 empty 5 strong 7 light 8 fast 10 dirty
> 15 high 17 old
> **ACROSS** 3 expensive 6 small 9 cold 11 different 12 short
> 13 beautiful 14 right 16 good 18 rich

- For **Activation**, put Sts in pairs and get them to cover the crossword and use the clues to test each other.

3A Verb phrases

Matching phrases and verbs

> **LANGUAGE**
> Common verb phrases: *listen to music, do exercise*, etc.

- Give each student a worksheet. Focus on the examples and make sure Sts understand them. Then give Sts time to complete the **VERB** column. Highlight that they need to use *do* and *play* twice.
- Check answers.

> **a** 4 have 5 do 6 go 7 drink 8 live 9 read 10 speak
> 11 take 12 study 13 work 14 listen 15 say 16 wear
> 17 do 18 play 19 watch 20 like 21 play 22 cook
> 23 drive

- For **Activation**, Sts test themselves or each other by covering the **VERB** column and saying the phrases.

EXTRA IDEA Put Sts in pairs and get them to take turns making true sentences with the verb and the first collocate in either the positive or negative.

3B Jobs

A crossword activity

> **LANGUAGE**
> Jobs: *waiter, pilot*, etc.

- Tell Sts that they are going to solve a crossword. Make sure they remember the meaning of *across* and *down*.
- You can either give each student a worksheet, or put Sts in pairs and give each pair a worksheet. Sts complete the crossword, using the photos.
- Check answers.

> **DOWN** 1 journalist 2 builder 3 musician 5 hairdresser
> 7 doctor 8 actor 9 engineer 11 cleaner 13 pilot 16 vet
> **ACROSS** 4 nurse 6 policewoman 10 architect 12 dentist
> 14 waiter 15 lawyer 17 receptionist 18 soldier

- For **Activation**, put Sts in pairs and get them to test themselves or each other by covering the crossword, looking at the pictures, and saying the jobs.

Practical English 2 Time

Practising writing times

> **LANGUAGE**
> Telling the time: *It's one o'clock, It's quarter past eight*

- Give each student a worksheet and get them to look at the pictures. Get them to answer the question *What time is it?* by writing the times for each picture.
- Check answers.

> **a** 2 It's ten past eleven.
> 3 It's quarter past two.
> 4 It's ten to five.
> 5 It's twenty-five to seven.
> 6 It's twenty-five past nine.
> 7 It's five past one.
> 8 It's half past twelve.
> 9 It's five to six.
> 10 It's quarter to three.
> 11 It's twenty past ten.
> 12 It's twenty to four.

- Sts test themselves or each other by covering the sentences and asking each other the times.

4A The family

Deciding if sentences are true or false

> **LANGUAGE**
> Family members: *father, son*, etc.

- Put Sts in pairs, **A** and **B**, and give each student a worksheet **A** or **B**.
- Sts look at the family tree and sentences 1–10. Sts write *T* (true) or *F* (false) for each sentence. Monitor and help if necessary.
- For **b**, tell Sts **A** to start by reading sentence 1 to Sts **B**, who must say if the sentence is true or false and correct it if it is false. Sts then swap roles and take turns reading their sentences.
- Check answers.

> **a** **Student A:** 1 F 2 F 3 T 4 T 5 F 6 F 7 T 8 F 9 T 10 T
> **Student B:** 1 F 2 T 3 T 4 F 5 T 6 F 7 T 8 F 9 T 10 F

- For **Activation**, put Sts in pairs and get them to test each other by asking questions, e.g. *Who is Sally's aunt?*

4B A day in the life of a fitness instructor

Telling a story from pictures

> **LANGUAGE**
> Everyday activities: *She wakes up at 6.00 a.m.*

- Give each student a worksheet and explain that this is the daily routine of a fitness instructor. Go through the sequence quickly to elicit the verbs. Focus on *-s* for the third person.

1. She wakes up at 6.00 a.m.
2. She gets up at 6.15 a.m.
3. She does exercise.
4. She has a shower.
5. She gets dressed.
6. She has breakfast.
7. She goes / cycles to work.
8. She gets to work at 9.30 a.m.
9. She teaches / works from 10.00 a.m. to 1.00 p.m.
10. She has lunch at 1.30 p.m.
11. She teaches / works from 3.30 p.m. to 5.30 p.m.
12. She goes / cycles home.
13. She cooks dinner.
14. She watches TV.
15. She goes to bed at 10.30 p.m.

• Put Sts in pairs and get them to describe the fitness instructor's day together. Encourage them to add information, e.g. *She has cereal and fruit for breakfast* (picture 6).

EXTRA CHALLENGE Elicit the sequence from the class and ask some extra questions, e.g. *Where does she have lunch? Does she go to work by bus?*

5A More verb phrases

A puzzle, completing verb phrases

LANGUAGE
Common verb phrases: *remember somebody's name, use the internet*, etc.

• Give each student a worksheet and ask Sts to complete the **VERBS** column with the correct verb, which must make sense with the phrase. Focus on the example and count the letters in the verb – there is a space for each letter.

• Check answers.

> **a** 2 use 3 swim 4 send 5 find 6 forget 7 tell
> 8 meet 9 look for 10 see 11 help 12 give
> 13 sing 14 take 15 wait for 16 try 17 draw
> 18 run 19 hear 20 call 21 buy 22 leave
> 23 paint 24 talk

• For **Activation**, put Sts in pairs and get them to cover the **VERBS** column and test their partner.

5C The weather

A pairwork activity describing the weather

LANGUAGE
Weather words and verbs: *It's sunny, It's raining*, etc.

• Put Sts in pairs, **A** and **B**, and give each student a worksheet **A** or **B**. Give Sts time to do the first exercise individually, and then check answers.

> 1 windy 2 sunny 3 cloudy 4 raining 5 snowing

• Focus on **b**. Remind Sts of the question *What's the weather like?* Explain that they are going to ask each other questions in pairs to complete the missing information in the **Weather**

and **Temperature** columns. Point out the example question and answer, and remind them of the word *degrees*.

• In their pairs, Sts take turns to ask and answer questions about the weather.

• When they have finished, Sts should compare charts.

6B Dates

A bingo game activity

LANGUAGE
Dates and months: *the sixth of July, the twentieth of February*

• Each worksheet has eight bingo cards. Make enough copies so each student has a bingo card.

• Tell Sts that they are going to play a bingo game. Give each student a bingo card. Tell them that you will read some dates. If they have the date on their card, they should cross it out. The first student to cross out all the dates should shout *Bingo!*

• Read out the dates at the top of the worksheet at random and tick them off as you go.

• When a student shouts *Bingo!*, check their card to make sure they crossed off the correct dates. The first student to cross out all the dates is the winner.

EXTRA IDEA If Sts need more practice, make some more copies of the cards and the dates and get Sts to play in groups with one of the Sts saying the dates. Remind them to tick off the dates as they read them.

7C *go, have, get*

Matching verbs and phrases

LANGUAGE
Expressions with *go, have, get*

• Put Sts in pairs, **A** and **B**, and give each student worksheet **A** or **B**. Give Sts time to complete the task individually. Check answers.

> **Student A** 1 go 2 get 3 have 4 get 5 go 6 get 7 go
> 8 have 9 have 10 go
>
> **Student B** 1 have 2 go 3 have 4 have 5 go 6 get 7 go
> 8 go 9 have 10 get

• Focus on **Activation** and get Sts to ask and answer their questions. Remind them to ask for more information and then to 'return' the questions, e.g. *What about you? / And you?*

8B Race around the house

Naming things in the house from definitions

LANGUAGE
Things in the house and furniture, rooms

- Put Sts in pairs and give each pair a worksheet. Tell them they have to identify house vocabulary as quickly as possible.
- Start the activity and set a time limit of ten minutes.
- Check answers. Pairs who have all the correct answers win.

1 armchair 2 lamp 3 pictures / paintings 4 mirror
5 bedroom 6 carpet 7 cooker 8 air conditioning
9 stairs 10 cupboard 11 fridge 12 bathroom
13 ceiling 14 washing machine 15 wardrobe 16 shelves
17 garden 18 garage 19 bath 20 central heating

- For **Activation**, tell Sts to cover the furniture words, look at the definitions, and then say the furniture words.

8C Prepositions of place
A describe-and-draw activity

LANGUAGE
Prepositions of place: *on*, *under*, *between*, etc., furniture

- Revise prepositions of place quickly, by making a drawing on the board or using the classroom. Remind Sts of *there is / are*, and *on the right* and *on the left*.
- Tell Sts they will each have a picture of a room which they have to describe to their partner. Their partner will draw furniture and objects into the picture exactly as their partner describes it.
- Put Sts in pairs, **A** and **B**, and give each student worksheet **A** or **B**. Tell Sts **A** to describe what is in Room 1 for Sts **B** to draw in. When they have finished, they swap roles for Room 2.
- Finally, get Sts to look at the originals and compare them with what they have drawn.

9A Food
Naming food from pictures

LANGUAGE
Food: *apple*, *bread*, etc.

- Give each student a worksheet and tell Sts to use the photos to find one food word for each of the letters. Point out the examples.
- You could do this as a race in pairs. In this case, make sure everyone starts at the same time, and set a time limit.

a apple b bread c carrots e egg f fish
h hamburger i ice cream j juice l lettuce
m mushrooms o onion p peas r rice s sandwich
t tomatoes v vegetables y yoghurt

- Check answers, getting Sts to spell the words.
- For **Activation**, put Sts in pairs, **A** and **B**. Tell Sts **A** to say the first letter of five food words for Sts **B** (with page face down) to guess. Then get them to swap roles.

9C Guess the number
A pairwork activity to practise saying and writing high numbers

LANGUAGE
High numbers: *two hundred and fifty-five*, *one thousand five hundred*, etc.

- Put Sts in pairs, **A** and **B**, and give each student a worksheet. Focus on the list of numbers, and elicit how to say them. Then give Sts time to individually read the sentences and complete them with a number from the list. They should not compare at this point. Monitor and help.
- When Sts have finished, get them to do **Activation** and compare answers. Sts **A** read sentence 1 to Sts **B**. If **B** doesn't agree with the number **A** has chosen, he / she says what he / she thinks the right number is. Monitor and help.
- Check answers. You could ask Sts if they were surprised by any of the answers. Encourage them to say why.

2 The total number of countries in the world is one hundred and ninety-six (196).
3 A person with a good level of English knows about five thousand (5,000) words.
4 A hippopotamus normally weighs about one thousand seven hundred (1,700) kilograms.
5 A normal person sleeps for about two thousand nine hundred and twenty (2,920) hours every year.
6 A day has eighty-six thousand four hundred (86,400) seconds.
7 An Olympic swimming pool has two million five hundred thousand (2,500,000) litres of water.
8 Sixty-four million one hundred thousand (64,100,000) people live in the UK.
9 The River Amazon is six thousand nine hundred and ninety-two (6,992) kilometres long.
10 The novel *Emma*, by Jane Austen, has one hundred and fifty-five thousand eight hundred and eighty-seven (155, 887) words.

EXTRA IDEA Ask Sts to look up information on their phones and modify the sentences to create their own. They can choose a book, for example, and look up the number of words on Google.

10A Places and buildings puzzle
Solving a puzzle to find a hidden phrase

LANGUAGE
Buildings and places: *post office*, *chemist's*, etc.

- Give each student a worksheet. Explain that Sts have to write the answers to the clues in the puzzle. If their answers are correct, they will find a phrase in the shaded area down the middle of the puzzle.
- Get Sts to do **a** and **b** individually or in pairs.
- Check answers.

a 1 post office 2 hospital 3 square 4 church 5 chemist's
  6 mosque 7 bridge 8 town hall 9 market 10 theatres
  11 museum 12 car park 13 river 14 station 15 art gallery
b Missing phrase: places in the city

- Get Sts to cover the puzzle, look at the definitions, and test themselves.
- For **Activation**, if Sts worked individually, put them in pairs and tell them to cover the puzzle, look at the definitions, and say the words.

1A VOCABULARY Days of the week / Numbers 0–20

a Find the numbers and days, and write the words in the right place in the lists.

AXTHREEYKGBEIGHTJQTFRIDAYOFIVEMAZTWELVECOELEVENSXON

DTHURSDAYDKLPTHIRTEENINSQTWENTYNBCMONDAYXOTUENINETEENEL

EVFOURTEENVCAAWSATURDAYFPUFIFTEENRUSHWEDNESDAYTWU

Numbers

0 ______	11 ______	
1 ______	12 ______	
2 ______	13 ______	
3 *three*	14 ______	
4 ______	15 ______	
5 ______	16 ______	
6 ______	17 ______	
7 ______	18 ______	
8 ______	19 ______	
9 ______	20 ______	
10 ______		

Days

1 ______
2 ______
3 ______
4 ______
5 ______
6 *Friday*
7 ______

b Complete the lists with numbers and days.

c Look at the code. Use it to write the words.

0 = P	1 = H	2 = R	3 = D	4 = N	5 = F	6 = M	7 = W	8 = U	9 = A	10 = T
11 = L	12 = E	13 = Y	14 = I	15 = S	16 = G	17 = V	18 = O	19 = B	20 = C	

1 **10 7 12 11 17 12** = ______   4 **7 12 11 20 18 6 12** = ______

2 **16 18 18 3 19 13 12** = ______   5 **4 14 4 12 10 12 12 4** = ______

3 **6 8 15 12 8 6** = ______   6 **15 9 10 8 2 3 9 13** = ______

ACTIVATION

Think of three words, days, or numbers and put them into the code.
Say the code numbers to your partner. He / she writes the words.

1B VOCABULARY The world

a Look at the pictures. Complete the names of the countries and write the nationalities.

Country: Sp*ain*
Nationality: Sp*anish*

Country: Fr__________
Nationality: __________

Country: Ger__________
Nationality: __________

Country: Ch__________
Nationality: __________

Country: Ar__________
Nationality: __________

Country: Tu__________
Nationality: __________

Country: Po__________
Nationality: __________

Country: Me__________
Nationality: __________

b Look at the pictures. Complete the sentences with a country or nationality.

  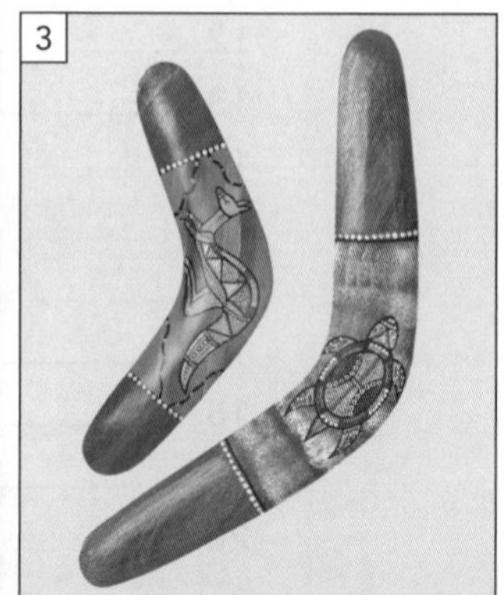 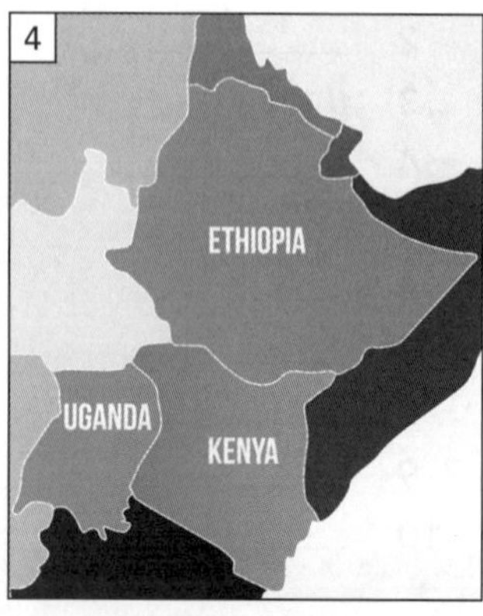

1 Geishas are from __________.
2 Samba is a __________ dance.
3 Boomerangs are from __________.
4 Uganda, Kenya, and Ethiopia are __________ countries.

5 Guinness is an __________ beer.
6 Moscow is the capital of __________.
7 Lindt is __________ chocolate.
8 Prague is the capital of the __________.

ACTIVATION

Look at the pictures and say the countries and nationalities.

1C VOCABULARY Classroom language

● Complete the conversations between a teacher and a student.

1

Student	How do you say 'kot' in English?
Teacher	It's 'cat'.
Student	How ____________ ____________ ____________ ____________ ?
Teacher	C-A-T.

2

Teacher	____________ ____________ ____________ , please.
Student	What ____________ ____________ ____________ ?
Teacher	Eighty-four.

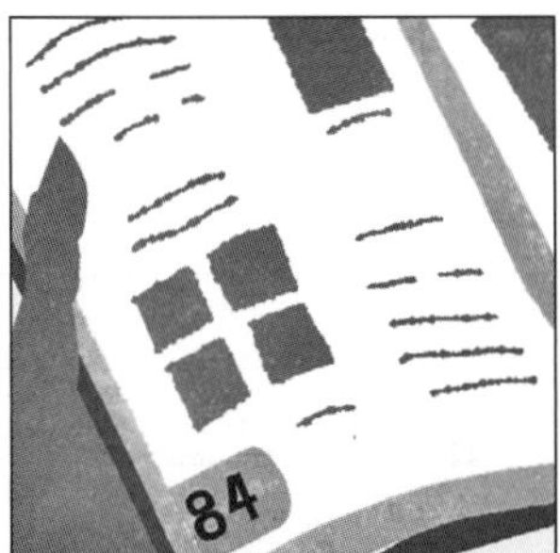

3

Student	Sorry ____________ ____________ !
Teacher	OK. ____________ ____________ .

4

Teacher	____________ ____________ questions.
Student	____________ ____________ ____________ me, ____________ ?
Teacher	Yes, what's the problem?

5

Teacher	____________ ____________ A. Can you match the words and definitions?
Student	I ____________ ____________ .

ACTIVATION

Practise the conversations with a partner.

English File fourth edition Teacher's Guide Elementary   Photocopiable © Oxford University Press 2019

2A VOCABULARY Things

● Look at the **ANAGRAMS**. Order the letters and write the words. Use *a / an* with the singular nouns. Match the words to pictures 1–15.

ANAGRAMS

a	enidytit arcd	**d**	tcwha	**g**	crossiss	**j**	salsseguns	**m**	ckitet
b	oicn	**e**	teawll	**h**	emnaigza	**k**	yek	**n**	pamst
c	urpes	**f**	life	**i**	platpo	**l**	riady	**o**	erumball

a	*an identity card* 7	**f**	____________	**k**	____________
b	____________	**g**	____________	**l**	____________
c	____________	**h**	____________	**m**	____________
d	____________	**i**	____________	**n**	____________
e	____________	**j**	____________	**o**	____________

ACTIVATION

Test a partner.

(*What's number 1?*

2B VOCABULARY Opposites crossword

● Look at the clues and complete the crossword.

DOWN ↓

1 the opposite of **dangerous**

2 the opposite of **easy**

4 the opposite of **full**

5 the opposite of **weak**

7 the opposite of **dark**

8 the opposite of **slow**

10 the opposite of **clean**

15 the opposite of **low**

17 the opposite of **young**

ACROSS →

3 the opposite of **cheap**

6 the opposite of **big**

9 the opposite of **hot**

11 the opposite of **the same**

12 the opposite of **tall**

13 the opposite of **ugly**

14 the opposite of **wrong**

16 the opposite of **bad**

18 the opposite of **poor**

ACTIVATION

Cover the crossword and test your partner.

What's the opposite of dangerous? *Safe.*

3A VOCABULARY Verb phrases

● Match the verbs in the list to phrases 1–23. Write them in the **VERB** column.

cook   do (x2)   drink   drive   ~~eat~~   go   have   like   listen   live   ~~need~~   play (x2)
read   say   speak   study   take   ~~want~~   watch   wear   work

		VERB
1	a new phone, new glasses	*need*
2	a coffee	*want*
3	vegetables, fruit	*eat*
4	a garden, two children	
5	exercise, yoga	
6	to the cinema, to the gym	
7	mineral water, tea, or coffee	
8	in a flat, in a big city	
9	a magazine, a book	
10	German, two languages	
11	an umbrella, your camera	
12	history, for an exam	
13	in an office, in a school	
14	to pop music, to the radio	
15	thank you, hello	
16	glasses, jeans	
17	housework, homework	
18	the guitar, the piano	
19	TV, a film	
20	animals, Mexican food	
21	tennis, chess	
22	dinner, pasta	
23	a car, a Toyota	

ACTIVATION

Test your memory. Cover the **VERB** column. Say phrases 1–23.

(*need a new phone*

English File fourth edition Teacher's Guide Elementary   Photocopiable © Oxford University Press 2019

3B VOCABULARY Jobs

Complete the crossword using the picture clues.

ACROSS →

DOWN ↓

ACTIVATION

Test a partner.

What's 1 Down?

PRACTICAL ENGLISH 2 VOCABULARY Time

Look at the pictures and write the times.

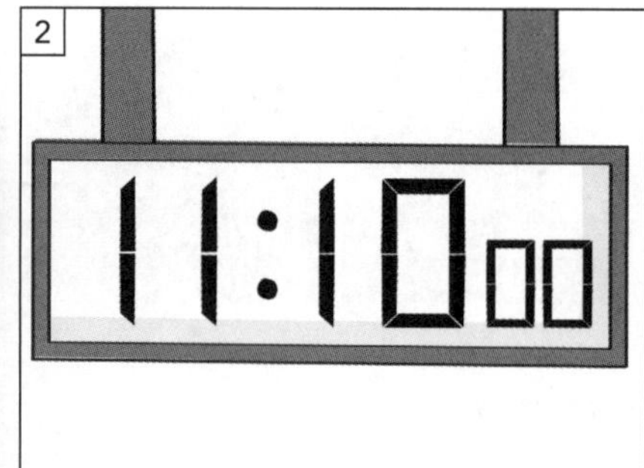

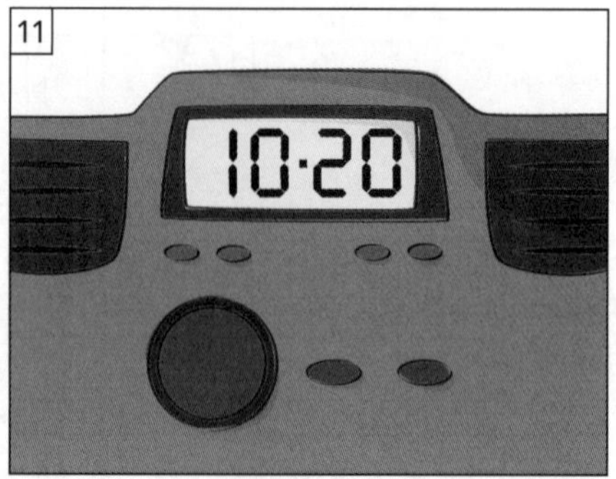

1 *It's eight o'clock.*

2 _______________

3 _______________

4 _______________

5 _______________

6 _______________

7 _______________

8 _______________

9 _______________

10 _______________

11 _______________

12 _______________

ACTIVATION

Work with a partner. Cover the sentences. Point to a clock and ask *What time is it?*

What time is it? *It's ten to five.*

4A VOCABULARY The family

a Look at sentences 1–10. Decide if they are true (**T**) or false (**F**).

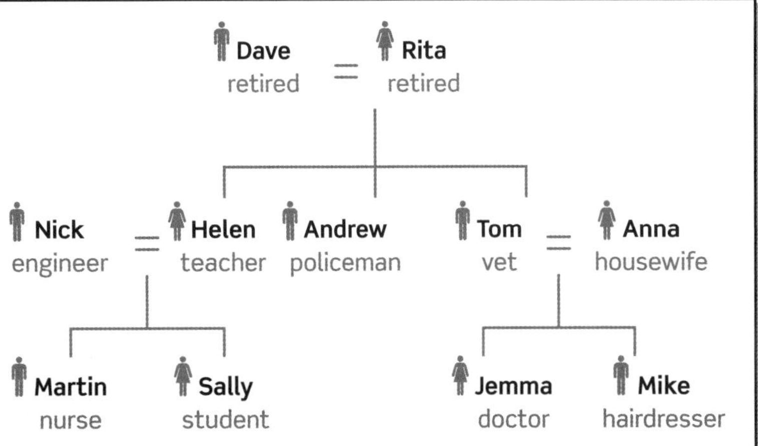

1 Martin is Jemma's brother.
2 Nick's wife is a doctor.
3 Mike's grandfather is Dave.
4 Rita has four grandchildren.
5 Helen's husband is a vet.
6 Tom is Nick's brother.
7 Andrew is Martin's uncle.
8 Nick and Helen have two sons.
9 Sally is Tom's niece.
10 Jemma is Dave and Rita's granddaughter.

b Read your sentences to your partner. He / She says if they are true or false.

Martin is Jemma's brother. *False. Martin is Sally's brother.*

Test your partner.

Who's Dave's wife? *Rita.*

- -

a Look at sentences 1–10. Decide if they are true (**T**) or false (**F**).

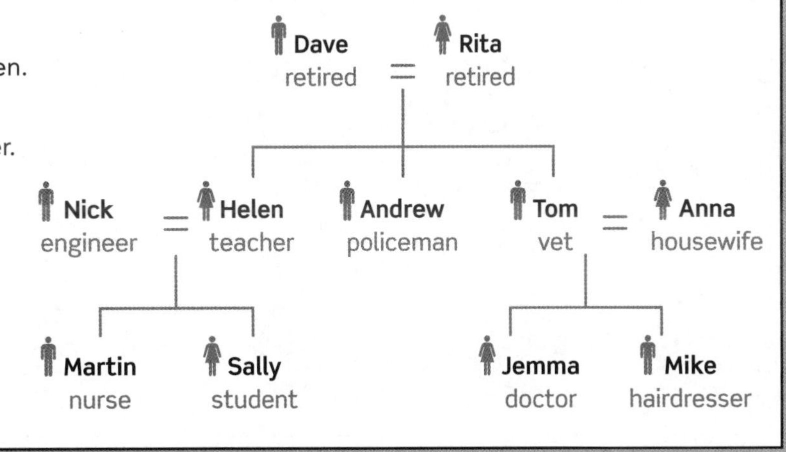

1 Mike's father is an engineer.
2 Dave and Rita have three children.
3 Mike is Martin's cousin.
4 Sally is Anna and Tom's daughter.
5 Andrew is Dave's son.
6 Martin is Nick's nephew.
7 Tom's sister is a teacher.
8 Andrew has two brothers.
9 Mike and Martin are Rita's grandsons.
10 Jemma's brother is a student.

b Read your sentences to your partner. He / She says if they are true or false.

Mike's father is an engineer. *False. Mike's father is a vet.*

Test your partner.

Who's Dave's wife? *Rita.*

4B VOCABULARY   A day in the life of a fitness instructor

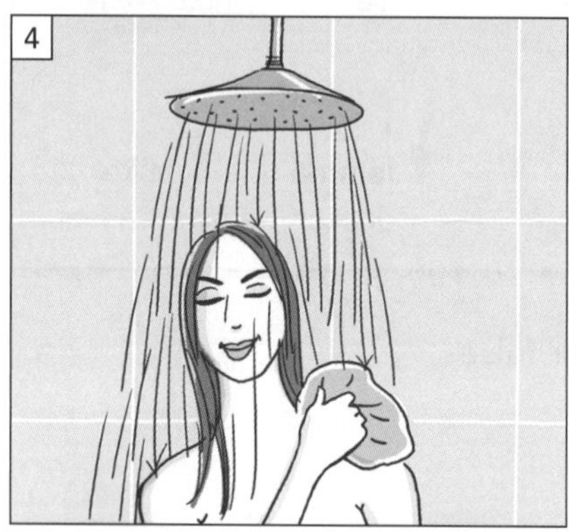

English File fourth edition Teacher's Guide Elementary   Photocopiable © Oxford University Press 2019

5A VOCABULARY More verb phrases

● Complete the phrases with the correct verb.

VERBS	PHRASE
1 r <u>e</u> <u>m</u> <u>e</u> <u>m</u> <u>b</u> <u>e</u> <u>r</u>	somebody's name, your friend's birthday
2 u _ _ _	the internet, Google maps
3 s _ _ _ _	in the sea
4 s _ _ _ _	a text message
5 f _ _ _ _	a parking space, a job
6 f _ _ _ _ _ _	somebody's name
7 t _ _ _ _	someone a secret, a story
8 m _ _ _ _	a friend
9 l _ _ _ _ f _ _	your keys, your wallet
10 s _ _	a film
11 h _ _ _ _	somebody, a friend
12 g _ _ _	somebody flowers
13 s _ _ _ _	a song
14 t _ _ _ _	a photo
15 w _ _ _ _ f _ _	a bus
16 t _ _	to do something difficult
17 d _ _ _ _	a picture
18 r _ _	a race
19 h _ _ _ _	a noise
20 c _ _ _ _	a taxi
21 b _ _	new clothes
22 l _ _ _ _ _	your bag on the train
23 p _ _ _ _ _	the walls, a picture
24 t _ _ _	to a friend

Work with a partner. Cover the **VERBS** and test your partner.

a photo) (*take a photo*

5C VOCABULARY The weather

a Look at the pictures. What's the weather like? Complete sentences 1–5.

1 It's __________. **2** It's __________. **3** It's __________. **4** It's __________. **5** It's __________.

b Ask **B** questions to complete your information.

(What's the weather like in Berlin?

City	Weather	Temperature
Berlin	__________	__________
Budapest	cloudy and windy	7°
Istanbul	__________	__________
Moscow	snowing	1°
Warsaw	__________	__________
Edinburgh	foggy	5°
Buenos Aires	__________	__________
Santiago	cloudy and hot	26°

c Answer **B**'s questions.

(It's cloudy and windy and it's 7 degrees.

---

a Look at the pictures. What's the weather like? Complete sentences 1–5.

1 It's __________. **2** It's __________. **3** It's __________. **4** It's __________. **5** It's __________.

b Answer **A**'s questions.

(It's cold and it's 4 degrees.

c Ask **A** questions to complete your information.

(What's the weather like in Budapest?

City	Weather	Temperature
Berlin	cold	4°
Budapest	__________	__________
Istanbul	cloudy and windy	14°
Moscow	__________	__________
Warsaw	raining	12°
Edinburgh	__________	__________
Buenos Aires	sunny and hot	29°
Santiago	__________	__________

6B VOCABULARY Dates

☐ 11th April ☐ 30th June ☐ 7th May ☐ 24th September ☐ 16th August

☐ 1st January ☐ 18th July ☐ 23rd February ☐ 15th April ☐ 27th March

☐ 19th March ☐ 25th December ☐ 6th July ☐ 22nd October ☐ 20th February

☐ 21st May ☐ 8th June ☐ 31st March ☐ 14th November ☐ 17th September

☐ 12th October ☐ 2nd November ☐ 9th January ☐ 29th August ☐ 8th December

---

BINGO

2/11	18/7	31/3	25/12	11/4
8/6	21/5	16/8	1/1	27/3

BINGO

1/1	12/10	23/2	16/8	2/11
15/4	30/6	7/5	24/9	31/3

BINGO

11/4	27/3	6/7	22/10	19/3
21/5	1/1	16/8	14/11	20/2

BINGO

25/12	24/9	8/6	9/1	15/4
29/8	20/2	22/10	6/7	7/5

BINGO

17/9	8/12	9/1	31/3	12/10
20/2	11/4	16/8	14/11	8/6

BINGO

23/2	29/8	1/1	7/5	19/3
30/6	11/4	6/7	22/10	25/12

BINGO

31/3	9/1	8/12	29/8	14/11
12/10	20/2	15/4	21/5	27/3

BINGO

29/8	2/11	31/3	9/1	22/10
11/4	17/9	20/2	30/6	6/7

Student A

Complete the questions with *go*, *have* or *get*.

1 What time did you ____ to bed last night?

2 Did you ____ up early yesterday?

3 What did you ____ for breakfast this morning?

4 How many emails did you ____ yesterday?

5 Did you ____ to the cinema at the weekend?

6 How often do you ____ a taxi?

7 When do you usually ____ shopping?

8 Do you usually ____ dinner with your family at Christmas?

9 How many brothers and sisters do you ____?

10 Do you usually ____ home after class?

ACTIVATION

Ask your partner the questions. Ask for more information.

Student B

Complete the questions with *go*, *have* or *get*.

1 Where did you ____ lunch last Saturday?

2 Did you ____ out last night?

3 Did you ____ a good time last weekend?

4 What car does your family ____?

5 Where did you ____ on holiday last year?

6 Do you usually ____ dressed before breakfast?

7 How do you usually ____ to work / school?

8 How often do you ____ to bed before midnight?

9 What did you ____ for dinner last night?

10 Do you ____ up at the same time during the week and the weekend?

ACTIVATION

Ask your partner the questions. Ask for more information.

8B VOCABULARY Race around the house

In 10 minutes write as many words as you can for the definitions.

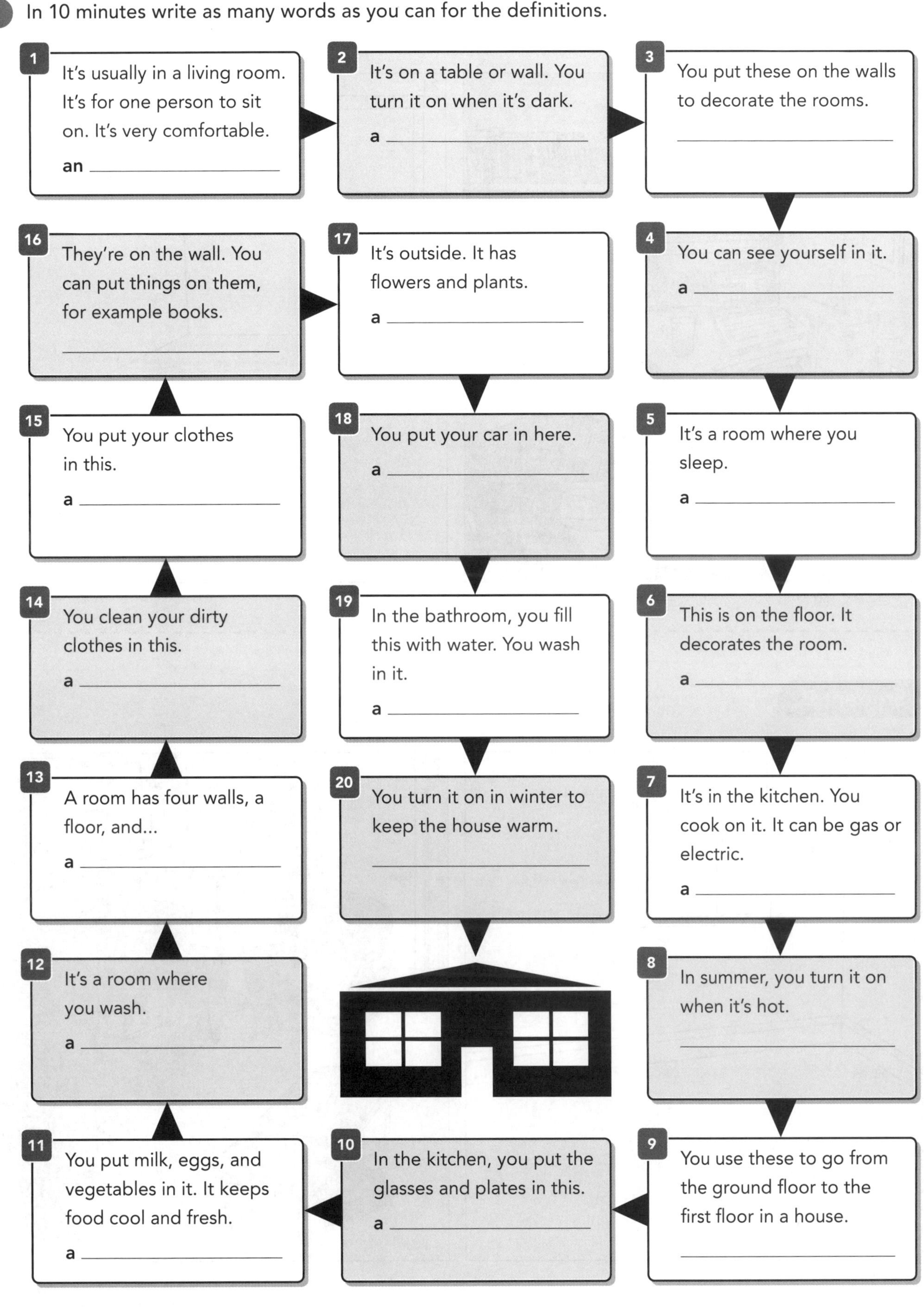

1 It's usually in a living room. It's for one person to sit on. It's very comfortable.

an ______________

2 It's on a table or wall. You turn it on when it's dark.

a ______________

3 You put these on the walls to decorate the rooms.

____

16 They're on the wall. You can put things on them, for example books.

____

17 It's outside. It has flowers and plants.

a ______________

4 You can see yourself in it.

a ______________

15 You put your clothes in this.

a ______________

18 You put your car in here.

a ______________

5 It's a room where you sleep.

a ______________

14 You clean your dirty clothes in this.

a ______________

19 In the bathroom, you fill this with water. You wash in it.

a ______________

6 This is on the floor. It decorates the room.

a ______________

13 A room has four walls, a floor, and...

a ______________

20 You turn it on in winter to keep the house warm.

____

7 It's in the kitchen. You cook on it. It can be gas or electric.

a ______________

12 It's a room where you wash.

a ______________

8 In summer, you turn it on when it's hot.

____

11 You put milk, eggs, and vegetables in it. It keeps food cool and fresh.

a ______________

10 In the kitchen, you put the glasses and plates in this.

a ______________

9 You use these to go from the ground floor to the first floor in a house.

____

ACTIVATION

Test your memory. Cover the words and the definitions. Say the words.

8C VOCABULARY Prepositions of place

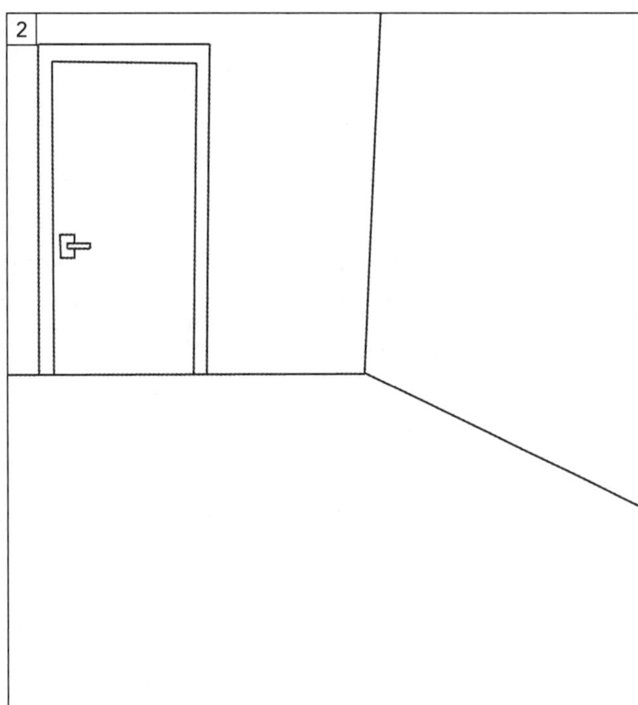

English File fourth edition Teacher's Guide Elementary   Photocopiable © Oxford University Press 2019

9A VOCABULARY Food

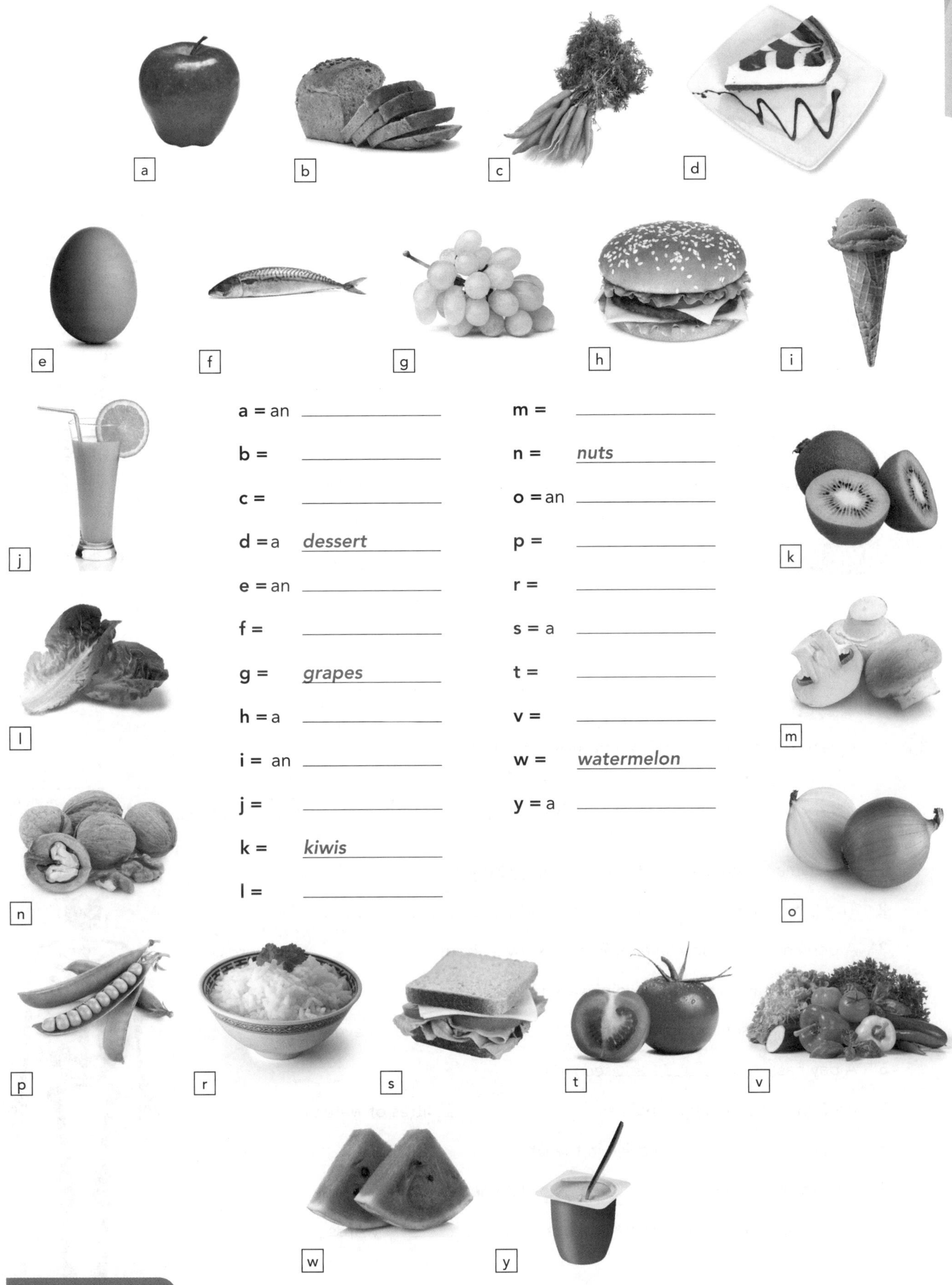

a = an _____________

b = _____________

c = _____________

d = a _dessert_

e = an _____________

f = _____________

g = _grapes_

h = a _____________

i = an _____________

j = _____________

k = _kiwis_

l = _____________

m = _____________

n = _nuts_

o = an _____________

p = _____________

r = _____________

s = a _____________

t = _____________

v = _____________

w = _watermelon_

y = a _____________

ACTIVATION

Work in pairs. **A** say the first letter of five words for food.
B (page face down) say the words. Then swap roles.

9C VOCABULARY Guess the number

● Complete the sentences with a number from the list.

196 ~~206~~ 1,700 2,920 5,000 6,992 86,400 155,887 2,500,000 64,100,000

1 The human body has _two hundred and six_ bones.

2 The total number of countries in the world is _________________.

3 A person with a good level of English knows about _________________ words.

4 A hippopotamus normally weighs about _________________ kilograms.

5 A normal person sleeps for about _________________ hours every year.

6 A day has _________________ seconds.

7 An Olympic swimming pool has _________________ litres of water.

8 _________________ people live in the UK.

9 The River Amazon is _________________ kilometres long.

10 The novel _Emma_, by Jane Austen, has _________________ words.

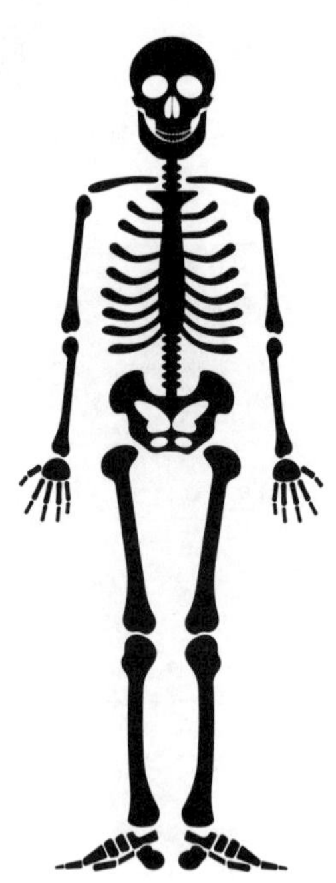

ACTIVATION

Work with a partner. Compare answers. Decide which answers you both think are correct.
Listen to your teacher and check your answers. Were you right?

● Complete the sentences with a number from the list.

196 ~~206~~ 1,700 2,920 5,000 6,992 86,400 155,887 2,500,000 64,100,000

1 The human body has _two hundred and six_ bones.

2 The total number of countries in the world is _________________.

3 A person with a good level of English knows about _________________ words.

4 A hippopotamus normally weighs about _________________ kilograms.

5 A normal person sleeps for about _________________ hours every year.

6 A day has _________________ seconds.

7 An Olympic swimming pool has _________________ litres of water.

8 _________________ people live in the UK.

9 The River Amazon is _________________ kilometres long.

10 The novel _Emma_, by Jane Austen, has _________________ words.

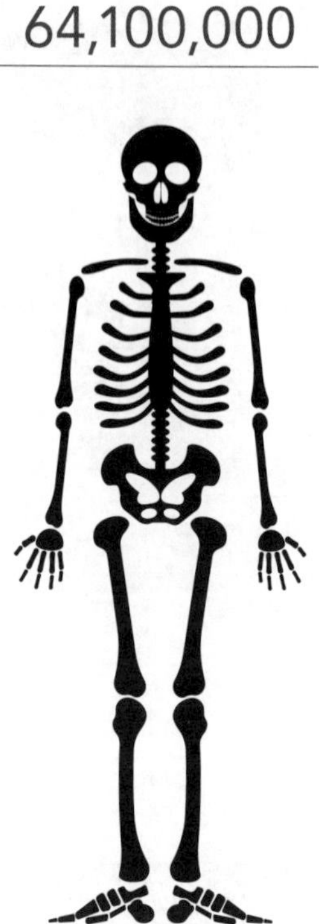

ACTIVATION

Work with a partner. Compare answers. Decide which answers you both think are correct.
Listen to your teacher and check your answers. Were you right?

English File fourth edition Teacher's Guide Elementary   Photocopiable © Oxford University Press 2019

10A VOCABULARY Places and buildings puzzle

a Read the clues and complete the puzzle.

1   If you need stamps or want to send a letter, you go here.
2   You go here if you are very ill or have an accident.
3   Trafalgar __________ is in London; Times __________ is in New York.
4   A religious building where Christians go.
5   You can buy aspirin or medicine here.
6   Similar to clue 4, but for Muslims.
7   To walk or drive across a river, you usually go over a __________.
8   A building where the local government offices are.
9   An open area of small stalls where you can buy fresh fruit, vegetables, and sometimes clothes.
10   Broadway in New York is a street with a lot of __________.
11   A building where you can see historical, scientific, or cultural objects.
12   An area where you can pay to leave your car.
13   The Thames is the __________ that goes through London.
14   You go here when you want to get a bus or a train.
15   You can see paintings and sculptures here.

b There is a phrase under the arrow. Find the missing phrase, which is the title of the puzzle.

ACTIVATION

Test your memory. Cover the puzzle and look at the definitions. Say the words.